A U D I T

GUIDE

OCTOBER 1, 2016

Assessing and Responding to Audit Risk in a Financial Statement Audit

AICPA®

A Resource of the
Enhancing Audit
Quality Initiative

★ ★ ★

18627-349

Copyright © 2016 by
American Institute of Certified Public Accountants, Inc.
New York, NY 10036-8775

All rights reserved. For information about the procedure for requesting permission to
make copies of any part of this work, please e-mail copyright@aicpa.org with your
request. Otherwise, requests should be written and mailed to the Permissions
Department, AICPA, 220 Leigh Farm Road, Durham, NC 27707-8110.

1 2 3 4 5 6 7 8 9 0 AAP 1 9 8 7 6

ISBN 978-1-94549-816-9

Printed in Canada

Preface

(Updated as of October 1, 2016)

About AICPA Audit Guides

This AICPA Audit Guide has been developed under the supervision of the AICPA Risk Assessment Audit Guide Task Force. The purpose of the guide is to help practitioners fulfill their responsibilities for assessing risk in a financial statement audit that is performed in accordance with generally accepted auditing standards (GAAS) (referred to as auditing standards herein) as established by the AICPA Auditing Standards Board (ASB) (United States). GAAS established by the ASB are applicable to audits of nonissuers. Audits of nonissuers are audits of the financial statements of those entities not subject to the oversight authority of the PCAOB (that is, entities not within its jurisdiction).

Auditing guidance related to GAAS included in an AICPA Audit Guide is recognized as an interpretive publication as defined in AU-C section 200, *Overall Objectives of the Independent Auditor and the Conduct of an Audit in Accordance With Generally Accepted Auditing Standards* (AICPA, *Professional Standards*). Interpretive publications are recommendations on the application of GAAS in specific circumstances, including engagements for entities in specialized industries.

An interpretive publication is issued under the authority of the ASB after all ASB members have been provided an opportunity to consider and comment on whether the proposed interpretive publication is consistent with GAAS. The members of the ASB have found the auditing guidance in this guide to be consistent with existing GAAS.

Although interpretive publications are not auditing standards, AU-C section 200 requires the auditor to consider applicable interpretive publications in planning and performing the audit because interpretive publications are relevant to the proper application of GAAS in specific circumstances. If the auditor does not apply the auditing guidance in an applicable interpretive publication, the auditor should document how the requirements of GAAS were complied with in the circumstances addressed by such auditing guidance.

The ASB is the designated senior committee of the AICPA authorized to speak for the AICPA on all matters related to auditing. Conforming changes made to the auditing guidance contained in this guide are approved by the ASB chair (or his or her designee) and the director of the AICPA Audit and Attest Standards Staff. Updates made to the auditing guidance in this guide exceeding that of conforming changes are issued after all ASB members have been provided an opportunity to consider and comment on whether the guide is consistent with the Statements on Auditing Standards (SASs).

Any auditing guidance in a guide appendix, while not authoritative, is considered an "other auditing publication." In applying such guidance, the auditor should, exercising professional judgment, assess the relevance and appropriateness of such guidance to the circumstances of the audit. Although the auditor determines the relevance of other auditing guidance, auditing guidance in an appendix to a guide or a guide chapter has been reviewed by the AICPA Audit and Attest Standards staff and the auditor may presume that it is appropriate.

Status of Other Material Included in the Guide

The guide includes numerous illustrative examples, interpretative flowcharts, observations, and suggestions. These materials have no authoritative status; however, they may help the auditor understand and apply the SASs. These materials have been reviewed by the AICPA Audit and Attest Standards staff and are presumed to be appropriate for the performance of an audit in accordance with the standards established by the ASB (United States).

Recognition

AICPA Senior Committee

Auditing Standards Board

Michael J. Santay, *Chair*

AICPA Senior Committee

Gerry Boaz

The AICPA gratefully acknowledges Lynford Graham who contributed significantly to the revision of this guide. Lyn's knowledge and generous effort were invaluable during the revision of this guide edition.

AICPA Staff

Nisha Gordhan
Technical Manager
Accounting and Auditing Content Development

Hiram Hasty
Senior Technical Manager
Audit and Attest Standards

Guidance Considered in This Edition

This edition of the guide has been modified by the AICPA staff to include certain changes necessary due to the issuance of authoritative guidance since the guide was last revised, and other revisions as deemed appropriate.

Authoritative guidance issued through October 1, 2016, has been considered in the development of this edition of the guide.

For this edition of this guide, authoritative guidance that is issued for entities with fiscal years ending on or before October 1, 2016, and effective on or before December 31, 2016 is incorporated directly in the text of this guide.

This guide has been conformed to the requirements of SAS No. 130, *An Audit of Internal Control Over Financial Reporting That Is Integrated With an Audit of Financial Statements* (AICPA, *Professional Standards*, AU-C sec. 940), effective for audits of financial statements for periods ending on or after December 15, 2016.

Users of this guide should consider guidance issued subsequent to the as of date of this guide edition to determine their effect on entities and engagements covered by this guide. In determining the applicability of recently issued guidance, its effective date should also be considered.

The changes made to this edition of the guide are identified in appendix N, "Schedule of Changes Made to the Text From the Previous Edition." The changes do not include all those that might be considered necessary if the guide were subjected to a comprehensive review and revision.

References to Professional Standards

In citing GAAS and their related interpretations, references use section numbers within the codification of currently effective SASs and not the original statement number, as appropriate.

Terms Used to Define Professional Requirements in This AICPA Audit Guide

Any requirements described in this guide are normally referenced to the applicable standards or regulations from which they are derived. Generally the terms used in this guide describing the professional requirements of the referenced standard setter (for example, the ASB) are the same as those used in the applicable standards or regulations (for example, *must* or *should*).

Readers should refer to the applicable standards and regulations for more information on the requirements imposed by the use of the various terms used to define professional requirements in the context of the standards and regulations in which they appear.

Certain exceptions apply to these general rules, particularly in those circumstances where the guide describes prevailing or preferred industry practices for the application of a standard or regulation. In these circumstances, the applicable senior committee responsible for reviewing the guide's content believes the guidance contained herein is appropriate for the circumstances.

Applicability of Quality Control Standards

QC section 10, *A Firm's System of Quality Control* (AICPA, *Professional Standards*), addresses a CPA firm's responsibilities for its system of quality control for its accounting and auditing practice. A system of quality control consists of policies that a firm establishes and maintains to provide it with reasonable assurance that the firm and its personnel comply with professional standards, as well as applicable legal and regulatory requirements. The policies also provide the firm with reasonable assurance that reports issued by the firm are appropriate in the circumstances. This section applies to all CPA firms with respect to engagements in their accounting and auditing practice.

AU-C section 220, *Quality Control for an Engagement Conducted in Accordance With Generally Accepted Auditing Standards* (AICPA, *Professional Standards*), addresses the auditor's specific responsibilities regarding quality control procedures for an audit of financial statements. When applicable, it also addresses the responsibilities of the engagement quality control reviewer.

Because of the importance of audit quality, we have added a new appendix, appendix M, *Overview of Statements on Quality Control Standards*, to this guide. Appendix M summarizes key aspects of the quality control standard. This summarization should be read in conjunction with QC section 10, AU-C section 220, and the quality control standards issued by the PCAOB, as applicable.

AICPA.org Website

The AICPA encourages you to visit the website at www.aicpa.org and the Financial Reporting Center at www.aicpa.org/FRC. The Financial Reporting Center supports members in the execution of high-quality financial reporting. Whether you are a financial statement preparer or a member in public practice, this center provides exclusive member-only resources for the entire financial reporting process, and provides timely and relevant news, guidance, and examples supporting the financial reporting process, including accounting, preparing financial statements and performing compilation, review, audit, attest, or assurance and advisory engagements. Certain content on the AICPA's websites referenced in this guide may be restricted to AICPA members only.

Select Recent Developments Significant to This Guide

AICPA's Ethics Codification Project

The AICPA's Professional Ethics Executive Committee (PEEC) restructured and codified the AICPA Code of Professional Conduct (code) so that members and other users of the code can apply the rules and reach appropriate conclusions more easily and intuitively. This is referred to as the AICPA Ethics Codification Project.

Although PEEC believes it was able to maintain the substance of the existing AICPA ethics standards through this process and limited substantive changes to certain specific areas that were in need of revision, the numeric citations and titles of interpretations have all changed. In addition, the ethics rulings are no longer in a question and answer format but rather, have been drafted as interpretations, incorporated into interpretations as examples, or deleted where deemed appropriate. For example,

- Rule 101, *Independence* [ET sec. 101 par. .01] is referred to as the "Independence Rule" [ET sec. 1.200.001] in the revised code.
- the content from the ethics ruling entitled "Financial Services Company Client has Custody of a Member's Assets" [ET sec. 191 par. .081–.082] is incorporated into the "Brokerage and Other

Accounts" interpretation [ET sec. 1.255.020] found under the subtopic "Depository, Brokerage, and Other Accounts" [ET sec. 1.255] of the "Independence" topic [ET sec. 1.200].

The revised code is effective December 15, 2014, and is available at http://pub .aicpa.org/codeofconduct/Ethics.aspx.

To assist users in locating in the revised code content from the prior code, PEEC created a mapping document. The mapping document is available in Excel format in appendix D in the revised code.

TABLE OF CONTENTS

Part III

Illustrative Audit Documentation Case Study

Part I

Authoritative and Nonauthoritative Guidance on the Auditor's Risk Assessment in a Financial Statement Audit

©2016, AICPA

Chapter 1

Overview of Applying the Audit Risk Standards

TABLE OF CONTENTS

Observations and Suggestions

Illustration 1-1
Overview of Applying the Audit Risk Model

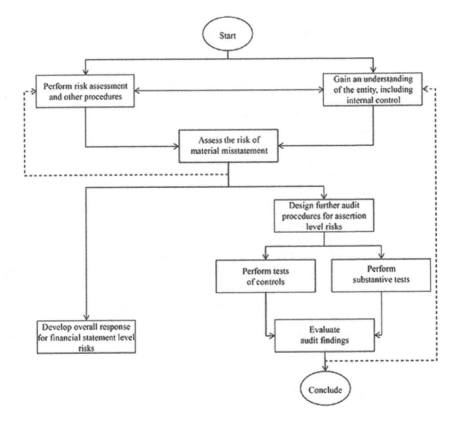

This illustration describes a high-level approach to the process that you follow to apply the audit risk standards to your audits by (1) assessing the risks of material misstatement, (2) using this risk assessment to plan and perform further audit procedures, and (3) evaluating the results of your procedures and reaching conclusions about the financial statements.

An Iterative Process. *Although the flowchart may indicate to some a linear audit process, an audit is, in fact, an iterative process in which you may repeat as the audit progresses the steps described in the flowchart as a result of new information obtained. In the flowchart, the dotted line connecting later steps in the process to earlier steps illustrates the potential iterative nature of the audit process.*

As indicated by the dotted line, the results of further audit procedures provide you with information that you use to confirm or modify your original risk assessment, which in turn, may lead to additional audit procedures or to a conclusion.

Perform Risk Assessment Procedures to Gain an Understanding of the Entity. *The first step in the process is to perform* risk assessment procedures *(for example, inquiry, observation, or inspection of documents) to gather information and gain an understanding of your client and its environment, including its internal control.*

Gain an Understanding of the Entity and Its Environment, Including Internal Control. *You should gain an understanding of the entity and its environment, including internal control, to identify and assess risks of material misstatement and to design further audit procedures. As you gather information about your client, you will begin to form an understanding of its business and the environment in which it operates. An important part of this understanding is your evaluation of the design of internal control and a determination of whether controls have been implemented (that is, placed in operation). This knowledge of the client, including the design of its internal control, may prompt you to seek additional information until you are satisfied with your level of understanding. Specifically, this knowledge and understanding of the client will enable you to assess whether there are risks of material misstatement in the financial statements that you are auditing. These risks should be expressed in terms of what can go wrong in specific classes of transactions, account balances, and disclosures and their relevant assertions.*

Materiality. *As you gather information and perform risk assessment procedures, you will want to have a materiality threshold in mind. Your risk assessment is responsive to judgments about financial statement materiality. Materiality is a critical judgment that affects all steps in the audit process. Because this judgment is not clearly associated with a specific phase and is responsive to some information you will be gathering before assessing the risks of material misstatement, it is not separately depicted in the illustration.*

Assess the Risks of Material Misstatement. *After identifying risks you will (1) relate them to what can go wrong in preparing the financial statements and (2) assess the likelihood and significance of the risk. When making these risk assessments, consider that*

- *the* risk of material misstatement (RMM) *is a combination of inherent and control risk. You are not required to perform a combined risk assessment, as you may choose to make separate assessments of inherent and control risk.*

- *risks of material misstatement can reside at either the financial statement level or the assertion level for classes of transactions, account balances, or disclosures. For example, a risk relating to the regulatory environment in which your client operates is a pervasive risk that affects many of the financial statement assertions in many accounts. On the other hand, a risk related to the valuation of inventory is restricted to that account and assertion and the related determination of cost of sales. Understanding the differences between the two types of risks is important because these differences drive your audit response. You will perform different procedures to understand and respond to financial statement level risks than you will need to understand and respond to assertion level risks.*

- *your assessment of risk at the assertion level should be specific to the unique circumstances of the entity. For example, assessing the* risk of material misstatement *relating to the existence assertion of an account as "high" in many cases would not be sufficient to design effective further audit procedures. Instead, in this example, your assessment of risk should describe* how *the existence assertion could contain a material misstatement, given the specific business processes, information processing, and controls in use at the particular client. It is common to use standard audit programs and example audit practice aids to complete your engagement. However, when using these standard programs and examples, it is important to consider carefully whether they appropriately reflect the unique circumstances of your client. To be effective, such programs are ordinarily tailored to each engagement.*

- *it is important that your risk assessments are supported by sufficient appropriate audit evidence. It is not appropriate to simply designate a risk to be at a given level without any support for the risk assessment. For example, why is the risk "low" and what supporting evidence do you have to support the assessment? This enumeration facilitates the review and communication value of the documentation.*

- *to the extent possible, even risks that reside at the financial statement level should be related to what can go wrong at the relevant assertion level for classes of transactions, account balances, or disclosures.*

Design Further Audit Procedures to Respond to Assessed Risks. *Once you have assessed the risks of material misstatement, you will design* further audit procedures *in response to these risks. There are two types of* further audit procedures: tests of controls and substantive procedures. *You may perform a combination of these two types of procedures. Of critical importance in performing an effective audit is to develop a clear link between the identified risks, the assessment of those risks, and the further audit procedures performed in response to the assessed risks. By relating risks of material misstatement to specific assertions, you will be able to establish this necessary linkage. Cross-references between assessed risks and further audit procedures facilitate the quality of the documentation and make working papers easier to review for quality assurance.*

> *Evaluate Audit Findings and Evidence. At the conclusion of the audit, you are required to evaluate the results of your audit procedures and reach a conclusion concerning whether the financial statements are free of material misstatement. You also should determine whether you have obtained sufficient appropriate audit evidence to support your audit opinion at a high level of assurance. Finally, you are required to evaluate identified control deficiencies and determine whether these deficiencies, individually or in combination, are significant deficiencies or material weaknesses.*

On every audit you are required to assess the risks that individual financial statement assertions are materially misstated. Other AICPA Audit and Accounting Guides may provide useful suggested risk assessment procedures if an entity is in a specialized industry or has transactions addressed within the specialized industry guides. The assessment of risk then serves as the basis for the design of further audit procedures.

This chapter provides an overview of this process, beginning with the information about the client and its environment that is necessary for you to identify risks, how you use that information to assess risk at the assertion level, and how that risk assessment helps you determine further audit procedures.

Subsequent chapters provide additional detail, as well as examples and illustrations of how the general guidance described here might be applied.

Practice Considerations for Auditors of Entities Using the COSO Framework

In May 2013, the Committee of Sponsoring Organizations of the Treadway Commission (COSO) published the updated *Internal Control—Integrated Framework* (COSO framework). The update of the original 1992 *Internal Control—Integrated Framework* (original COSO framework) became necessary due to the increasing complexity of business, evolving technologies, and changing expectations of stakeholders. The COSO framework updated in 2013 supersedes the original COSO framework after December 15, 2014.

Although the auditing standards do not require the application of a specific internal control framework, the COSO framework is widely used by entities[1] for designing, implementing, and conducting internal control. The COSO framework provides guidance that is useful and relevant to auditors charged with evaluating the design and implementation of controls (for example, as part of their risk assessment procedures) during a financial statement audit. The discussion in the following chapters of this guide are reflective of the fact that auditing standards are written without reference to a specific controls framework.

The auditing standards recognize 5 components of internal control that, for purposes of generally accepted auditing standards, provide a useful framework for auditors when considering how different aspects of an entity's internal control may affect the audit. Chapter 2, "Key Concepts Underlying the Auditor's Risk Assessment Process," and appendix C, "Internal Control Components," of this guide further explain these 5 components and the elements of

---

[1] *Standards for Internal Control in the Federal Government*, known as the "Green Book," sets the standards for an effective internal control system for federal agencies and may also be used by state and local governments and quasigovernmental entities, as well as not-for-profit entities.

those components that are relevant to the audit. These components are consistent with the components recognized in the COSO framework. However, the COSO framework includes not only 5 separate components but also 17 principles representing the fundamental concepts associated with the components.

In order for an entity's system of internal control to be effective, the COSO framework states that each of the five components of internal control and relevant principles should be *present* (designed appropriately and placed in operation) and *functioning* (effectively operating) and that the five components be operating together in an integrated manner. A major deficiency exists in an entity's system of internal control when the entity's management has determined that a component and one or more principles are not present and functioning or that components are not operating together. A *major deficiency* according to the COSO framework is an internal control deficiency or combination of deficiencies that severely reduces the likelihood that the entity can achieve its objectives. As discussed in the COSO framework, when a major deficiency exists, an entity cannot conclude that it has an effective system of internal control.

Observations and Suggestions

The COSO framework uses the terms *component, principle, points of focus,*[2] *approaches,* and *examples* to assist users in applying the framework. The auditing literature in many cases uses the term *objective* to help users comprehend the controls assessment process. This audit guide follows the terminology in the Statements on Auditing Standards, but may clarify how certain terms relate to the COSO framework. For example, companies may set financial reporting "objectives" as part of Principle 6, which is different from the "objective" of having controls over the revenue account.

In addition, the COSO framework notes two deficiency assessment levels: deficiency and severe deficiency. However this guide uses the categorizations of deficiency, significant deficiency, and material weakness as set out in AU-C section 265, *Communicating Internal Control Related Matters Identified in an Audit* (AICPA, *Professional Standards*).

Chapter 7, "Evaluating Audit Findings, Audit Evidence, and Deficiencies in Internal Control," of this guide provides guidance on the evaluation and communication of control deficiencies in the context of the auditing standards.

Points of focus are also provided within the COSO framework. There is no requirement that an assessment be performed to determine whether all points of focus are present and functioning. Management may determine that some points of focus are not suitable or relevant to the entity. Similarly, management may identify other suitable and relevant points of focus in addition to those provided in the COSO framework.

The fundamental concepts of an effective control are the same whether the entity is large or small. The auditing standards do not set up a lower standard

---

[2] *Points of focus* are important characteristics of principles that assist management in designing, implementing, and conducting internal control and in assessing whether the relevant principles are, in fact, present and functioning.

for small businesses or separate standards for different industries. Additionally, the auditing standards have no measures for achieving effective internal control that apply only to certain businesses. Similarly, the COSO framework views the 5 components and 17 principles as suitable to all entities. The COSO framework presumes that principles are relevant because they have a significant bearing on the presence and functioning of an associated component. Accordingly, if a relevant principle is not present and functioning, the associated component cannot be present and functioning. Therefore, in the context of risk assessment for a financial statement audit of an entity using the COSO framework, the consideration of the COSO components and principles is applicable regardless of the size of the entity being audited.

Appendix C of this guide specifies the 5 COSO components of internal control and the 17 COSO principles representing the fundamental concepts associated with the components.

COSO has also published the following companion documents to the COSO framework:

- *Internal Control—Integrated Framework Illustrative Tools for Assessing Effectiveness of a System of Internal Control*
- *Internal Control—Integrated Framework Internal Control over External Financial Reporting: A Compendium of Approaches and Examples*

Although not authoritative, these resources may be useful to auditors charged with evaluating the design and implementation of controls (as well as the operating effectiveness thereof) in conjunction with a financial statement audit.

Entities that have adopted the COSO framework and their auditors may find the transition to it, or the first time adoption of it, challenging in some respects. For example, the auditing standards currently do not explicitly recognize the 17 principles that COSO introduced in the COSO framework, although the principles for the most part align with the elements of internal control outlined in AU-C section 315, *Understanding the Entity and Its Environment and Assessing the Risks of Material Misstatement* (AICPA, *Professional Standards*). This guide can help relate the framework to the auditing standards and acts as a bridge to help entities and their auditors transition from the original COSO framework.

The Purpose of This Audit Guide

1.01 You, as the auditor, are required to perform risk assessment procedures, which include gaining an understanding of systems of internal control, to provide a basis for the identification and assessment of risks of material misstatement at the financial statement and relevant assertion levels. (Throughout this guide the auditor is referred to as "you.") This risk assessment then serves as the basis for you to design the nature, timing, and extent of further audit procedures. (AU-C sec. 315 par. .05 and AU-C sec. 300 par. .09)

1.02 The further audit procedures you design and perform should be appropriate in the circumstances for the purpose of obtaining sufficient appropriate audit evidence to be able to draw a reasonable conclusion on which to base your opinion. (AU-C sec. 500 par. .01 and .06)

1.03 This guide provides guidance, primarily on performing risk assessment procedures referred to in paragraph 1.01 and obtaining sufficient appropriate audit evidence referred to in paragraph 1.02. As such, this guide illustrates how to gather information needed to assess risk, evaluate that information to assess risk at the assertion level, and design and perform further audit procedures based on that assessed risk, evaluate the results, and reach conclusions. In addition, guidance on evaluating and communicating findings is also included.

Observations and Suggestions

The preceding paragraph describes a process in which there is a link between information gathering, the identification and assessment of risk, and the design and performance of further audit procedures. Each step in this process serves as the basis for performing the subsequent step. For example, your determination of what can go wrong at the assertion level helps you determine the nature, timing, and extent of your substantive procedures.

This linkage between the various stages in the risk assessment process is vital to performing an effective and efficient audit.

Financial statement assertions allow you to develop this link between the various stages of the risk assessment process. For example, your substantive procedures and tests of controls are directed at what can go wrong in specific assertions. For those audit procedures to be clearly linked to risks of material misstatement, those risks also should be expressed at that same level of detail: what can go wrong in the financial statement assertions.

Your documentation of the risks and associated procedures should be clear, to enable an experienced auditor with no prior association with the audit to understand the intended linkage.

1.04 Understanding the entity and its environment includes obtaining an understanding of its internal control. (This guide uses the term *client* to refer to the entity being audited.) This understanding of internal control should be sufficient to allow you to evaluate the design of controls and to determine whether they have been implemented (placed in operation). (Unless otherwise indicated, this guide uses the term *internal control* to mean "internal control over financial reporting, including the relevant controls over safeguarding assets.")

Overview of the Risk Assessment Process

1.05 This chapter provides a summary of the risk assessment process followed in an audit. Even though some requirements and guidance are presented in a way that suggests a sequential process, risk assessment involves a continuous process of gathering, updating, and analyzing information throughout the audit. Accordingly, you may implement the requirements and guidance in a different sequence from that presented in this guide or you may revisit steps when updated information is available.

Observations and Suggestions

Auditing is a nonlinear process, and different auditors may have different judgments about which steps should be performed first. For example, some auditors may determine that it first is necessary to obtain an understanding of the client and its environment to develop an appropriate audit strategy. Other auditors may determine that it first is necessary to determine appropriate materiality levels, which then serve to guide them through the information gathering process.

Neither approach is inherently more effective or efficient than the other. Within the audit process, it is common for different steps to interact dynamically with one or more other steps. The determination of materiality drives audit procedures, which produce results, which in turn influence materiality levels.

In that sense, it may not matter where you start in the process as long as you continue to revisit the procedures you performed and confirm the judgments made earlier in your engagement as you discover new information. For example, a practical point at which to revisit the judgments made to date and their interactions is when assessing the *risks of material misstatement*. At that point, the materiality and risk assessment procedures come together in determining the further audit procedures, and the assessment of the risks of material misstatement is an important determinant of the procedures to be applied to the audit risks.

1.06 The following is an overview of the audit process described in this guide:

- Perform risk assessment procedures by *gathering information about the entity and its environment, including internal control.* You should gather information about those aspects of the client and its environment that will allow you to identify and assess *risks of material misstatements* of the client's financial statements. The client's internal control is an integral part of its operations, and your evaluation of the design of internal control is an important part of your understanding of the client.

- *Gain an understanding of the entity and its environment, including its internal control.* You need to develop an understanding of specific aspects of the entity, its environment, and internal control to identify and assess risk and design and perform further audit procedures. Based on the information gathered, you should be able to identify what can go wrong in specific classes of transactions, account balances, and disclosures and their relevant assertions.

- *Assess risks of material misstatement.* Next, you will use your understanding of the client and its environment to assess the risks of material misstatement that relate to relevant assertions. Paragraph .27 of AU-C section 315, states that, to assess RMM, you should

  — identify risks through the process of obtaining an understanding of the entity and its environment, including relevant controls that relate to the risks, by considering the classes of transactions, account balances, and disclosures in the financial statements;

  — assess the identified risks and evaluate whether they relate more pervasively to the financial statements as a whole and potentially affect many assertions;

- relate the identified risks to what can go wrong at the relevant assertion level, taking account of relevant controls that the auditor intends to test; and

- consider the likelihood of misstatement, including the possibility of multiple misstatements, and whether the potential misstatement is of a magnitude that could result in a material misstatement.

- *Design further audit procedures (an audit response).* You should address the risks of material misstatement at both the financial statement level and the relevant assertion level. These risks are described subsequently. (The auditing standards use the term *relevant assertions* to describe the specific assertions that are related to a given account, class of transactions, or disclosure. This guide uses the term *assertions* in the same manner in which the auditing standards use the term *relevant assertions*.)

  - Risks of material misstatement at the financial statement level have a more pervasive effect on the financial statements and affect many accounts and assertions. In addition to developing assertion-specific responses, these types of risks may require you to develop an overall, audit-wide response, such as your choice of audit team members.

  - Assertion level risk pertains to specific accounts and assertions and should be considered when you design and subsequently perform further audit procedures. These further procedures often encompass a combined approach using both tests of activity-level controls (this guide uses the term *activity-level controls* to refer to the controls that pertain to assertion level risks) and substantive procedures directed at individual account balances, classes of transactions, and disclosures and their relevant assertions. It is important that auditors are mindful that some risks may relate to more than one assertion.

- *Perform further audit procedures.* Further audit procedures include tests of controls and substantive procedures. The nature, timing, and extent of these procedures should be designed in a way that is responsive to your assessed risks. Once designed, you will perform these procedures to gather sufficient appropriate audit evidence to support your opinion on the financial statements.

- *Evaluate audit findings.* You will evaluate the results of further audit procedures and the audit evidence obtained to reach a conclusion about whether the client's financial statements are free of material misstatement or whether such a conclusion can be reached.

Audit documentation is an important part of every audit, and each chapter in this guide summarizes the documentation requirements that pertain to each phase in the audit.

(AU-C sec. 230 par. 08, AU-C sec. 315 par. .03, and AU-C sec. 500 par. .06)

Information Gathering

Information Needed About the Client and Its Environment to Identify and Assess Risks of Material Misstatement

1.07 Obtaining an understanding of your client and its environment, including internal control, is a continuous, dynamic process of gathering, updating, and analyzing information throughout the audit. This understanding establishes a framework that allows you to plan the audit and exercise professional judgment throughout the audit when, for example, you are

- assessing risks of material misstatement of the financial statements;
- determining materiality;
- considering the appropriateness of the client's selection and application of accounting policies and adequacy of its financial statement disclosures;
- identifying areas where special audit consideration may be necessary (for example, related party transactions);
- developing expectations for performing analytical procedures;
- responding to the assessed risks of material misstatement, including designing and performing further audit procedures to obtain sufficient appropriate audit evidence; and
- evaluating the sufficiency and appropriateness of audit evidence obtained.

1.08 Not all information about a client or its environment is relevant for your audit. Often, the information you are required to gather about your client is that which allows you to assess the risk that specific assertions could be materially misstated. AU-C section 315 defines the aspects of the client for which you should gather information and obtain an understanding. Table 1-1 summarizes these aspects. Chapter 3, "Planning and Performing Risk Assessment Procedures," of this guide provides more detail and examples of the information you should gather.

Table 1-1
Understanding the Client and Its Environment, Including the Entity's Internal Control

On every audit you should gather (or update) information and obtain an understanding of the client and its environment including an understanding of the

- relevant industry, regulatory, and other external factors affecting the client;
- nature of the client;
- client's selection and application of accounting policies;
- client's objectives and strategies and those related business risks that may result in risks of material misstatement

(continued)

Understanding the Client and Its Environment, Including the Entity's Internal Control—*continued*

- measurement and review of the client's financial performance; and
- the client's internal control relevant to the audit.

(AU-C sec. 315 par. .12–.13)

Relevant industry factors may include the market and competition, supplier and customer relationships, energy supply and cost, and technological developments.

Regulatory factors may include relevant accounting pronouncements, the regulatory framework, laws, taxation, governmental policies, and environmental requirements that affect the industry and client.

Other external factors may include general economic conditions, interest rates, inflation, and availability of financing.

Understanding the nature of the client, may include, among other matters, its operations, ownership, governance, the types of investments it makes and plans to make, how it is financed, and how it is structured. Numerous other matters you may consider are included in paragraph .A31 of AU-C section 315.

The client's selection and application of accounting policies may encompass the methods used for significant and unusual transactions, changes in accounting policies, new accounting standards and their adoption, and the financial reporting competencies of personnel. You should evaluate whether the client's accounting policies are appropriate for its business and consistent with the applicable financial reporting framework and those used in the client's industry. (AU-C sec. 315 par. .12)

The client sets strategies in the context of its industry, regulatory, and other external factors. Those strategies are the approaches to achieving its business objectives. Objectives and strategies are related to business risks. An understanding of business risks increases the likelihood of identifying risks of material misstatement because most business risks eventually have financial consequences that in turn affect the client's financial statements. You are not responsible to identify or assess all business risks because not all of them give rise to risks of material misstatement. Paragraph .A39 of AU-C section 315 includes numerous examples of objectives, strategies, and business risks.

The metrics used by management to measure and review financial performance provide you with information about the aspects of the entity that management considers to be important.

Internal Control

1.09 Not all of the client's internal controls are relevant to your audit. When performing a financial statement audit, your consideration of internal control is limited to those controls that are deemed to be "relevant to the audit." Operational controls, for example, over production and other business functions, may affect but often are not directly related to financial reporting. Accordingly, early in the audit process, you will determine which controls are relevant to the audit. For example, production quality control issues may affect estimates of warranty costs. Paragraph .A69 of AU-C section 315 lists many factors that you might consider in making a professional judgment about whether a control, individually or in combination with others, is relevant to the audit. The factors include materiality, the size of the entity, the diversity and complexity of its operations, and how a specific control prevents, or detects and corrects, potential material misstatements.

1.10 There are some controls that are relevant to every audit. These controls relate to

a. elements of the five internal control components that chapter 2 of this guide describes. On each audit, you should gain an understanding of certain, specified elements relating to each of the five components.

b. antifraud programs and controls. AU-C section 240, *Consideration of Fraud in a Financial Statement Audit* (AICPA, *Professional Standards*), directs you to evaluate the design and implementation of antifraud programs and controls.

c. controls related to "significant risks." Some significant risks arise on most audits, and the controls related to these risks are relevant to your audit. Significant risks are discussed in paragraph 1.30.

d. controls related to circumstances when substantive procedures alone will not provide sufficient appropriate audit evidence.

e. other controls that you determine to be relevant to your audit.

In addition, when obtaining an understanding of the company and its environment, the design and implementation of controls over the most significant revenues and significant expenditures will, in many cases, be relevant. Chapters 3 and 4, "Understanding the Client, Its Environment, and Its Internal Control," further describe these categories of relevant controls in more detail.

Risk Assessment Procedures

1.11 You should perform risk assessment procedures to provide a basis for your identification and assessment of risks of material misstatement at the financial statement level and relevant assertion level. Risk assessment procedures include

a. inquiries of management, appropriate individuals within the internal audit function (if such function exists), and others at the client who, in the auditor's professional judgment, may have information that is likely to assist in identifying risks of material misstatement due to fraud or error,

b. analytical procedures, and

c. observation and inspection.

(AU-C sec. 315 par. .06)

Observations and Suggestions

You should perform risk assessment procedures to support your assessment of the risks of material misstatement. Your risk assessment procedures provide the audit evidence necessary to support your risk assessments, which, in turn, drive the nature, timing, and extent of further audit procedures. Thus, the results of your risk assessment procedures are an integral part of the audit evidence you obtain to support your opinion on the financial statements. It is not acceptable to simply deem risk to be "at the maximum" without evidence or support unless such an assessment is supported by the facts. By defaulting to maximum risk without adequate understanding of actual controls in place, you are not determining specifically what, exactly, the risks are, and which assertions they affect. For example, is it likely that all assertions of accounts payable are equally risky? If that were so, extensive tests of existence and valuation would be required as well as the common tests of completeness and accuracy, and this is unlikely to result in an efficient audit. You may also overlook conditions or weaknesses that indicate a fraud risk. Example or illustrative audit programs may not be sufficient to address all possible risks of material misstatement that might be specific to this entity.

Further, even at the assertion level, for example, an inventory existence risk could be high, but it could result from a number of different causes, not all of which may be applicable at your client (for example, theft, shrinkage, cut-off issues, short deliveries). Without understanding and documenting what, exactly, is the source of this risk, you are not necessarily able to design the appropriate nature, timing, and extent of procedures to address the risk. Procedures designed to address a risk of theft may be different from procedures designed to address a risk of short deliveries or cut-off, even though both could be described as high risk pertaining to existence of inventory.

A Mix of Procedures

1.12 You are not required to perform *all* the risk assessment procedures (for example, inquiries, analytical procedures, observations, and so on) for *each* aspect of the client's internal control and its environment listed in table 1-1. However, in the course of obtaining the required understanding about the client, including internal control, you should perform all the risk assessment procedures.

(AU-C sec. 315 par. .A5)

Procedures to Obtain an Understanding of Internal Control

1.13 Inquiry may allow you to gather information about internal control design, but inquiry alone is not sufficient to determine whether the control has been implemented (placed in operation). Thus, when inquiry is used to obtain information about the design of internal control, you should corroborate the responses to your inquiries by performing at least one other risk assessment procedure to determine that client personnel are using the control. That additional procedure may be further observations of the control operating, inspecting documents and reports, or tracing transactions through the information system relevant to financial reporting.

1.14 Although AU-C section 500, *Audit Evidence* (AICPA, *Professional Standards*), notes that corroboration of evidence obtained through inquiry is often of particular importance, in the case of inquiries about the control environment and "tone-at-the-top," the information available to support management's responses to inquiries may be limited. When better audit evidence is not available from any other sources, corroborative inquiries made of multiple sources may sometimes be a source of evidence available to determine whether a control has been implemented (that is, placed in operation). When no more effective procedures can be identified, corroborating inquiries of different knowledgeable persons can be an effective procedure when the results of the inquiries are consistent with observed behaviors or past actions. For example, making inquiries of an owner-manager about the implementation of the company's code of conduct will not, by itself, allow the auditor to obtain a sufficient understanding of that aspect of the control environment. However, corroborating the owner manager's response with additional inquiries or a survey of other company personnel, and observing consistent behaviors or other evidence with respect to the results of those inquiries, may provide the auditor with the requisite level of understanding. As another example, if it is represented to the auditor that no instances of ethics code violations were reported and evidence of that is not otherwise observable, corroborating inquiry and the lack of contradictory evidence or observations may be the only viable alternative evidence. The auditor may consider his or her experience in dealing with management in this area as well as other areas, and consider whether any results from applying audit procedures are consistent with or might contradict such evidence before accepting the inquiries.

Observations and Suggestions

As will be discussed later, inquiry is often the starting point for understanding controls but is supported by observation, examining documentary evidence, or a walkthrough. These are common audit procedures that provide evidence that a control is in place.

Other Procedures That Provide Relevant Information About the Client

1.15 *Assessing the risks of material misstatement due to fraud.* AU-C section 240 directs you to perform certain audit procedures to assess the risks of material misstatement due to fraud. Some of these procedures also may help gather information about the entity and its environment, particularly its internal control. For this reason, it may be helpful to

- coordinate the procedures you perform to assess the risks of material misstatement due to fraud (for example, brainstorming) with your other risk assessment procedures, and

- consider the results of your assessment of fraud risk when identifying the risks of material misstatement.

The COSO framework specifies, under the risk assessment component, principles and associated points of focus addressing the entity's consideration of the potential for fraud during risk assessment procedures (principle 8).

1.16 *Other information.* When relevant to the audit, you also should consider other knowledge you have of the client that can help you assess risk. This other information may include either or both of the following:

- Information obtained from prior audits or from your client acceptance or continuance process

- Experience gained on other engagements performed by the engagement partner for the client, for example, the audit of the client's pension plan.

(AU-C sec. 315 par. .07–.08)

Updating Information From Prior Periods

1.17 If you intend to use information about the client you obtained from previous experience with the client and from audit procedures performed in previous audits, you should determine whether changes have occurred since then that may affect the relevance of the information to the current audit. To make this determination, you may make inquiries and perform other appropriate audit procedures, such as walkthroughs of relevant systems. (AU-C sec. 315 par. .10)

Gaining an Understanding of the Client and Its Environment

1.18 The gathering of information, by itself, does not provide you with the understanding of the client that is necessary for you to assess risk. For you to assess the risks of material misstatement and design further audit procedures, you will want to assimilate and synthesize the information gathered to determine how it might affect the financial statements. For example,

- information about the client's industry may allow you to identify characteristics of the industry that could give rise to specific misstatements. For example, if your client is a construction contractor that uses long-term contract accounting, your understanding of the client should be sufficient to allow you to recognize that the significant estimates of revenues and costs create risk, and without proper controls, there would be risks of material misstatement.

- information about the ownership of your client, how it is structured, and other elements of its nature assists you to identify related-party transactions that, if not accounted for properly and adequately disclosed, could lead to a material misstatement.

- your identification and understanding of the business risks facing your client increase the chance that you will identify financial reporting risks. For example, your client may face an imminent risk that a new company has recently entered its market, and that new entrant could have certain business advantages (for example, economies of scale or greater brand recognition). The potential risk related to this business risk might be obsolescence or overproduction of inventory that could only be sold at a discount. Thus, you might need to understand how the client understands and controls the risk in order to assess the risks of material misstatement.

- information about the performance measures used by client management may lead you to identify differences in internal control or pressures or incentives that could motivate client personnel to misstate the financial statements.

- information about the design and implementation of internal control may lead you to identify a deficiency in control design. Such an improperly designed control may represent a significant deficiency or material weakness.

- appendix B, "Understanding the Entity and Its Environment," of this guide suggests factors that may be relevant in understanding the entity and its environment, and is reproduced from paragraph .A156 of AU-C section 315.

Understanding Internal Control

Observations and Suggestions

The "extent" of your understanding of controls describes the level of knowledge you should obtain about the controls. There are two basic levels of knowledge:

    a. The design (presence) of the controls and whether they have been implemented. You should obtain this level of understanding on all engagements.

    b. The operational effectiveness (functioning) of those controls. You should obtain this level of understanding only when you plan to rely on internal control to modify the nature, timing, and extent of your substantive procedures or in the circumstance when substantive procedures alone do not provide sufficient audit evidence.

The second level, the operational effectiveness of controls, requires a more in-depth testing of internal control that addresses how well the control performed during the audit period. To determine operational effectiveness, you first need to understand how the controls are designed and assess whether they appear to have been implemented (that is, placed in operation). In other words, any knowledge of operational effectiveness builds upon your evaluation of control design and implementation.

1.19 At a minimum, your understanding of internal control allows you to do the following:

    a. Evaluate control design. Evaluating the design of a control involves determining whether the control is capable of either

        i. effectively preventing material misstatements, or

        ii. effectively detecting and correcting material misstatements.

    b. Determine whether a control has been implemented. Implementation of a control means that the control exists and that the entity is using it.

(AU-C sec. 315 par. .14)

Procedures Related to Controls at a Service Organization

1.20 When your client uses a service organization to process some of its transactions, you may need to obtain an understanding of the information system and related controls that reside at the service organization. To help obtain that understanding, you may wish to obtain a report on the service organization's controls, prepared by the service organization's auditors.

Service organizations (including sub-servicers, if applicable) play an increasing role in the financial accounting and reporting of many entities. Relevant services that are performed by these organizations may be applicable regarding the *risks of material misstatement* of the entity they serve. The COSO framework contains a pervasive discussion of service organizations and the effect thereof on the considerations that may be made relevant to certain principles.

1.21 Just because your client uses a service organization to process some of its transactions does not, in itself, require you to obtain a service auditor's report. If certain conditions are met, such as sufficient company input and output controls on the information processed by the service organization, you may meet the requirements for understanding internal control without obtaining a service auditor's report on controls at a service organization. Paragraphs 3.78–.85 of this guide provide additional guidance on this matter.

Discussion Among the Audit Team

1.22 The engagement partner and other key members of the audit engagement team should discuss the susceptibility of the client's financial statements to material misstatement. The engagement partner should determine which matters are to be communicated to the engagement team members not involved in the discussion. (AU-C sec. 315 par. .11)

This discussion

- provides an opportunity for more experienced team members to share their insights;
- allows team members to exchange information about the client's business risks;
- assists team members to gain a better understanding of the potential for material misstatement resulting from fraud or error in areas assigned to them; and
- provides a basis upon which the team members communicate and share new information obtained throughout the audit that may affect the assessment of risks of material misstatement or the audit procedures to address those risks.

1.23 This discussion among the audit team could be held at the same time as the discussion among the team related to fraud, as described by AU-C section 240. In many cases this discussion may be held after the auditor obtains the understanding of the entity and its controls. If held earlier, the brainstorming might need to be repeated or updated.

Observations and Suggestions

The discussion among the engagement team about the susceptibility of the entity's financial statements to material misstatement and the annual brainstorming session specific to fraud can become stale over time. To keep the sessions thoughtful and effective, auditors may vary the format and focus of discussions. In some cases, fraud specialists or firm owners may be invited to participate in the engagement discussion to provide a fresh perspective.

Assessing the Risks of Material Misstatement

Observations and Suggestions

To assess the risk of "material" misstatement, you will need to determine an appropriate materiality level. Over the course of your audit, as you perform audit procedures and evaluate the results, you may revise your determination of materiality. If your judgments of materiality do change, you also may want to reevaluate your assessment of the risks of material misstatement. For example, if your audit procedures result in you lowering your materiality level for a particular assertion, certain conditions that you previously did not consider to result in a risk of a material misstatement could be reassessed as risks of material misstatement.

1.24 The *risk of material misstatement* of the financial statements prior to the audit consists of the following two components:

- *Inherent risk* is the susceptibility of an assertion about a class of transaction, account balance, or disclosure to a misstatement that could be material, either individually or when aggregated with other misstatements, before consideration of any related controls (that is, assuming that there are no related controls). For example, the inherent risk of uncollectible accounts receivable might be high but such risk might be mitigated with effective controls over the granting of credit and the collection of outstanding accounts receivable.

- *Control risk* is the risk that a misstatement that could occur in an assertion about a class of transaction, account balance, or disclosure and that could be material, either individually or when aggregated with other misstatements, will not be prevented or detected and corrected on a timely basis by the entity's internal control.

(AU-C sec. 200 par. .14)

1.25 Inherent risk and control risk are the client's risks; that is, they exist independently of your audit. Thus, your risk assessment procedures help you better assess these client risks, but they do not alter the client's existing inherent or control risks. This guide refers to the *risk of material misstatement* as your combined assessment of inherent risk and control risk; however, you may make separate assessments of inherent risk and control risk.

Observations and Suggestions — Assessing Versus Testing Controls

There is a difference between assessing and testing controls. For example, say that you have assessed the controls as effective based on your review of their design and an observation that they have been implemented (that is, placed in operation). Based solely on that assessment, you would not necessarily have an adequate basis for considering control risk is low (or even moderate) as part of your audit strategy, as you would need further evidence of the effective operation of the controls through sufficient tests of controls to reach that conclusion.

Observations and Suggestions — The Audit Risk Model

Chapter 2 of this guide provides a model of audit risk (AR) in which:

$$AR = RMM \times DR$$

where RMM is the risk of material misstatement and DR is detection risk.

The risk of material misstatement is described as "the client's risk," which means that it is independent of your audit. You can control detection risk by changing the nature, timing, and extent of your substantive procedures. For example, to decrease the planned level of detection risk, you could perform more extensive and detailed analytical procedures and detailed substantive procedures, such as increasing sample sizes. Illustrations of how these risks can be managed to achieve a low overall audit risk can also be noted in table 4-2 in chapter 4, "Nonstatistical and Statistical Audit Sampling for Substantive Tests of Details," of the AICPA Audit Guide *Audit Sampling*.

You cannot control the risk of material misstatement as you can detection risk. The risk of material misstatement exists separately from your audit procedures. However, to properly control detection risk, you are required to assess the risk of material misstatement. The risk assessment process described in this guide is designed to allow you to gather information to assess the risk of material misstatement so you can design further audit procedures.

The Risk Assessment Process

1.26 You use your understanding of the client and its environment—which includes your evaluation of the design and implementation of internal control—to identify and assess the risks of material misstatement at the financial statement level and the relevant assertion level for classes of transactions, account balances, and disclosures. (AU-C sec. 315 par. .26) To make this assessment, you should

    a. identify risk throughout the process of obtaining an understanding of the entity and its environment, including relevant controls that relate to the risks, by considering the classes of transactions, account balances, and disclosures in the financial statements;

    b. assess the identified risks and evaluate whether they relate more pervasively to the financial statements as a whole and potentially to many assertions;

    c. relate the identified risks to what could go wrong at the assertion level, considering relevant controls that you intend to test; and

    d. consider the likelihood of misstatement and whether the potential misstatement is of a magnitude that could result in a material misstatement.

(AU-C sec. 315 par. .27)

Financial Statement Level and Assertion Level Risks

1.27 You should identify and assess the risks of material misstatement at both the financial statement level and the relevant assertion level for classes of transactions, account balances, and disclosures. (AU-C sec. 315 par. .26)

    a. *Financial statement level risks and controls.* Some risks of material misstatement relate pervasively to the financial statements as a whole and potentially affect many relevant accounts and assertions. The risks at the financial statement level may be identifiable with specific assertions at the class of transaction, account balance or disclosure level. In this guide, we use the term *entity-level controls* to describe those controls that pertain to financial statement level risks.

b. *Relevant assertion level risks and controls.* Other risks of material misstatement relate to specific classes of transactions, account balances, and disclosures at the assertion level, for example, the valuation of a long-term unconditional promise to give in a not-for-profit organization. Your assessment of risk at the assertion level provides a basis for considering the appropriate audit approach for designing and performing further audit procedures, which include substantive procedures and may also include tests of controls. This guide uses the term *activity-level controls* to refer to the controls that pertain to assertion level risks.

Observations and Suggestions

You express an audit opinion on the financial statements *as a whole*, and the audit risk model describes audit risk for the overall financial statements (and for assertions). However, in executing the audit, you apply the audit risk model and assess risk at a more granular level, namely the assertion level. To accomplish this detailed level of risk assessment, you will consider what can be misstated in specific accounts, classes of transactions, and disclosures and their relevant assertions.

Risk that exists at the financial statement level, for example, those that pertain to a weak control environment or to management's process for making significant accounting estimates, should be related to specific assertions, if possible. For example, risk related to the client's process for making accounting estimates would affect those assertions where an accounting estimate was necessary (for example, the valuation of assets).

In other instances, it may not be possible for you to relate your financial statement level risk to a particular assertion or group of assertions. For example, it may not be possible for you to determine which assertions will or will not be affected by an overall weak control environment. Financial statement level risk such as a weak control environment that cannot be related to specific assertions often will require you to make an overall engagement response, such as the way in which the audit is staffed or supervised, or the timing of further audit procedures. It might also mean that risk might be assessed as high for many or all accounts and assertions.

Careful consideration of potential financial statement level risk during the brainstorming may indicate that there are cost-effective ways to limit your response to the risk. For example, a weak accounting function may only be a significant risk for unusual or new transactions or when new accounting standards are implemented. Effective accounting for routine transactions may be well evidenced. By focusing audit procedures on the points in the accounting process where these issues can create risk, a more cost- and risk-effective audit can be designed.

How to Consider Internal Control When Assessing Risks

1.28 Your evaluation of internal control design and the determination of whether controls have been implemented are integral components of the risk assessment process. When making risk assessments, you should identify the controls that are likely to either prevent, or detect and correct material misstatements in specific assertions. For example, procedures relating to the client's physical inventory count may relate specifically to the existence or completeness of inventory.

1.29 Individual controls often do not address a risk completely by themselves. Often, only multiple control activities, together with other components of internal control (for example, the control environment, risk assessment, information and communication, or monitoring), will be sufficient to address a risk. For this reason, when determining whether identified controls are likely to prevent or detect and correct material misstatements, you may organize your risk assessment procedures according to significant transactions and business processes, rather than general ledger accounts.

Identification of Significant Risks

1.30 Paragraph .04 of AU-C section 315 defines *significant risk* as follows: "A significant risk is an identified and assessed risk of material misstatement that, in the auditor's professional judgment, requires special audit consideration." (The defined term *significant risk* is italicized in this guide to remind readers of its definition and limited application.) As part of your risk assessment, you should determine whether any risks identified are, in your professional judgment, a *significant risk*. In making this judgment you exclude the effects of identified related controls (that is, assume there are no related controls). *Significant risks* are those that require special audit consideration. For example, because of the nature of your client and the industry in which it operates, you might determine that revenue recognition requires special audit consideration. For other clients, the valuation of intangible assets or the identification and required disclosure of related party transactions may be considered *significant risks*. Significant risk often arises with unusual transactions. Moreover, one or more *significant risks* arise on most audits. (Note: In practice, auditors may confuse significant risk with high risk. Not all high risks are *significant risks*. For example, the collectability of accounts receivable may be a high risk but not a *significant risk*; that is, no special audit consideration is required beyond extensive but customary substantive procedures of collectability.) (AU-C sec. 315 par. .28)

1.31 Special audit consideration for *significant risks* means you should

    a. obtain an understanding of your client's controls relevant to that risk and, based on that understanding, evaluate the design of related controls, including relevant control activities, and determine whether they have been implemented. (AU-C sec. 315 par. .30)

    b. perform other appropriate procedures that are linked clearly and responsive to the risk. Moreover, when your approach to *significant risks* consists *only* of substantive procedures, you should include tests of details.

        Substantive procedures related to *significant risks* should not be limited solely to analytical procedures. For other risks, effective analytical procedures alone may sometimes provide sufficient evidence.

        Note that if you *are* testing controls over *significant risks*, you may be able to limit your substantive procedures to only analytical procedures.

        (AU-C sec. 330 par. .22)

    c. If you intend to rely on controls related to a *significant risk,* you should test the operating effectiveness of those controls in the current period. Reliance on tests of controls performed in a prior period is not appropriate for a *significant risk.* (AU-C sec. 330 par. .15)

    d. Document those risks you have identified as *significant risks* (AU-C sec. 315 par. 33*d*).

    1.32 The determination of *significant risks* is a matter for your professional judgment. In exercising that judgment, you should first consider only inherent risk and not control risk. Paragraphs 5.30–.37 of this guide provide more guidance on how to determine *significant risks.* (AU-C sec. 315 par. .29)

Responding to Assessed Risks

    1.33 The risk assessment process culminates with your articulation of the account balances, classes of transactions, or disclosures where material misstatements are most likely to occur and how those misstatements may occur, given the unique circumstances of your client. This assessment of the risk of material misstatement, which relates identified risks to what can go wrong at the assertion level, provides a basis for designing and performing further audit procedures.

    1.34 You perform further audit procedures to obtain the audit evidence necessary to support your audit opinion. Further audit procedures are defined as tests of controls and substantive procedures. Often, a combined approach using both tests of controls and substantive procedures is an effective approach.

    1.35 In determining the nature, timing, and extent of further audit procedures, you should design and perform further audit procedures whose nature, timing, and extent are responsive to the assessed risks of material misstatement at the assertion level. You should provide a clear linkage between the risk assessments and the nature, timing, and extent of the further audit procedures. (AU-C sec. 330 par. .06)

    1.36 Audit procedures performed in previous audits and suggested procedures provided by illustrative audit programs may help you understand the types of further audit procedures it is possible for you to perform. However, prior year procedures and example audit programs do not provide a sufficient basis for determining the nature, timing, and extent of audit procedures to perform in the current audit. Your assessment of the risks of material misstatement in the current period is the primary basis for designing further audit procedures in the current period.

Identification and Communication of Internal Control Matters

    1.37 Your objective in an audit is to form an opinion on the client's financial statements as a whole. Your audit objective is not to identify all deficiencies in internal control, and you are not required to perform procedures to identify all deficiencies in internal control. Nevertheless, your application of audit procedures or communications with management or others may make you aware of deficiencies in the client's internal control. (AU-C sec. 265 par. .02)

1.38 A deficiency in internal control over financial reporting exists when the design or operation of a control does not allow management or employees, in the normal course of performing their assigned functions, to prevent, or detect and correct misstatements on a timely basis. (AU-C sec. 265 par. .07) You should evaluate the deficiencies in internal control you identify during the course of your audit and determine whether these deficiencies, individually or in combination, are significant deficiencies or material weaknesses. (AU-C sec. 265 par. .09) You are required to communicate in writing to management and those charged with governance those deficiencies in internal control that, in your judgment, constitute significant deficiencies or material weaknesses. (AU-C sec. 265 par. .11) Chapter 7 of this guide provides guidance on the evaluation and communication of deficiencies.

Audit Documentation

1.39 AU-C section 230, *Audit Documentation* (AICPA, *Professional Standards*), provides requirements that apply to the risk assessment process. Your audit documentation should be sufficient to enable an experienced auditor, having no previous connection to the audit, to understand

- the nature, timing, and extent of the audit procedures performed,
- the results of the audit procedures performed, and the evidence obtained, and
- the significant findings or issues, and conclusions reached, and professional judgments made.

Subsequent chapters of this guide illustrate the application of the audit documentation requirements.

(AU-C sec. 230 par. .08)

1.40 The form and extent of audit documentation is for you to determine using professional judgment. AU-C section 230 provides general guidance regarding the purpose, content, and ownership and confidentiality of audit documentation. Examples of common documentation techniques include narrative descriptions, questionnaires, checklists, and flowcharts. These techniques may be used alone or in combination.

1.41 The form and extent of your documentation are influenced by the following:

- The nature, size, and complexity of the entity, its controls, and its environment
- The availability of information from the entity
- The specific audit methodology and technology used in the course of the audit

Observations and Suggestions

For example, documentation of the understanding of a complex information system in which a large volume of transactions are electronically initiated, recorded, processed, or reported may include flowcharts, questionnaires, or decision tables. For an information system for which few transactions are processed (for example, long-term debt), documentation of the system in the form of a memorandum may be sufficient. In many cases, the more complex the entity and its environment, and the more extensive the audit procedures performed by the auditor, the more extensive your documentation should be.

The existence of good client documentation can also help reduce the extent of required audit documentation as you document your understanding of the controls. Where the client has good documentation, it can minimize the cost of producing audit documentation about entity processes through leveraging the existing documentation using references and focusing auditor documentation on the assessment of the controls over those processes.

You may relate your client's controls to objectives (for example, principles) and assertions for the most significant processes of an entity, regardless of the way control processes are documented by the client. By documenting your evaluation of controls using the concepts in the controls framework, you will more easily identify important gaps in control that are not fully addressed by the client's system of internal control. When your client directly relates their documentation to the terms and structure of an appropriate framework (for example, components, principles, and points of focus), savings in audit time can be achieved.

The specific audit methodology and technology used in the course of the audit will also affect the form and extent of documentation. For example, a firm may require the use of a risk matrix (for example, by account and by assertion) to summarize the elements of the risks of material misstatement. That may simplify the documentation and linkage process. Also, firms may require the use of electronic working papers and the use of active electronic links, which may facilitate the documentation process and navigation between working papers.

Summary

1.42 Illustration 1-2 summarizes the guidance provided in this chapter.

Chapters 3–6 of this guide provide more detailed guidance, examples, and illustrations of the overview material described in this chapter. To apply this guidance on your audit, you will need to have a working knowledge of key risk assessments and terms. The next chapter of this guide provides you with this knowledge.

Illustration 1-2
Summary of the Risk Assessment Process

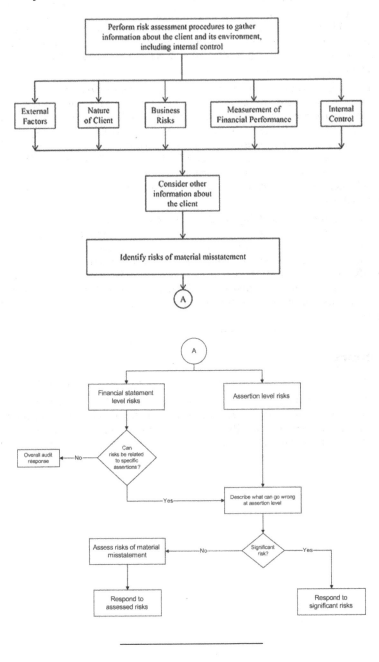

Chapter 2

Key Concepts Underlying the Auditor's Risk Assessment Process

TABLE OF CONTENTS

_____

This guide describes how you as the auditor assess and respond to audit risk in a financial statement audit in practice. It describes a process to gather information, assess and respond to identified risks, and evaluate evidence on your audits.

To appropriately apply this process to your audits, you will need to have a working knowledge of the key concepts upon which the process is built. The purpose of this chapter is to provide working definitions of those key concepts.

Reasonable Assurance

2.01 The auditing standards make numerous references to your responsibility for obtaining *reasonable assurance*. For example, your audit opinion states that generally accepted auditing standards (GAAS) require you to "obtain reasonable assurance about whether the financial statements are free of material misstatement." For this reason, it is important that you have a working knowledge of the term.

2.02 Reasonable assurance is a high—but not absolute—level of assurance. Put another way, you should plan and perform your audit in such a way that audit risk is reduced to an acceptably low level. The auditor is not expected to obtain absolute assurance that the financial statements are free from material misstatement due to fraud or error. (AU-C sec. 200 par. .06)

Audit Risk and the Risks of Material Misstatement

2.03 *Audit risk* is the risk that the financial statements are materially misstated and the auditor expresses an inappropriate opinion. You should perform your audit to reduce audit risk to an acceptably low level. You will consider audit risk at all stages of your audit. (AU-C sec. 200 par. .14)

2.04 Audit risk is a function of two components:

    a. *Risks of material misstatement*, which are the risks that a class of transaction, account balance, or disclosure contains a material misstatement.

    b. *Detection risk*, which is the risk that the auditor will not detect such misstatements.

(AU-C sec. 200 par. .14)

2.05 To reduce audit risk to an acceptably low level you will

    a. assess the risks of material misstatement, and

    b. based on that assessment, design and perform further audit procedures to detect material misstatements.

Assessing the Risks of Material Misstatement

2.06 To assess the risks of material misstatement you should obtain an understanding of the client and its industry. The understanding should include understanding the following:

- The industry, its regulatory environment, and other external factors
- The nature of the entity, for example its operations, ownership, and financing

©2016, AICPA

- The entity's selection and application of accounting policies
- The entity's objectives, strategies, and related business risks
- How management measures and reviews the entity's financial performance
- The entity's internal control relevant to the audit

(AU-C sec. 315 par. .12–.13)

Thus, the first step in assessing the risks of material misstatement is to gather information and gain an understanding of these matters.

2.07 You are required to assess risks of material misstatement at the financial statement level and at the assertion level for classes of transactions, account balances, and disclosures. (AU-C sec. 315 par. .26)

- Risks of material misstatement at the financial statement level refer to risks that relate pervasively to the financial statements as a whole and potentially affect many different assertions. For example, a lack of qualified personnel in financial reporting roles (an element of the client's control environment) may affect many different accounts and several assertions.
- Risks of material misstatement at the assertion level relates to one or more specific assertions in an account or in several accounts, for example, the valuation of inventory or the occurrence of sales.

2.08 Your specific response to assessed risk may differ depending on whether they reside at the financial statement or assertion level.

- Financial statement level risk in many cases requires an overall response, such as providing more supervision to the engagement team or incorporating additional elements of unpredictability in the selection of your audit procedures.
- Assertion level risk is addressed by the nature, timing, and extent of further audit procedures, which may include substantive procedures or a combination of tests of controls and substantive procedures.

For this reason, you should assess the risks of material misstatement at both the financial statement and the assertion level. (AU-C sec. 315 par. .26)

Observations and Suggestions

In some instances, it may be possible to relate financial statement level risk to an individual assertion or small group of assertions. For example, the selection and application of accounting policies many times is thought of as a financial statement level risk because it has the potential to affect the financial statements as a whole. However, at your client, you may determine that the selection and application of accounting policies is a risk only for revenue recognition, as all other accounting policies that are relevant to the client (for example, depreciation policies) do not pose a risk. You may decide that implementing new accounting standards is an area of risk and may focus experienced auditor attention on this aspect of risk. In the forthcoming transition to the new Revenue Recognition standard (Topic 606) entities may assess revenue recognition as a high risk.

> To the extent possible, you will want to relate financial statement level risks to individual assertions, as this will help you design more effective further audit procedures.

2.09 Your assessment of the risks of material misstatement (at both the financial statement and the assertion level) should be directly linked to your overall audit response and to the design and performance of further audit procedures. For example, if your understanding of the client and its environment, including internal control, leads you to assess that there is a significant risk that inventory quantities are overstated, you would design further audit procedures to specifically respond to that risk.

Risks of Material Misstatement at the Assertion Level

2.10 The *risks of material misstatement* consist of two components:

   a. *Inherent risk,* which is the susceptibility of an assertion about a class of transaction, account balance, or disclosure to a misstatement that could be material, either individually or when aggregated with other misstatements, before consideration of any related controls. Inherent risk is higher for some assertions and related account balances, classes of transactions, and disclosures than for others. Table 2-1 provides examples of some factors that affect inherent risk.

   b. *Control risk,* which is the risk that a misstatement that could occur in an assertion about a class of transaction, account balance, or disclosure, and that could be material, either individually or when aggregated with other misstatements, will not be prevented, or detected and corrected, on a timely basis by the entity's internal control. Control risk is a function of the effectiveness of the design, implementation, and maintenance of the client's internal control.

(AU-C sec. 200 par. .14)

Table 2-1
Inherent Risk Factors

Factor	Comments	Example
Volume	Voluminous transactions may increase the risk of misstatement.	High volume may create a strain on most processing systems.
Complexity	Complex calculations used to determine the account balance or disclosure are more likely to be misstated than simple calculations.	The accuracy assertion of a sales transaction that involves a stated number of items at a set price is less likely to be misstated than the same assertion for gain on the sale of a loan that requires present value calculations of variable cash flow streams.

(continued)

Inherent Risk Factors—*continued*

Factor	Comments	Example
Susceptibility of the asset to theft	Accounts that report the balance of assets that are highly susceptible to theft or misappropriation are more likely to be misstated than other accounts.	The existence assertion related to an office building is less likely to be materially misstated because of theft than the existence of inventory items that are small and easily transportable, such as microprocessors.
Estimates	Accounts consisting of amounts derived from accounting estimates, including fair valuations, that are subject to significant measurement uncertainty pose a greater risk than do accounts consisting of relatively routine, factual data.	The valuation assertion related to fixed assets such as a building is less likely to be materially misstated than the valuation assertion for technology-sensitive inventory.
Industry circumstances	Industry or general economic conditions may create risks of material misstatement.	Technological developments, changes in processes, or regulatory action might make a particular product obsolete, thereby increasing the inherent risk related to the valuation assertion of inventory.
Other external circumstances	Factors in the entity and its environment that relate to several or all of the classes of transactions, account balances, or disclosures may influence the inherent risk related to a specific relevant assertion.	A company that provides goods to a declining industry characterized by a large number of business failures may have increased inherent risk related to the valuation assertion of accounts receivable.

The Primary Direction of Inherent Risk

2.11 Your evaluation of inherent risk also might indicate the primary direction of the risk, that is, whether an account will most likely be overstated or understated. For example, you may determine that inherent risk for inventory is related primarily to overstatement, whereas the risk for accounts payable is understatement. Understanding the direction of inherent risk for an account or a class of transactions can help you evaluate control design and plan and perform further audit procedures.

2.12 Inadvertent, random errors rarely favor one direction or another. However, in most audits, there is a primary direction of overall inherent risk resulting principally from factors that tend to influence management's judgments with regard to selecting accounting policies or making estimates. (Since the financial statements are often used by investors and lenders to evaluate performance, the primary direction is usually, but not always overstatement of assets and income.) The possibility of management or employee fraud causes other factors to influence the direction of risk.

2.13 To determine the primary direction of inherent risk you may wish to consider factors such as

- how the financial statements are likely to be used. For example, the owners of a privately held company often are concerned with tax savings, particularly when profitable and in strong financial condition, which indicates an incentive to understate income.
- management's business or financing plans or other objectives. For example, substantial management bonuses based on earnings or the need to present a strong financial position to obtain financing both indicate greater incentive to overstate income.
- your prior experience with the client. You may consider the predominant direction of misstatements found in prior audits, and whether they were consistent with the primary direction of your auditing in those years, as a possible predictor of what you can expect to find this year.

In combination with the assessment of the risk of misstatement and an assessment of the magnitude of possible exposure, the primary direction of the misstatement risk can be used to guide you in the selection of efficient and effective procedures when determining their nature, timing, and extent.

Detection Risk

2.14 Detection risk relates to the nature, timing, and extent of the auditor's procedures that are determined by the auditor to reduce audit risk to an acceptable level. It is a function of the effectiveness of your audit procedures and how you apply them. (AU-C sec. 200 par. .13)

Observations and Suggestions

Detection risk addresses the need for the audit procedures applied to detect misstatement and does not include the risk that the auditor may draw the wrong conclusion from the audit evidence. The latter risk is managed by, for example, effective engagement planning, proper assignment of personnel to the engagement team, and supervision and review of the audit work performed.

2.15 In accordance with paragraph .21 of AU-C section 315, *Understanding the Entity and Its Environment and Assessing the Risks of Material Misstatement* and paragraph .A39 of AU-C section 200, *Overall Objectives of the Independent Auditor and the Conduct of an Audit in Accordance With Generally Accepted Auditing Standards* (AICPA, *Professional Standards*) detection risk relates to your further audit procedures and is managed by how you respond to the *risks of material misstatement* at both the financial statement and the assertion level:

- *Financial statement level risks.* Some financial statement level risks affect most, if not all, accounts and their relevant assertions. For those types of pervasive risks, it may not be practicable to develop assertion level risks for all affected assertions. Therefore, in response to pervasive financial statement level risks, you will make choices related to the assignment of personnel to the engagement team, the emphasis of the application of professional skepticism, and the supervision and review of the audit work performed. Appropriate choices related to these matters will help you mitigate the risk that you might select an inappropriate audit procedure, misapply audit procedures, or misinterpret the results.

- *Assertion level risks.* In response to assertion level risks, you will choose the test you wish to perform, and determine the timing of the test and its extent. The nature, timing, and extent of your further audit procedures should be appropriate to respond to the assessed risk.

Thus, the effectiveness of further audit procedures depends on how closely they are driven by or linked to your assessment of the risks of material misstatements.

2.16 Detection risk has an inverse relationship to the risks of material misstatement at the assertion level. The greater the risks of material misstatement, the less the detection risk that you can accept, and, accordingly, the more persuasive the audit evidence required by the auditor.

2.17 Conversely, when the risks of material misstatement are low, you can accept a greater detection risk. However, you should design and perform substantive procedures for material account balances, classes of transactions, and disclosures, regardless of your assessment of the risks of material misstatement for the relevant assertions. (AU-C sec. 330 par. .18)

2.18 The model Audit Risk = Risk of Material Misstatement x Detection Risk expresses the general relationship of audit risk and its components. You may find this model useful when planning appropriate detection risk levels for your audit procedures, keeping in mind your overall desire to reduce audit risk to an acceptably low level. Table 4-2 in chapter 4, "Nonstatistical and Statistical Audit Sampling for Substantive Tests of Details," of the AICPA Audit Guide *Audit Sampling* provides further illustration of how different audit strategies can reduce audit risk to an acceptably low level.

Materiality, Performance Materiality, and Tolerable Misstatement

The Concept of Materiality

2.19 The concept of materiality recognizes that some matters are more important for the fair presentation of the financial statements than others. In performing your audit, you are concerned with matters that, individually or in the aggregate, could be material to the financial statements. Your responsibility is to plan and perform the audit to obtain reasonable assurance that you detect all material misstatements, whether caused by error or fraud. (AU-C sec. 320 par. .02, .06, and .A1)

2.20 The auditor's determination of materiality is a matter of professional judgment and is affected by the auditor's perception of the financial information needs of the users of the financial statements. Table 2-2 summarizes the assumed characteristics of the users that you should consider when determining materiality. (AU-C sec. 320 par. .04) The amount that users may consider material is influenced by several factors including the nature of the entity (for profit or not-for-profit) and its current and past performance. As such, it is unlikely that a single benchmark or percentage, or both, could adequately address user needs for all entities and circumstances. Professional judgment considers the various relevant factors when determining materiality for a specific entity. Paragraphs .A5–.A9 in AU-C section 320, *Materiality in Planning and Performing an Audit* (AICPA, *Professional Standards*), include a discussion of the use of benchmarks in determining materiality. Materiality is also addressed in chapter 3, "Planning and Performing Risk Assessment Procedures," of this guide.

Table 2-2
Characteristics of Financial Statement Users

The evaluation of whether a misstatement could influence economic decisions of users, and therefore be material, involves consideration of the characteristics of those users. Users are assumed to

    a. have a reasonable knowledge of business and economic activities and accounting.

    b. have a willingness to study the information in the financial statements with reasonable diligence.

    c. understand that financial statements are prepared and audited to levels of materiality.

    d. recognize the uncertainties inherent in the measurement of amounts based on the use of estimates, judgment, and the consideration of future events.

    e. make reasonable economic decisions on the basis of the information in the financial statements.

The determination of materiality, therefore, takes into account how users with such characteristics could reasonably be expected to be influenced in making economic decisions.

(AU-C sec. 320 par. .04)

Observations and Suggestions

Materiality is derived from user needs. It is not a mechanical calculation based on a table. In many cases auditors first consider the base (for example, revenues, expenses, assets, net assets, net free cash flow, net income, and so on) that relates best to user needs and then determine an amount or percentage of that base appropriate to the needs of users. The determination of materiality could adversely affect the effectiveness or efficiency of the audit if not carefully considered.

How Materiality Is Used in Your Audit

2.21 Though defined by the accounting literature, materiality also is an audit concept of critical importance. From the auditor's perspective, materiality represents the maximum amount that you believe the financial statements could be misstated and still fairly present the client's financial position, results of operations, and cash flows. Materiality affects the following:

a. *The nature, timing, and extent of audit procedures.* During audit planning, you should determine a materiality level for the financial statements as a whole. This initial determination of materiality will help you determine performance materiality, which will help you

— make judgments when identifying and assessing the risks of material misstatement, and

— determine the nature, timing, and extent of your tests of controls (if any) and your substantive audit procedures.

Chapter 3 of this guide provides more detail on how to determine and use materiality and performance materiality for audit planning purposes. Chapter 5, "Risk Assessment and the Design of Further Audit Procedures," of this guide describes how your initial determination of materiality may change as your audit progresses.

b. *The evaluation of audit findings.* To form an opinion about the financial statements, you will need to evaluate audit findings and determine whether the misstatements that are not corrected by the client are material to the financial statements. Chapter 6, "Performing Further Audit Procedures," of this guide provides detailed guidance on how to use materiality to evaluate audit findings.

Quantitative and Qualitative Considerations

2.22   Although materiality commonly is expressed in quantitative terms, your determination of materiality is a matter of professional judgment that includes both quantitative and qualitative considerations. As described in more detail in chapter 7, "Evaluating Audit Findings, Audit Evidence, and Deficiencies in Internal Control," of this guide, qualitative considerations mostly influence your evaluation of audit findings and the determination of whether uncorrected misstatements are material. During the course of your audit, you should be alert for misstatements that could be qualitatively material. However, it ordinarily is not practical to design audit procedures to detect misstatements that qualitatively are material, and for that reason, materiality used for planning purposes considers primarily quantitative matters. (AU-C sec. 200 par. .07)

Performance Materiality

2.23   As described in paragraph 2.21, during audit planning you should determine an initial level of materiality for the purposes of designing and performing your audit procedures. This initial determination of materiality is made for the financial statements as a whole. However, in designing your audit procedures, the possibility exists that several misstatements of amounts less than planning materiality could—in the aggregate—result in a material misstatement of the financial statements. (AU-C sec. 320 par. .A14)

2.24   For example, suppose that for planning purposes you determined materiality to be $100,000, and you designed your audit to obtain reasonable assurance that misstatements of that magnitude were detected. Because of the way you designed your audit, you may not detect a misstatement of $80,000, which is acceptable because the amount is not considered material. However, what if you failed to detect 2 misstatements of $80,000? Individually, each misstatement would not be material, but when aggregated, the total misstatement is greater than materiality. Thus, materiality for the financial statements as a whole would not be appropriate for assessing risk and performing further audit procedures at the assertion level.

2.25   Performance materiality is the adjustment (reduction) of financial statement materiality to the account or assertion level. This adjustment is necessary to make an allowance for misstatements that might arise in other accounts as well as make a provision for possible misstatements that might exist in the financial statements, but were not detected by the audit procedures. Performance materiality effectively creates a margin for error in your audit plan to take into consideration misstatements that are not detected as part of the audit.

2.26   *Performance materiality* is defined as the amount or amounts set by the auditor at less than materiality for the financial statements as a whole to reduce to an appropriately low level the probability that the aggregate of uncorrected and undetected misstatements exceeds materiality for the financial statements as a whole. If applicable, *performance materiality* also refers to the amount or amounts set by the auditor at less than the materiality level or levels for particular classes of transactions, account balances, or disclosures. For each class of transactions, account balance, and disclosure, you should determine at least one level of performance materiality. For example, if your overall financial statement materiality for audit planning purposes was $100,000, you might determine performance materiality for aggregating accounts or testing receivables to be $70,000. Appendix J, "Matters to Consider in Determining Performance Materiality," of this guide provides further discussion and guidance on this point. The AICPA Audit Guide *Audit Sampling* also provides additional discussion on the relationship of performance materiality and tolerable misstatement.

Performance materiality can also be used to identify significant accounts as well as (when aligned with tolerable misstatement) design effective, sufficient substantive samples and other audit procedures, and evaluate audit results.

(AU-C sec. 530 par. .05)

Tolerable Misstatement

2.27   As described in paragraph .A6 of AU-C section 530, *Audit Sampling* (AICPA, *Professional Standards*), *tolerable misstatement* is the application of performance materiality to a particular sampling procedure. Tolerable misstatement may be the same amount or an amount smaller than performance materiality.

Observations and Suggestions

When there are multiple samples or procedures involving estimation to be applied to a specific account balance or class of transactions, you may set tolerable misstatement for each test at less than performance materiality for the same reasons that performance materiality is specified at less than materiality (for example, to make a provision for possible misstatements that might exist, but were not detected by the audit procedures in reaching conclusions on

---

the account as discussed in paragraph 2.24). Each test may need to seek misstatements smaller than the performance materiality for the account balance or class of transactions, so that when aggregated, the procedures provide the desired assurance that the risk of material misstatement has been reduced to an acceptably low level.

For example, in an audit of inventory balances, several procedures may be performed related to the overall balance. Tests may be applied to verify the physical existence of the inventory quantities, other tests may be performed to verify the costs associated with inventory items, and independent tests may also be performed to determine whether the inventories might require a write-down for obsolescence or other issues. Setting tolerable misstatement (for example, $60,000) at less than performance materiality (for example, $70,000) for each of the tests provides some assurance that the combined test results will provide the desired assurance that performance materiality has not been exceeded.

The more tests performed, the greater the likelihood that some misstatement will be identified. The greater the likelihood that misstatements may be identified, the more "cushion" is needed (lower tolerable misstatement) relative to the performance materiality. For example, the performance of multiple tests, a likelihood of encountering misstatements, and management's reluctance to make adjustments may warrant reduction of tolerable misstatement to $50,000 from $60,000.

When performance materiality and tolerable misstatement are the same, the tolerable misstatement amount (allowing for possible but undetected misstatements at the test level) should be used for performance materiality. Otherwise, adequate allowance for misstatements at the test level, when aggregated with other tests and accounts, might not provide an adequate allowance for undetected misstatements. Therefore, the use of a separate performance materiality and tolerable misstatement might be more efficient.

Additional guidance on the relationship between performance materiality and tolerable misstatement is noted in chapter 4 of the AICPA Audit Guide *Audit Sampling*. That discussion and other examples in that guide also provide illustrations of how these two concepts might be different and which factors might be used to gauge their relative values. The critical requirement is that performance materiality be less than full materiality (see appendix J in this guide for factors) and that tolerable misstatement be equal to or less than performance materiality.

In the AICPA Audit Guide *Audit Sampling*, a range of Tolerable Misstatement relative to materiality of 50 percent to 75 percent is suggested as applicable in many instances, however engagement circumstances may support setting higher percentages than this range when the factors noted in appendix J of this guide absent, or lower percentages when all are present.

Observations and Suggestions

When AU-C section 600, *Special Considerations—Audits of Group Financial Statements (Including the Work of Component Auditors)* (AICPA, *Professional Standards*), applies, the auditor is directed to modify the previously discussed concepts to identify group materiality, component materiality, component performance materiality, and tolerable misstatement at the testing level. Further guidance on these requirements can be found in AICPA Audit Risk Alert *Understanding the Responsibilities of Auditors for Audits of Group Financial Statements*.

See appendix L for additional discussion of group audits.

Financial Statement Assertions

Observations and Suggestions

Your audit is designed to result in an opinion on the financial statements *as a whole*, and audit risk is expressed as a risk that relates to the entire set of financial statements. However, to reach this opinion on the financial statements, most of your audit procedures should be directed at a much more detailed level, the class of transaction, account balance, and assertion level.

Put another way, you can view the financial statements as an accumulation of a large number of individual accounts and assertions. Individual assertions may be aggregated to form an account or disclosure item, and several accounts or disclosure items may then be aggregated to form a line item on the financial statements or a disclosure. Many of your audit procedures are performed not on the financial statements as a whole nor even at the account or disclosure level, but rather, they are directed at individual assertions within a class of transactions, account balance, or disclosure.

Relating identified risks to misstatements that might occur at the assertion level is necessary for you to properly link assessed risk to your tests of controls and substantive audit procedures. Assertions help you to ensure your audit procedures are related to the risks you have identified.

Appendix E, "Illustrative Financial Statement Assertions and Examples of Substantive Procedures Illustrations for Inventories of a Manufacturing Company," of this guide may be helpful to you in illustrating the linking of assertions to specific substantive procedures designed to address them.

2.28 An assertion is a declaration or a positive statement. In presenting their financial statements, management makes implicit or explicit assertions about the information presented. For example, by presenting the information "Cash....$XXX" in the financial statements, management may be making the following assertions:

- The cash truly exists, and the company has the right to use it (existence).
- The amount presented represents *all* the company's cash (completeness).
- The amount presented is accurate (accuracy).

2.29 Assertions may relate to the way in which financial statement information is

- recognized,
- measured,
- presented, and
- disclosed.

2.30 Table 2-3 provides a summary of how assertions might be grouped into various categories. You may express these assertions differently, as long as your descriptions encompass all of the aspects described in table 2-3.

Observations and Suggestions

For example, some auditors may call rights and obligations "ownership" and others may subsume the rights and obligations assertion within the existence assertion. Some may treat cut-off as either an existence or a completeness issue and not identify it as a separate assertion. In any case, as long as the assertions used cover the risks, there is no requirement to use one specific convention for naming assertions.

Table 2-3
Categories of Assertions

	Description of Assertions		
	Classes of Transactions and Events During the Period	*Account Balances at the End of the Period*	*Presentation and Disclosure*
Occurrence/ Existence	Transactions and events that have been recorded have occurred and pertain to the entity.	Assets, liabilities, and equity interests exist.	Disclosed events and transactions have occurred and pertain to the entity.
Rights and Obligations	—	The entity holds or controls the rights to assets, and liabilities are the obligations of the entity.	—
Completeness	All transactions and events that should have been recorded have been recorded.	All assets, liabilities, and equity interests that should have been recorded have been recorded.	All disclosures that should have been included in the financial statements have been included.
Accuracy/ Valuation and Allocation	Amounts and other data relating to recorded transactions and events have been recorded appropriately.	Assets, liabilities, and equity interests are included in the financial statements at appropriate amounts and any resulting valuation or allocation adjustments are recorded appropriately.	Financial and other information is disclosed fairly and at appropriate amounts.
Cut-off	Transactions and events have been recorded in the correct accounting period.	—	—

(continued)

Categories of Assertions—*continued*

	Description of Assertions		
	Classes of Transactions and Events During the Period	*Account Balances at the End of the Period*	*Presentation and Disclosure*
Classification and Under-standability	Transactions and events have been recorded in the proper accounts.	—	Financial information is appropriately presented and described and information in disclosures is expressed clearly.

Relevant Assertions

2.31 For any given account, some assertions will be relevant whereas others may not be. For example, valuation may not be relevant for cash (denominated in the same currency that the entity uses for financial reporting, like dollars). As they relate to cash, completeness and existence/occurrence always are relevant. However, valuation would be relevant to cash if the presentation of cash involved a currency translation.

2.32 To conduct your audit, you will exercise professional judgment to determine which assertions are relevant and whether they have a meaningful bearing on whether the account balance, class of transactions, or disclosures that are the subject of your audit procedures are fairly stated.

2.33 To identify relevant assertions, you may determine the most likely ways that the given account, class of transactions, or disclosure could be misstated by considering the nature of the assertion, the volume of transactions, and nature and complexity of the systems, including the use of IT, by which the entity processes and controls information supporting the assertion. For example, the gross balance of accounts receivable could be misstated if

- one or more individual receivables did not exist at the balance sheet date (existence),
- the client failed to record a receivable that did exist at the balance sheet date (completeness),
- a long-term receivable was presented as a current asset (classification), or
- a long-term receivable was not accurately reported, for example, by inappropriately discounting the receivable (valuation).

Observations and Suggestions

In many cases, multiple sources of risk can cause an assertion to be misstated.

For example, completeness may not be achieved if transactions are not captured in the accounting system or if they are captured, but not processed on a timely basis or incorrectly classified. Thus the completeness assertion could relate to more than one defined risk. Thus, assertions do not necessarily have a one-to-one correlation with risks, but are still a helpful aid in ensuring that audit procedures are related to the identified risks.

It may be necessary to design several procedures related to completeness to fully address the risk in an account for the completeness assertion.

How You Use Assertions on Your Audit

2.34   Most of your tests of controls and substantive audit procedures are directed at specific assertions. For example, observation of inventory quantities provides strong, direct evidence about the existence of inventory and it may provide some evidence about valuation of the allowance for inventory obsolescence.

For this reason, to establish a clear link between your assessment of the *risks of material misstatement* and further audit procedures, your risk assessment procedures should be performed at the assertion level as well. This will directly assist with determining the nature, timing, and extent of further audit procedures to obtain sufficient appropriate audit evidence.

For example, if the risk of obsolescence (a valuation risk) is important in valuing inventory, the explicit use of the valuation assertion when assessing the risk, documenting the controls, and designing for the audit plan further tests such as evaluating turnover by product or selecting specific items to test for valuation issues, will help establish the linkage of the risk and the related audit procedures.

Observations and Suggestions

The conceptual audit risk model is expressed at the overall financial statement level. However, in the conduct of your audit, you can apply the model at the account and relevant assertion level. That is, at the assertion level, audit risk is the risk that in an account or transaction stream, the *assertion* could be materially misstated and you fail to detect the misstatement.

This is helpful to keep in mind when designing tests. A receivables confirmation procedure may provide no assurance about completeness and little about valuation, but may provide assurance on existence. Other tests and procedures need to be designed to address the assertions not addressed or weakly addressed by the confirmation.

Certain accounts and assertions in accounts may be more susceptible to overstatement than understatement, or vice versa. Consideration of this susceptibility can be helpful in designing appropriate audit procedures to address the risk. For example, in auditing the accuracy of inventory costing, both overstatement and understatement might be encountered, however if testing the existence of inventories, overstatement might be the focus of the risk. Further, to test the completeness of liabilities at year-end, it may be necessary to test subsequent payments for unrecorded liabilities, because understatement might be the focus of the risk as it relates to the year under audit.

As a quick check, every relevant assertion in an account may have a link to one or more of the auditor's procedures as a basis for the auditor's conclusion. The absence of any procedure to address, say, completeness or existence, may indicate an incomplete strategy.

Definition of Internal Control

2.35   As defined in AU-C section 315, *internal control* is a process—effected by those charged with governance, management, and other personnel—that is designed to provide reasonable assurance about the achievement of the entity's objectives with regard to the reliability of financial reporting, effectiveness and efficiency of operations, and compliance with applicable laws and regulations. Further, internal control over safeguarding of assets against unauthorized acquisition, use, or disposition may include controls relating to financial reporting and operations objectives. In summary, internal controls fall into three categories: financial reporting, operations, and compliance with laws and regulations. In general, when performing a financial statement audit, you are most concerned with the client's financial reporting objectives, which relate to the preparation of reliable published financial statements. Only when operating and compliance activities affect financial reporting are these aspects relevant to you. (AU-C sec. 315 par. .04)

How the Definition of Internal Control Is Relevant to Your Audit

A Process

2.36   Internal control is not one event or circumstance, but a series of actions that permeate an entity's activities. These actions are pervasive and are inherent in the way management runs the business. As described more completely in chapter 3 of this guide, your understanding of the client and its environment, including internal control, is audit evidence that ultimately supports your opinion on the financial statements. An understanding of internal control assists you in identifying types of potential misstatements and factors that affects the risks of material misstatement and in designing the nature, timing, and extent of further audit procedures.

Implemented by Entity Personnel

2.37   Internal control is put in place by those charged with governing the client (for example, the board of directors), management, and other client personnel. Client management is responsible for adopting sound accounting policies and for establishing and maintaining effective internal control. The results of your audit procedures may provide evidence about the effectiveness of internal control, but these procedures are not part of the entity's internal control. For example, your detection of a material misstatement in the financial statements that was not identified by the entity indicates that there may be a significant deficiency in internal control, notwithstanding the fact that management of the entity expects the audit to identify and correct such misstatements. The Committee of Sponsoring Organizations of the Treadway Commission (COSO) framework indicates that the auditor is not an element in the controls of the entity. Chapter 7 provides additional guidance on the evaluation and communication of control deficiencies. (AU-C sec. 330 par. .16)

The Achievement of Management's Objectives

2.38   Every client establishes objectives it wants to achieve. In trying to achieve its objectives, your client faces certain risks. Internal control helps the entity achieve its objectives by mitigating the risk of "what can go wrong" in the pursuit of an entity's objectives. Thus, there is a direct link between your client's objectives, the risk to achieving those objectives, and internal control. Your assessment of internal control effectiveness is a consideration of whether the controls effectively mitigate financial reporting risks.

Observations and Suggestions

Many entities from different types of industries will share the same objectives. (Principle 6 of the COSO framework addresses the expectation that the entity has set objectives, such as the presentation of generally accepted accounting principles [GAAP] compliant financial statements). For example, all entities will want to make sure that their cash disbursements were for legitimate business expenses that were properly authorized; businesses will want to make sure that all legitimate revenue transactions get recorded properly under GAAP.

However, the way in which the entity achieves these objectives—that is, the actual control procedures themselves—can vary greatly. For example, the way in which a bank controls its revenue transactions will be much different from the procedures followed by a retail sales business or a not-for-profit entity. Even within the same industry, companies can satisfy the same principles[1] using different controls.

Your clients may not have stated explicitly all their principles, points of focus or assertions, particularly for transaction processing. To help articulate any implicit objectives, consider referencing the GAAS financial statement assertions. For example, for revenue transactions, implicit objectives may include ensuring that *all* valid sales are captured and processed by the system (completeness assertion) and that *only* valid transactions are captured and processed (occurrence/existence assertion).

2.39 In many cases, an entity has a multitude of objectives and controls. You are not required to gain an understanding of *all* controls, only those that are "relevant to the audit." In most cases, controls that are relevant to an audit pertain to the client's objective of preparing financial statements and disclosures for external purposes that are fairly presented in conformity with GAAP. Relevant controls also may include controls over safeguarding company assets against unauthorized acquisition, use, or disposition. (AU-C sec. 315 par. .13)

2.40 Controls relating to operations and compliance objectives may be relevant to an audit if they pertain to information or data the auditor evaluates or uses in applying audit procedures or if they have an effect on financial reporting or disclosure. For example, the following may be relevant to an audit:

a. Controls pertaining to nonfinancial data that management uses to operate the business and that the auditor uses in analytical procedures (for example, production statistics)

b. Controls over compliance with income tax laws and regulations that affect the income tax provision, which pertain to detecting noncompliance with laws and regulations that may have a direct and material effect on the financial statements

---

[1] Principles per the Committee of Sponsoring Organizations of the Treadway Commission (COSO) framework are described in appendix C, "Internal Control Components," of this guide.

c. Controls over production or sales data used to estimate returns and allowances and warranty reserves

d. Controls over compliance with other laws and regulations (for example, labor laws, environmental regulations, or restrictions on doing business in specific parts of the world) that could give rise to financial statement accruals or required disclosures

---

Observations and Suggestions

The situations described in paragraph 2.40 may not be easy to identify early in the audit process. Rather, you may identify these situations only later in the audit, while performing fieldwork. For example, you may be performing an analytical procedure related to inventory and become aware of production statistics that will help you create more reliable analytical procedures.

In those situations, you may want to consider the completeness and accuracy of the report you are using to perform your analytical procedure. It is helpful to start by understanding, for example, how the report was prepared, the source of the information used to prepare the report, and who or by what means it was prepared. This background information will help you understand "what can go wrong" in maintaining the completeness and accuracy of the report. This process may cause you to identify as relevant some controls that you previously did not think were relevant to the audit.

Auditing is iterative. The performance of certain procedures may cause you to revisit procedures you performed or conclusions you reached earlier in the audit.

The Top-Down Approach to Understanding Internal Control

2.41 Although not defined by the standards, you may use the "top-down" approach for understanding internal control. This approach is a framework for applying risk assessment procedures needed to understand the five components of internal control sufficient to assess the risks of material misstatement of the financial statements and to evaluate the design and implementation of controls relevant to an audit of financial statements. The top-down approach is helpful in driving both audit effectiveness and audit efficiency. Illustration 2-1 describes this approach.

Illustration 2-1
Diagram of the Top-Down Approach

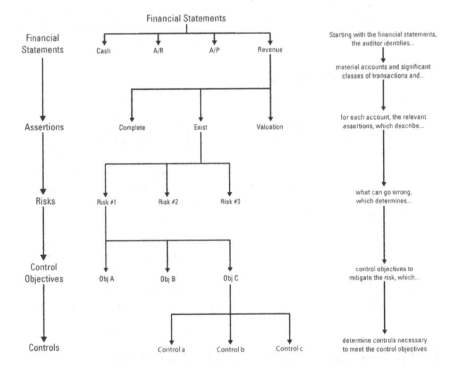

Applying the Top-Down Approach

2.42 To apply the top-down approach, start with the financial statements at the "top" of the diagram and work "down" to the individual controls.

- The top-down approach begins at the financial statement level and with your understanding of the overall risks of material misstatement.

- The next step is to identify the material accounts and classes of transactions in the client's operations that are significant to the financial statements. Identify the relevant assertions related to those accounts.

- At the assertion level, the risk of material misstatement (or "what can go wrong") is another way of stating the opposite or the reverse of the assertion. For example, the risk associated with the completeness assertion may be phrased as the risk that not all valid transactions are captured by the system.

- Identifying what can go wrong allows you to understand the relationship between objectives and related assertions. In this example, "ensure that all valid transactions are captured" is an objective that relates to the completeness assertion and the risk is that not all valid transactions are captured.

- Once you identify the relevant assertion, you then can better identify those controls that mitigate the risk that the objective and the assertion will not be achieved.

2.43 The top-down approach can help you properly scope the audit. You are not required to assess *all* the control activities that exist at the client. By focusing on objectives related to the relevant assertions for material accounts and significant classes of transactions, the top-down approach helps you identify and focus on key controls. (AU-C sec. 315 par. .21)

2.44 The top-down approach helps you better assess design effectiveness. If objectives are not being met, for example because of missing controls or poorly designed ones, then a control deficiency exists and needs to be evaluated pursuant to AU-C section 265, *Communicating Internal Control Related Matters Identified in an Audit* (AICPA, *Professional Standards*). Additionally, knowledge of the control deficiency will assist you in designing the nature, timing, and extent of your substantive procedures to appropriately respond to those higher risks.

Observations and Suggestions

In addition, the top-down approach includes the early consideration of entity level controls such as the control environment and common control processes across a complex organization, as well as the effectiveness of IT general controls.

Failures of these controls can preclude the effectiveness of other controls that are dependent on their operation. For example, if controls over segregation of duties are not operating effectively, reconciliations and exception report follow-up may be incapable of operating effectively.

By first considering the effectiveness of these more pervasive controls, or controls that affect other controls, you may be able to better plan your tests to achieve a low risk at a more efficient cost. Conversely, when deficiencies are identified in such controls, you might reconsider whether testing the more detailed controls that depend on these controls is justified until such deficiencies are corrected.

Key Characteristics of Internal Control

2.45 It is important for you to understand the key characteristics of internal control that serve as the foundation for the way in which you consider internal control in an audit. The purpose of this section is to provide you with that understanding.

The Five Components of Internal Control

2.46 AU-C section 315 requires you to obtain an understanding of internal control relevant to the audit. Components of internal control described in paragraph .A57 of AU-C section 315 are presented in the following:

- a. *Control environment* sets the tone of an organization, influencing the control consciousness of its people. It is the foundation for all other components of internal control, providing discipline and structure.

b. *Risk assessment* is the entity's identification and analysis of relevant risk to achievement of its objectives, forming a basis for determining how the risk should be managed.

c. *Information and communication systems* support the identification, capture, and exchange of information in a form and time frame that enable people to carry out their responsibilities.

d. *Control activities* are the policies and procedures that help ensure that management directives are carried out.

e. *Monitoring* is a process that assesses the quality of internal control performance over time.

Appendix C, "Internal Control Components," of this guide contains a discussion of the internal control components required by the auditing standards. In addition to the components of internal control, the COSO framework identifies 17 principles which need to be satisfied by the entity in order to assert that the entity's system of internal control is effective.

2.47 This division of internal control into five components provides a useful framework for you to consider how different aspects of your client's internal control may affect the audit. When performing an audit, your objective in considering internal control is not to classify controls into a particular component. Rather, your understanding of internal control centers around whether and how a specific control has been designed and implemented to prevent or detect and correct material misstatements.

2.48 The way in which an entity designs and implements internal control varies with its size and complexity. If your client lacks some of the detailed control elements described in appendix C of this guide, you may consider the absence of these control elements within the context of the circumstances at the entity. For example, a small, relatively noncomplex entity with active management involvement in the financial reporting process may not have extensive descriptions of accounting procedures or detailed written policies. Therefore, the components of internal control may not be clearly distinguished within smaller entities, but their underlying purposes are equally valid.

Observations and Suggestions

This guide and the related auditing standards may describe how the design of internal control (and therefore your evaluation of the effectiveness of that design) may vary for "smaller entities with *active management involvement in the financial reporting process* [emphasis added]."

When applying the guidance in these paragraphs and others relating to "smaller entities," it is important that you consider whether management truly is involved actively in the financial reporting process. Similarly, you should not mistake an owner-manager's active involvement in the operations of the business with active involvement in financial reporting.

In general, if you base your conclusions about internal control design on the owner-manager's active participation in the financial reporting process, you will need to obtain audit evidence that supports your conclusions about the owner-manager's active participation in financial reporting.

While small entities may sometimes enjoy the benefits of more active and direct management oversight, there is a corresponding risk of management override that must be considered.

The existence of documentation of entity processes and controls is helpful to the auditor when assessing controls and identifying changes in controls over time. Entity documentation can be developed by the entity or derived from auditor or consultant documentation of the processes and controls.

Entity Versus Activity-Level Controls

2.49   Your client's financial reporting risk (and therefore its controls) may relate

   a.   to specific classes of transactions, account balances, and disclosures, or

   b.   more pervasively to the financial statements taken as a whole.

2.50   Controls designed to address pervasive risks are referred to in this guide as *entity-level* controls. Those that address risk related to specific classes of transactions, account balances, and disclosures are *activity-level* controls.

2.51   For example, the control environment is pervasive to the entity and potentially affects many assertions. In contrast, a control to ensure that all valid purchases are captured and recorded is restricted to specific accounts and classes of transactions and thus operates at the assertion level.

2.52   As described more completely in chapter 5, you should assess the *risks of material misstatement* at both the financial statement and the assertion level. To appropriately make that assessment, you will evaluate both entity- and activity-level controls.

2.53   Understanding whether a control is an entity- or activity-level control may help you determine the following:

   ●   *The sequencing of your audit procedures.* Because entity-level controls are pervasive, it usually is more effective and efficient to evaluate the design and assess the implementation of entity-level controls *before* evaluating activity-level controls. This is because the failure to satisfy entity-level control objectives undermines any perceived effectiveness of activity-level controls. As an example, suppose there may likely be good detailed controls over the revenues and cash cycle at the activity level. However, if there is a weak control environment caused by recent management overrides of controls, this factor could negate the potentially effective cash controls. Therefore, even though you still need to understand the controls at the activity level, there is no point in planning to test their operating effectiveness and rely on them.

   ●   *The nature of tests you may perform to gather audit evidence.* Some entity-level controls may not be documented directly. For example, elements of the control environment include management's operating philosophy, their integrity, and ethical values. The range of audit procedures available to you to evaluate the design and implementation of these elements will be much different from the procedures that you may perform to evaluate other control procedures, such as the preparation of a bank reconciliation or the matching of a shipping report to an invoice.

   ●   *An appropriate audit response.* Your further audit procedures (that is, tests of controls and substantive procedures) are performed at the assertion level. Strengths and weaknesses in activity-level controls will shape the further audit procedures directed at the related assertions. For example, if the client has well-designed and implemented controls over the recording of all payables that exist at the balance sheet date, the effectiveness of those controls will affect the design of your search for unrecorded liabilities.

On the other hand, entity-level controls potentially affect many assertions. To the extent possible, you will first try to relate entity-level controls to what can go wrong at the financial statement level. For example, if the client has poor controls over the preparation of all accounting estimates, you can determine which accounts and related assertions are affected by estimates, and with that knowledge, adjust the nature, timing, and extent of your audit procedures in those areas accordingly.

However, some entity-level controls may not be able to be related to what can go wrong at the assertion level. Weaknesses in the design or implementation of these controls may require you to develop an overall response to how you perform the audit. For example, if your client has a weak accounting staff, that weakness may cause you to reconsider how you staff the engagement.

Other Characteristics of Internal Control That May Affect Your Audit

Some Controls Are More Critical Than Others

2.54   Individual control policies and procedures are designed to achieve specific internal control objectives. In any internal control system, some controls may be more critical to achieving the control objective than others. For example, suppose that a controller uses an aging of accounts receivable to prepare an estimate of a valuation allowance. That estimate is reviewed for overall reasonableness and approved by the owner-manager of the company. The control performed by the owner-manager is important, but you may determine that the controls over the completeness and accuracy of the aging report are even more critical to achieving a reasonable estimate because without reliable underlying information, the chances for preparing a reasonable estimate are diminished greatly.

2.55   When planning the audit, it is helpful to identify those controls that are most critical to achieving financial reporting objectives. By identifying these critical (or *key*) controls, you can help ensure that the audit team gathers sufficient information about the design and implementation of the most significant aspects of the client's internal control.

2.56   Key controls in many cases have one or both of the following characteristics:

- Their failure could materially affect the relevant assertion, but might not be detected in a timely manner by other controls, and/or

- Their operation might prevent other control failures or detect such failures before they have an opportunity to become material to the organization's objectives.

Complementary Controls

2.57 To evaluate the effectiveness of control design, the auditing standards direct you to determine whether the control "individually or in combination with other controls" is capable of effectively preventing or detecting and correcting material misstatements. When considering and evaluating a combination of controls, it is helpful to distinguish between controls that are complementary and those that function jointly to achieve the same control objective.

2.58 In some instances, multiple control procedures are required to completely address a given control objective.

2.59 *For example, the City of Anytown collects a tax from each restaurant in the city based on a percentage of revenue. There are a large number of restaurants in the city, many of which go out of business and are replaced by new ones. One of the control objectives for the city is to make sure that all restaurants will report their revenue (completeness) and pay the required tax (accuracy). To address the completeness risk, the city has a list of all restaurants that paid the tax in the previous year. Current year remittances are compared against this list to help ensure that all restaurants required to pay the tax have paid. This control is only partly effective at achieving the completeness control objective because it does not fully address the addition of new restaurants or the closing of restaurants from the previous year. Information from this control needs to be followed up to determine whether nonpayers represent closed restaurants. However, the city has another control procedure that captures the granting of new restaurant licenses. These new licensees are then monitored during their first year of operation to ensure that they comply with a variety of city laws, including the requirement to pay the required tax. In this example, the monitoring of new restaurants and the comparison of remittances to a list of existing restaurants are complementary controls over completeness.*

In this situation, each control has a direct but limited effect on achieving the control objective, but in combination, the two controls do achieve the control objective. Because both of these control procedures are necessary to completely satisfy the control objective, you should determine that both of these controls have been suitably designed and appropriately implemented.

2.60 Complementary controls may not directly address a control objective but rather, they enable the effective functioning of the controls that do directly address the objective. In general, you should obtain an understanding of the design and implementation of controls that are directly related to an assertion. However, the effectiveness of controls that are directly related to an assertion may depend on other, complementary controls that are only indirectly related to an assertion. As discussed more completely in chapter 6 of this guide, when designing tests of controls for the purpose of relying on them as part of your audit strategy, you may consider the need to obtain evidence supporting the effective operation of both (*a*) the controls directly related to the assertion and (*b*) other, complementary controls on which these direct controls depend.

2.61 *For example, a credit manager may review an exception report of credit sales that exceed the customer's authorized credit limit. This control is designed to address risk related to unauthorized credit sales. But the effectiveness of this control procedure depends on the completeness and accuracy of the exception report that is reviewed by the credit manager. That is, evidence concerning the completeness and accuracy of the credit report is also relevant when evaluating* *the control design and designing tests of the operating effectiveness of the credit manager's review of the exception report.*

Preventive Versus Detective Controls

2.62 Controls can be categorized as one of two types:

- *Preventive controls* are designed to identify misstatements as they occur and prevent them from further processing. Preventive controls are performed more timely and help ensure that misstatements are never recorded in the accounting records to begin with. However, to design and perform preventive controls at each step in the processing stream may be costly.

- *Detective controls* are designed to detect and correct misstatements that already have entered the system. Detective controls in many cases are cheaper to design and perform. However, the drawback to detective controls is that they are performed after the fact, sometimes well after the fact. The lack of timely performance of a detective control could mean that misstatements remain undetected in the accounting records for extended periods of time.

2.63 Whether preventive or detective, an effectively designed control contains both an error-detection and a correction component. The fact that a control procedure can identify a misstatement does not make the control effective. It is the process of communicating identified misstatements to individuals who can then make corrections that makes the control complete.

2.64 Preventive and detective controls can be equally effective at achieving control objectives. However, as a practical matter, it is considered better by many controls experts to prevent a misstatement from entering the accounting system rather than relying on detecting and correcting one that has entered the system.

2.65 Most internal control systems rely on a combination of preventive and detective controls, and it is common to build some redundancy into the system, in which more than one control meets the same objective, especially when the inherent risk is high.

How Information Technology Affects Internal Control

Observations and Suggestions

Understanding how your client uses and manages IT is central to understanding its internal control. IT is used in many different ways, for example, to initiate transactions, store data, or process information. How the technology is deployed can range from simple, off-the-shelf PC-based applications to much more complex, globally interconnected systems.

The purpose of the following section of this guide is to help you understand the key aspects of IT you may consider when gaining your understanding of internal control.

The COSO framework specifically identifies effective IT general controls as a principle (principle 11) that needs to be satisfied by the entity in order to assert that a system of internal control is effective.

Information Capture, Storage, and Processing

2.66 Understanding how the client's information system captures, stores, and processes information is critical to gain an understanding of the client, evaluate the design and implementation of controls, and design further audit procedures. Illustration 2-2 describes one common way in which your client's system may be configured. This diagram does not reflect all systems, but it is useful for the discussion that follows.

- Inside the main box is the client's IT system. The two ovals that reside outside the box illustrate external parties that interface with the system. In this illustration, there are two such parties: customers and suppliers.

- In this system, the diagram depicts four separate applications or *modules*: order management, customer relationship management (CRM), purchasing, and inventory management.

- Each of these application modules captures data and may perform some processing. The application then accesses the central database to store the resulting information. For example, if a customer places an order, the order management system captures the relevant data, processes it, and then stores the resulting information in the database.

- Once the information has been stored in the database, it can be used by other applications. For example, the inventory management system may query the database for new orders and process this information to determine if the items are on hand or to take further steps to process the order, such as sending the relevant information to the warehouse.

- The client's financial management system includes the general ledger and other accounting functions such as billing, accounts receivable management, and cash receipts and disbursements.

- The financial management system also interacts with the database to gather and store relevant information. However, the financial management system can be accessed directly through journal entries, bypassing the applications.

- How the previously mentioned steps occur in a given environment can vary, emphasizing the need for you to gain a clear understanding to identify risk and design your audit tests.

Illustration 2-2
Diagram of Typical IT System

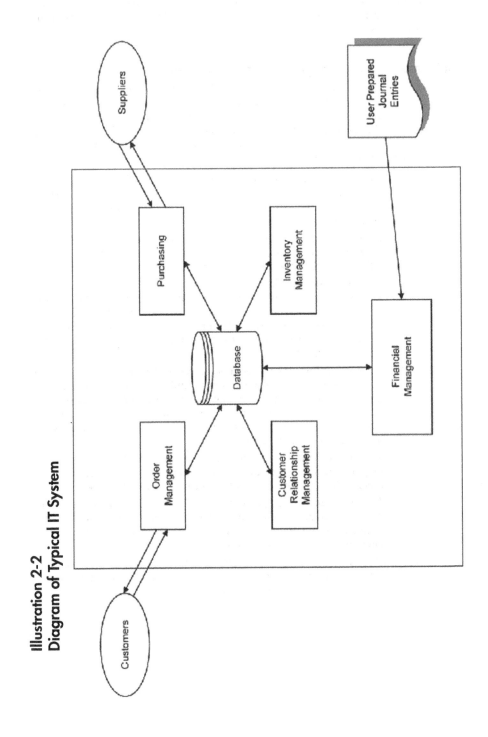

©2016, AICPA

2.67 In a system, for example the one described in paragraph 2.66, it is critical that the client retain the integrity of the information contained in the database. Illustration 2-2 shows that only applications access the database. However, a database administrator may have the ability to bypass the applications and make changes directly to the database. This functionality may be necessary to maintain the database, but left uncontrolled, access or unmonitored changes may expose the company to the risk of fraud or error through unauthorized data manipulation.

2.68 The reports you use during your audit may be generated from individual applications. Alternatively, the client may have a separate report-writing application that accesses the database directly. When evaluating controls such as program change controls or when considering the completeness and accuracy of those reports, you may want to consider how those reports were generated and how system changes are controlled and monitored.

Integration of Applications From Different Vendors

2.69 For a system such as the one in the preceding paragraph to function properly, data that is captured and processed in one application must be properly "mapped" to the data used in other applications. For example, the order processing system may use a unique customer number to identify customers. The CRM system, which provides information about customers such as their address and credit limits, will use the same customer number, assuming the data resides in the same database. To function properly (for example, for the financial management system to prepare an invoice) that unique customer number is used.

2.70 Problems can arise when the numbers assigned to the same customer are not the same. In those situations they can be "mapped" in tables that translate the numbers in one system to another. Without proper mapping, unlike applications, or those using different databases will not be able to share necessary information.

2.71 When your client uses applications that are integrated during their development, the risk related to improper mapping is reduced significantly. This is more commonly found when the same vendor is responsible for different components of the system, such as Oracle Financials or Systems Applications and Products. Also called an *application suite*, they share a database, so that each customer has one unique set of records, containing a number of data elements. Each application module may not use all of the data elements that relate to a customer, but will access those that are necessary.

2.72 However, it is common for companies to use applications provided by different software vendors. For example, in illustration 2-2, the company may have an order management and CRM application provided by one vendor, a purchasing application from another vendor, and the inventory management system may be a legacy system that the company has had for years.

Server-Client Configurations

2.73 When businesses first started using computers to process data, computer processing was highly centralized. For example, a mainframe computer typically performed all of the processing, which was monitored and controlled by a centralized electronic data processing department. Over time, information processing became more decentralized. Later, as local computers appeared on all users' desks, a central *server* hosted various *clients* that could be other servers or local desktops. As company information systems became more accessible, access was granted to a wide number of users. In this configuration, information can be processed both centrally and remotely. The client/server model is not implemented the same way in each company, so you have to find out where processing actually occurs. In addition, a large number of companies are using Internet-based systems that can change the configuration even more.

2.74 In general, the more visible or usable by outsiders a system is, the greater the risk from threats such as

- unauthorized access to applications or data.
- incorrect or inappropriate processing of information, which then is communicated throughout the entire system.
- lack of physical access controls to computer equipment and other physical risks to the system.
- transmission of computer viruses, which can destroy data.

Information Processed Outside the Accounting Applications

2.75 It is not uncommon for clients to process financial information outside the accounting application, accessing the database to extract information, which they then process independently. For example, accounting department personnel may be responsible for preparing information for the notes to the financial statements. Where the accounting application does not provide this information in a format suitable for preparation of the required disclosures, the individual responsible for the disclosure may access the database and extract the raw data. He or she imports this data into a spreadsheet, which is then used to sort, combine, or otherwise manipulate the data to provide the necessary disclosure information.

2.76 The development and use of spreadsheets may not be supported by the formal IT controls associated with purchased applications. While auditors understand that spreadsheets are nevertheless processes that should be controlled, in most instances

- people who develop and use spreadsheets are not trained application programmers.
- the spreadsheets may not be tested formally and may contain unknown errors.
- it is impossible to build in data checking routines (called *programmed edit checks*) such as are found in applications, so errors are introduced easily and can be hard to track down.
- access to the spreadsheets (including the underlying formulas) is not controlled.
- changes to spreadsheets are not controlled effectively.
- several versions of the same spreadsheet may be in use at the same time.

For these reasons, depending on the nature and use of the spreadsheet, the risk to the client posed by use of spreadsheets in its financial reporting process may be significant. Greater awareness of the risk associated with spreadsheets has prompted development of procedures and processes by entities to control them better, but due to the intrinsic nature of entering data into the cells of a spreadsheet, no matter how well the client thinks the controls are working, there is a higher risk of error when spreadsheets are being used.

2.77 The term *information system* as used in this guide encompasses both formal accounting applications and the ad hoc information systems that exist outside the accounting application.

Observations and Suggestions

Understanding your client's IT system will help you perform a more knowledgeable risk assessment by identifying risk of fraud or error. The effectiveness of IT General Controls is contained in a specific principle in the COSO framework (principle 11).

In more sophisticated entity environments, the assistance of an IT specialist to assist in the assessment may be warranted.

In addition, the client's maintenance of information in electronic format may allow you to use computer assisted auditing techniques to gather highly relevant and reliable audit evidence about an assertion, for example, by testing aspects of an entire class of transactions or account balance. For example, an entire file of payments can be compared to an approved vendor list to identify payments made to any unapproved vendor.

Benefits and Risks of Using IT

2.78 How IT is deployed varies among entities. For example, your client may use IT as part of discrete systems that support only particular business units, functions, or activities, such as a unique accounts receivable system for a particular business unit or a system that controls the operation of factory equipment. Alternately, other entities in the same industry may have complex, highly integrated systems that share data and are used to support all aspects of the company.

2.79 Your client's use of IT creates both benefits and risks that are relevant for your audit. Table 2-4 summarizes some of these benefits and risks.

Table 2-4
Benefits and Risks of Using IT

Benefits of Using IT	Risks of Using IT
IT can enhance internal control because it enables your client to • consistently apply predefined business rules and perform complex calculations in processing large volumes of transactions or data. • enhance the timeliness, availability, and accuracy of information. • facilitate the additional analysis of information.	IT poses specific risks to your client's internal control, including • reliance on systems or programs that are processing data inaccurately, processing inaccurate data, or both. • unauthorized access to data that may result in destruction of data or improper changes to data, including the recording of unauthorized or nonexistent transactions or inaccurate recording of transactions.

(continued)

Benefits and Risks of Using IT—*continued*

Benefits of Using IT	Risks of Using IT
• enhance the ability to monitor the performance of the entity's activities and its policies and procedures. • reduce the risk that controls will be circumvented. • enhance the ability to achieve effective segregation of duties by implementing security controls in applications, databases, and operating systems.	• unauthorized changes to data in master files may be more difficult to detect than similar changes to manual records. • unauthorized changes to systems or programs. • failure to make necessary changes to systems or programs. • inappropriate manual intervention when security is not effective. • potential loss of data or inability to access data as required.

2.80   In addition to the benefits and risks described in table 2-4, you also may consider that the client's use of IT may affect the availability of information you need for your audit. When client data is processed electronically, you may be

- prevented from using only substantive procedures to obtain audit evidence. For example, if the evidence regarding the transaction is not maintained in paper form or observable in the historical record, it may not be observable in the transaction record that the transaction was authorized by management electronically, thus requiring that the authorization systems and controls be examined directly for proper application of the control procedure.

- enabled to use electronic data extraction and other computer assisted audit techniques to gather audit evidence, for example, by examining an entire population of an account balance.

How Your Consideration of Fraud Is Related to the Consideration of Internal Control

Observations and Suggestions

Many of the procedures that AU-C section 240, *Consideration of Fraud in a Financial Statement Audit* (AICPA, *Professional Standards*), require you to perform can provide you with audit evidence about the design and implementation of internal control, particularly the control environment. To achieve both audit efficiency and effectiveness, you should consider the requirements to understand internal control and to assess fraud risk not as two separate and unconnected audit objectives, but rather, as two objectives whose achievement are interrelated and reinforce each other.

Prior studies of fraud and audit failures have shared the conclusion that the root cause of these incidents is weaknesses in internal control.

The following section of this guide provides guidance on how you can integrate the AU-C section 240 requirements with the requirements to understand internal control.

2.81 Fraud is a broad legal concept, and auditors do not make legal determinations of whether fraud has occurred. Rather, your interest primarily relates to acts that result in a material misstatement of the financial statements. That is, you have a responsibility to plan and perform the audit to obtain reasonable assurance about whether the financial statements are free of material misstatements, including misstatements caused by fraud. (AU-C sec. 240 par. .03)

2.82 Ineffective controls or the absence of controls or fraud awareness at your client provide an opportunity for a fraud to be perpetrated. Thus, areas of overlap exist between your consideration of internal control and your consideration of fraud. (AU-C sec. 240 par. .16)

2.83 The procedures you perform related to internal control may provide audit evidence that is relevant to your assessment of the risks of material misstatement due to fraud. For example, when evaluating the design of internal control or determining whether it has been implemented, you may obtain audit evidence about the existence of events or conditions that indicate opportunities to carry out a fraud. (These conditions are referred to as *fraud risk factors*.) Examples of fraud risk factors are provided in appendix A, "Examples of Fraud Risk Factors," of AU-C section 240.

2.84 Conversely, the performance of audit procedures you perform to assess the risks of material misstatement due to fraud may provide you with an understanding of internal control. For example, AU-C section 240 directs you to make inquiries of management and others within the entity about the risk of fraud. Responses to these inquiries and further corroborations may provide audit evidence about the design of certain controls, whether those controls have been implemented, or possibly the operating effectiveness of those controls.

2.85 Thus, audit procedures performed primarily for one objective (for example, understanding internal control) may provide evidence relating to a second audit objective (for example, assessing the risks of material misstatement due to fraud) and vice versa. For this reason, you may choose to consider this relationship when planning and performing related audit procedures. For example, knowing that inquiries of management and others relating to the risk of fraud at the entity may provide evidence about certain elements of the control environment, you may consider asking follow-up questions and obtaining further evidence that the controls were implemented (that is, placed in operation), in addition to the questions specifically required by AU-C section 240, directed toward achieving the second audit objective.

Considering Antifraud Programs and Controls

2.86 Paragraph .41 of AU-C section 240 requires you to communicate with those charged with governance any other matters related to fraud that are, in your professional judgment, relevant to their responsibilities. For example, the absence of programs or controls to address the risks of material misstatement due to fraud that are significant deficiencies or material weaknesses should be discussed with those charged with governance.

Observations and Suggestions

The COSO framework includes a principle (principle 8) and associated points of focus specific to an entity's consideration of the potential for fraud during risk assessment related to the achievement of the entity's objectives.

Appendix D, "Exhibit—Management Antifraud Programs and Controls," of this guide discusses examples of programs and controls your client might implement to create a culture of honesty and ethical behavior, and that help to prevent, deter, and detect fraud. This exhibit was originally published with Statements on Auditing Standards No. 99, *Consideration of Fraud in a Financial Statement Audit* (AICPA, *Professional Standards*, AU sec. 316).

The semi-annual fraud survey of the Association of Certified Fraud Examiners ("Report to the Nations on Occupational Fraud and Abuse") tracks the reported effectiveness of various anti-fraud measures. The latest (2016) survey is available for free download at: www.acfe.com/rttn2016.aspx.

Deficiencies in Internal Control

2.87 During the course of your audit, you may become aware of deficiencies in internal control over financial reporting. A deficiency in internal control over financial reporting exists when the design or operation of a control does not allow management or employees, in the normal course of performing their assigned functions, to prevent, or detect and correct, misstatements on a timely basis. Table 2-5 summarizes the definitions of these two types of deficiencies. (AU-C sec. 265 par. .07)

Table 2-5
Internal Control Design and Operating Deficiencies

Design Deficiencies	*Operating Deficiencies*
A deficiency in internal control design exists when either	A deficiency in the operation of a control exists when either
• a control necessary to meet the control objective is missing or • an existing control is not properly designed so that, even if the control operates as designed, the control objective is not met.	• a properly designed control does not operate as designed, or • when the person performing the control does not possess the necessary authority or qualifications to perform the control effectively.

2.88 You *should* evaluate identified deficiencies in internal control over financial reporting and determine whether the deficiencies, individually or in combination, are deficiencies, significant deficiencies, or material weaknesses.

   a. *Material weakness.* A *material weakness* is a deficiency, or combination of deficiencies in internal control over financial reporting, such that there is a reasonable possibility that a material misstatement of the financial statements will not be prevented or detected and corrected on a timely basis by the entity's internal control.

   b. *Significant deficiency.* A *significant deficiency* is a deficiency in internal control over financial reporting, or a combination of deficiencies, that is less severe than a material weakness yet important enough to merit attention by those charged with governance.

(AU-C sec. 265 par. .07 and .09)

2.89 The evaluation of the severity of a deficiency is a matter of professional judgment that depends on

- the magnitude of the potential misstatement resulting from the deficiency or deficiencies; and

- whether there is a reasonable possibility (that is, more than remote) that the entity's controls will fail to prevent, or detect and correct a misstatement of an account balance or disclosure.

Limitations of Internal Control

2.90 Internal control, no matter how effective, can provide an entity only reasonable assurance about achieving the entity's financial reporting objectives. Reasonable assurance is a high level of assurance. The likelihood that an entity will achieve its objectives is affected by limitations inherent to internal control. These inherent limitations include the realities that human judgment in decision making can be faulty and that breakdowns in internal control can occur because of human failures such as simple errors or mistakes. For example

- if an entity's personnel do not sufficiently understand how an order entry system processes sales transactions, they may design changes to the system that will erroneously process sales for a new line of products. On the other hand, such changes may be correctly designed but misunderstood by individuals who translate the design into program code.

- controls may be designed to automatically identify and report transactions over a specified amount for management review, but individuals responsible for conducting the review may not understand the purpose of such reports and, accordingly, may fail to review them or investigate unusual items.

- individuals may perform procedures less attentively on some days than others, based on, for example, the level of distractions, workload, and personal factors such as attitude and health.

2.91 Additionally, controls, whether manual or automated, can be circumvented by the collusion of two or more people or by inappropriate management override of internal control. For example, management may enter into undisclosed side agreements with customers that alter the terms and conditions of the entity's standard sales contracts that may result in improper revenue recognition. Also, edit checks in a software program that are designed to identify and report transactions that exceed specified credit limits may be overridden or disabled.

2.92 By its nature, management override of controls can occur in unpredictable ways. To address the risk of management override, you should:

a. test the appropriateness of journal entries recorded in the general ledger and other adjustments made in the preparation of the financial statements, including entries posted directly to financial statement drafts. In designing and performing audit procedures for such tests, the auditor should

    i. obtain an understanding of the entity's financial reporting process and controls over journal entries and other adjustments, and the suitability of design and implementation of such controls;

 ii. make inquiries of individuals involved in the financial reporting process about inappropriate or unusual activity relating to the processing of journal entries and other adjustments;

 iii. consider fraud indicators, the nature and complexity of accounts, and entries processed outside the normal course of business;

 iv. select journal entries and other adjustments made at the end of a reporting period; and

 v. consider the need to test journal entries and other adjustments throughout the period.

 b. review accounting estimates for biases and evaluate whether the circumstances producing the bias, if any, represent a risk of material misstatement due to fraud. In performing this review, the auditor should

  i. evaluate whether the judgments and decisions made by management in making the accounting estimates included in the financial statements, even if they are individually reasonable, indicate a possible bias on the part of the entity's management that may represent a risk of material misstatement due to fraud. If so, the auditor should reevaluate the accounting estimates taken as a whole, and

  ii. perform a retrospective review of management judgments and assumptions related to significant accounting estimates reflected in the financial statements of the prior year. Estimates selected for review should include those that are based on highly sensitive assumptions or are otherwise significantly affected by judgments made by management.

 c. evaluate, for significant transactions that are outside the normal course of business for the client or that otherwise appear to be unusual given your understanding of the client and its environment and other information obtained during the audit, whether the business rationale (or lack thereof) of the transactions suggests that they may have been entered into to engage in fraudulent financial reporting or to conceal misappropriation of assets.

(AU-C sec. 240 par. .32)

Audit Evidence

The Nature of Audit Evidence

2.93 Audit evidence is all the information you use to arrive at the conclusions that support your audit opinion. Audit evidence includes both information obtained in the accounting records underlying the financial statements and other information. Audit evidence is cumulative in nature. For example, your evidence regarding payables begins with you performing risk assessment procedures relating to the client and its environment, including its internal control. These risk assessment procedures provide audit evidence to support your conclusion about the risks of material misstatement for payables. Based on this risk assessment, you then perform further audit procedures, which include substantive procedures and may include tests of controls. The results of these further audit procedures provide audit evidence that, when considered in conjunction with the evidence from risk assessment procedures, allow you to form a supportable conclusion about payables. You then repeat this process for other accounts, classes of transactions, and disclosures, and the aggregation of your conclusions provides a basis for your opinion on the financial statements as a whole. (AU-C sec. 500 par. .05)

2.94 You should design and perform audit procedures for the purpose of obtaining sufficient appropriate audit evidence. Appropriate audit evidence is relevant and reliable. The procedures that you perform on your audit provide audit evidence, but they are not the only source of audit evidence. For example, previous audits and your firm's client acceptance and continuance procedures also may be sources of audit evidence. (AU-C sec. 500 par. .05–.06)

2.95 You should determine what modifications or additions to audit procedures are necessary if

- audit evidence obtained from one source is inconsistent with that obtained from another, or
- you have doubts about the reliability of the information to be used as audit evidence.

(AU-C sec. 500 par. .10)

2.96 A lack of consistency among individual items of audit evidence may indicate that one of the items is not reliable. For example, management may describe the company's year-end financial reporting process as following certain steps, but others at the company may describe the process differently. When audit evidence obtained from one source is inconsistent with that obtained from another, you should document how you resolved the inconsistency. (AU-C sec. 230 par. .12)

2.97 You may obtain more assurance from consistent audit evidence obtained from *different* sources or of a different nature than from items of evidence considered individually. For example, reading minutes of the board and other documentation and making inquiries of several individuals about matters included in disclosures usually provides more reliable evidence than that provided by making inquiries of one individual.

Tests of Accounting Records

2.98 As described in subsequent chapters of this guide, you may perform tests of the accounting records, for example, through analysis and review, reperforming procedures followed in the financial reporting process, or testing the client's reconciliation of significant accounts. Performing these types of tests may allow you to determine that the accounting records are consistent with each other and that they agree to the financial statements, which provides some audit evidence. However, accounting records alone do not provide sufficient audit evidence on which to base your audit opinion on the financial statements. Table 2-6 provides examples of other information you may use as audit evidence.

Table 2-6
Examples of Information You May Use as Audit Evidence

The tests you perform on the client's accounting records provide some audit evidence but not enough to support an opinion on the financial statements. Other information that you may use as audit evidence includes

- minutes of meetings.
- confirmations from third parties.
- industry analysts' reports.
- comparable data about competitors.
- controls manuals.
- information you obtain from audit procedures, such as inquiry, observation, or inspection.
- other information developed by or available to you that allows you to reach conclusions through valid reasoning.

The Sufficiency and Appropriateness of Audit Evidence

Sufficiency of Audit Evidence

2.99   You are required to design and perform audit procedures to obtain sufficient appropriate audit evidence. The sufficiency of audit evidence relates to its quantity. For example, the auditor who tests 8 of the 12 monthly reconciliations between a general ledger control account and the related subsidiary ledger will obtain more evidence about the operating effectiveness of the control than the auditor who tests 2 of the 12 reconciliations. (AU-C sec. 500 par. .06)

2.100   Paragraph .28 of AU-C section 330, *Performing Audit Procedures in Response to Assessed Risks and Evaluating the Audit Evidence Obtained* (AICPA, *Professional Standards*), requires you to conclude on whether sufficient appropriate audit evidence has been obtained. The amount of audit evidence you need to support your conclusion is affected by the risks of material misstatement and the quality of the audit evidence obtained as follows:

- The higher the risk of material misstatement, the more audit evidence likely to be required to support a conclusion.
- The higher the quality of the evidence, the less that may be required. However, obtaining more audit evidence may not compensate for its poor quality.

Appropriateness of Audit Evidence

2.101   The appropriateness of audit evidence relates to its quality. The quality of audit evidence is a function of its relevance and its reliability in providing support for, or detecting misstatements in, your audit.

2.102   *Relevance of audit evidence.* Tests of controls may provide audit evidence that is relevant to certain assertions but not others. For example, tests of controls related to the proper authorization of a transaction will provide evidence about the occurrence assertion but not about the completeness assertion.

Obtaining audit evidence relating to a particular assertion, in this example, the occurrence of a transaction, is not a substitute for obtaining audit evidence regarding another assertion, in this example, completeness.

2.103 *Reliability of audit evidence.* The reliability of audit evidence is influenced by its source and by its nature. Reliability also depends on the individual circumstances under which it is obtained, including its timing.

2.104 Generalizations about the reliability of various kinds of audit evidence can be made, and these are presented in table 2-7. However, when considering such generalizations, keep in mind that they are subject to important exceptions. Even when audit evidence is obtained from sources external to the client, circumstances may exist that could affect the reliability of the information obtained. For example, audit evidence obtained from an independent external source may not be reliable if the source is not knowledgeable. While recognizing that exceptions may exist, the following generalizations about the reliability of audit evidence may be useful:

- Audit evidence is more reliable when it is obtained from knowledgeable independent sources outside the entity.
- Audit evidence that is generated internally is more reliable when the related controls being used by the entity are designed and operate effectively.
- Audit evidence obtained directly by the auditor (for example, observation of the application of a control) is more reliable than audit evidence obtained indirectly or by inference (for example, inquiry about the application of a control).
- Audit evidence is more reliable when it exists in documentary form than when it is evidence obtained orally (whether paper, electronic, or other medium). For example, a contemporaneously written record of an audit committee meeting that described the actions taken by the members to oversee the financial reporting process is more reliable than a subsequent oral representation of the matters discussed at the meeting.
- Audit evidence provided by original documents is more reliable than audit evidence provided by photocopies, facsimiles, or documents that have been filmed, digitized, or otherwise transformed into electronic form.

Table 2-7
The Reliability of Audit Evidence

The following generalizations about the reliability of audit evidence will be useful to you when designing audit procedures.

	Reliability of Audit Evidence	
Consideration	More Reliable	Less Reliable
Source of evidence	Knowledgeable, independent sources outside the entity	Sources inside the entity Sources that are not knowledgeable
Reliability of client's internal control (when evidence is generated internally)	Effective	Ineffective
How evidence is obtained	Obtained directly by the auditor	Obtained indirectly or by inference
Format of evidence	Documentary form, either written or electronic	Oral or otherwise undocumented
Availability of evidence	Original evidence available for inspection	Evidence available only as a photocopy or facsimile of original

2.105 You may obtain more assurance from consistent audit evidence obtained from different sources or of a different nature than from audit evidence considered individually. For example, if the company lacks documentation to support its intent with regard to equity securities (which affect how those securities are classified and presented in the financial statements), you may have no choice but to rely on management's verbal statements regarding their intent. Verbal statements may be less reliable than a written record, but if you obtain statements or representations from several sources, and these statements or representations are consistent with the client's past history of selling equity investments, you may find the consistency from different sources to be persuasive.

2.106 An increased quantity of audit evidence cannot compensate for audit evidence that lacks relevance. For example, a confirmation of the existence of an account receivable is not directly relevant to the valuation of the allowance account. Increasing the number of receivables confirmations may not provide you with any additional evidence relating to their collectability and the allowance for doubtful accounts.

Observations and Suggestions

Past performance by management, actions of management before the financial statements are issued, and reviewing meeting minutes of management discussion of the issue, among other things, can provide corroboration of critical representations made by management upon which you are relying for the audit. Critical representations can also be made part of the management representation letter to better document the representation. Reliance on the general wording of the representation letter may not be sufficient to address the specific representation need.

AU-C section 580, *Written Representations* (AICPA, *Professional Standards*), contains further discussion regarding representations of management.

Determining Whether You Have Obtained Sufficient, Appropriate Audit Evidence

2.107 Whether sufficient appropriate audit evidence has been obtained to reduce audit risk to an acceptably low level and, thereby, enable the auditor to draw reasonable conclusions on which to base the auditor's opinion, is a matter of professional judgment.

Assessing and Responding to Risk in a Small Business Audit

2.108 The guidance provided in this guide applies to all audits regardless of the size of the audited entity. However, the nature of a smaller entity, the environment in which it operates, and its internal control may differ from larger entities. These differences may create different types of risks, which in turn may require different audit strategies. Auditor judgment always is needed to apply the guidance provided in this guide to specific situations, including those that may be unique to a small business.

Characteristics of a Small Business

2.109 It is difficult to precisely define a *small business*. As the term is used in this guide, it refers to an entity that has one or more of the following characteristics:[2]

- One line of business and few product lines
- A single location
- Led by founders or a small group of owners who dominate management of the business
- Limited in-house accounting resources
- Financial reporting systems built on less sophisticated, general purpose bookkeeping software and supplemented with spreadsheets for sub-ledgers and other accounting records
- Less complex, perhaps undocumented transaction processing systems
- Fewer personnel, many having a wider range of duties

Internal Control at a Small Business

2.110 Small businesses face certain challenges in implementing effective internal control, particularly if management of the business views internal control as something to be "added on" rather than integrated with core processes. These challenges to implementing effective internal control include

---

[2] These criteria were adapted from volume II of the COSO "Internal Control over Financial Reporting—Guidance for Smaller Public Companies" document.

- management's ability to dominate activities. This increases opportunities for improper management override of processes in order to appear that financial reporting objectives have been met.
- obtaining qualified accounting personnel to prepare and report financial information.
- management's view that the primary value of internal control is in preventing the misappropriation of assets while underestimating the importance of control objectives related to financial reporting.
- obtaining sufficient resources to achieve adequate segregation of duties.
- informal, largely undocumented decision-making processes, including risk assessment and the monitoring of internal control.
- attracting independent, outside parties with financial and operational expertise to serve on the board of directors and on the audit committee.
- controlling information technology. Controls over information systems, particularly application and general IT controls, present challenges for smaller businesses.
- ad hoc, undocumented entity-level control policies and procedures.

Observations and Suggestions

Smaller companies may exhibit increased reliance on the control environment, as there is more direct oversight and reinforcement of the "tone at the top" by management. Management may rely more on its control environment and their own active participation in or monitoring of the controls over financial reporting. For example, active management oversight may only partially compensate for inadequate segregation of duties. For example, management may provide a monitoring and oversight function that would preclude the occurrence of a material skimming of cash receipts, but might not be sufficient to preclude all skimming.

In those instances where management involvement may compensate for deficiencies in the design of other controls, consider that

- management's involvement in the operations of the business (for example, in managing relationships with significant customers, or obtaining financing) is not the same as its involvement in the controls over financial reporting.
- management's active involvement in controls also increases the risk of management override of controls and the manipulation of financial reporting.

While there may be less direct reliance on control activities in smaller companies, there are certain foundational control activities that need to be in place in every company. Both smaller and larger companies will have similar control activities including reconciliations of material accounts, approvals of large transactions, and various input controls.

2.111 In order for an entity's system of internal control to be effective, the COSO framework states that each of the five components of internal control and 17 relevant principles should be present and functioning and that the five components operate together in an integrated manner. The COSO framework has stated its view that the components and principles of internal control are applicable to all types and sizes of entities. If a principle or component is not present and functioning, a *major deficiency* (as defined in the COSO framework) exists. Chapter 7 of this guide discusses the evaluation of deficiencies based on the auditing standards (specifically AU-C section 265). Entities should implement a control structure to reduce risk to an acceptable level. Sometimes, smaller companies do not perceive that they have sufficient resources to fully implement segregation of duties or other controls that are more preventive in nature. Thus, smaller businesses may rely more on detective rather than preventive monitoring and personal involvement by top management in setting a control environment that brings in sufficient competence and trust to assist in reducing risk. All companies, regardless of size, need to have all five components present and functioning, but the relative reliance on each component may be different in smaller companies than it is in larger companies.

2.112 Notwithstanding the challenges faced by smaller companies in documenting and implementing effective internal control, the fundamental concepts of good control are the same whether the company is large or small. Fundamental controls, such as reconciliations, management review, and basic input controls, remain the same. The auditing standards do not set up a lower standard for small businesses in the form of measures to achieving effective internal control that only apply to small businesses. All components of internal control should be in place—in some form or another—to achieve effective internal control.

2.113 Auditors of small businesses face certain challenges in gathering information about internal control design and implementation, assessing control risk and evaluating deficiencies in internal control. These challenges may themselves be deficiencies in controls that should be assessed for their severity. These challenges include those situations where the client

- lacks sufficient documentation of its internal control, particularly: entity-level control policies, performance of control activities, including monitoring of control performance, policies and procedures for accounting for nonrecurring transactions.
- is highly susceptible to management override of internal control.
- lacks adequate segregation of duties.
- lacks sufficient in-house accounting experience, especially in dealing with nonrecurring transactions, new or complex accounting standards, or new business practices.

Audit Strategy for Audits of a Small Business

2.114 Audit strategies used on larger entities may not be practical for audits of a small business. For example, auditors of a large business with significant in-house resources may be able to rely on client personnel, including its internal auditor function, to provide assistance during the audit. Auditors of a small business that lacks such resources would not be able to adopt a similar audit strategy.

2.115 Auditors of a small business may encounter certain challenges that affect their audit strategy. These challenges include

- accounting records that require significant adjustments prior to the start of significant auditing procedures.

- significant transactions with unaudited related parties.
- internal controls that include one or more of the characteristics described in paragraph 2.112.
- the need to adapt standardized audit practice aids developed for larger entities to the conditions that exist on a small business audit.

Observations and Suggestions

The unique demands of a small business audit in many cases requires significant involvement of the most experienced auditors during the audit planning process. More experienced auditors will be able to make important judgments about audit strategy, including

- the nature, timing and extent of risk assessment procedures designed to gather information about the client and its environment, including internal control.
- the assessment of risks of material misstatement.
- the nature and extent of the auditor's documentation of assessed risks.
- the nature and extent of the documentation of the client's internal control.
- the choice of further audit procedures that are clearly linked to assessed risks.
- the allocation of audit resources to those areas of the audit that present the most risk.

The significant involvement of the most experienced auditors early in the audit process should improve both audit quality and efficiency.

Observations and Suggestions

A potential area of confusion in practice is the issue of independence when the auditor also performs certain services in conjunction with an attest engagement such as preparation of financial statements. As part of the revisions to paragraph .06 of "Scope and Applicability of Nonattest Services" interpretation (AICPA, *Professional Standards*, ET sec. 1.295.010) (formerly Interpretation No. 101-3, "Nonattest Services") effective for engagements covering periods beginning on or after December 15, 2014, the Professional Ethics Executive Committee clarified that activities such as financial statement preparation, cash-to-accrual conversions, and reconciliations are considered outside the scope of the attest engagement and, therefore, constitute nonattest services that are subject to the interpretations under the "Nonattest Services" subtopic (AICPA, *Professional Standards*, ET sec. 1.295) of the "Independence Rule," including the requirements of the "General Requirements for Performing Nonattest Services" interpretation (AICPA, *Professional Standards*, ET sec. 1.295.040).

The interpretations under the "Nonattest Services" subtopic provide guidance and requirements applicable to the performance of nonattest services, including the availability of safeguards for the auditor's consideration in determining whether the auditor is independent to issue an audit opinion.

When performing any such services the auditor may reference and consider the knowledge, skills, and experience of the entity resource taking responsibility for such procedures.

Also new for auditors who provide nonattest services to their audit clients is the "Cumulative Effect on Independence When Providing Multiple Nonattest Services" interpretation (AICPA, *Professional Standards*, ET sec. 1.295.020). This interpretation is effective for engagements covering periods beginning on or after December 15, 2014, and calls for the auditor to evaluate, prior to agreeing to perform nonattest services, whether the performance of multiple nonattest services by the member or member's firm in the aggregate creates a significant threat to the member's independence that cannot be reduced to an acceptable level by the application of the safeguards in the "General Requirements for Performing Nonattest Services" interpretation.

Summary

2.116 Chapters 3–6 of this guide describe an audit process that revolves around the assessment and response to the risks of material misstatement. This *risk of material misstatement* begins with the risk that a misstatement exists in an account balance, class of transactions, or disclosure without consideration of internal controls. This *inherent risk* exists independently of the client's system of internal control.

2.117 For example, suppose that the client has transactions with related parties that should be disclosed in the financial statements. There is a risk—irrespective of any controls—that the person who prepares the financial statements will omit the disclosure or draft one that is incomplete or not understandable.

However, suppose the client has implemented internal controls over financial reporting. These controls have been designed and operate in a way that will either prevent or identify and correct the misstated or omitted related party disclosure. For example, the person responsible for preparing the disclosure may be properly trained and supervised, and client management may review the draft disclosures to make sure they are complete and understandable. In this way, the client's internal control mitigates the risk that is inherent in the account balance, class of transactions, or disclosures.

2.118 The client's internal control is bounded by two important thresholds: accounting materiality and reasonable assurance. Internal control—no matter how well designed and operated—can only provide management with reasonable (not absolute) assurance that the financial statements are free of material misstatement.

2.119 Thus, the risk that the financial statements are materially misstated—before considering the performance of any audit procedures—is a function of inherent risk and the risk that the client's internal control will fail to either prevent or detect and correct a material misstatement.

2.120 Both the risk assessment procedures and the further audit procedures allow you to gather *audit evidence*, which supports your opinion on the financial statements.

2.121 The performance of risk assessment and further audit procedures also is bounded by two thresholds: audit materiality and reasonable assurance. *Audit materiality* is the maximum amount that you believe the financial statements could be misstated and still fairly present the client's financial position and results of operations.

Reasonable assurance is the fundamental threshold you use to design and perform your audit procedures. Reasonable assurance is a high—but not an absolute—level of assurance. To obtain reasonable assurance, the auditor should obtain sufficient appropriate audit evidence to reduce audit risk to an acceptably low level and thereby enable the auditor to draw reasonable conclusions on which to base the auditor's opinion.

2.122 The ideas presented in this chapter are the key concepts underlying the risk assessment process that is central to every audit. Chapters 3–7 of this guide describe that process in detail. The next chapter builds on your understanding of these key concepts to introduce the first step in the risk assessment process, the performance of risk assessment procedures.

                                        ©2016, AICPA

Chapter 3

Planning and Performing Risk Assessment Procedures

TABLE OF CONTENTS

Observations and Suggestions

Illustration 3-1
Planning and Performing Risk Assessment Procedures

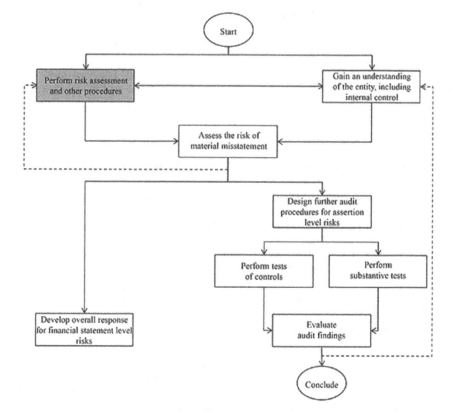

This chapter focuses on planning an audit of financial statements and performing risk assessment procedures.

Your risk assessment procedures include gathering information about a wide range of matters to enable you to understand your client. Some of these matters relate directly to the financial reporting process, but many of them relate to the broader business issues such as the current status of the client's industry and its business objectives and strategies. Your client's internal control is an integral part of its business and as such, your risk assessment procedures in many cases will also relate to the relevant portions of the internal control system.

As sufficient information is gathered, ordinarily you will begin to form an understanding of the client and how the specific conditions and circumstances pertaining to the client may affect the preparation of the client's financial statements.

Ultimately, the information you gather and the resulting understanding you gain about the client provide audit evidence to support your assessment of the risks of material misstatement and your opinion on the financial statements.

In the early stage of your audit you may often gain an understanding of the client and its environment, including internal control. This understanding should be sufficient to allow you determine materiality and to identify and assess the risks of material misstatement. To form a meaningful understanding of your client, you are required to perform risk assessment and other procedures to gather the information you need (see AU-C section 315 par. .05 and .12–.13).

This chapter provides guidance on how to gather information about your client and how to use that information to understand the client in a manner that allows you to appropriately assess the risks of material misstatements. This understanding of your client provides audit evidence that is necessary to support your risk assessments.

A Note Concerning the Use of the COSO Framework

The auditing standards recognize 5 components of internal control that, for purposes of generally accepted auditing standards (GAAS), provide a useful framework for auditors when considering how different aspects of an entity's internal control may affect the audit. Chapter 2, "Key Concepts Underlying the Auditor's Risk Assessment Process," and appendix C, "Internal Control Components," of this guide further explain these 5 internal control components, the related 17 principles per the Committee of Sponsoring Organizations of the Treadway Commission (COSO) framework and the elements of those components per the auditing standards that are relevant to the audit.

Points of focus are also provided within the COSO framework. Points of focus may facilitate the design, implementation and assessment of internal controls. There is no requirement that an assessment be performed to determine whether all points of focus are present and functioning. Management may determine that some points of focus are not suitable or relevant to the entity. Similarly, management may identify other suitable and relevant points of focus in addition to those provided in the COSO framework.

The fundamental concepts of a good system of internal control are the same whether the entity is large or small. The auditing standards do not set a lower standard for small businesses or separate standards for different industries. Additionally, GAAS has no measures for achieving effective internal control that apply only to certain businesses. Similarly, the COSO framework views the 5 internal control components and its related 17 principles as suitable to all entities. The COSO framework presumes that principles are relevant because they have a significant bearing on the presence and functioning of an associated component. Accordingly, if a relevant principle is not present and functioning, the associated component cannot be present and functioning.

COSO has also published the following companion documents to the COSO framework that was updated in 2013:

- *Internal Control—Integrated Framework Illustrative Tools for Assessing Effectiveness of a System of Internal Control*
- *Internal Control—Integrated Framework Internal Control over External Financial Reporting: A Compendium of Approaches and Examples*

Although not authoritative, these resources may be useful to auditors charged with evaluating the design and implementation of controls (as well as the operating effectiveness thereof) in conjunction with a financial statement audit.

Entities that have adopted the COSO framework and their auditors may find the transition to it, or the first time adoption of it, challenging in some respects. For example, GAAS currently does not explicitly recognize the 17 principles that COSO introduced in the COSO framework, although the principles for the most part align with the elements of internal control outlined in AU-C section 315, *Understanding the Entity and Its Environment and Assessing the Risks of Material Misstatement* (AICPA, *Professional Standards*). This audit guide helps relate the COSO framework to GAAS and provides guidance to help entities, and their auditors, transition from the original COSO framework.

Audit Planning

3.01 Audit planning is not a discrete phase of the audit, but rather an iterative process that continues throughout the engagement to its completion. A revision of the overall audit strategy or the audit plan may be necessary as a result of evidence obtained from the performance of planned audit procedures. Any modifications to your initial audit strategy should be documented.

An audit strategy developed before you have an understanding of the business and the risks of material misstatement may require updating, or a whole new strategy.

Forming an Overall Audit Strategy

3.02 Forming an overall audit strategy is an integral part of audit planning. You should establish an overall audit strategy on each engagement that sets the scope, timing, and direction of the audit that guides the development of the audit plan. Table 3-1 describes some elements of an overall audit strategy. In addition to the matters in table 3-1, you also should consider the experience you have from performing other engagements by the engagement partner for the client, as well as the results of preliminary audit activities, such as client acceptance and continuance procedures. (AU-C sec. 300 par. .07–.08)

Table 3-1
Developing an Overall Audit Strategy

The overall audit strategy involves the determination of ...	Examples of which include ...
the characteristics of the audit that define its scope.	• the basis of reporting. • industry-specific reporting requirements. • the locations of the client.
the reporting objectives of the engagement related to the timing of the audit and the required communications.	• deadlines for interim and final reporting. • key dates for expected communications with management and those charged with governance.
factors significant to directing the audit team's efforts.	• appropriate materiality and performance materiality levels, considering AU-C section 600, *Special Considerations—Audits of Group Financial Statements (Including the Work of Component Auditors)* (AICPA, *Professional Standards*), when applicable. Additional guidance regarding group audits is provided in appendix L, "The Effect of Group Audits on Planning and Determining Materiality," of this guide. • preliminary identification of areas where there may be higher risks of material misstatement. • preliminary identification of material locations and account balances. • plans, if any, to obtain evidence about the operating effectiveness of internal control at the assertion level. • how the entity uses IT to capture, store, and process information and whether the use of an IT specialist is necessary for the engagement. • recent, significant, and entity-specific developments related to the client's industry, financial reporting requirements, or other relevant matters.

3.03 Your overall audit strategy helps you determine the resources necessary to perform the audit, which include

- the human resources to assign to specific audit areas, such as the use of appropriately experienced team members for high-risk areas or the involvement of experts on complex matters.

- whether an IT, valuation, or other specialist should be part of the engagement team.

- the resources to assign to specific audit areas, such as the number of team members necessary to observe the inventory count at material locations, the extent of review of other auditors' work, or the audit budget in hours to allocate to high-risk areas.

- when these resources are assigned, such as whether at an interim audit period or at key cut-off dates.

- how such resources are managed, directed, and supervised, such as when team briefing and debriefing meetings are expected to be held, how engagement partner and manager reviews are expected to take place (for example, on-site or off-site), and whether to complete engagement quality control reviews.

Observations and Suggestions

Establishing an overall audit strategy varies according to the size of the entity and the complexity of the audit.

In audits of small entities, a very small audit team may conduct the entire audit. With a smaller team, coordination and communication between team members are easier. Consequently, establishing the overall audit strategy need not be a complex or time-consuming exercise.

For example, the auditor of Ownco developed her audit strategy for the year X2 audit at the completion of the X1 audit. Based on a review of the audit documentation she highlighted the issues identified in the X1 audit and prepared a brief memo of the overall audit strategy for X2. At the beginning of the X2 audit, she updated and changed the strategy developed in X1 based on discussions with the owner-manager.

Appendix A, "Considerations in Establishing the Overall Audit Strategy," of this guide is a useful reference regarding this issue. It was reproduced from the appendix, "Considerations in Establishing the Overall Audit Strategy," of AU-C section 300, *Planning an Audit* (AICPA, *Professional Standards*).

As smaller entities continue to refine and improve internal control, there may be more opportunities to provide efficiencies in audit strategies by incorporating reliance on controls into parts of the audit.

The Audit Plan

3.04 An audit plan is a more detailed, tactical plan that addresses the various audit matters identified in the audit strategy. (The audit plan was called the "audit program" in previous literature.) You should develop and document an audit plan for every audit. The audit plan includes the nature, timing, and extent of the audit procedures to be performed by your engagement team members. (AU-C sec. 300 par. .09)

3.05 Each successive phase of your audit depends on the results of the audit procedures that precede it. For example, your determination of the nature, timing, and extent of your substantive procedures depends on the results of your tests of controls (if any), which in turn depend on the results of your risk assessment. Table 3-2 lists the items that, at a minimum, should be included in your audit plan. (AU-C sec. 300 par. .09)

Table 3-2
Items to Be Included in Your Audit Plan

Your audit plan should include the following:

- A description of the nature and extent of planned risk assessment procedures. Because these procedures normally are the first procedures you perform to gather audit evidence to support your opinion, in many cases you will plan your risk assessment procedures first, or early in the audit.

- A description of the nature, timing, and extent of planned further audit procedures at the relevant assertion level for each material class of transactions, account balance, and disclosure. The plan for further audit procedures should reflect your decision whether to test the operating effectiveness of controls, and the nature, timing, and extent of planned substantive procedures. Because your design of further audit procedures depends on the results of your assessment of the risks of material misstatement, you may not develop your plan for further audit procedures until you have completed your risk assessment procedures.

- A description of other audit procedures to be carried out for the engagement to comply with GAAS (for example, seeking direct communication with the entity's lawyers). Your plan for these procedures may evolve over the course of the audit, as you begin to gather audit evidence.

Observations and Suggestions

It is common for example audit plans (programs) to include a step for audit planning. Example forms also are used to facilitate the documentation of the matters listed in table 3-2.

When using these example forms and checklists, it is important to remember the iterative nature of planning. The completion of example forms once, at the beginning of the engagement, is inconsistent with the notion that planning is an iterative process, reassessed continuously throughout the engagement.

Materiality in Planning an Audit

3.06 As part of developing an overall audit strategy, you should determine a materiality level for the financial statements as a whole, which is used to help you plan your audit. This materiality is used to determine performance materiality, which helps you make judgments about

- a. the identification of risks of misstatement,
- b. the assessment of whether those risks are material, and
- c. the determination of the nature, timing, and extent of further audit procedures. Properly designed further audit procedures increase the likelihood that you will detect any material misstatement that exists in the financial statements.

(AU-C sec. 320 par. .10–.11)

3.07   Materiality in the planning stage may be different from the level of materiality determined for evaluating audit results. Because it is not feasible for you to anticipate *all* the circumstances (for example, final net income) that may influence your determination of materiality at the completion of the audit, the materiality level you use for planning purposes may change. Materiality does not establish a monetary threshold below which identified misstatements always are to be considered immaterial when evaluating misstatements. The circumstances related to some identified misstatements (for example, misstatements due to fraud) may cause you to evaluate them as material even though they are below materiality or performance materiality.

Observations and Suggestions

When the materiality used to evaluate audit findings differs from that used to plan the audit, clear documentation is expected of how you re-assessed and supported the revised materiality in reaching your audit opinion. Also, when materiality used to evaluate misstatements is less than that used in planning the audit, additional evidence may be needed to support the audit opinion.

See chapter 7, "Evaluating Audit Findings, Audit Evidence, and Deficiencies in Internal Control," of this guide for a further discussion of materiality when used to evaluate audit findings.

3.08   Your judgments about materiality include both quantitative and qualitative information. However, it ordinarily is not practical to design audit procedures to detect misstatements that qualitatively could be material unless you have identified specific risks of qualitative misstatements. For this reason, the materiality used for planning purposes is primarily determined using quantitative considerations. (AU-C sec. 320 par. .06)

3.09   The determination of materiality for planning purposes is a matter of your informed, professional judgment and is affected by your perception of the financial information needs of users of the financial statements. You may apply a percentage to an appropriate benchmark, such as total revenues, income before taxes, or net assets, as a step in determining materiality for the financial statements as a whole. (AU-C sec. 320 par. .04)

3.10   The relative appropriateness of a benchmark used to establish materiality depends on the nature and circumstances of your client and, in particular, who the users of the financial statements are and how they use the financial statements. For example, income before taxes may be an appropriate benchmark for a for-profit entity, but inappropriate for a not-for-profit entity or for an owner-managed business where the owner takes much of the pretax income out of the business in the form of compensation. For asset-based entities, an appropriate benchmark might be net assets. Other entities might use other benchmarks. Table 3-3 provides a list of factors that may be relevant when determining an appropriate benchmark for materiality.

Observations and Suggestions

As indicated in paragraph 3.10, the determination of materiality depends on the nature and circumstances of the client, including how the financial statement users use the financial statements. What may be an appropriate benchmark (or base) for determining materiality for one entity may not be appropriate for another.

For example, the auditor of a for-profit entity may use a benchmark of 5 percent of income before taxes as a starting point for determining materiality. (However, auditors of for-profit entities operating near breakeven ordinarily would not use income before taxes as a basis.) Users of a not-for-profit organization ordinarily do not make judgments based on the organization's "profit," and accordingly, the auditor of the organization may use revenues or expenditures as a base for determining materiality. Governments may find it more appropriate and relevant to its users to use a percentage of expenditures as a "base" for determining materiality.

Similarly, users of the financial statements of a mutual fund may be most interested in the value of the assets being managed by the fund, and the auditor may use a base of total or net assets, rather than income before taxes, as a starting point for determining materiality.

As noted in chapter 2, it is unlikely that a single benchmark and percentage or rule-of-thumb could adequately reflect user perspectives for all entities and circumstances.

Table 3-3
Considerations When Determining a Benchmark for Materiality

Factors that may affect the identification of an appropriate benchmark include

- the elements of the financial statements (for example, assets, liabilities, equity, income, and expenses).
- whether there are financial statement items on which, for the particular entity, users' attention tends to be focused (for example, profit, revenue, free cash flow, or net assets).
- the nature of the entity, where it is in its life cycle, and the industry and economic environment in which it operates.
- the size of the entity, its ownership structure, and the way it is financed.
- the relative volatility of the benchmark.

3.11 When choosing an appropriate benchmark for determining materiality, you may consider the circumstances underlying the benchmark and make any adjustments you consider necessary.

For example, suppose that the auditor of Young Fashions determined that total revenue was an appropriate basis for determining materiality. However, during the audit period, the company acquired a manufacturer of children's clothes, which had a significant effect on the revenues during the year. Because of the unusual circumstance that gave rise to the revenue increase in the current period, the auditor determined that rather than using current period revenues, a more appropriate benchmark would be normalized revenues based on past results for the aggregate of the two companies that are now together.

3.12 Other factors that you may consider when evaluating the underlying circumstances of a chosen benchmark for materiality include the following:

- Who the users of the financial statements are and what they are likely to consider important
- Prior periods' financial results and financial positions
- The period-to-date financial results and financial position
- Budgets or forecasts for the current period
- Significant changes in the client's conditions, or the conditions of the industry and economy as a whole

---

Observations and Suggestions

Ultimately, you should plan and perform your audit to obtain reasonable assurance about whether the financial statements are free of material misstatement. "Reasonable assurance" is a high level of assurance.

The danger in setting materiality too high is that you may not gather sufficient relevant audit evidence to provide that low risk of material misstatement, if materiality is assessed at a lower level later in the audit. For that reason, it is important to consider carefully the benchmarks used to determine materiality for the financial statements as a whole and also for any performance materiality levels determined for particular items or elements.

Lesser Performance Materiality for Particular Items

3.13 In some instances it may be appropriate to establish a lower threshold performance of materiality for particular items that is less than performance materiality for the financial statements as a whole. For example, given the specific circumstances of the client and the needs of the users of its financial statements, you should establish a lower threshold for one or more particular classes of transactions, account balances, or disclosures if a lesser amount than performance materiality could reasonably be expected to influence the economic decisions of those users. (AU-C sec. 320 par. .09–.10)

3.14 In making judgments about whether a lower materiality threshold is appropriate for particular classes of transactions, account balances, or disclosures, you may consider factors such as

- whether the accounting standards, laws, or regulations affect users' expectations regarding the measurement or disclosure of certain items.
- the key disclosures in relation to the industry and the environment in which the client operates.
- whether attention is focused on the financial performance of a particular business segment that is separately disclosed in the financial statements. (For example, revenues might be used to determine royalty payments. As such, revenues might be audited to a higher degree of precision than otherwise appropriate.)

3.15 To identify those particular classes of transactions, account balances, or disclosure for which it may be appropriate to reduce performance materiality, it may be helpful to consider the views and expectations of those charged with governance. However, it is matter for the auditor's professional judgment.

Observations and Suggestions

Performance materiality is often the mechanism by which the lower materiality threshold is applied to the class of transaction, account or disclosure to assist in the design of effective, efficient audit procedures.

When performance materiality is reduced from materiality for an account, balance or disclosure, then tolerable misstatement used to test a sample from the population is also reduced. Chapter 2 of this guide contains information related to the relationship between performance materiality and tolerable misstatement.

Note that the guidance provided in paragraph 3.15 applies only to the *reduction* of materiality. The views and expectations of management may not determine initial levels of materiality and performance materiality but may elicit considerations that the auditor had not initially thought about.

Gathering Information About the Client and Its Environment

3.16 Obtaining an understanding of your client and its environment, including internal control, is an essential part of every audit. It is a dynamic process which allows you to exercise professional judgment related to

- assessing risks of material misstatements;

- determining materiality and performance materiality;

- considering the appropriateness of the client's selection and application of accounting policies and the adequacy of its financial statement disclosures;

- identifying areas where special audit consideration may be necessary (for example, related-party transactions);

- developing expectations for performing analytical procedures;

- responding to the assessed risks of material misstatement, including designing and preforming further audit procedures; and

- evaluating the sufficiency and appropriateness of audit evidence obtained.

3.17 It is not acceptable to simply deem risk to be "at the maximum." The risk assessment procedures you perform to gather information and obtain an understanding of the client provide a measure of audit evidence that supports your risk assessment. In turn, your risk assessments support your determination of the nature, timing, and extent of further audit procedures such as your substantive procedures. Thus, the results of your risk assessment procedures are an integral part of the audit evidence you obtain to support your opinion on the financial statements. However, risk assessment procedures by themselves do not provide sufficient appropriate audit evidence on which to base your audit opinion. (AU-C sec. 315 par. .05)

Breadth and Depth of Your Understanding

Observations and Suggestions

It can be helpful to think of your "understanding" of the client consisting of two components: breadth and depth.

The breadth of your understanding describes its span, those aspects of the client and its environment about which you should have some understanding. The depth of your understanding describes the level of knowledge you should have about the subject matter.

Breadth of Understanding

3.18 As described in more detail in paragraphs 4.02–.25 of this guide, your understanding of the client should encompass the following.

- Relevant industry, regulatory, and other external factors, including the financial reporting framework

- The nature of the client, including its operations, ownership and governance structures, types of investments that it is making or plans to make (including those to accomplish specified objectives), and the way it is structured and how it is financed to enable you to understand the classes of transactions, account balances, and disclosures to be expected in the financial statements;

- The client's objectives and strategies and resulting business risks that may result in risks of material misstatement; and

- The client's measurement and review of the entity's financial performance

3.19 You should obtain an understanding of internal control relevant to the audit. The breadth of your understanding extends to all five components of internal control, and other controls you determine to be relevant to the audit. Paragraphs 3.48–.111 of this guide discuss the breadth of your understanding of internal control in more detail.

Depth of Understanding

3.20 You should use your judgment to determine the depth of the understanding about your client and its environment, including internal control, to identify and assess the risks of material misstatement to provide a basis for designing and implementing responses to the assessed risks of material misstatement. In many cases, that understanding

- is less than that needed by management to manage the entity, but

- sufficient enough to allow you to

  — assess the risk that specific assertions could be materially misstated (for example, what can go wrong), and

  — plan and perform further audit procedures, which may include tests of controls, substantive analytical procedures, tests of details, or any combination of the three.

3.21 When obtaining an understanding of controls that are relevant to your audit, you evaluate the design of a control and determine whether it has been implemented.

> a. *Evaluation of control design.* Evaluating the design of a control involves determining whether the control—either individually or in combination with other controls—is capable of effectively preventing, or detecting and correcting material misstatements.
>
> b. *Determination of whether a control has been implemented.* Implementation of a control means that the control exists and that the entity is using it.

(AU-C sec. 315 par. .14)

Chapter 4, "Understanding the Client, Its Environment, and Its Internal Control," of this guide provides a more detailed discussion of your required understanding of your client's internal control.

Performing Procedures to Gather Information

Observations and Suggestions

AU-C section 315 requires you to obtain an understanding of your client and its environment, including internal control. The procedures you perform to gain that understanding are referred to as *risk assessment procedures.*

For this guide we have separated the process of obtaining an understanding of your client into two steps: (1) gathering or updating information and (2) using that information to develop an understanding of the client. In practice the two parts are often performed together. The following sections describe the procedures you perform to gather information. Chapter 4 of this guide describes the requirements for using the information gathered to form an understanding of the client.

The separation of the process is done just for the convenience of presenting the material and should not be construed to imply a linear process of discrete steps. Obtaining an understanding of the client, its environment, and its internal control is a continuous dynamic process of gathering, updating, and analyzing information throughout the audit.

3.22 The audit procedures you perform to obtain an understanding of the entity, its environment, and its internal control are referred to as *risk assessment procedures.* Risk assessment procedures include

> a. inquiries of management, appropriate individuals within the internal audit function (if such function exists), and others at the client,
>
> b. analytical procedures,
>
> c. observation and inspection.

(AU-C sec. 315 par. .06)

3.23 Risk assessment procedures are designed to gather and evaluate information about the client and are not specifically designed as substantive procedures or as tests of controls. Nevertheless, in performing risk assessment procedures, you may obtain evidence about relevant assertions or the effectiveness of controls.

Observations and Suggestions

As risk assessments in many cases involve the gathering and weighing of evidence, you can take "credit" for these procedures to adjust and reduce other audit procedures and still achieve the objectives of the audit.

As audit evidence, such procedures should include support for the assessments. For example, a practice aid listing example risk factors and prompting for risk level ratings in many cases will prompt for the documentation of the procedures performed, evidence examined and conclusions reached, to support these assessments.

The Risk Assessment Procedures

Inquiry of Management, Appropriate Individuals Within the Internal Audit Function, and Others

3.24 Although much of the information you obtain by inquiry can be obtained from management, accounting personnel, and others involved in the financial reporting process, it is often helpful to direct inquires to others within the entity. For example, people who work in production, sales, or the internal audit function, as well as individuals employed at different levels within the organization can provide you with a different perspective that helps identify *risks of material misstatement*. Inquiries of others can also help corroborate or provide additional details to the statements and representations made by management and accounting personnel. Table 3-4 provides examples of other individuals within the entity who might be able to help you identify and assess the *risks of material misstatement*.

Table 3-4
Examples of Inquiries of Others Within the Entity

Inquiries of these individuals (outside of management the financial reporting process)…	May help you understand…
those charged with governance	• the environment in which the financial statements are prepared. • whether they have knowledge of any fraud or suspected fraud. • how they exercise oversight of the entity's programs and controls that address fraud. • their views on where the company is most vulnerable to fraud. • how financial statements are used.

(continued)

Examples of Inquiries of Others Within the Entity—*continued*

Inquiries of these individuals (outside of management the financial reporting process)...	*May help you understand...*
the internal audit function	• the design and operating effectiveness of internal control (including identified control deficiencies or risks). • the internal audit function's activities related to internal control over financial reporting. • whether management has responded satisfactorily to the internal audit function's findings. • matters raised by the internal audit function with those charged with governance. • their views on where the company is most vulnerable to fraud. • the outcome of the function's own risk assessment process.
employees involved in the initiation, processing, or recording of complex or unusual transactions	• the controls over the selection and application of accounting policies related to those transactions. • the business rationale for those transactions.
IT systems users	• how IT users identify changes to IT systems and how frequently those changes occur. • how users "work around" IT systems for those circumstances where the IT system does not support them. • how logical access to data and applications is controlled. • how remote access to the system is controlled. • excessive system down time and other indicators that the system is not functioning properly.
in-house legal counsel	• litigation. • compliance with laws and regulations. • fraud or suspected fraud. • warranties. • post sales obligations. • arrangements such as joint ventures. • the meaning of certain contract terms.

     ©2016, AICPA

Examples of Inquiries of Others Within the Entity—*continued*

Inquiries of these individuals (outside of management the financial reporting process)...	May help you understand...
marketing, sales, or production personnel	• marketing strategies. • sales trends. • production strategies. • contractual arrangements with customers. • any pressures to meet budgets or change reported performance measures.

3.25 Paragraph .17 of AU-C section 240, *Consideration of Fraud in a Financial Statement Audit* (AICPA, *Professional Standards*), states that the auditor should make inquiries of management and others in the entity relating to fraud. As a matter of audit effectiveness, it is helpful to integrate these inquiries with the ones described in paragraph 3.24.

Observations and Suggestions

Inquiries are an important element in information gathering and involve skills other than technical accounting and auditing knowledge. Appendix I, "Suggestions for Conducting Inquiries," of this guide was developed to assist you in conducting effective and meaningful inquiries. Many frauds discovered by auditors have been identified during an interview process.

Analytical Procedures

3.26 AU-C section 520, *Analytical Procedures* (AICPA, *Professional Standards*), requires the use of analytical procedures in planning the audit. The objective of these procedures is to help you understand the client and its environment and, ultimately, to assess the *risks of material misstatement*. As such, you may consider the analytical procedures performed during audit planning to be a risk assessment procedure that provides some broad audit evidence to support your opinion on the financial statements. (AU-C sec. 315 par. .06)

Observations and Suggestions

When you perform analytical procedures during planning, it is common to use data that is aggregated at a high level. For example, you might base your analysis on total revenues rather than revenues by product line or geographic region.

Analyses that rely on highly aggregated data may provide only a broad initial indication of whether a material misstatement may exist. Accordingly, in such cases, consideration of other information that has been gathered when identifying the *risks of material misstatement* together with the results of such analytical procedures may assist the auditor in understanding and evaluating the results of the analytical procedures.

In addition, analyses made prior to recording accruals, adjustments, eliminations, and corrections may result in variations that are not useful or may be limited in providing sufficient appropriate audit evidence.

3.27 Please refer to paragraphs .A14–.A16 of AU-C section 315 for additional guidance on the performance of analytical procedures in planning the audit.

3.28 The results of analytical procedures may help you obtain an understanding of the entity. For example, analytical procedures may be helpful in identifying the following:

- The existence of unusual transactions or events, which may indicate the presence of significant risks (which are described in more detail in paragraphs 5.30–.37).
- Amounts, ratios, and trends that might indicate matters that have financial statement and audit implications. For example, an unexpected amount, ratio, or trend may be the result of a misstatement that was not prevented or detected and corrected by the client's internal control.

Observations and Inspection of Documents

3.29 You may use observation and the inspection of documents to support the responses you receive to your inquiries of management, appropriate individuals within the internal audit function (if such function exists), and others. Additionally, your observations and inspections in many cases will provide you with further information about the entity and its environment that you might not otherwise obtain.

3.30 The procedures you perform to observe activities and inspect documents may include

- observing client activities and operations.
- visiting the client's premises and plant facilities.
- inspecting documents, records, and internal control manuals.
- reading reports prepared by management (such as quarterly management reports and interim financial statements).
- reading minutes of board of directors' meetings and other documents prepared by those charged with governance.
- tracing transactions through the financial reporting information system.

Risk Assessment Procedures for IT Controls

3.31 Table 3-5 provides examples of risk assessment procedures you may perform to assess the design and implementation of IT controls (general controls and application controls).

The effectiveness of IT general controls is specified in the COSO framework in principle 11. IT general controls can have a pervasive effect on related application controls and are often included early on in the "top down" controls assessment approach.

Table 3-5

Examples of Risk Assessment Procedures to Assess the Design and Implementation of IT Controls

Risk Assessment Procedure	Application for IT Controls
Inspection	• Inspecting change management policies and procedures • Inspecting documentation of change management controls • Inspecting log files to determine what user access rights were associated with movement of new objects to production environment • Review of a system-generated administrative access rights list
Observation	• Conducting a walkthrough review of the entity's data center to observe physical and environmental controls, and general orderliness of the data center • Observing automated controls being performed for situations that are required per the design of the control
Inquiry	• Interviewing personnel to determine if responsibilities regarding performance of control activities are understood and the person(s) are capable of effectively performing the control(s)
Reperformance	• Performing a function within an application (for example, creating a test environment) to confirm the existence of an automated control

A Mix of Procedures

3.32 You are not required to perform *all* the procedures noted in paragraph 3.22 for *each* aspect of the client's internal control and its environment listed in table 1-1. However, in the course of gathering information about the client, you are required to perform all the risk assessment procedures in accordance with the auditing standards. Please refer to paragraphs .06 and .A5 of AU-C section 315 for additional guidance.

Other Procedures That Provide Relevant Information About the Client

3.33 *Obtaining information from sources outside the entity.* Information from sources external to the client may be helpful in understanding the client and identifying risks of material misstatement. Examples of information sources external to the client that may be helpful include

- external legal counsel.
- experts that the client has used who may be relevant for financial reporting purposes, for example a valuation expert. (Please refer to AU-C section 620, *Using the Work of an Auditor's Specialist* [AICPA, *Professional Standards*], for guidance relating to the client's use of a specialist. AU-C section 540, *Auditing Accounting Estimates, Including Fair Value Accounting Estimates, and Related Disclosures* [AICPA, *Professional Standards*], also may provide relevant guidance relating to the client's and auditor's use of an expert to provide information relating to fair values.)
- reports prepared by analysts, banks, or rating agencies.
- trade and economic journals.
- regulatory or financial publications.
- reports from service organizations used by the client (see AU-C section 402, *Audit Considerations Relating to an Entity Using a Service Organization* [AICPA, *Professional Standards*]).

3.34 *Assessing the risks of material misstatement due to fraud.* AU-C section 240 requires you to perform certain audit procedures to assess the risks of material misstatement due to fraud. Some of these procedures also may help you gather information about the entity and its environment, particularly its internal control. For this reason, it is helpful to

- coordinate the procedures you perform to assess the risks of material misstatement due to fraud with your other risk assessment procedures, and
- consider the results of your assessment of fraud risk when identifying the risks of material misstatement.

The AICPA Practice Aid *Fraud Detection in a GAAS Audit* (Revised Edition) provides guidance on performing procedures directed toward identifying, assessing, and responding to risks of material misstatement due to fraud.

3.35 *Other information.* When relevant to the audit, you also should consider other knowledge you have of the client that can help you assess risk. This other information may result from the following:

- Your client acceptance or continuance process; and
- Other engagements performed by the engagement partner for the client

(AU-C sec. 315 par. .07–.08)

Discussion Among the Audit Team

Observations and Suggestions

The gathering of information about aspects of the client and its environment, in and of itself, does not provide audit evidence to support your assessment of risks. When the information gathered is supported by observations and other forms of corroboration, that information becomes audit evidence. From that evidence of the client and its environment, you form the basis for your risk assessment.

    ©2016, AICPA

In addition to the objectives described in paragraph 3.36, the required discussion among team members also may be used to exchange information about the client and its environment that the team has gathered and to form a common understanding of the client that may often be useful for assessing risks of material misstatement. The discussion also provides an opportunity for more experienced team members, including the engagement partner, to share their insights about the client.

AU-C section 240 directs you to perform a similar discussion among team members to specifically address the risks of material misstatement due to fraud. You are not required to have two separate discussions—the discussion described in paragraph 3.36 can be held concurrently with the discussion required by AU-C section 240. However, because of the unique characteristics of fraud (for example, it is a result of an intentional act), it is recommended that you clearly distinguish between your discussion of possible material misstatements due to error and your discussion of how and where the client's financial statements might be susceptible to material misstatement due to fraud.

3.36 You and your audit team should discuss the susceptibility of the client's financial statements to material misstatement. The objectives of this discussion are for team members to

- gain a better understanding of the potential for misstatements in the specific areas assigned to them, and
- understand how the results of the audit procedures they perform may affect other aspects of the audit, including the decisions about the nature, timing, and extent of further audit procedures.

(AU-C sec. 315 par. .11)

Table 3-6 lists the items that may be the topics of your discussion.

Table 3-6
Topics for Audit Team Discussion

You and your audit team should discuss the susceptibility of the client's financial statements to material misstatements. The extent of this discussion is influenced by the roles, experience, and information needs of the audit team. Matters you may discuss include

- areas of significant risks of material misstatement, including susceptibility to fraud or error.
- unusual accounting procedures used by the client.
- important control systems.
- significant IT applications and how the client's use of IT may affect the audit.
- areas susceptible to management override of controls.
- materiality at the financial level and performance materiality.
- how performance materiality and tolerable misstatement will be used to determine the extent of testing.

(continued)

Topics for Audit Team Discussion—*continued*

- the application of generally accepted accounting principles to the client's facts and circumstances and in light of the entity's accounting policies.
- the need to
  - exercise professional skepticism throughout the engagement.
  - remain alert for information or other conditions that indicate that a material misstatement due to fraud or error may have occurred.
  - follow up rigorously on any indications of a material misstatement.

3.37 You should exercise your professional judgment to determine logistical matters relating to the audit discussion, such as who should participate, how and when the discussion should occur, and its extent. The engagement partner and other key members of the audit team should be involved in the discussion. (AU-C sec. 315 par. .11)

3.38 When considering who should participate in the discussion, you also may determine that an IT specialist or other individual possessing specialized skills should be included.

Observations and Suggestions

Multiple discussions among the audit team may help facilitate an ongoing exchange of information that may allow for a more effective assessment of risks of material misstatement and tailored responses to those risks.

Gathering Information About Internal Control

3.39 On all audits you should evaluate the design and implementation of your client's internal control relevant to the audit of the financial statements. The procedures you perform to make this evaluation may ordinarily be more complex and comprehensive than those necessary to obtain an understanding of the other elements of the client and its environment listed in paragraph 3.18. The following sections of this guide provide guidance on planning and performing risk assessment procedures directed toward gathering the information necessary to evaluate the design and implementation of internal control.

Observations and Suggestions

You should evaluate the design and implementation of your client's internal control on *all* audits, even if you intend to design a substantive audit approach and not rely on the operating effectiveness of controls when designing further audit procedures.

Evaluating internal control design involves more than assigning a value (for example, "effective" or "ineffective") to control risk. Understanding your client's internal control also involves a subjective consideration of "what can go wrong?" in your clients' processing of its financial information.

See paragraph 4.29 of this guide for an example of how an auditor might consider the qualitative aspects of internal control design.

Understanding "what can go wrong" is critical if you are to design and perform further audit procedures that are clearly linked to assessed risks, which is why you should evaluate internal control even when you plan a purely substantive audit. Paragraphs 5.24–.25 of this guide describe and provide examples of how your qualitative assessment of internal control design and implementation affect the nature, timing, and extent of substantive procedures.

Management's Documentation of Internal Control

3.40 The form, content, and extent of an entity's documentation of its internal control may affect your assessment of the design of the client's internal control and the nature of your audit procedures. Because of these effects, you may consider the client's documentation when planning your risk assessment procedures and evaluating the design of the client's internal control.

Observations and Suggestions

An entity's documentation of internal control in many cases achieves two types of objectives:

    a. Documenting the design of internal control, for example, through accounting manuals, flowcharts, or descriptions of company policies or control procedures. This type of documentation may help you evaluate the design of the entity's controls.

    b. Documentation of the performance of the control, which can help you determine whether the control has been implemented.

It helps to carefully distinguish between these two types of documentation when gaining an understanding of the client's internal control. You often can overcome a lack of detail in the documentation about the design of internal control, for example, by performing inquiries or observations to understand design. However, if the client has not provided documentation showing the performance of the control, it may often be difficult to determine that the control has been implemented, that is, that client employees are applying the control. For example, if the required approvals for all checks over $1,000 are not evidenced, it is difficult to establish that the control was performed.

The COSO framework guidance notes that while documentation may not always be present in an effective system of internal control, it may be required by regulators or others that the performance of certain controls be evidenced in some manner.

3.41 Management's documentation of internal control can vary greatly among entities. The quantity of documentation at some entities may be limited; at others it may be more extensive. It may be helpful to think of documentation as existing along a continuum between these two extremes, neither totally nonexistent, nor totally complete. Some smaller companies and organizations may have an accounting or procedures manual, and some may have flowcharts or narratives of procedures.

3.42 In general, the quantity and appropriateness of management's documentation may have several implications for your audit. For example, insufficient or inappropriate documentation may

- limit your ability to assess controls design and to gather audit evidence that the controls are placed in operation.

- result in the need for you to create additional documentation to document your understanding of the design of internal control.

- indicate to you that the client's controls are largely ad hoc or not communicated or understood, and therefore may not operate consistently throughout the year.

Your Ability to Assess Control Design

3.43 Risk assessment procedures related to understanding internal control consist of inquiry, observation, and the inspection of documentation. The client's lack of sufficient or appropriate documentation of internal control may restrict your ability to obtain audit evidence by inspecting documents. For example, if your client has not documented its ethical values, you may have to rely on inquiry and observation, to understand the design of this important element of the company's control environment. In some instances, observation of a control may not be possible, and you may have to determine whether corroborative inquiries made of multiple sources is sufficient to determine whether a control has been implemented. The lack of appropriate evidence that a control is in place and operating effectively may preclude the auditor from relying on that aspect of controls when designing an audit strategy. See paragraphs 3.117–.118 for a further discussion on the limits of inquiry as a risk assessment procedure.

Observations and Suggestions

Risk assessment procedures provide you with direct information about internal control design. *Indirect information* also may be a valuable source for gathering information about your client's internal control.

Indirect information is all other information available to you that may indicate a change or flaw in the design (or operation) of controls. It can include, but is not limited to, (1) operating statistics, (2) key risk indicators, (3) key performance indicators, and (4) comparative industry metrics.

Indirect information can help you identify deviations from normal or expected results that may signal a control change or failure and warrants further investigation. Indirect information does not, however, provide an unobstructed view of control operation, thus it is less able than direct information to identify deficiencies in internal control. Existing deficiencies may not yet have resulted in errors significant enough to be identified as deviations, or the indirect information may have lost its ability over time to identify deviations. Indirect information is therefore limited to the level of evidence it can provide on its own, especially over a long period of time.

The value of indirect information in monitoring depends on several factors, including the following:

- *Its level of precision.* More-precise indirect information is better able to identify anomalies that indicate a control failure.

- *The degree of variability in the outcomes.* Indirect information is better able to identify anomalies in processes that ordinarily generate consistent, predictable results.

- *The adequacy of the follow-up procedures.* The skills and experience of people responsible for investigating anomalies, and the diligence with which they conduct their follow-up procedures, affect the ability of indirect information to identify a control failure.

- *The length of time since the operation of the underlying controls was last validated through persuasive direct information.* As time passes and operating environments change, indirect information loses its ability to detect control failures. Periodically reestablishing the control baseline using direct information helps evaluators validate or modify the nature, timing, and extent of indirect information.

The Auditor's Documentation of the Design of the Entity's Internal Control

3.44 You should document the key elements of your understanding of the client's internal control, including each of the five components of internal control. When management has documented the design of its internal control, you may choose to use management's documentation as a basis for documenting your understanding of internal control design. For example, if the client has prepared flowcharts and other documentation related to the process and controls for significant transactions, you may use that documentation as a base from which to describe your understanding of internal control. (AU-C sec. 315 par. .33)

3.45 When management's documentation is insufficient or inappropriate for audit purposes, you may need to create more documentation than you would have had management's documentation been greater or otherwise more appropriate.

Observations and Suggestions

You may wish to encourage your clients to develop basic documentation in advance of your audit. In consultation with its auditor, an entity can develop basic procedures and control documentation that may be more cost-effective than if the documentation was developed by the auditor.

As described in paragraphs 3.133–.134, you may use information obtained from prior periods as audit evidence in the current period, provided that you can determine that no changes have occurred either in the client's processes or its controls. The client's maintenance of its documentation of its controls can help you identify changes in subsequent audits, which also may be more cost-effective than if you maintain the documentation. In addition, client employees need the documentation to understand the system and maintain continuity in the application of controls.

The Design of the Communication Component of the Entity's Internal Control

3.46 The communication component of an entity's internal control involves providing an understanding of individual roles and responsibilities pertaining to internal control. It includes the extent to which personnel understand how their activities in the financial reporting information system relate to the work of others and the means of reporting exceptions to an appropriate higher level within the entity. Open communication channels help ensure that exceptions are reported and acted on. Your understanding of the design of the client's internal control includes evaluating whether the client's communication methods are capable of meeting these control objectives.

3.47 Communication may be written or oral. Absent sufficient or appropriate documentation of internal control, evaluation of internal control design may often include a determination of whether management can meet its internal control communication objectives with oral communication alone. That determination is a matter of informed professional judgment that depends on a number of factors, including

- the nature of the entity, including its size and the relative complexity of its operations and financial reporting systems.
- the relative effectiveness of the oral communication, which may be influenced by, among other factors, its content, frequency, and the individual providing the communication.

Observations and Suggestions

In many cases, clients will need some level of documentation of controls for effective communication of internal control roles and responsibilities as well as to assist in achieving consistency in its accounting and reporting. This need for documentation is especially true for business continuity, when personnel with key internal control responsibilities leave, retire, or are absent from work.

The COSO framework states the auditor is *not* an element of internal control; in other words, internal control is not the responsibility of the external auditor. As such, the lack of adequate documentation about internal control design can be a control deficiency, and if it rises to the level of a significant deficiency or a material weakness, it should be communicated to management and those charged with governance. Chapter 7 provides additional guidance on evaluating control deficiencies and communications to management about internal control matters.

Making an Initial Determination of the Overall Scope of Your Evaluation of Internal Control

3.48 You do not have to evaluate the design of *all* your client's controls, only those that are relevant to the audit. Early in the audit process, you will need to identify those controls that in your professional judgment are relevant and therefore should be included within the initial scope of your understanding. (AU-C sec. 315 par. .13)

3.49 Your professional judgment about whether a control, individually or in combination with others, is relevant to the audit may include factors such as

- materiality.

- significance of the related risk.

- the size of the entity.

- the nature of the client's business, including its organization and ownership characteristics.

- the diversity and complexity of the client's operations.

- applicable legal and regulatory requirements.

- circumstances and the applicable component of internal control.

- the nature and complexity of the systems that are part of the client's internal control, including the use of service organizations.

- whether and how a specific control, individually or in combination with other controls, prevents, or detects and corrects, material misstatements.

3.50 It is common for some redundancy to be built into a system of internal control. When several control activities all achieve the same control objective, it may not be necessary to obtain an understanding of each of the control activities.

3.51 *For example, one of the control objectives at Ownco is to ensure that all purchases are properly authorized. Several distinct control activities all achieve this objective, including the procedures related to issuing and accounting for purchase orders and the review of all cash disbursements over a stated amount.*

In this situation, the auditor does not have to evaluate all of the control activities related to the given control objective. Rather, the auditor uses judgment to determine the control (or combination of controls) that achieves the objective and may limit his or her evaluation to that control, or combination of controls.

Thus, some auditors prefer to start with risks or "what can go wrong" and identify and understand the specific controls that satisfy the risk.

Consideration of the Client's IT Systems

3.52 To plan your audit you may often want to obtain an up-front understanding of the effect of IT on internal control. Information that may be useful for this purpose includes the following:

- *The role of IT in the initiation, authorization, recording, processing, and reporting of transactions.* In many cases, you will want to identify and obtain an understanding of financial reporting and information systems that are, directly or indirectly, the source of financial transactions or the data used to generate financial transactions and financial reporting. These information systems may include

  — packaged applications,

  — custom developed applications, or

  — end-user computing (for example, spreadsheets) that are used for accounting functions or transaction cycles (for example, revenue recognition) that drive accounting data (for example, revenue and A/R entries).

- *How the client manages IT.* This includes the person(s) and third parties that support the IT infrastructure (applications and supporting networks and servers), and the person(s) that have responsibility for managing the deployment and integrity of the IT infrastructure. In general you would expect to see staffing and skills commensurate with the complexity of the deployed systems and the entity's information system's needs.

3.53 How your client uses IT in to process financial information affects its internal control. For example:

- Multiple users may access a common database of information. In these circumstances, a lack of control at a single user entry point might compromise the security of the entire database, potentially resulting in improper changes to or destruction of data.
- When IT personnel or users are given, or can gain, access privileges beyond those necessary to perform their assigned duties, a breakdown in segregation of duties can occur. This breakdown could result in unauthorized transactions or changes to programs or data that affect the financial statements.

The following paragraphs describe those characteristics of IT use that may affect a financial statement audit.

General Versus IT Application Controls

3.54 As discussed previously, controls can operate at two levels, either at the specific assertion level, or more pervasively, at the entity level, with the potential to affect many different accounts and assertions.

3.55 *IT general controls.* General controls are policies and procedures that relate to many applications and support the effective functioning and continued proper operation of information systems. For example, your client's administration of passwords can potentially affect many applications. If passwords for a given user can be stored on that person's unsecured computer, the effectiveness of internal control may be compromised because any one who gained access to the computer could inappropriately gain access to the application, the related data, or both. The COSO framework identifies a specific principle (principle 11) regarding the effectiveness of IT general controls.

3.56 General controls are internal controls implemented and administered by an organization's IT department. The objectives of general controls are to

- ensure the proper operation of the applications and availability of systems.
- protect data and programs from unauthorized changes.
- protect data from unauthorized access and disclosure.
- provide assurance that applications are developed and subsequently maintained, such that they provide the functionality required to process transactions and provide automated controls.

3.57 General controls commonly include controls over data center and network operations; system software acquisition, change, and maintenance; access security; and application system acquisition, development, and maintenance. These controls apply to all types of IT environments. Table 3-7 provides examples of general controls.

3.58 *Application controls.* Application controls are applied only to specific applications, for example accounts payable, payroll, or the general accounting application. Application controls apply to the processing of individual transactions. These controls help ensure that transactions occurred, are authorized, and are completely and accurately recorded and processed. Table 3-7 provides examples of application controls that may be relevant to your audit.

3.59 Application controls help ensure

- proper authorization is obtained to initiate and enter transactions.
- applications are protected from unauthorized access.
- users are only allowed access to data and functions in an application they should have access to.
- errors in the operation of an application will be prevented—or detected and corrected—in a timely manner.
- application processing operates as intended.
- application output is protected from unauthorized access or disclosure.
- reconciliation activities are implemented when appropriate to ensure that information is complete and accurate.
- high-risk transactions are appropriately controlled.

Application controls are, in many cases, assessed with the accounts or stream of transactions to which they relate. In the COSO framework, these transactions are assessed in conjunction with principle 12, which addresses the deployment of controls through policies and procedures.

Table 3-7
Examples of General and Application Controls

Example General Controls	*Example Application Controls*

Examples of such general controls that may be relevant to your audit are
 	
- program change controls that include how changes are made to information systems, applications, and supporting infrastructure.
- controls that restrict access to the system it-self, programs or data.
- controls over the implementation of new releases of packaged software applications.
- controls over system software that restrict access to or monitor the use of system utilities that could change financial data or records without leaving an audit trail.
	Application controls that may be relevant to the audit include those relating to
	
	- the rights granted to specific users to
	  — access the application or data.
	  — delete transactions or data that had previously been processed by the application.
	  — originate a new transaction or record (for example, authorized vendor, approved customer, or new employee).
	- the integrity of data input into the system.
	- the completeness and accuracy of the processing of data.
	- the integrity of reports and information that are the products of the processing.

Observations and Suggestions

Many small to medium-sized entities choose not to develop a formal access or security framework that describes in detail which individuals should be granted access to which information or applications. As a matter of convenience, entity management may decide that it is faster and easier to grant all users access to all applications and data.

A lack of access control ordinarily is a control deficiency of some magnitude and, depending on the circumstances, may be a material weakness if it is broad enough and serious enough to create a risk that access to the accounting system is "wide open." Lack of access controls, in many cases, may be considered when you evaluate the risks of material misstatement at the entity level. In many cases, a lack of access controls or security may preclude reliance on general and application controls and may preclude reliance on manual (user) controls that depend on information processed by IT. You may seek to understand what mitigating controls might be in place when you identify a lack of access control.

Access Controls

3.60 Logical access controls may reside at various levels within an IT system. For example, assume that a company's website is maintained on the same network that stores the company's applications and data. To prevent unauthorized logical access, the company may have several different layers of access controls, for example, it may deploy

- a firewall to control access from the external Internet users to the company's network.
- access controls that reside on the company's main computer that controls overall access to the system.
- application-level access controls that control the access to individual applications.
- access controls over the database, which limit the applications and individuals who can access data.

3.61 A system needs to be analyzed to understand how access is controlled and the effectiveness of the control. Different approaches can be equally effective in achieving control objectives for IT. Once the initial access to applications and data has been assigned to individuals, the ongoing management and maintenance of these access assignments is a critical component of the control. For example:

- It is common for the software vendor to have universal access to the company's system for a short time after installation, to help transition the company to a new system. Once the vendor ceases to help in the transition, the vendor's access to the system should be removed.
- Employees who leave the company should have their access privileges terminated.
- Individuals who change jobs should have their access reevaluated to ensure that they are granted access only to the data and applications they need to perform their new jobs.

3.62 Unauthorized access to computer equipment also may pose a risk to the company. For example, an individual with physical access to the company's server may be able to inappropriately manipulate data. For this reason, the company usually will want to control the physical access to its server and other critical hardware components, for example, by keeping such equipment in a locked space.

Observations and Suggestions

Logical access controls may affect the *risks of material misstatement*, in that they can be structured to restrict access to system components such as networks, applications, databases, and end-user computing such as spreadsheets supporting the financial reporting process.

In certain circumstances, the absence of effective logical access controls (for example, access rights to the financial database, or access rights to the general ledger), could increase the *risks of material misstatement* so significantly that a prudent auditor would assess control risk as high for all of the output produced by a business application.

Program Change Controls for Off-the-Shelf Programs

3.63 The objective of program change controls is to help ensure that new or modified programs operate as designed and that they are appropriately tested and validated prior to being placed into production. Program change controls may include changes related to

- the operating system, including updates and patches,
- applications,
- database schemas, and
- how the database presents data to the application.

3.64 Even in circumstances where your client uses unmodified, off-the-shelf programs and does not modify these programs, controls are still relevant. For example, your client may want to ensure that

- updated versions of operating systems or application software are properly installed.
- new or modified applications, even if received from the vendor, are tested to ensure they function properly and capture and process the data properly from prior versions before being put into production.
- users are involved in a meaningful way in testing new applications or new versions of existing applications.

Documentation of Mapping of Data Among Different Applications

3.65 As described in paragraph 2.69 of this guide, when a company uses applications developed by different software vendors, data among applications may need to be "mapped." It is common for an application vendor to take responsibility for mapping the data to ensure the application integrates properly with the company's system. In other circumstances, company personnel may map the data. As a best practice, regardless of who performs the task, the mapping or interface between the applications is recommended to be documented. Without adequate documentation, the company may have difficulty adding other applications or making other modifications to the system. The importance of general controls over new system development or changes to systems includes controls that require documentation of the mapping and testing to ensure the mapping is implemented correctly.

3.66 For example, this might be less of an issue if the new program is the next version of the existing software (for example, QuickBooks Version x to QuickBooks Version x+1), but more of an issue if the new program is an upgrade from several versions back, is from a different vendor (for example, Peachtree) or is self-developed software. In such cases it may not be appropriate to simply rely on the claims of the vendor or developer regarding importing data from other applications. The completeness, classification, and accuracy of the data may need to be tested before relying on the new software.

The Relationship Between Manual and IT Application Controls

3.67 IT application controls almost always require a complementary manual control to be effective. For example, one of your client's control objectives may be to ensure that items are shipped to customers only if the customer provides a purchase order. Toward that end, your client's IT system may produce an exception report of all shipments to which no purchase order was matched. By itself, production of the exception report does not satisfy the control objective. To achieve the objective, the client must have a complementary manual control—that is, an individual to perform a timely review of the exception report and follow-up on all reported items.

Similarly, effective functioning of an IT control may depend on the effective functioning of a manual follow up component. For example, suppose the IT system compares key information on a sales order to an approved purchase order. Any differences are identified and placed in a suspense file. That control procedure is effective only if the suspense file is reviewed on a timely basis and the items identified are investigated and resolved in an appropriate manner.

3.68 The effective functioning of a manual control may depend on the effective functioning of certain IT controls. For example, a sales manager periodically reviews the commissions paid to sales people to determine whether the amounts paid seem reasonable. To perform the review, he or she uses a sales report that breaks down sales volume by sales person per month. In this example, the manual control procedure (reviewing commissions paid for reasonableness) depends on the completeness and accuracy of the information provided to the sales manager about sales volumes. Thus, the IT controls related to the accuracy and completeness of this information are relevant to the audit, even though the information itself does not flow directly to the financial statements. Both the manual procedure and the IT controls are relevant.

3.69 Because of the close relationship between manual and IT controls, your understanding of the client's internal control includes consideration of both types of controls.

Consideration of IT Skills Needed to Perform the Audit

3.70 The use of professionals possessing IT skills is a significant aspect of many audit engagements. An IT professional may help to

- determine the effect of IT on the audit,
- identify and assess IT risks,

- understand IT controls,
- identify IT control deficiencies that would prevent you from relying on controls to modify the nature, timing, and extent of your substantive procedures,
- design and perform tests of IT controls, or
- design and perform substantive procedures or dual-purpose tests covering both, for example using computer assisted auditing techniques (CAATs).

3.71 Table 3-8 describes examples of the factors you may consider when determining whether an IT professional is needed on your audit team.

Table 3-8
Examples of Factors to Consider Regarding Use of an IT Professional

	Likelihood of Needing an IT Professional on the Audit	
Factor	*More Likely*	*Less Likely*
Complexity of the client's IT systems	Relatively complex IT systems and custom applications	Relatively simple IT systems and purchased software
Changes to existing systems	Significant changes	Minor, if any, changes
Implementation of new systems	Implementation of significant new systems	Minor or no new systems
Data sharing	Significant sharing of data among systems	Little sharing of data among systems
E-commerce activities	Significant	Minimal
Use of emerging technologies	Significant use of emerging technologies to process financial information	Minimal use of emerging technologies to process financial information
Availability of audit evidence	Significant audit evidence available only in electronic form	Most or all audit evidence available in hard copy

Observations and Suggestions

The more complex the entity's systems and IT environment, the more likely that an IT professional should be an integral part of the audit team during the planning process and may need to be involved in performing the audit. In these cases, an IT professional with sufficient understanding of financial statement audit objectives and methodology (for example, the AICPA Certified Information Technology Professional or ISACA Certified Information Systems Auditor) may be helpful in determining the need to use additional professionals possessing a sufficient understanding of the technologies being used by the entity in support of its financial processes to understand the effect of IT on the audit.

As a best practice, the IT specialist would participate in the risk and fraud brainstorming, understand the risks identified by the engagement team, and understand the role of IT in the entity and how that relates to the preparation of the financial statements. This understanding, along with proper coordination with the engagement team, will more likely result in a focused, effective and efficient participation by the IT specialist.

3.72   When using an IT professional on your engagement, it may be appropriate to include that professional in your audit team discussions to help design those segments of the audit strategy and plan that include the IT audit objectives, resources required, and time line. Specific objectives that may be established for the IT professional may include

- assessing the entity-level IT functions and controls.
- assessing the role of third parties including inherent risk and adequacy of mitigating controls.
- documenting the role of IT applications used to support one or more financial statement accounts, financial statement preparation, and the reporting process. This may include the preparation of documentation to depict the flow of financial information from transaction initiation, through various stages of processing and reporting.
- assessing activity-level inherent risk and the adequacy of mitigating controls for one or more IT applications used to support one or more financial statement accounts, financial statement preparation, and the reporting process.
- identifying relevant IT processes that support the relevant applications and inherent general control risks, and the adequacy of controls to mitigate these risks.
- planning and performing tests of IT controls.
- identifying opportunities to leverage CAATs in the execution of tests for fraud and substantive procedures.

3.73   If you plan to use an IT professional on your audit, that professional ordinarily functions as a member of the audit team, and your responsibilities with respect to him or her are the same as those for other assistants. That is, you should have sufficient knowledge to

- communicate the objectives of the IT professional's work,
- evaluate whether the specified audit procedures will meet your objectives, and
- evaluate the results of the audit procedures applied as they relate to the nature, timing, and extent of further planned audit procedures.

(AU-C sec. 300 par. .12)

3.74   It is common for companies to operate several different IT systems, some of which may integrate directly with the accounting system and others that are stand-alone. For the purpose of planning the scope of your risk assessment procedures, it is helpful to obtain an understanding of the number and types of IT systems the client uses and which of these systems are relevant to the audit. Your consideration of IT "systems" includes standalone, PC-based applications that process information used in the financial reporting process, such as spreadsheets.

3.75 Ordinarily, IT systems that are relevant to the audit are those that capture, store, access, or process data that is used in the preparation of financial information. On the other hand, systems that pertain exclusively to nonfinancial information that is not used by management in the financial reporting process normally are not within the scope of your audit. However, the example previously mentioned shows the possibility of such systems' effect on the financial statements even when it is not readily apparent.

3.76 *For example, Young Fashions uses the following IT systems to manage its business:*

- Customer relationship management. *This system maintains a database of customer contact information, purchase history, outstanding orders, approved credit limits, and other information needed by sales personnel to service the account. The system captures sales and return information, which it stores and makes available to the company's general accounting software. The system runs off of the company's main server.*

- Garment design system. *The company's designers use a computerized garment design system, in addition to hand drawings, to help design fabrics and individual garment product lines and to determine the quantities and types of materials to order. The system is a standalone, which is producing information that is used by the system only for production planning purposes.*

- Communications systems. *The company has several systems that manage its in-house network and its website, including the e-commerce function. This system captures sales made over the Internet. To date, the company has not been successful at integrating this system with its customer relationship management system or its accounting system. As a result, Internet sales are entered manually into the accounting system (via journal entry) and into the customer relationship management system (by the sales reps).*

- Accounting system. *The company has an off-the-shelf general accounting software package. Except for sales, this system is used to capture all routine business transactions, process these transactions and maintain the general ledger.*

- Utilities, Online Analytical Processing (OLAP), and Standalone User Systems. *The company uses several utilities and OLAP programs to access data maintained either in the customer database or the various databases maintained by the general accounting system. Certain individuals within the company use these applications to access data for further analysis. Some of these spreadsheets are used to prepare accounting processing in a spreadsheet program, financial statement disclosures, or other financial information.*

3.77 *By obtaining an overall understanding of the various IT systems, the auditor of Young Fashions is better able to plan which of these systems is relevant for the audit and how the use of these systems will affect the audit. For*

example, controls over the garment design system are used for operational pur-
poses only and have no interaction with financial information. All other systems
are involved in the capture, storage, access, or processing of financial informa-
tion, either directly or indirectly. These systems are relevant to the audit, and the
auditor should perform the risk assessment procedures to include obtaining ad-
ditional information about the general and application specific controls related
to them.

Your initial determination of which IT systems are relevant to the audit may
change as the audit progresses. For example, you may decide to use the information produced by the garment design system to perform analytical procedures
relating to purchases or cost of sales.

In that case, when you use information produced by the client's IT system to
perform audit procedures, you obtain audit evidence about the completeness
and accuracy of that information, which may require you to evaluate the controls over the system that produces that information.

This may be effectively and efficiently done in conjunction with your required
overall assessment of the information and communication component of internal control.

Principle 13 within the information and communication component of the
COSO framework addresses the entity's use of relevant information in developing its financial reporting and disclosure data. Principle 14 addresses the adequacy of data used in internal communications (including data used by management to manage or monitor the entity). The use of data that is possibly
inaccurate or not best suited to the purpose could generate a deficiency related
to these principles and might also affect principles that focus on monitoring
activities, depending on the data.

Consideration of Controls at a Service Organization

3.78 Services provided by a service organization (including subservicers,
if applicable) are relevant to the audit of a user entity's financial statements
when those services and the controls over them affect the user entity's information system, including related business processes, relevant to financial reporting. Although most controls at the service organization are likely to relate
to financial reporting, other controls also may be relevant to the audit, such as
controls over the safeguarding of assets. A service organization's services are
part of a user entity's information system, including related business processes,
relevant to financial reporting if these services affect any of the following:

> *a.* The classes of transactions in the user entity's operations that are
>   significant to the user entity's financial statements;
>
> *b.* The procedures within both IT and manual systems by which the
>   user entity's transactions are initiated, authorized, recorded, pro-
>   cessed, corrected as necessary, transferred to the general ledger,
>   and reported in the financial statements;
>
> *c.* The related accounting records, supporting information, and spe-
>   cific accounts in the user entity's financial statements that are
>   used to initiate, authorize, record, process, and report the user en-
>   tity's transactions. This includes the correction of incorrect infor-
>   mation and how information is transferred to the general ledger;
>   the records may be in either manual or electronic form;

  d. How the user entity's information system captures events and conditions, other than transactions, that are significant to the financial statements;

  e. The financial reporting process used to prepare the user entity's financial statements, including significant accounting estimates and disclosures; and

  f. Controls surrounding journal entries, including nonstandard journal entries used to record nonrecurring, unusual transactions, or adjustments.

 3.79 The nature and extent of work to be performed by the user auditor regarding the services provided by a service organization depend on the nature and significance of those services to the user entity and the relevance of those services to the audit.

(AU-C sec. 402 par. .03–.04)

 3.80 The objectives of the user auditor, when the user entity uses the services of a service organization, are to

  a. obtain an understanding of the nature and significance of the services provided by the service organization and their effect on the user entity's internal control relevant to the audit, sufficient to identify and assess the risks of material misstatement.

  b. design and perform audit procedures responsive to those risks.

(AU-C sec. 402 par. .07)

 3.81 For example, many organizations use a service organization to process their payroll transactions and for many entities—particularly not-for-profit organizations—payroll is a significant class of transactions. In many cases, the payroll processor merely records and processes the transactions and data and does not initiate or authorize payroll. If the entities put into place user controls related to both the information it sends to the payroll processor and the information it receives from the processor, the auditor may choose to gain an understanding of these controls rather than rely on the ones at the payroll processor. However, from a practical standpoint, it is often cost-effective to seek assurance from a type 2 SOC 1® report[1] under AU-C section 402 when it is available and relevant.

 3.82 When obtaining an understanding of the user entity in accordance with AU-C section 315, the user auditor should obtain an understanding of how the user entity uses the services of a service organization in the user entity's operations, including the following:

  a. The nature of the services provided by the service organization and the significance of those services to the user entity, including their effect on the user entity's internal control

  b. The nature and materiality of the transactions processed or accounts or financial reporting processes affected by the service organization

  c. The degree of interaction between the activities of the service organization and those of the user entity

---

[1] SOC: Service organization controls.

©2016, AICPA

    d. The nature of the relationship between the user entity and the service organization, including the relevant contractual terms for the activities undertaken by the service organization

3.83 When obtaining an understanding of internal control relevant to the audit in accordance with AU-C section 315, the user auditor should evaluate the design and implementation of relevant controls at the user entity that relate to the services provided by the service organization, including those that are applied to the transactions processed by the service organization.

3.84 The user auditor should determine whether a sufficient understanding of the nature and significance of the services provided by the service organization and their effect on the user entity's internal control relevant to the audit has been obtained to provide a basis for the identification and assessment of risks of material misstatement. (AU-C sec. 402 par. .09–.11)

Observations and Suggestions

An effective and efficient way to determine the effect a service organization has on your audit is to focus on the complementary user entity controls maintained by your client. A type 2 SOC 1 report under AU-C section 402 may include a discussion of complementary user entity controls the service auditor believes should be in place at your client. This information may be helpful to your evaluation of the design of the client's controls over transactions processed by the service organization.

If the user auditor plans to use a type 1 or type 2 SOC 1 report as audit evidence to support the user auditor's understanding about the design and implementation of controls at the service organization, the user auditor should

    a. evaluate whether the type 1 SOC report is as of a date, or in the case of a type 2 SOC report, is for a period that is appropriate for the user auditor's purposes;

    b. evaluate the sufficiency and appropriateness of the evidence provided by the report for the understanding of the user entity's internal control relevant to the audit; and

    c. determine whether complementary user entity controls identified by the service organization are relevant in addressing the risks of material misstatement relating to the relevant assertions in the user entity's financial statements and, if so, obtain an understanding of whether the user entity has designed and implemented such controls.

3.85 In certain situations, the transactions processed and the accounts affected by the service organization initially may not appear to be material to your client's financial statements. However, the nature of the transactions processed may require you to obtain an understanding of those controls. For example, assume that a service organization provides third-party administration services to an entity that is self-insured with regard to health insurance benefits to its employees. Although the administrative transactions processed by the service organization may not appear to be material to the user organization's financial statements, the user auditor may need to gain an understanding of the controls at the third-party administrator because improper processing may result in a material understatement of the liability for unpaid claims.

Observations and Suggestions

Outsourcing

It has become increasingly common for entities to "outsource" some of their operations to third-party service providers. As described in paragraph 3.78, your client's outsourcing of all or a portion of its information system does not relieve you of your responsibility to understand the controls related to those outsourced functions.

However, it may be difficult to determine whether the functions that your client has outsourced are part of its information system or constitute your client's engagement of a specialist to provide a service. This distinction is important because

- if your client has outsourced part of its information system, you should obtain an understanding of the processes and controls directly related to the outsourced system, as described in paragraph 3.78.

- on the other hand, if your client has engaged a specialist, you do not need to obtain an understanding of the controls maintained by that specialist, but instead would consider the controls maintained by the client related to the specialist's work, including those related to

  — the selection of the specialist (for example, reputation, qualifications, or certifications).

  — the accuracy of data supplied to the specialist.

  — the review of the specialists work and conclusion that results are reasonable.

To determine whether your client has outsourced a portion of its information system or has engaged a specialist, it is helpful to refer to the definition of a *specialist*. As defined in the auditing literature (AU-C sec. 620 par. .06), "a specialist is a person (or firm) possessing special skill or knowledge in a particular field other than accounting or auditing." Using that definition, your client's use of a third-party payroll processor would constitute the outsourcing of a portion of its information system. The payroll processor is not a specialist because payroll is a common function within the field of accounting and auditing.

As a general rule, if a client is using a specialist, it is in a discipline that requires some sort of certification or licensure other than a CPA (for example, attorneys, actuaries, appraisers, valuation specialists, engineers, or geologists). For example, a client that uses an appraiser to determine the fair value of an asset would be engaging a specialist, not outsourcing a part of its information system.

The role assumed by the third party is also critical. An outsourced IT function is an extension of entity operations in many instances, and, as such, the vendor is not acting in the role of a specialist.

The COSO framework includes discussion of IT in association with 14 of the 17 principles, and service organization considerations in connection with 12 of the 17 principles. This focus distinguishes current business practices from the environment reflected in the original COSO framework where these topics were given less attention.

Consideration of Multiple Operating Units or Business Functions

3.86 Internal control may apply to the entity as a whole or to any of its operating units or business functions. Determining which operating units or business functions should be included in your understanding of internal control is a matter of informed professional judgment. In general, if a segment or operating unit of the company could have a material effect on the income statement or the balance sheet, the unit's controls may be relevant.

3.87 Factors that may influence your judgment about whether to gather information and evaluate the controls of a particular operating unit or business function include

- the significance of the transactions initiated, authorized, recorded, or processed by the operating unit or business function.
- the risks of material misstatement of specific assertions related to the operating unit or business function.

Observations and Suggestions

Once you have made an initial determination of the overall scope of your risk assessment procedures, in many cases, you will then be able to begin gathering information about specific control objectives and related controls.

Remember that your understanding of the client and assessment of the risks of material misstatement may evolve as the audit progresses and you obtain results from your audit procedures.

This guide distinguishes between controls that operate at the entity-level and address risks to the financial statements as a whole, and those that operate at the activity-level and address risks of misstatement of specific assertions.

The auditing standards do not dictate the order in which you gather information and obtain an understanding of these two categories of controls. However, in most cases it may be more effective and efficient to gain an understanding of entity-level controls *first* before the activity-level controls.

Observations and Suggestions

For auditors of group financial statements, additional guidance may be found in the AICPA's Audit Risk Alert *Understanding the Responsibilities of Auditors for Audits of Group Financial Statements*. The purpose of this alert is to provide guidance on implementing AU-C section 600, *Special Considerations—Audits of Group Financial Statements (Including the Work of Component Auditors)* (AICPA, *Professional Standards*).

In addition to the considerations in assessing risks for a specific component of a group audit discussed in AU-C section 315 and AU-C section 320, *Materiality in Planning and Performing an Audit* (AICPA, *Professional Standards*), additional risks may exist that result from activities involved in managing a group, such as risks related to the consolidation process.

AU-C section 600 contains explicit requirements for the group auditor that are intended to address these risks.

                                        ©2016, AICPA

Appendix L, "The Effect of Group Audits on Planning and Determining Materiality," of this guide provides some additional guidance about when AU-C section 600 applies and some of its requirements. Some auditors have had difficulty identifying engagements that this standard applies to because it is much broader in scope than the previous standard on using the work of other auditors.

Entity-Level Controls That Are Relevant to Your Audit

3.88 There are several categories of entity-level controls that are relevant to your audit. The following section discusses these categories in the following order:

- Elements of the five control components that are defined by AU-C section 315 as being relevant to the audit
- IT general controls
- Antifraud programs and controls, the understanding of which is required by AU-C section 240
- Controls related to significant financial statement level risks
- Other entity-level controls that you determine are relevant

Elements of the Control Components

3.89 On each audit, you should obtain an understanding of certain, specified elements relating to each of the five components of internal control required by the auditing standards. (Chapter 2 of this guide describes these components.) Table 3-9 summarizes those elements that operate at the entity-level and for which you may gather information.

Table 3-9
Examples of Entity-Level Controls Elements of the Components for Which You May Gather Information

Control Component	Control Element
Control Environment	• The attitudes, awareness, and actions of those charged with governance concerning the entity's internal control and its importance in achieving reliable financial reporting.
Management's Risk Assessment Process	• How management considers risks relevant to financial reporting objectives and decides about actions to address those risks.
Information and Communication	• How the information system captures events and conditions, other than classes of transactions, that are significant to the financial statements.

(continued)

Examples of Entity-Level Controls Elements of the Components for Which You May Gather Information — *continued*

Control Component	Control Element
	• The procedures the client uses to prepare financial statements and related disclosures, and how misstatements may occur. • How the entity communicates financial reporting roles and responsibilities and significant matters relating to financial reporting.
Monitoring	• The major types of activities that the entity uses to monitor internal control over financial reporting, including the sources of the information related to those activities, and how those activities are used to initiate corrective actions to its controls.

The COSO framework specifies how the 17 principles and associated points of focus are distributed within the elements described previously and in AU-C section 315. Please refer also to appendix C regarding the relationship between the elements contained in the auditing standards and the principles contained in the COSO framework.

IT General Controls

3.90   IT general controls are policies and procedures that relate to many applications and support the effective functioning of application controls by helping to ensure the continued proper operation of information systems. IT general controls commonly include controls over

- data center and network operations;
- system software acquisition, change, and maintenance;
- access security; and
- application system acquisition, development, and maintenance.

Observations and Suggestions

The auditor may wish to consult reference works on IT general controls from the Information Systems Audit and Control Association (ISACA), the Institute of Internal Auditors, the U.S. Government Accountability Office and other organizations. For example, the IT Governance Institute, in conjunction with the ISACA published *IT Control Objectives for Sarbanes-Oxley*. This publication is intended for IT professionals to help them gain an understanding of and test IT controls for the purposes of relating that understanding to requirements of Section 404 of the Sarbanes-Oxley Act of 2002. However, the concepts, control objectives, and example control policies and procedures may be a helpful reference for auditors performing a GAAS audit.

Antifraud Programs and Controls

3.91 Your client may have antifraud programs and controls that are relevant to the audit. If so you may evaluate whether they are suitably designed and placed in operation to address identified risks of material misstatement due to fraud. The COSO framework specifies, under the risk assessment component, principles, and associated points of focus related to antifraud controls (principle 8).

3.92 At the entity level, your client may have established broad programs designed to prevent, deter, and detect fraud, for example, programs to promote a culture of honesty and ethical behavior. These controls in many cases function at the financial statement level and often require you to develop an overall response in terms of how you plan, staff, and conduct the audit. Appendix D, "Exhibit—Management Antifraud Programs and Controls," of this guide provides additional details and examples of entity-level antifraud programs and controls.

Controls Related to Significant Financial Statement Level Risks

3.93 *Significant risks* are risks of material misstatement that require special audit consideration. One or more significant risks arise on most audits, and the controls related to these risks are relevant to the audit. At the financial statement level, *significant risks* often relate to significant nonroutine transactions and judgmental matters such as estimates. Paragraphs 4.65–.66 of this guide provide guidance on the controls related to nonroutine transactions and judgmental matters. Chapter 5, "Risk Assessment and the Design of Further Audit Procedures," of this guide provides more detailed guidance on the identification of *significant risks*. (AU-C sec. 315 par. .29)

Other Entity-Level Controls That May Be Relevant to Your Audit

3.94 Other entity-level controls that may be relevant to your audit include those relating to the following:

- *The selection and application of significant accounting policies.* Management is responsible for adopting appropriate accounting policies. Risks of material misstatement of the financial statement arise if management's selection or application of its accounting policies is inappropriate. Paragraphs 4.68–.69 of this guide provide guidance on controls relating to the selection and application of significant accounting policies.

- *The participation of those charged with governance.* The responsibilities of those charged with governance are of considerable importance. Their participation in the financial reporting process affects your client's overall control consciousness. Paragraphs 4.70–.71 of this guide provide guidance on controls relating to the responsibilities of those charged with governance.

Observations and Suggestions

The risk assessment standards use the term *those charged with governance.* Governance describes the role of a person or persons entrusted with the supervision, control, and direction of the entity. In a smaller entity, the responsibilities of governance may reside with only one individual, the owner-manager.

This guide uses the phrase *those charged with governance* simply to be consistent with the standards. The use of the word *those* should not be construed to mean that all entities must have a group, independent from management, responsible for governing the entity.

In the COSO framework, an effective governance function is addressed broadly within the control environment component and incorporated into most of the 5 specific principles underlying that component (see appendix C of this guide for these principles).

The COSO framework contains principles specific to the board of directors' oversight of the development and performance of internal control (principles 2 and 3). Further, the oversight activities of the board of directors apply to the development and performance of internal control across COSO components.

AU-C section 265, *Communicating Internal Control Related Matters Identified in an Audit* (AICPA, *Professional Standards*), states that an ineffective governance function in many cases is an indicator of a material weakness.

Activity-Level Controls That Are Relevant to Your Audit

3.95 The following section discusses activity-level controls that are relevant to your audit in the following order:

- Elements of the five control components that are defined by AU-C section 315 as being relevant to the audit
- Activity-level anti-fraud controls, the understanding of which is required by AU-C section 240
- Controls related to significant assertion level risks
- Other activity-level controls that you determine are relevant

Observations and Suggestions

Distinguishing Between a Process and a Control

The steps in a financial reporting process are different from the controls related to that process. Understanding these differences may help you design appropriate audit procedures to obtain your understanding of internal control.

Processes. The processing of financial information is transformative in nature. Data or information is changed as a result of a process. For example, an entity may process its sales transactions, and one of the steps in the process may involve preparing an invoice based on the number of units shipped and the price per unit. The extension of unit prices by number of units sold is a process. When information is processed, the risk of misstatement is introduced. For example, the calculation of an invoice may be based on incorrect prices.

Controls. In contrast, the primary objective of a control is not to transform information. The objective of a control is to either (1) prevent or (2) detect and correct misstatements that may be introduced as a result of performing a process. For example, if one of the things "that can go wrong" in preparing an invoice is the use of an incorrect price, a procedure involving the check of invoices to make sure that correct prices have been used is a control.

Elements of the Components of Internal Control and Antifraud Controls

Information Systems and Control Activities

3.96 Your knowledge of the presence or absence of control activities obtained from understanding the control environment, and other control components assists you in determining whether it is necessary to devote additional attention to obtaining an understanding of control activities. Ineffective control environments and unreliable accounting systems may overshadow any benefit of examining controls activities in any significant detail.

3.97 However, when the auditor finds it appropriate to examine relevant control activities, an audit does not require you to obtain an understanding of all the information processing and activity-level controls related to each class of transactions, account balance, and disclosure in the financial statements or to every relevant assertion. Rather, your understanding of activity-level controls should be focused on significant classes of transactions and accounts. Also, you should obtain an understanding of the process of reconciling detailed records to the general ledger for material account balances. (AU-C sec. 315 par. .21)

3.98 *Information systems.* For those significant classes of transactions, you should obtain an understanding of

   a. how significant transactions are initiated, authorized, recorded, processed, and reported and the related accounting records, supporting information, and specific accounts. (AU-C sec. 315 par. .19)

   b. how the incorrect processing of transactions is resolved.

   c. if applicable, control activities relating to authorization, segregation of duties, safeguarding of assets, and asset accountability.

Observations and Suggestions

Determining which transactions are "significant" at your client is a matter of professional judgment. Factors you might consider in determining whether a class of transactions is significant for financial statement purposes include

- the volume and value of transactions and
- the relative importance of the transactions to the company's day-to-day operations and to the financial statements.

Examples of significant classes of transactions on many audits include revenue or sales transactions, purchases, payroll, cash receipts, and cash disbursements.

3.99 *Material account balances.* You should obtain an understanding of the entity's process of reconciling detailed records to the general ledger for material account balances. (AU-C sec. 315 par. .21)

3.100 *Antifraud controls.* You should evaluate the design of specific controls to mitigate specific risks of fraud and determine that they have been implemented for example, controls to address specific assets susceptible to misappropriation via theft. (AU-C sec. 240 par. .27)

IT Application Controls

3.101 Under paragraph .22 of AU-C section 315 you should obtain an understanding of how the client has responded to risks arising from IT. As such, you may obtain an understanding of IT application controls. Such controls are manual or automated and in many cases operate at a business process level and apply to the processing of transactions by individual transactions. Application controls can be preventive or detective and are designed to ensure the integrity of the accounting records. They relate to procedures used to initiate, authorize, record, process, and report transactions or other financial data. For example, application controls help ensure that transactions occurred, are authorized, and are completely and accurately recorded and processed. Another example is edit checks of input data, numerical sequence checks, and manual follow-up of exception reports.

Observations and Suggestions

IT application controls may include those relating to

- data input controls over transactions (including those rejected) to determine that they are authorized, and that transactions accepted are processed correctly and completely.

- output controls that assess whether input errors are reported and corrections are made or data is resubmitted, preventing the possibility of incomplete or inaccurate data.

- testing packaged software updates before they are put into production. For example, testing that key reports from both the old and new software reflect the same information is one way to test the completeness and accuracy of information transfer between the software packages. However, controls over systems implementation are in most cases considered part of IT general controls (principle 11).

- using a more formal process for selecting new applications, for example, consideration of application controls, security requirements, or data conversion requirements.

- storing critical applications or data in secure locations or on secured file servers. However, controls over system access are in most cases considered part of IT general controls (principle 11).

However, without good IT general controls where they are relevant, the auditor may have little basis to rely on application controls.

Revenue Recognition

3.102 Revenue recognition demands special audit consideration on many audits. The Audit Guide *Auditing Revenue in Certain Industries* states that "revenue recognition issues pose significant risk to auditors." AU-C section 240 directs the auditor to "ordinarily presume that there is a *risk of material misstatement* due to fraud relating to revenue recognition." For these reasons, controls relating to revenue recognition are, in many cases, relevant to your audit.

Table 3-10
Controls Over Revenue Recognition

The AICPA Audit Guide *Auditing Revenue in Certain Industries* provides guidance on the understanding of controls relating to revenue recognition and describes the following revenue recognition controls as ordinarily being relevant to the audit:

1. Policies and procedures for
     a. receiving and accepting orders
     b. extending credit
     c. shipping goods
     d. relieving inventory
     e. billing and recording sales transactions
     f. receiving and recording sales returns
     g. authorizing and issuing credit memos
2. Procedures for determining the proper cutoff of sales at the end of the accounting period
3. The computer applications and key documents used during the processing of revenue transactions
4. The methods used by management to monitor its sales contracts, including
     a. the company's policy about management or other personnel who are authorized to approve nonstandard contract clauses
     b. whether those personnel understand the accounting implications of changes to contractual clauses
     c. whether the entity enforces its policies regarding negotiation and approval of sales contracts and investigates exceptions
5. The application of accounting principles
6. The entity's financial reporting process to prepare the financial statements, including disclosures

Observations and Suggestions

In July 2016, a risk alert titled *Revenue Recognition: Accounting and Auditing Considerations—2016/17* was issued. This publication addressed accounting and general auditing considerations in the transition to FASB *Accounting Standards Codification* (ASC) 606, *Revenue with Contracts from Customers*, scheduled for 2018–2019 implementation for all entities. It is anticipated at the time of this revised guide that an Audit and Accounting Guide related to revenue recognition with updated information and some industry accounting guidance for selected industries will be released late in 2016. These publications on revenue recognition contain risk assessment, controls and other planning guidance specific to revenue recognition. Upon the implementation of FASB ASC 606, the existing industry-specific revenue recognition guides will be superseded.

©2016, AICPA

Controls Related to Significant Activity-Level Risks

3.103 *Significant risks* are risks that require special audit attention. You should obtain an understanding of the controls, including control activities, related to these risks. Paragraph 5.37 of this guide provides additional guidance on identifying *significant risks* at the assertion level. (AU-C sec. 315 par. .30)

Identify Other Controls That Are Relevant to the Audit

Circumstances When Substantive Procedures Alone Will Not Provide Sufficient Appropriate Audit Evidence

3.104 In some circumstances, substantive procedures alone will not provide sufficient appropriate audit evidence about an assertion. In those circumstances, you should evaluate the design and implementation of controls related to that assertion. Further, as described in chapter 6, "Performing Further Audit Procedures," of this guide, you should test these controls to obtain evidence of their operating effectiveness. (AU-C sec. 315 par. .31 and AU-C sec. 330 par. .08)

Observations and Suggestions

Circumstances where "substantive procedures alone will not provide sufficient appropriate audit evidence" may arise when significant transactions (for example, revenues, purchases, cash receipts, or cash disbursements) are initiated and processed electronically or when data is stored without manual intervention or a traceable "audit trail."

It is your understanding of the client's information system and business practices that enables you to identify these circumstances.

The Identification and Examples of Circumstances When Substantive Procedures Alone Will Not Provide Sufficient Appropriate Audit Evidence

3.105 In some cases, your client may initiate, record, process, or report a significant amount of information electronically. In those circumstances, it may not be possible to design effective substantive procedures that, by themselves, are capable of providing sufficient, appropriate audit evidence. (AU-C sec. 315 par. .31)

3.106 *Risks of material misstatement* may relate directly to the recording of routine classes of transactions or account balances. Such risks may include risks of inaccurate or incomplete processing for routine and significant classes of transactions such as sales. When determining whether substantive procedures alone are sufficient to gather the appropriate audit evidence you may consider the following:

   a. *Characteristics of available audit evidence.* When the processing of a significant amount of client's information is highly automated with little or no manual intervention, audit evidence may be available only in electronic form. When audit evidence exists only electronically, a paper or electronic "audit trail" may not exist. Absent this trail, your ability to determine whether the electronic information provides appropriate and sufficient audit evidence in many cases depends on the effectiveness of controls over its accuracy and completeness.

 b. *Greater risks of material misstatement.* The *risks of material misstatement* may be greater if information is initiated, recorded, processed, or reported only in electronic form and appropriate controls are not operating effectively. For example, inappropriate transactions may be initiated, or electronically stored information may be altered when there is little or no manual intervention on the initiation or processing of transactions. Because of this increased risk, you may determine that it is not possible to reduce audit risk to an acceptable level solely by performing substantive procedures.

 3.107 *For certain finished goods of its JY Sport line, Young Fashions initiates purchase orders based on predetermined rules of what to order and in what quantities. These rules are programmed into its IT system, and transactions are entered into automatically, without further approval or any other type of manual intervention. No other documentation of orders placed for these goods is produced or maintained, other than through the IT system. Any differences between the amounts received and ordered should be identified and reconciled at the time the shipment is received (and the purchase order is matched to the receipt of goods).*

In this example, audit evidence for purchase orders is available only in electronic format. However, evidence of the receipt of goods is available. The auditor may be able to perform substantive audit procedures to address some assertions but not others. For example, obtaining confirmations of purchases from suppliers may provide evidence concerning the occurrence of the transaction and its amount. The inventory count process also provides evidence of existence of inventory quantities. However, to reach a conclusion concerning whether all valid purchase orders were captured by the system (a completeness assertion) the auditor may have no better choice than to rely on the controls relating to the IT system in conjunction with controls related to the receiving process. Because an unfilled purchase order does not give rise to a liability, the auditor assessed the risk of a misstatement associated with such a situation to be low.

 3.108 *Ownco makes retail sales online. The company's IT system authorizes the transaction, invoices the customer, and collects the amount due by charging the customer's credit card.*

As with the previous example, the auditor may not be able to obtain evidence relating to the completeness assertion for revenue without testing the controls related to the IT system.

Controls Over Processes Not Directly Related to Financial Reporting

 3.109 Ordinarily, controls that are relevant to an audit pertain to the preparation of the client's financial statements and may include controls over safeguarding of assets against unauthorized acquisition, use, or disposition. Similarly, compliance with regulatory requirements or laws may have financial implications, so the effectiveness of a company's programs over compliance may be relevant. Failure to comply with laws and regulations may give rise to contingencies, or other financial statement footnote disclosure.

 3.110 Controls relating to the client's operations and compliance with laws and regulations may be relevant to your audit as serious noncompliance may misstate information or data that is reported to shareholders. An example is the risk of unmeasured costs that may arise due to fines. On the other hand, the auditor in many cases examines the programs the client places into effect to achieve these objectives and the results of regulatory actions to assess their effectiveness rather than the auditor testing compliance directly.

3.111 *For example, controls pertaining to nonfinancial data that management uses in monitoring its financial reporting results or that you use in analytical procedures (for example, production statistics) or controls pertaining to detecting noncompliance with laws and regulations that may have a direct and material effect on the financial statements (for example, controls over compliance with income tax laws and regulations used to determine the income tax provision) may be relevant to your audit.*

Perform Risk Assessment and Other Procedures

Performing Risk Assessment Procedures to Gather Information About Internal Control

3.112 To obtain the necessary understanding of internal control, you should perform risk assessment procedures, which should include

   a. inquiries of management, appropriate individuals within the internal audit function (if such function exists), and others within the client who, in your professional judgment, may have information that is likely to assist in identifying risks of material misstatement;

   b. analytical procedures; and

   c. observation and inspection.

Note: See paragraphs 3.78–.85 for guidance when the entity uses a service organization to process transactions.

(AU-C sec. 315 par. .06)

3.113 In addition to these risk assessment procedures, when you perform other procedures they may help you identify *risks of material misstatement*. For example, you read analysts' reports or make inquiries of the client's legal counsel.

Observations and Suggestions

The auditing standards describe the procedures listed in paragraph 3.112 as risk assessment procedures. In fact, these procedures are designed to gather the information that then allows you to understand internal control. The procedures described are information-gathering procedures. The performance of these procedures does not provide you with the requisite understanding of internal control, only the information necessary to form your understanding. An understanding of internal control is a function of information gathering and its subsequent analysis and synthesis.

As discussed in the COSO framework, the determination of risks related to financial reporting drives the population of controls that are expected to be in place. Thus, effective risk assessment is a fundamental prerequisite to the assessment of a system of the internal control and identification of any important gaps in their design. When entities perform an effective risk assessment related to their financial statements, auditors may consider that assessment, along with their own assessments.

Inquiries and Their Limitations

3.114 Inquiry may allow you to gather information about internal control design, but inquiry alone is not sufficient to determine whether the control has been implemented. Thus, when inquiry is used to obtain information about the design of internal control, you may corroborate the responses to your inquiries by performing at least one other risk assessment procedure in order to determine that client personnel are using the control. That additional procedure may be further observations of the control operating, inspecting documents and reports, or tracing transactions through the information system relevant to financial reporting. When no other procedure is more effective, corroborating inquiries, combined with observations, consideration of past actions or other evidence supporting the inquiries, may together provide sufficient evidence.

3.115 When audit evidence is not available from any other sources, corroborative inquiries made of multiple sources may still have significant value when determining whether a control has been implemented. For example, making inquiries of the owner-manager about the implementation of the company's code of conduct will not, by itself, allow the auditor to obtain a sufficient understanding of that aspect of the control environment. However, corroborating the owner manager's response with additional inquiries of company personnel or a survey in conjunction with observations or other evidence the auditor may gather through other audit procedures that support the veracity of the inquiries, may provide the auditor with the requisite level of understanding. For example, AU-C section 500, *Audit Evidence* (AICPA, *Professional Standards*), notes that corroboration of evidence obtained through inquiry is often of particular importance. In the case of inquiries about the control environment and "tone-at-the-top," the information available to support management's responses to inquires may be limited. In these cases, further inquiries or surveys of company personnel are often designed to provide further evidence regarding the implementation or the effectiveness of such controls. Observing behaviors, understanding management's past history of carrying out its stated intentions with respect to control environment issues such as ethical policies and fraud intolerance, and management's ability to pursue a specific course of intended action may provide relevant information supporting the results of the inquiries.

Even in the case of very small businesses where there are, for example, only two or three employees, inquiries may be supplemented with auditor observations or other evidence supporting the results of inquiries.

Observations and Suggestions

Sometimes auditors overlook the indirect evidence that is gathered continuously by being on-site and interacting on a regular basis with company personnel and management. An effective practice of some engagement teams is a meeting to discuss observations about the control environment or specific principles in the controls framework. The contribution by individual engagement team members to a common document that summarizes such information may also be useful. Such evidence can be particularly helpful in supporting certain principles for which tangible evidence is more difficult to gather.

3.116 Much of the information you obtain by inquiry can be obtained from management and those responsible for financial reporting. However, inquiries of others within the entity, such as production personnel and the internal audit function, if the entity has such a function, and other employees with different levels of authority, also may be useful. Paragraph 3.24 and table 3-4 provide additional guidance on making inquiries of others within the entity.

Analytical Procedures

3.117 Paragraphs 3.26 and 3.28 provide guidance on how analytical procedures may help you gather information and gain an understanding of the client, its environment, and its internal control. The application of analytical procedures may lead you to identify unusual transactions or events, which may indicate the presence of significant risks (as discussed in chapter 5 of this guide). Paragraph 3.93 addresses controls related to significant risks.

Observation and Inspection

3.118 Observation and inspection may support inquiries of management, appropriate individuals within the internal audit function (if such function exists), and others, and also provide information about internal control. Such audit procedures ordinarily include

- observing entity activities and operations;

- inspecting documents (business plans and strategies), records, and internal control manuals;

- reading reports prepared by management, the internal audit function (if, as a result of the inquiries with appropriate internal audit function personnel, items are noted that are deemed relevant to the audit, the auditor may consider reading related internal audit reports), and those charged with governance (such as minutes of board of directors' meetings); and

- visiting the client's premises and plant facilities.

3.119 The observation of the performance of a control procedure may not be possible when the control is performed on an as-needed basis, and you are not present to observe it. For example, the way in which management responds to a violation of the company's code of conduct may be an element of the control environment that you cannot plan to observe.

3.120 When inspecting the documentation of a control, it is helpful to distinguish between the documentation of the design of the control and evidence of its performance, which addresses the implementation of the control. For example,

- a written code of conduct describes the design of an element of the control environment. However, by itself, it does not provide evidence about how the control has been implemented.

- the "sign-off" by the accounting staff that a reconciliation was performed will help you determine whether the control was implemented. However, the sign-off alone does not allow you to understand the design of the control and how the procedure should have been performed. It also does not establish what the signer did to review the transaction, other than to sign.

Other Procedures

Procedures Performed to Assess Misstatements Caused by Fraud

3.121 AU-C section 240 directs you to perform certain audit procedures to assess the risks of material misstatement due to fraud. Some of these procedures will complement your understanding of the implementation of internal control. These audit procedures include the following:

a. Inquiries of management and others within the entity about the risk of fraud, knowledge of any fraud or suspected fraud, programs and controls to mitigate fraud risks (AU-C sec. 240 par. .17–.19)

b. Inquiries of management about whether and how they communicate to employees its views on business practices and ethical behavior (AU-C sec. 240 par. .17d)

c. Communications from management to the audit committee on how the entity's internal control serves to prevent, deter, or detect material misstatements due to fraud (AU-C sec. 240 par. .17c)

d. Inquiries of others within the entity about how effectively management has communicated standards of ethical behavior to individuals throughout the entity (AU-C sec. 240 par. .17d)

e. Audit procedures relating to revenue recognition performed in response to the presumption that revenue recognition is a fraud risk (AU-C sec. 240 par. .26)

f. Audit procedures performed to obtain an understanding of the entity's financial reporting process and the controls over journal entries and other adjustments (AU-C sec. 240 par. .32a)

g. Audit procedures performed to evaluate the business rationale for significant unusual transactions (AU-C sec. 240 par. .32c)

Walkthroughs

Observations and Suggestions

Evaluating the design of a control involves considering whether the control is capable of effectively preventing, or detecting and correcting material misstatements. Implementation of a control means that the control exits and the client is using it. Risk assessment procedures to obtain audit evidence about the design and implementation of a control may include inquiring, observing, inspecting documentation, and tracing transactions through the information system. This activity is commonly referred to as a *walkthrough*. The following commentary on walkthroughs describes a process as rigorous and thorough as any other audit procedure you perform to gather audit evidence. Walkthroughs need to be well-planned and performed with due care and an appropriate level of professional skepticism. To perform a thorough walkthrough, you would plan to

- make inquiries of people who actually perform the procedure, not just someone at a supervisory level.
- corroborate the responses to inquiries by performing additional procedures such as the inspection of relevant documents or accounting records, or corroborating inquiries made of others.

Merely tracing information through the client's accounting system is not considered a walkthrough. A properly performed walkthrough will allow you to confirm the design of controls over the processing of the information and to gain some evidence that the controls exist and that client personnel are using them.

It is relatively easy to document a set of controls that "should" be in place, but the walkthrough provides evidence that the design reflects the way the control works. Anecdotal evidence indicates that differences between documented and implemented controls may be more common than expected.

Walkthrough documentation is intended to focus on controls. Walkthrough documentation that contains a lot of process description may detract from the purpose of the walkthrough and be inefficient.

There is no requirement to perform a walk through to document business processes.

Although specific content of walkthrough documentation is not specified by the auditing standards, some elements of a good walkthrough often contain

- an efficient format. Forms or matrices are sometimes used to document the walkthrough and its elements.
- a design so that the walkthrough covers several related controls to encourage efficiency in documentation and to follow the "trail" of controls over the processing of a transaction.
- identification of the assertions addressed by the controls.
- indication of who performed the walkthrough and the date thereof.
- indication of to whom the engagement team spoke.
- evidence observed or examined.
- observations regarding whether the employee spoken to seemed to be competent and knowledgeable of the control and its implications.
- consideration of any IT or service organization involvement.
- consideration of any risks associated with the transactions being processed.
- linkages to control descriptions and verification that the walkthrough agreed with the descriptions of controls.

3.122 The purpose of a walkthrough is to help

- confirm your understanding of key elements of the client's information processing system and related controls.
- evaluate the effectiveness of the design of internal control.
- determine whether certain controls have been implemented.

3.123 A walkthrough may be designed to provide evidence regarding the design and implementation of controls. However, a walkthrough may be designed to include procedures that are also tests of the operating effectiveness of relevant controls (for instance, inquiry combined with observation, inspection of documents, or reperformance). See paragraphs 6.65–.68 of this guide for additional guidance on the use of walkthroughs to gather evidence about the operating effectiveness of controls.

3.124 There are several ways to perform a walkthrough to achieve your audit objectives. For example, you could

- select a single transaction and trace its processing through the company's information processing system and all the way through to its reporting in the financial statements.

- identify the key steps in the client's processing of a class of transactions, from initiation through to financial reporting. For each of these steps, you then perform risk assessment procedures to gain an understanding of the design of the process and the related controls and to determine that the controls have been implemented. At each step in the process you would perform the procedures for a given transaction, but not necessarily the same transaction at each step.

3.125 Although inquiries of management and those involved in the financial reporting process ordinarily are a significant component of a walkthrough, they are not the only component. Walkthroughs provide more reliable and relevant audit evidence when you corroborate responses of a single individual with inquiries of others, observations of the performance of control procedures, and inspection of accounting records and other documentation.

3.126 Inquiries related to the following may be helpful in gaining the necessary understanding of internal control:

- The individual's understanding of the client's stated procedures and controls

- Whether the processing and control procedures are performed as required and on a timely basis

- Specific situations in which the individual or others do not perform the company's prescribed control procedures

- The individual's understanding of the information processing and control procedures performed on information (a) before he or she receives it and (b) after he or she has transferred the information to the next processing step

3.127 You may corroborate the response to your inquiries through observation and inspection, or example by

- observing the individual perform their assigned information processing or control procedure.

- reperforming the information processing or control procedure using the same documents and IT that company personnel use to perform the procedures.

Using Service Auditors' Reports to Gather Information About Controls at a Service Organization

3.128 As described in paragraph 3.79, in some situations, you may need to gain an understanding of the design and implementation of controls at a service organization. To gain this understanding you may wish to obtain at least a type 2 SOC 1 report from the client's service organization. Table 3-11 summarizes the objectives of the two types of service auditor reports and how you might use these on your audit. When the audit strategy is to rely on the controls at a service organization, a type 2 SOC 1 report under AU-C section 402 (design and implementation and effectiveness) is necessary.

Table 3-11
Summary of Service Organization Control Reports®

Title	Contents	Relevance to User Auditors
Reports on management's description of a service organization's system and the suitability of the design of controls (Type 1 SOC 1 report)	• Includes management's description of the service organization's system and a report by the service auditor that includes an opinion on whether such description is fairly presented and related controls are suitably designed to achieve specified control objectives • Is *as of* a specified date	• Assists the auditor in obtaining a sufficient understanding of the nature and significance of the services provided by the service organization and their effect on the user entity's internal control relevant to the audit
Report on management's description of a service organization's system and the suitability of the design and operating effectiveness of controls (Type 2 SOC 1 report)	• Includes all elements of a type 1 SOC 1 report and also includes the service auditor's opinion on whether the controls included in the description were operating effectively • Is for a specified period	• Has the same utility as a type 1 SOC 1 report and also provides evidence of the operating effectiveness of the relevant controls to support the user auditor's risk assessment

Observations and Suggestions

In addition to the broad recognition of the role of service organizations in today's business environment across 12 of the 17 COSO principles, the COSO framework discusses the expectation that an entity will communicate to its service organization the entity's standards of conduct and seek to confirm the service organization understands and is in compliance with the entity's policies.

3.129 Illustration 3-2 summarizes the process for gathering information about internal control.

Illustration 3-2
Process for Understanding Internal Control

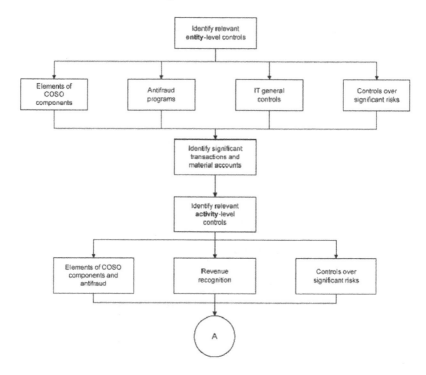

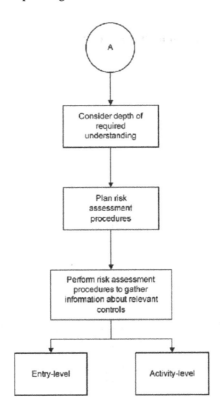

©2016, AICPA

Information Obtained in Prior Audits

3.130 For continuing engagements, your previous experience with the entity contributes to your understanding of its internal control. For example, audit procedures performed in previous audits may often provide

- audit evidence about the client's organizational structure, business, and internal control.
- information about past misstatements.
- whether past misstatements were corrected on a timely basis.

All of this information can help you assess risks of material misstatement.

3.131 However, if you intend to use the information obtained in prior audits to support your risk assessments in the current period audit, you should determine whether the information from prior audits remains relevant. Changes may have occurred that affect the relevance of such information in the current audit. To determine whether changes have occurred that may affect relevance, you may make inquiries and perform other appropriate audit procedures, such as walkthroughs of systems to confirm the results of inquiries. (AU-C sec. 315 par. .10)

3.132 The nature, timing, and extent of the procedures you perform to update your understanding of the client obtained in prior periods may depend on matters such as

- the significance of the changes to the entity or its environment that have occurred since the prior period. (Note that a change in personnel at the company could be a significant change even if the client's processes or its internal control procedures did not change. For example, a change in the person responsible for a significant control activity or for monitoring the database could be significant.)
- the relative significance of the risks of material misstatement that could be affected by changes to the entity or its environment.
- the reliability of evidence available to support your conclusions about changes or lack of changes from the prior period. (Documented controls may be more reliable evidence when supported by observations and inquiry than if only inquiry is available to assess controls changes.)

3.133 For example, XYZ company manufactures technology used in wireless telephones. During the period between audits, three of the changes to the entity and its environment were

- the company leased additional office space;
- a competitor introduced new technology that was vastly superior to XYZ's; and
- the company revised its accounts payable procedures.

The auditor initially learned of these developments through an inquiry of company management. However, as described in paragraph 3.36, to determine what changes have occurred and assess how these changes affect the relevance of audit evidence from prior periods, the auditor may make inquiries and perform other appropriate procedures.

For example, given the nature of the changes at XYZ, the other procedures the auditor might perform include the following:

- Observing company employees at work in the new office space. The auditor determined that entering into a routine lease agreement of this nature did not pose significant risks of material misstatement and that the observation of operations and controls in the new space was sufficient to corroborate that the company occupied the new space. Accounting for the lease and other related costs might require information concerning the dates of occupation.

- Reading an article in a trade journal about the competitor's release of its new product. This release could significantly change the auditor's assessment of the risks of material misstatement, perhaps due to product obsolescence risks. The auditor believed the public information was sufficient to corroborate the representation that the release occurred.

- Making inquiries of employees in accounting and in purchasing, examined revised documentation to reflect the revised controls, and performed a full walkthrough of the new accounts payable system. Because of the magnitude of the change and its potential effect on the assessment of the risks of material misstatement, the auditor determined that these procedures were necessary to evaluate the design and implementation of internal control.

Identifying and Evaluating Change

3.134 In some situations, changes in the client or its environment require changes to the client's internal control. For example, if the company expands its operations to other locations, internal control should be expanded to those new locations. Control deficiencies may arise when changes in the entity or its environment are not matched by corresponding changes to controls. Thus, when determining whether changes have occurred that may affect the relevance of information about internal control obtained in a previous audit, you may consider *both* of the following:

a. Whether the company has changed its controls

b. Whether there have been changes to the entity or its environment that should have resulted in changes to control

3.135 Your client's ability to appropriately modify internal control depends on the effectiveness of its risk assessment process. A failure to appropriately modify internal control in response to changes in the entity or its environment may indicate a deficiency in the client's risk assessment process.

Table 3-12 provides examples of changes to the entity or its environment that may create new risks and therefore the need for changes to existing controls.

                                        ©2016, AICPA

Table 3-12
Changes in the Client or Its Environment That May Require Changes in Internal Control

Changes in the client or its environment may create new financial reporting risks, which in turn require modifications to internal control. In determining whether information about internal control that was obtained in a prior audit continue to be relevant in the current audit, it is helpful to consider whether the client made changes to internal control in response to circumstances such as the following:

- Changes in operating environment
- New personnel
- New or revamped information systems
- Rapid growth
- New technology
- New business models, products, or activities
- Corporate restructurings
- Expanded foreign operations
- New accounting pronouncements
- Changes in economic conditions

Management's failure to appropriately modify internal control for changes such as the ones listed here may indicate a deficiency in their risk assessment process as well as result in deficiencies in their control activities.

Observations and Suggestions

When you have audited an entity in the prior period, you are not required to "reinvent the wheel" when it comes to understanding internal control for the current period audit. You do not have to start from scratch and ignore all you have learned in the prior period. Once you have established an appropriate basis for assessing the controls, the update of that assessment in following periods may not be as costly in time and effort.

However, you cannot simply carry forward your understanding from the prior period under an unsupported assumption that everything is the "same as last year."

To determine whether your understanding of internal control remains relevant you may consider *both* of the following:

- Changes to internal control that have been made since the last audit
- Changes to internal control that *should have been made* but were not (for example, changes in the business or its operations that resulted in new risks and therefore should require new controls)

The procedures you perform to determine whether your previous understanding of internal control remains relevant may be less time-consuming than those procedures you performed in the initial audit. However, these subsequent procedures should be performed with the same level of professional skepticism and due care as they were when first performed.

The COSO framework states that the entity is expected to identify and assess significant changes such as those discussed previously. This is articulated within principle 9 and the associated points of focus under the risk assessment component.

A Process for Identifying and Evaluating Change

3.136 Illustration 3-3 describes a process you may use to identify and evaluate change as a means for determining the nature, timing, and extent of the risk assessment procedures you will perform to update your understanding of internal control obtained in a previous audit.

- Beginning at the top of the diagram, the risk assessment procedures you perform to obtain an understanding of the entity and its environment should allow you to gather information about matters that have changed since your previous audit.

- Information about change can be used to identify changes in inherent risk. For example, an economic downturn may create inherent risk for your client that was not present before the downturn.

- If inherent risk remains unchanged or new risks are appropriately addressed by controls that were in place in prior years, then you may want to perform risk assessment procedures to verify that controls have not changed.

3.137 As shown in illustration 3-3, there are three different approaches you might take to determine the nature, timing and extent of risk assessment procedures to perform to update your understanding of the client obtained in previous audits. The approach you select depends, in part, on your assessment of risk in the current year. For example

- if the controls in place during the prior year would have been effective in addressing the current year's risks, then a good deal of the audit evidence obtained in prior audits may be relevant to the current audit. Once you determine that there have been no changes to those controls, then your understanding of internal control may be sufficient for you to assess risks of material misstatement.

- if prior year's controls would have been effective in addressing current year's risks but you discover that the design or implementation of those controls has changed, then you will want to assess the changes to those controls that have occurred since your previous audit. Assessing these changes and determining whether the revised controls adequately address the inherent risk present in the current year can enable you to support your assessment of the risks of material misstatement.

- in some instances, you may identify new or significantly changed inherent risk that could not be effectively addressed by prior year's controls. If this is the case, the information you obtained in prior audits may have very little relevance in the current audit, and you will most likely perform more extensive risk assessment procedures to gain an understanding of the design and implementation of control.

Observations and Suggestions

Decisions about the nature, timing, and extent of the risk assessment procedures you perform to update your understanding of the client are made on a process-by-process basis and not globally for the entire audit.

For example, assume that in previous audits you performed walkthroughs for many significant classes of transactions, including accounts receivable and inventory. In the current period, the conditions at your client may lead you to determine that inquiries of selected client personnel and examination of some evidence of the controls through observations may be sufficient to update your understanding of controls over accounts receivable, but inquiry, a walkthrough, and other procedures may be necessary to update your understanding of controls over inventory.

Determining Whether to Perform a Walkthrough Each Year

3.138 You are required to obtain an understanding of internal control to evaluate the design of controls and to determine whether they have been implemented. To do that, performing a walkthrough would be a good practice. Accordingly, auditors might perform a walkthrough of significant accounting cycles every year.

3.139 In some situations, you may rely on audit evidence obtained in prior periods to help satisfy some of the requirements for understanding the design and implementation of internal control in the current period. In those situations, you are required to perform audit procedures to establish the continued relevance of the audit evidence obtained in prior periods. That is, it ordinarily would be inappropriate to rely completely on audit procedures performed in prior audits as audit evidence supporting your understanding of internal control design and implementation in the current period.

3.140 A walkthrough may be helpful in determining whether and how internal control design and implementation have changed since the prior period. However, you may determine that a walkthrough is not required. Rather, it is important that you first understand the audit objective (establish the continued relevance of the audit evidence obtained in prior periods) and then determine the audit procedure(s) that can meet that objective.

3.141 When determining the nature, timing, and extent of procedures to perform to update your understanding of internal control from the prior year, you may wish to consider the following:

- *Effectiveness of the client's control environment, management's risk assessment, monitoring, and general controls.* The more effective these controls, the more appropriate it may be for you to use prior year's audit evidence to support your current understanding of internal control.
- *Reliance on automation.* The more automated the performance of the control the more appropriate it may be for you to use prior year's audit evidence to support your current understanding of internal control (assuming effective general controls.)
- *Changes in client circumstances.* The fewer the changes in client circumstances (for example, personnel, changes in business practices) the more appropriate it may be for you to use prior year's

audit evidence to support your current understanding of internal control.

- *Risks of material misstatement.* The lower the risks of material misstatement for the relevant assertion, the more appropriate it may be for you to use prior year's audit evidence to support your current understanding of internal control.

- *Length of time since performing extensive risk assessment procedures.* The shorter the period of time since your initial evaluation on internal control design and implementation the more appropriate it may be for you to use prior year's audit evidence to support your current understanding of internal control.

Continuous Reevaluation

3.142 As your audit progresses, additional audit evidence you obtain from the performance of risk assessment or further audit procedures may either confirm or disconfirm your understanding of the changes that have occurred since the prior period. Disconfirming audit evidence may lead you to revise your audit strategy or audit plan.

Illustration 3-3
Process for Assessing Changes in an Entity's Internal Control

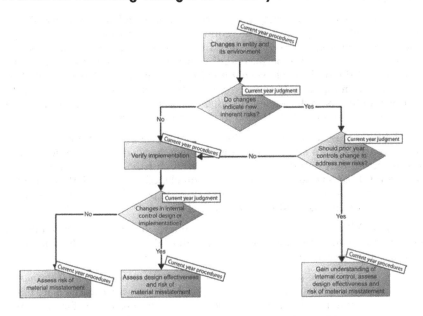

       ©2016, AICPA

Audit Documentation

3.143 This chapter provides guidance on certain matters relating to the planning of the audit, including the determination of materiality and performance materiality. It also describes how you perform risk assessment procedures to gather an understanding of the client and how you should plan for the performance of those procedures. With regards to these matters, you should document

a. the preliminary overall audit strategy and any significant revisions to it. (AU-C sec. 300 par. .14c)

b. the audit plan, including the audit procedures to be used that, when performed, are expected to reduce audit risk to an acceptably low level. The documentation should include a description of the nature, timing, and extent of planned

    i. risk assessment procedures.

    ii. further audit procedures.

    iii. other audit procedures necessary to comply with GAAS.

(AU-C sec. 300 par. .09)

c. the level of materiality for the financial statements as a whole, which you used to plan your risk assessment procedures including

    i. the basis on which those levels were determined, and

    ii. any changes to those levels.

(AU-C sec. 320 par. .14)

d. the levels of performance materiality, including the basis of those levels and any changes made over the course of the audit. (AU-C sec. 320 par. .14)

e. the discussion among the audit team regarding the client's financial statements to material misstatement due to error or fraud. This documentation should include the following matters.

    i. How and when the discussion occurred

    ii. The subject matter discussed

    iii. The audit team members who participated in the discussion

    iv. Significant decisions reached about the teams planned responses, both at the financial statement and the assertion level

(AU-C sec. 315 par. .33)

f. the risk assessment procedures you performed to gather information about the client. (AU-C sec. 315 par. .33)

g. the sources you used to gather information of the client. (AU-C sec. 315 par. .33)

h. the key elements of your understanding of the client's risks, including each of the aspects of the client and its environment. With regard to internal control, your documentation should include each of the five elements of internal control. (AU-C sec. 315 par. .33)

Paragraphs 1.39–.41 provide additional, more general guidance on the preparation of audit documentation.

©2016, AICPA

Observations and Suggestions

Paragraph 3.136 describes the requirement to document your understanding of each of the five elements of internal control. As described in paragraph 4.26, "understanding" internal control means evaluating internal control design and determining whether the controls have been implemented.

Accordingly, your documentation of internal control should include this evaluation and a determination that the controls are implemented. Appendix K, "Illustrative Audit Documentation Case Study: Young Fashions, Inc.," of this guide provides some examples of controls documentation.

If you are auditing an entity using the COSO framework, your audit documentation may indicate how the 17 principles were addressed in your procedures. In addition, your documentation may reflect how the integrated nature of internal controls and relationships between principles were considered when analyzing control deficiencies identified by your procedures.

Summary

3.144 This chapter provides guidance on the procedures—risk assessment procedures—that you perform to gain the understanding of your client, including the identification of inherent risks, that is necessary for you to first assess and then to respond to risks of material misstatement.

3.145 As a prelude to performing these risk assessment procedures, you will need to plan for them. Among other things, your planning may involve

- developing an audit strategy and a more detailed plan for gathering information, which may help you allocate resources to the engagement and make a preliminary determination of the risk assessment procedures you will perform;

- determining a materiality level for the financial statements as a whole, which will be used for audit planning purposes; and

- determining performance materiality, which is necessary to adjust materiality for the financial statements as a whole to a level that is appropriate for performing your audit at the assertion level.

3.146 Once you have planned for your risk assessment procedures, in many cases you will perform them. This constitutes the first step in your gathering of audit evidence to support your opinion on the financial statements. Chapter 4 of this guide describes how you use the information gathered through your risk assessment procedures to form an understanding of the client and its environment, including its internal control.

Observations and Suggestions

Risk assessment procedures are essentially information gathering procedures. As you obtain information, you begin to form an understanding of the entity and its internal control. This process of information gathering and gaining an understanding is iterative in nature. Throughout the audit, you are continuously gathering and evaluating information and adding depth to your understanding of the client.

                                    ©2016, AICPA

As you incorporate the guidance in this chapter into your audits, you may wish to consider the following:

- Your initial understanding of the client and its environment may be reinforced or possibly challenged by the subsequent gathering of additional information. Some of this information may come from the results of your substantive procedures. For example, the discovery of audit differences in a particular account should lead you to question whether your initial understanding of controls related to that account was accurate. Audit differences do not just result in proposed adjustments to the general ledger. They also should prompt you to consider the controls that failed to prevent or detect and correct the error you discovered.

- Audit team members need to share information with each other to ensure that the understanding of internal control is made with full knowledge of all available information. AU-C section 315 requires a brainstorming session to facilitate this exchange of information, but you do not have to limit the sharing of information to the one brainstorming session early in the audit. Consider structuring your audit to include the regular sharing of information among audit team members.

- Your client is a primary source of the information you need to form an understanding internal control. Your ability to obtain timely, high quality information from your client, in many cases will affect greatly the efficiency and effectiveness of your audit.

Appendix—Answers to Frequently Asked Questions About Audit Planning and Risk Assessment Procedures

Question	See Paragraphs
What is an audit strategy and what is an audit plan? How are they different?	3.02–.05
What should I include in my audit strategy?	3.02 and appendix A of this guide
What should I include in my audit plan?	3.05
How do I determine materiality?	3.07–.12
What is my overall objective in obtaining an understanding of the client?	3.16
How much of an understanding of my client and its environment should I obtain?	3.18–.21
What are *risk assessment procedures*?	3.22
Can I use other procedures, in addition to risk assessment procedures, to obtain information about my client and its environment?	3.33
Can I use information gathered in previous audits as a basis for my understanding of the client in the current year? How should I update that understanding from year-to-year?	3.133–.142
What is the purpose of the audit team discussion? What topics should be included in this discussion?	3.36–.38
How does the client's internal control documentation or lack of documentation affect my audit?	3.40–.47 and 4.36–.38
What IT controls most typically affect my audits?	3.54–.69
When should I consider using an IT audit professional on my audits?	3.70–.77
My client uses a third party service organization to process some of its transactions. How does this arrangement affect my audit?	3.78–.85
What is a service auditors' report and what sort of information will it provide me about my client's internal control?	3.128–.129
Which entity-level controls are most likely to fall within the scope of my audit?	3.88–.94

Question	See Paragraphs
What general types of activity-level controls would I most likely want to include within the scope of my audit?	3.95–.111
How can I best use inquiries to gather information about my client and its environment, including its internal control?	3.112–.121
What is a walkthrough? How can I use walkthroughs on my audit?	3.122–.127 and 3.138–.140
What audit planning matters should I document?	3.143

Chapter 4

Understanding the Client, Its Environment, and Its Internal Control

TABLE OF CONTENTS

_____

Observations and Suggestions

Illustration 4-1
Understanding the Client, Its Environment,
and Its Internal Control

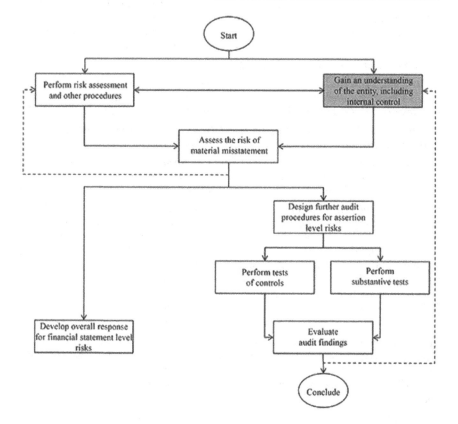

After you develop a preliminary audit strategy, you will often perform risk assessment procedures to gather information to gain an understanding of your client. Some of the information you need to understand about your client may be carried forward from your previous experience or from other procedures, such as the process you follow to decide on client acceptance or continuance.

Information About the Entity and Its Environment

You will gather information about a wide range of matters relating to your client. Some of these matters relate directly to the financial reporting process, but many of them relate to the broader business issues, such as the current status of the client's industry and its business objectives and strategies.

Information About Internal Control

Your client's internal control is an integral part of its business. On every audit, you will gain an understanding of internal control that allows you to evaluate its design and determine whether controls are being used at the entity.

Using Your Understanding of the Client, Its Environment, and Its Internal Control

As you gather information, you will begin to form an understanding of the client and how the specific conditions and circumstances pertaining to their business may affect the preparation of the client's financial statements.

Ultimately, the information you gather and the understanding you gain about the client at this phase of the process provides audit evidence to support your assessment of the risks of material misstatement and, ultimately, your opinion on the financial statements. As you become knowledgeable about your client, in many cases you will discover you need additional information to gain an understanding that is sufficient enough to enable you to assess the risks of material misstatement. Thus, the gathering of information and creation of knowledge about your client is a continuous, nonlinear process.

To assess risk and design appropriate substantive procedures and other procedures, you need to have a good understanding of your client and its environment, including internal control. To form a meaningful understanding of your client, you will perform risk assessment and other procedures to gather the information you need.

This chapter provides guidance on how to gather information about your client and how to use that information to understand the client in a way that allows you to appropriately assess the risks of material misstatements. This understanding of your client provides information that is necessary to support your risk assessments.

Introduction

Observations and Suggestions

The mere documentation of information that you gather about the client and its environment is not sufficient to support an assessment of the risks of material misstatement. You then evaluate that information and use it to form an understanding of your client that will allow you to assess risk and design appropriate other audit procedures.

This section has been organized to help you bridge the gap between gathering information and forming an understanding. The auditing standard directs you to gain an understanding of five different components of the client and its environment. For each of these aspects, this section of the guide lists the information that should be gathered and then explains how this information should be used to form a more in-depth understanding of the company that will allow you to assess the risks of material misstatement.

4.01 Risk assessment procedures help you gather information about your client and its environment. As you gather this information, you will need to synthesize and evaluate it to form a meaningful understanding of the client, one that will allow you to assess the risks of material misstatement. This understanding of the client and its environment provides the information necessary to support your risk assessments.

4.02 As described in chapter 3, "Planning and Performing Risk Assessment Procedures," of this guide, your understanding of the client and its environment consists of an understanding of the following aspects:

- *a.* Industry, regulatory, and other external factors
- *b.* Nature of the entity
- *c.* Selection and application of accounting policies
- *d.* Objectives and strategies and the related business risk that may result in a material misstatement of the financial statements
- *e.* Measurement and review of the entity's financial performance
- *f.* Internal control relevant to the audit

Paragraphs 4.04–.25 provide guidance on items *a–d.*

4.03 Obtaining an understanding of internal control involves evaluating the design of controls and determining whether they have been implemented (that is, placed in operation). Paragraphs 4.26–.38 provide guidance on understanding internal control.

Obtaining an Understanding of the Entity and Its Environment

Understanding the Industry, Regulatory, and Other External Factors

Breadth of Understanding

4.04 You should obtain an understanding of

- the client's relevant industry, regulatory, and other external factors, including the applicable financial reporting framework.
- the nature of the client.
- the client's selection and application of accounting policies, including the reasons for changes thereto.

- the client's objectives and strategies and those related business risks that may result in risks of material misstatement.
- the measurement and review of the client's financial performance.

(AU-C sec. 315 par. .12)

How Your Understanding Helps You Assess the Risks of Material Misstatement

4.05 The information you gather about the industry, regulatory, and other external factors should help your form an understanding of the client that will help you identify and *assess risks of material misstatements*.

Industry factors include industry conditions such as the competitive environment, supplier and customer relations, and technology developments. Examples you may consider include

- the market and competition.
- cyclical or seasonal activity.
- product technology.
- energy supply and cost.

Relevant regulatory factors include the regulatory environment which encompasses, among other matters, the applicable financial reporting framework and the legal and political environment. Examples you may consider follow:

- Accounting principles and industry-specific practices
- Regulatory framework for a regulated industry
- Laws and regulations that significantly affect the client's operations
- Taxation
- Government policies affecting the conduct of the client's business
- Environmental requirements affecting the client's industry and business

Industry conditions, the degree of regulation or other external factors may subject your client to specific risks of material misstatement. Also, industry regulations may specify certain financial reporting requirements, which, if not complied with, would result in a material misstatement of the financial statements.

For example, many years ago the government standards were changed for configuration of civil band mobile radios. Manufacturers of parts for these radios had inventories of these parts they were producing under the old standard. Some of these parts became obsolete the day the new regulation was announced.

Understanding the Nature of the Entity

Breadth of Understanding

4.06 The nature of an entity includes

a. its operations;

b. its ownership and governance structure;

c. the types of investments it is making and plans to make;

d. the way it is structured and how it is financed.

Understanding the nature of the client enables you to understand the classes of transactions, account balances, and disclosures to be expected in its financial statements. This may include an entity formed by your client to accomplish a narrow purpose (for example, a variable interest entity). (AU-C sec. 315 par. .12)

How Your Understanding Helps You Assess the Risks of Material Misstatement

4.07 The information you gather with respect to the items listed in paragraph 4.06 will help you understand the matters about the client that may affect the *risks of material misstatement*. For example,

- the account balances, classes of transactions, and disclosures expected to be in the financial statements. (AU-C sec. 315 par. .12*b*)
- complex organizational structures that increase the risks of material misstatements, for example, the allocation of goodwill to subsidiaries or the accounting for variable interest entities.
- transactions with related parties.

4.08 With regard to the client's selection and application of accounting policies, your understanding of the client includes understanding

- the methods the client uses to account for significant and unusual transactions.
- the effect of significant accounting policies in controversial or emerging areas for which there is a lack of authoritative guidance or consensus.
- changes in the client's accounting policies.

For each of these matters you should evaluate whether the client's selection and application of accounting policies are appropriate and consistent with generally accepted accounting principles (GAAP) and accounting policies used in the client's industry. When the client changes its accounting policies, you also should obtain an understanding of the reason for the change.

(AU-C sec. 315 par. .12*c*)

Understanding Sales Transactions

4.09 Sales are often a significant class of transactions for many of your clients, and for that reason, it may often be important for you to obtain an understanding of matters relating to sales that may affect your client's revenue recognition. With regard to assertions about revenue, you might consider obtaining information relating to the following matters:

- The kinds of products and services sold
- Whether seasonal or cyclical variations in revenue may be expected
- The marketing and sales policies customary for the client and the industry
- Policies regarding pricing, sales returns, discounts, extension of credit, and normal delivery and payment terms
- Who, particularly in the marketing and sales functions, is involved with processes affecting revenues including order entry, extension of credit, and shipping

- Whether there are compensation arrangements that depend on the company's recording of revenue, for example, whether the sales force is paid commissions based on sales invoiced or sales collected, and the frequency with which sales commissions are paid, might have an effect on the recording of sales at the end of a period

4.10   Paragraphs 4.11–.13 discuss some of these matters. The AICPA Audit Guide *Auditing Revenue in Certain Industries* provides additional guidance on matters which you may need to consider with regard to your level of understanding about your client's sales transactions.

4.11   *Your client's customers.* Obtaining an understanding of the classes and categories of your client's customers is important. For example, if sales to distributors are material, it is important to understand whether concessions have been made in the form of return product rights or other arrangements in the distribution agreements the client has entered into. For example, distribution agreements in the high-technology industry might include such terms as price protection, rights of return for specified periods, rights of return for obsolete product, and cancellation clauses, such that the real substance of the agreement is that it results in consignment inventory.

4.12   *Assistance provided to distributors.* Other factors that may be relevant to your understanding include whether the client assists distributors in placing product with end users, and how the company manages, tracks, and controls its inventory that is held by distributors. For example, the client may take physical inventories of product held by distributors or receive periodic inventory reports from distributors that are reconciled to the client's records.

4.13   *Selection and application of accounting principles.* You may consider the need to understand the accounting principles that are appropriate for the client's sales transactions, including special industry practices. In considering the appropriateness of recognizing revenue on sales to distributors, for example, you should bear in mind that a sale is not final until the distributor accepts the product and the risks and rewards of ownership have been transferred. In some cases, the distributor does not take ownership but only transfers ownership to its customers when the product is sold.

Understanding of IT Systems

4.14   Although many engagements will require the use of an IT specialist to gather information and assess risk related to the client's IT system, non-IT auditors may be able to gather information and obtain a basic understanding of IT-related risks. Table 4-1 provides an example of information that may be gathered and how it may help assess risk.

Table 4-1
Information That May Be Gathered About IT Systems

Information About IT	How This Information Helps Assess Risk
List of applications (including operating system), the vendor, and version number	• Provides a general understanding of the complexity of the client's system and the scope of your work. • Identifies applications that were provided by different vendors. (See paragraph 2.74 of this guide for a discussion of the risks related to the use of applications from different vendors.) • Comparison of information between audit periods can identify installation of new applications or upgrades to existing applications that were performed during the year.
Network policies such as password protocols	• Provide an overall understanding of the parameters the entity has established for its network and whether these fall within a typical range. • Identify weaknesses that might lead to risks of fraud or error.
List of key hardware components	• Provides a general understanding of the overall complexity of the system.
Systems configuration diagram	• Provides a visual summary of the hardware and software configuration of the system. • Forms a basis for the auditor's understanding of the financial reporting process. • Information about data storage can help design data extraction applications using software.
Documentation of IT general or application controls	• Provides information about the design of general controls such as access controls. • Information about application controls can be used to design risk assessment or further audit procedures. • Provides a basis for assessing changes over time that could affect performance. • Provides a basis for the walkthrough of the process that may be performed to confirm implementation of the control.

Understanding Your Client's Objectives, Strategies, and Related Business Risks

4.15 In accordance with AU-C section 315, *Understanding the Entity and Its Environment and Assessing the Risks of Material Misstatement* (AICPA, *Professional Standards*), obtain an understanding of the business risk your client faces because most business risk will eventually have financial consequences and therefore an effect on the financial statements. An understanding of business risk increases the likelihood of identifying risks of material misstatement. Paragraph .A158 of AU-C section 315 provides examples of conditions and events that may indicate risks of material misstatement. The Committee of Sponsoring Organizations of the Treadway Commission (COSO) principle 6 identifies the entity's objectives as important for the entity to identify.

4.16 You should obtain an understanding of your client's objectives and strategies because it will help you gain a more meaningful understanding of the client's business risks:

- *Objectives* are the overall plans for the client. Management and those charged with governance set these plans in response to internal and external factors affecting the business.

- *Strategies* are the operational approaches that the client uses to reach its objectives.

(AU-C sec. 315 par. .12*d*)

Observations and Suggestions

It is helpful to compare management's stated objectives with its actions. A "disconnect" between the two may indicate a risk of material misstatement either due to error or fraud. For example, a business that seems only marginally profitable and inconsistent with the owner's stated objectives may be a "front" for a disreputable business.

Breadth of Understanding

4.17 Business risk is broader than and inclusive of the *risks of material misstatement* of the financial statements. You do not have a responsibility to identify or assess all business risks because not all business risks give rise to *risks of material misstatement*. (AU-C sec. 315 par. .12*d*)

4.18 Your responsibility is to identify and assess the potential *risks of material misstatement* of the financial statements. Within that context, your current understanding of the client's key business objectives and strategies is your basis for understanding the most significant business risks facing the client. Once you identify these significant business risks and the client's strategy for dealing with them, it is important that you determine which of them, in light of the client's unique and specific circumstances, may result in a material misstatement.

                                      ©2016, AICPA

How Your Understanding Helps You Assess the Risks of Material Misstatement

4.19 When identifying business risks, be alert for

   a. changes in the client's business strategies, for example, introducing a new product or expanding into a new market, frequently create business risks. Additionally, changes in external or internal conditions that the client does *not* respond to also can create risk. For example, if the client's product is aimed solely at a particular market, and the characteristics of that market shift, the client may face certain business risks if it fails to respond to this market shift. COSO principle 9 addresses the entity's awareness and responses to change.

   b. operational complexities also may create business risk. For example, the nature of a long term construction project creates risk in the areas of percentage of completion, pricing, costing, design, and performance control.

(AU-C sec. 315 par. .12*d*)

4.20 Business risk may affect the financial statements in a variety of ways. They may have an immediate effect, or one that is long term. They may affect the financial statements as a whole, or individual assertions. For example

*   the business risk arising from a contracting customer base caused by industry consolidation may increase the risk of misstatement associated with the valuation of accounts receivable or obsolescence in the valuation of inventories (an immediate consequence for a specific assertion).

*   the business risk of significant transactions with related parties may increase the risk of misstatement of a range of significant account balances and assertions (an immediate consequence for multiple assertions).

*   the business risk of a decline in your client's industry may affect the client's ability to continue as a going concern[1] (a long term consequence that affects the financial statements as a whole).

(AU-C sec. 315 par. .12*d*)

Management's Responsibilities for Assessing Business Risks

4.21 In many cases, management identifies business risks and develops approaches to address them. This process for managing risk is an element of the client's internal control and should be understood as part of your procedures to gain an understanding of internal control. (AU-C sec. 315 par. .12*d*)

---

[1] AU-C section 570, *The Auditor's Consideration of an Entity's Ability to Continue as a Going Concern* (AICPA, *Professional Standards*), addresses the auditor's responsibilities in an audit of financial statements with respect to evaluating whether there is substantial doubt about the entity's ability to continue as a going concern. Auditors should also consider AU-C section 9570, *The Auditor's Consideration of an Entity's Ability to Continue as a Going Concern: Auditing Interpretations of Section 570* (AICPA, *Professional Standards*, AU-C sec. 9570 par. .01–.10) that addresses (1) definition of *substantial doubt about an entity's ability to continue as a going concern*, (2) definition of *a reasonable period of time*, (3) interim financial statements, and (4) consideration of financial statement effects. FASB Accounting Standards Update No. 2014-15, *Presentation of Financial Statements—Going Concern (Subtopic 205-40): Disclosure of Uncertainties about an Entity's Ability to Continue as a Going Concern*, requiring entities to make certain disclosures regarding going concern becomes effective for financial statements issued after December 15, 2016.

4.22 In a smaller entity, management may not have a formal risk assessment process and may lack documentation of these matters. That your client lacks documentation or a formal process does not relieve you of your responsibilities to gain an understanding of how the client manages business risk. If it is not possible to inspect documentation related to the client's business risk management, you may obtain your understanding through inquiries of management and observation of how the client responds to business risks.

Understanding Your Client's Measurement and Review of the Client's Financial Performance

Breadth of Understanding

4.23 You should obtain an understanding of how management measures and reviews the entity's performance to determine whether performance is meeting their objectives. Table 4-2 lists examples of internal and external performance measures that may provide information that is useful to your understanding of the client and its environment. (AU-C sec. 315 par. .12e)

Table 4-2
Examples of Internal and External Performance Measures

You should obtain an understanding of the measurement and review of your client's financial performance. This information will help you gain a more in-depth understanding of the client and its environment, and you may obtain this information from both internal and external sources.

Internally generated measures that you may find helpful include

- financial and nonfinancial performance indicators.
- budgets and variance analyses.
- segment information and divisional, departmental, or other level performance reports.
- comparisons of your client's performance with that of its competitors.

Externally generated measures that you may find helpful include

- analysts' reports.
- credit rating agency reports.

Observations and Suggestions

The way in which management monitors internal control is one of the components of internal control. You should be careful to distinguish between measurement and review of financial performance from the monitoring of internal control. (AU-C sec. 315 par. .12e)

For example, management may review key ratios related to inventory levels. This review may tell management a great deal about the financial performance of the entity but little, if anything, about the effectiveness of controls over inventory. Your understanding of the client's methods for reviewing financial performance may not meet the requirement you have to understand the design and implementation of the monitoring component of internal control.

                                          ©2016, AICPA

How Your Understanding Helps You Assess the Risks of Material Misstatement

4.24 Your understanding of how management measures and reviews the client's financial performance can further your understanding of the client and its environment in a number of ways, including the following:

- Performance measures, whether external or internal, create pressures on the entity that, in turn, may motivate management to take action to improve the business performance. Also, as described in paragraph .A1 of AU-C section 240, *Consideration of Fraud in a Financial Statement Audit* (AICPA, *Professional Standards*), pressure or incentive provides a reason to commit fraud. Your understanding of your client's performance measures will help you consider whether such pressures could result in management or employee actions that may have increased the *risks of material misstatement*, whether due to error or fraud. (AU-C sec. 315 par. .12*e*)

- Performance measures may indicate a risk of misstatement of related financial statement information. For example, performance measures may indicate that the client has unusually rapid growth or profitability when compared to other entities in the same industry. This information, particularly if combined with other factors such as performance-based bonus or incentive remuneration, may indicate the presence of fraud risk factors relating to fraudulent financial reporting. (AU-C sec. 315 par. .12*e*)

- Internal measures may highlight unexpected results or trends, which may indicate the existence of a misstatement in the financial statements. (AU-C sec. 315 par. .12*e*)

4.25 Once you gain an understanding of the measurements your client uses to measure and review financial performance, you may decide to use some of these measures in your audit, for example, as part of your analytical procedures. When you use management's performance measurements in your audit, you should evaluate the reliability of the data. (AU-C sec. 520 par. .05*b*)

Observations and Suggestions

Your responsibility for obtaining an understanding of internal control may have been clarified and may have increased significantly with the issuance of AU-C section 315. As described in the following sections, a sufficient understanding of internal control is one that allows you to evaluate the design of controls and to determine whether controls have been implemented (placed in operation). This threshold suggests a substantial understanding of internal control.

Does this definition mean that your understanding of internal control should enable you to identify all material weaknesses in internal control? No. That high threshold is reserved for an attestation of internal control effectiveness.

When performing a financial statement audit, your understanding of internal control will not allow you to provide reasonable assurance that all material weaknesses have been identified. However, the evaluation of control design and determination that controls have been implemented is a significant threshold (less than reasonable assurance) that may result in you identifying

---

material weaknesses in the design of internal control as a result of your obtaining an understanding of internal control in a financial statement audit.
This depth of understanding of internal control is necessary to make a fully
informed assessment of the risks of material misstatement.

Evaluating the Design and Implementation of Internal Control

4.26 On every audit, you should obtain an understanding of internal control that is sufficient to enable you to

    a. evaluate the design of controls that are relevant to the audit
and determine whether the control—either individually or in
combination—is capable of effectively preventing or detecting and
correcting material misstatements.

    b. determine that the control has been implemented, that is, that the
control exists and that the entity is using it.

(AU-C sec. 315 par. .13–.14)

Observations and Suggestions

Your evaluation of internal control design and the determination of whether
controls have been implemented are critical to your assessment of the *risks
of material misstatement* and the design of further audit procedures. It is not
possible to develop a reliable assessment of the risks of material misstatement absent a sufficient understanding of internal control. For this reason,
you are required to perform risk assessment procedures to gather information and form an understanding of internal control on every audit. Even if
your initial audit strategy contemplates performing only substantive procedures for all classes of transactions, account balances, and disclosures, you
still should evaluate the design of internal controls and determine whether
they have been implemented in order to plan your audit procedures to appropriately address the risks.

Identification of specific risks related to financial reporting, without any associated entity controls, may lead to a conclusion that the missing control(s)
is (are) a significant deficiency or a material weakness. This may affect the
nature and extent of audit procedures, and lead to required communications
with management and governance.

Evaluating Control Design

4.27 The process for evaluating control design includes your consideration
of

    • the risk of what can go wrong at the assertion level.

    • the likelihood and significance of the risks, irrespective of internal
control considerations.

    • the design of relevant controls and assertions addressed.

    • the controls, either individually or in combination, that mitigate
each financial reporting risk.

4.28 To evaluate whether controls have been designed appropriately, consider whether

- the control or combination of controls would—if operated as designed—likely address the risk at the assertion level.

- the control or combination of controls necessary to address the risk at the assertion level are in place.

The design of internal controls to address identified risks is embodied in principle 10 in the COSO framework.

4.29 *Financial statement assertions can help you evaluate the effectiveness of control design over classes of transactions. For example, one of Ownco's objectives is to ensure that payables and purchases are complete and valid (occurrence). The company uses a purchase order (PO) system to manage the purchase of raw materials used in the manufacture of its fishing lures. Before ordering any materials, the operations manager enters the order into the system and receives a PO number. Suppliers are instructed to include this number in the invoices they send to Ownco.*

In this example, one of the things that can go wrong in recognizing and reporting purchases is that the company could process the same purchase transaction more than once, thus overstating inventory (prior to the physical count) and ultimately cost of goods sold (after the physical count). To mitigate this risk, the IT system matches the PO number on the vendor's invoice to the file of outstanding POs. Any invoice that contains a PO that is not considered outstanding is not paid and is put into a suspense file for further follow up.

This control procedure is effective at addressing a risk related to the occurrence assertion. However, there are other "things that can go wrong" related to purchases. For example, the system may fail to capture all authorized purchases (completeness assertion). To evaluate whether the client has effectively designed controls over purchases, the auditor will usually consider the controls related to completeness as well as all other relevant assertions.

Determining If the Control Has Been Implemented

4.30 Determining whether a control has been implemented is important because it confirms your understanding of control design and helps ensure that your risk assessment is based on accurate information. However, it is not unusual for client personnel to apply a control differently from the way the control is described in a policy manual or in response to inquiries you make of someone else. For example, your client's accounting policy manual may state that physical inventory accounts are performed annually. However, because of increases in the volume of transactions, the client deviates from this stated policy and counts some inventory items twice a year. This practice is not reflected in the policy manual and is not known by all individuals in the company.

4.31 The determination of whether a control has been put in place and is implemented involves obtaining evidence about whether those individuals responsible for performing the prescribed procedures have

- an awareness of the existence of the procedure and their responsibility for its performance, and

- a working knowledge of how the procedure should be performed.

Determining whether the control has been implemented does not require you to determine whether the control was performed properly throughout the audit period.

4.32 *For example, Smith, CPA, makes inquiries of client employees regarding the reconciliation of general ledger control totals to the underlying subsidiary ledgers. During the course of one of his interviews, Smith learns that the employee responsible for reconciling the accounts receivable subsidiary ledger to the general ledger was on a three-month extended leave of absence, during which time the duty was performed by someone with incompatible functions.*

Once, once the information is obtained, Smith should assess it and use it to design further audit procedures.

Distinguishing Between the Evaluation of Design (and Implementation) and the Assessment of Operating Effectiveness

Observations and Suggestions

In practice, misunderstandings sometimes arise over the procedures auditors should perform on all audits, regardless of their audit strategy, and those they should perform only when they intend to rely on controls to modify the nature, timing, and extent of substantive audit procedures.

On all audits, you should evaluate internal control design and determine whether controls have been implemented.

If you intend to rely on controls as part of your audit strategy, you should test them to assess their operating effectiveness.

Paragraphs 4.33–.35 are intended to clarify the differences between evaluating control design and implementation (discussed in this chapter) and testing controls to assess their operating effectiveness (discussed in chapter 6, "Performing Further Audit Procedures," of this guide).

4.33 Obtaining an understanding of the design and implementation of internal control is different from assessing its operating effectiveness:

- *Understanding design and implementation* should be performed on every audit as a prerequisite for assessing the risks of material misstatement. (AU-C sec. 315 par. .14)
- *Assessing operating effectiveness* builds on your understanding of internal control design and implementation and is necessary only when the design of your substantive procedures relies on the effective operation of controls or when substantive procedures alone will not provide you with the audit evidence needed to form a conclusion about the financial statements.

Table 4-3 summarizes the differences between design and operating effectiveness.

4.34 In many cases, the procedures necessary to understand the design and implementation of manual controls are not sufficient to serve as tests of the operating effectiveness of those controls. For example, obtaining audit evidence about the implementation of a manually operated control at a point in time does not provide audit evidence about the operating effectiveness of that control at other times during the period under audit.

4.35 Examples of situations where the procedures you perform to understand the design and implementation of controls may be sufficient to support a conclusion about their operating effectiveness include

- controls that are automated to the degree that they can be performed consistently, provided that the auditor is satisfied that IT general controls operated effectively during the period.

- controls that operate only at a point in time rather than continuously throughout the period. For example, if the client performs an annual physical inventory count, your observation of that count and other procedures to evaluate its design and implementation provide you with evidence that you consider in the design of your substantive procedures.

Table 4-3
Design Versus Operating Effectiveness

Audit Evidence Should Support Your	Design and Implementation	Operating Effectiveness
Understanding of how the control is designed	X	X
Evaluation of whether the design is effective	X	X
Determination that the control procedure has been implemented	X	X
Understanding of how the control procedure was applied throughout the period		X
Determination that the control was applied consistently throughout the period		X
Understanding of who or by what means the control was applied throughout the audit period		X

Evaluating Design and Implementation in the Absence of Control Documentation

4.36 For smaller companies, the company's evidence supporting the design and implementation of some elements of internal control may not be available in documentary form. For example, the entity may lack

- a written code of conduct that describes management's commitment to ethical values.

- a formal risk assessment process.

4.37 Without adequate documentation of controls, the risk assessment procedures available to you to understand control design may be limited to inquiry and observation. As risk assessment procedures, both inquiry and

©2016, AICPA

observation have limitations, as described in paragraphs 3.114 and 3.119. Accordingly, absent adequate documentation, you might consider whether the information you have gathered about internal control is sufficient to evaluate its design.

4.38 Inadequate documentation of the components of internal control also may be a control deficiency as defined in AU-C section 265, *Communicating Internal Control Related Matters Identified in an Audit* (AICPA, *Professional Standards*). For example, the lack of appropriate documentation may impair management's ability to communicate control procedures to those responsible for their performance or to monitor control performance effectively. If the client does not document a control, you may document your understanding of the control as part of your risk assessment procedures to identify and assess the risks of material misstatements. Paragraphs 3.44–.46 of this guide provide additional guidance on evaluating internal control in the absence of control documentation.

Observations and Suggestions

The client's lack of adequate documentation does not necessarily mean that controls do not exist, nor does the lack of documentation relieve you of your responsibility to gain an understanding of the controls being used by client personnel and evaluating their design. Without adequate documentation, you may gain this understanding through inquiry and observation.

To evaluate whether inadequate documentation is a control deficiency and, if so, the severity of that deficiency, it is helpful to consider whether the client can meet its responsibility to maintain a system of internal control without adequate documentation. In some circumstances the company may achieve its objectives without formal documentation, for example, at small entity where most communication—even critical information—is done orally. In other circumstances, the company's ability to meet its control objectives may be hindered significantly in the absence of the documentation of control policies and procedures. As summarized in table 3-9, an important element of the communication element of your client's internal control is whether it can communicate effectively financial reporting roles and responsibilities and significant matters relating to financial reporting.

Under an AICPA Ethics Interpretation, it is acceptable for the auditor to assist the audited entity in gathering internal control documentation. However, such a service may involve a non-attest service that may be assessed in combination with other non-attest services as they relate to independence. Once developed, such documentation may be maintained and updated by the entity. If the entity is unable to understand or maintain such documentation, the auditor should assess the severity of this deficiency in internal control, and whether communication to those charged with governance is required. If the auditor assists the entity in preparing internal control documentation and shares information obtained in the audit process, care should be taken not to share auditor assessment techniques and methodology or actual assessments such that the client has insight to how the auditor did or will evaluate controls. Sharing such information could result in a risk of undetectable fraud.

Management is responsible for maintaining and documenting its system of controls, but the auditor is responsible for understanding and assessing the

---

         ©2016, AICPA

controls. From an efficiency standpoint, this may mean that client documentation may need to be more extensive than auditor documentation and include more process descriptions along with the controls descriptions. Vice-versa, auditor documentation may not be adequate to fully describe the processes and internal controls of an entity.

Evaluating Entity-Level Controls

The Control Environment

4.39 You should obtain sufficient knowledge of the control environment to understand the attitudes, awareness, and actions of management and those charged with governance concerning the entity's internal control and its importance in achieving reliable financial reporting. Table 4-4 summarizes those elements of the control environment that you may consider when gaining an understanding of the control environment. (AU-C sec. 315 par. .15)

Table 4-4
Elements of the Control Environment

In evaluating the design of your client's control environment, you may consider the following elements and how they have been incorporated into the entity's processes:

  a. *Communication and enforcement of integrity and ethical values.* Essential elements that influence the effectiveness of the design, administration, and monitoring of controls.

  b. *Commitment to competence.* Management's consideration of the competence levels for particular jobs and how those levels translate into requisite skills and knowledge.

  c. *Participation of those charged with governance.* Independence from management, the experience and stature of its members, the extent of its involvement and scrutiny of activities, the information it receives, the degree to which difficult questions are raised and pursued with management, and its interaction with the internal audit function (if any) and external auditors.

  d. *Management's philosophy and operating style.* Management's approach to taking and managing business risks, and management's attitudes and actions toward financial reporting, information processing and accounting functions, and personnel.

  e. *Organizational structure.* The framework within which an entity's activities for achieving its objectives are planned, executed, controlled, and reviewed.

  f. *Assignment of authority and responsibility.* How authority and responsibility for operating activities are assigned and how reporting relationships and authorization hierarchies are established.

  g. *Human resource policies and practices.* Recruitment, orientation, training, evaluating, counseling, promoting, compensating, and remedial actions.

Observations and Suggestions

It is preferable to evaluate the control environment early on in the audit process using the "top-down" approach. This is because the results of your evaluation affect your overall risk assessment at the financial statement level which in turn could affect the nature, timing, and extent of other planned audit procedures.

For example, weaknesses in the control environment may undermine the effectiveness of other control components and, therefore, be negative factors in your assessment of the risks of material misstatement, in particular in relation to the risk of fraud. It may also cause you to perform more extensive procedures as of year-end rather than as of an interim date.

Please refer to appendix C, "Internal Control Components" for a mapping of control environment principles in the COSO framework to the control environment elements described in AU-C section 315.

Evaluating Design and Implementation

4.40 When obtaining an understanding of the control environment, you may consider the collective effect of all control environment elements rather than a single element in isolation. Strengths in one element or principle may compensate for deficiencies in others. Conversely, weaknesses in one element or principle may diminish strengths in another. For example, the client's design and implementation of controls related to management's philosophy and operating style and participation of those charged with governance may compensate for some deficiencies in the design of controls related to the entity's commitment to competence.

4.41 Management's strengths and weaknesses may have a pervasive effect on internal control. For example,

- owner-manager controls may mitigate a lack of segregation of duties, or an active and independent board of directors may influence the philosophy and operating style of senior management in larger entities.
- management's failure to commit sufficient resources to address the access and security risk presented by IT may adversely affect internal control by allowing improper changes to be made to computer programs or to data, or by allowing unauthorized transactions to be processed.
- human resource policies and practices directed toward hiring competent financial, accounting, and IT personnel may not mitigate a strong bias by top management to overstate earnings.

4.42 The existence of a satisfactory control environment can be a positive factor when you assess the *risks of material misstatement*. Although an effective control environment will not guarantee the absence of misstatements, it may help reduce the *risks of material misstatements* of the financial statements. For example, the effective oversight of those charged with governance combined with an effective internal audit function may constrain improper conduct by management.

4.43 Conversely, weaknesses in the control environment may undermine the effectiveness of other control components and therefore be negative factors in your assessment of the risks of material misstatement, in particular in relation to the risk of fraud. For example, when the nature of management incentives increases the *risks of material misstatement* of financial statements, the effectiveness of control activities may be reduced.

Observations and Suggestions

In smaller entities, the control environment might be less formal than larger entities. Irrespective of the relative formality of the control environment and the documentation of related policies and procedures, you still should gain an understanding of all five components of internal control, including the control environment. Even in audits of smaller entities, you may be able to place some reliance on the control environment to determine the nature, timing, and extent of further audit procedures assuming you have tested the control environment and found it to be effective.

When entity documentation is lacking, you may need to produce more robust documentation of your understanding of internal control to serve as a basis for the determination of the nature, timing, and extent of further audit procedures. You may also request the entity to provide more observable or documentary evidence of implementation, or the operation of controls to support your reliance on controls. This documentation may benefit both the auditor and client, and may result in more efficiency in the audit process. Regulatory bodies may also require more formal documentation of controls to meet their compliance requirements.

The Client's Risk Assessment Process

4.44 You should obtain sufficient knowledge of your client's risk assessment process to understand how management considers risk relevant to financial reporting objectives and decides about actions to address that risk. (AU-C sec. 315 par. .16)

Evaluating Design and Implementation

4.45 In evaluating the design and implementation of your client's risk assessment process, you should obtain an understanding of whether client management has a process to

    a. identify business risk relevant to financial reporting.

    b. estimate the significance of the risks.

    c. assess the likelihood of their occurrence.

    d. decide upon actions to manage them.

(AU-C sec. 315 par. .16)

4.46 Your client may not have established a highly effective risk assessment process or you may have identified risks of material misstatement in the financial statements that management failed to identify. In such cases, you should consider why the client's risk assessment process failed to identify those risks and whether their process is appropriate to the client's circumstances. Paragraphs 7.48–.59 provide additional guidance on evaluating control deficiencies related to the client's risk assessment process. (AU-C sec. 315 par. .18)

4.47 *For example, Ownco does not have a highly effective risk assessment component to internal control.[2] Consequently, the auditor's overall approach to the engagement involves significant procedures to identify and assess the financial reporting risk relating to changes (principle 9) in*

- *the company's operating environment.*
- *new personnel or IT system.*
- *new technology.*
- *new accounting pronouncements.*

To properly consider these items, the auditors conduct extensive inquiries of management, company employees, the company's lawyers, and external parties whose interactions with the company may affect financial reporting. These third parties include: suppliers, creditors, and customers. To the extent that market factors might influence the business, these would be considered. If Ownco had a more robust risk assessment process, the auditors would be able to reduce the extent of the procedures performed to understand internal control.

Inquiries of Management About Identified Business Risks

4.48 You should obtain an understanding of whether the client has a process for identifying business risks relevant to financial reporting objectives. If the client has such a process you should obtain an understanding of it and the results thereof. If your client has an effective risk assessment process, it can help you identify risks of material misstatement. For example, client management already may have identified business risk prior to the start of your audit. For this reason, you may ask them about business risk that they have identified, and you should consider whether this business risk may result in material misstatement of the financial statements. (AU-C sec. 315 par. .16–.17)

Critical to the assessment of the design of controls is the identification of business and financial reporting objectives and the identification of risks of not achieving those objectives.

Information and Communication

4.49 Under AU-C section 315 paragraph .19, you should obtain a sufficient knowledge to assess the risks of material misstatement of the client's information and communication system, including the related business processes relevant to financial reporting, including

a. the classes of transactions which are significant to the financial statements.

b. the procedures within both IT and manual systems by which those transactions are initiated, authorized, recorded, processed, corrected as necessary, transferred to the general ledger, and reported in the financial statements.

c. the related accounting records used in *b*.

d. how the information system captures events and conditions, other than transactions, that are significant to the financial statements.

---

[2] For example, it may not fully specify its objectives (principle 6), its risks of not achieving its objectives (principle 7) its anti-fraud procedures (principle 8) or changes in its risk (principle 9).

    e. the process used to prepare the client's financial statements, including significant accounting estimates and disclosures.

    f. controls surrounding journal entries, including nonstandard journal entries used to record nonrecurring, unusual transactions, or adjustments.

Under AU-C section 315 paragraph .20, you should obtain an understanding of how the client communicates financial reporting roles and responsibilities and significant matters relating to financial reporting, including

    a. communications between management and those charged with governance and

    b. external communications, such as those with regulatory authorities.

Observations and Suggestions

The COSO framework identifies three principles related to Information and Communication. They relate to the generation of relevant information (principle 13), effective internal communication (principle 14) and effective external information (principle 15). Some auditors integrate or combine their testing of information system data to evidence support underlying principles of the COSO framework with tests of system data used in analytical procedures as an efficiency measure.

Evaluating Design and Implementation

4.50 Examples of events and conditions significant to your client's financial statements that the financial information system captures may relate to

- an asset impairment;
- a contingent liability;
- the classification of an asset or liability;
- the client's ability to continue as a going concern;[3] and
- subsequent events required to be disclosed to keep the financial statements from being misleading.

4.51 The information system relevant to financial reporting objectives consists of the procedures and records designed and established to

- initiate, authorize, record, process, and report entity transactions;
- resolve incorrect processing of transactions (For example, automated suspense files accompanied by procedures to investigate and resolve them on a timely basis. Also, when planning the audit you should be aware that when IT is used to transfer information automatically, there may be little or no visible evidence of inappropriate intervention.);
- process and account for system overrides or bypasses of controls;
- transfer information from transaction processing systems to the general ledger;

---

[3] See footnote 1.

©2016, AICPA

- capture information relevant to financial reporting for events and conditions other than transactions (for example, depreciation); and

- ensure information required to be disclosed by the applicable financial reporting framework is accumulated, recorded, processed, summarized, and appropriately reported in the financial statements.

Journal entries are ordinarily part of the client's information system and its financial reporting process. Such entries includes standard and nonstandard journal entries. Standard journal entries might be used to record accruals and depreciation or to record some routine accounting estimates. Nonstandard entries might be used to record nonrecurring or unusual transactions or adjustments such as a business combination or disposal, or a nonrecurring estimate such as asset impairment.

4.52 The information system relevant to financial reporting includes the client's communication of financial reporting roles and responsibilities. (AU-C sec. 315 par. .A97)

4.53 Your understanding of the communication component of the client's information system also includes assessing the extent to which personnel understand

    a. how their activities in the financial reporting system relate to the work of others.

    b. the means of reporting exceptions to an appropriate higher level within the entity so that they may be acted on.

Monitoring of Controls

4.54 You should obtain an understanding of

    a. the major types of activities that the entity uses to monitor internal control over financial reporting, including the sources of the information related to those activities.

    b. how those activities are used to initiate corrective actions to the entity's controls.

(AU-C sec. 315 par. .23)

Evaluating Design and Implementation

4.55 Monitoring is a process to assess the effectiveness of internal control performance over time. It involves assessing both (*a*) the design and operating effectiveness of controls on a timely basis and (*b*) taking necessary corrective actions. Monitoring may ensure that controls continue to operate effectively. For example, if the timeliness and accuracy of bank reconciliations are not monitored, personnel are likely to stop preparing them. Management accomplishes monitoring of controls through ongoing activities, separate evaluations of the entire internal control system, or a combination of the two.

COSO identifies two principles relating to monitoring: performing ongoing and separate monitoring procedures (principle 16) and following up and communicating control issues raised (principle 17).

4.56 Changes in the entity or its environment may require changes in internal control. Thus management's monitoring of controls also includes a consideration of whether controls are modified as appropriate for changes in the entity or its environment. (AU-C sec. 315 par. .A157)

4.57 In many entities, much of the information used in monitoring may be produced by the entity's information system. If management assumes that data used for monitoring are accurate without having a basis for that assumption, misstatements may exist in the information, potentially leading management to incorrect conclusions from its monitoring activities. For this reason, when evaluating the design and implementation of the monitoring component of internal control, you may

> *a.* identify the sources of the information management uses to monitor control effectiveness.
>
> *b.* determine whether management has a sufficient basis for concluding that these sources are reliable for that purpose.

4.58 *For example, the comparison of budget to actual is a significant part of the monitoring activities performed by management and the board of directors of Young Fashions. If either the budgeted amounts or the actual amounts are inaccurate, the monitoring function will be ineffective. Thus, to evaluate the effectiveness of the design of the control, the auditor may consider whether management and the board have a sufficient basis for relying on the budgeted and actual amounts by obtaining evidence about the accuracy and completeness of the information.*

4.59 Management's monitoring activities may include using information from communications from external parties such as customer complaints and regulator comments that may indicate problems or highlight areas in need of improvement. The extent to which management uses this information to make corrections or improvements to internal control may be an indication of their attitude and awareness of internal control matters, which have a bearing on the effectiveness of the control environment. For example, if management receives information from an external party about a significant deficiency in internal control and fails to evaluate or act on that information, that failure may be a control deficiency. (AU-C sec. 315 par. .A157)

4.60 If the entity has an internal audit function, you should obtain an understanding of (*a*) the nature of the internal audit function's responsibilities and how the internal audit function fits in the client's organizational structure and (*b*) the activities performed or to be performed. (AU-C sec. 315 par. .24) If the entity has an internal audit function, obtaining an understanding of that function contributes to the external auditor's understanding of the entity and its environment, including internal control; this also includes the role that the function plays in the entity's monitoring of internal control over financial reporting. This understanding, together with the information obtained from the external auditor's other inquiries, may also provide information that is directly relevant to the external auditor's identification and assessment of the *risks of material misstatement*. When obtaining an understanding of the internal audit function, you should follow the guidance in AU-C section 610, *Using the Work of Internal Auditors* (AICPA, *Professional Standards*). (AU-C sec. 315 par. .A157)

4.61 Your understanding of management's monitoring of controls may help you identify more detailed controls or other activities that you may consider in making risk assessments.

©2016, AICPA

Other Entity-Level Controls

Antifraud Programs and Controls

4.62 The primary responsibility for the prevention and detection of fraud and error rests with those charged with governance and your client's management. In obtaining an understanding of the control environment, you may consider the design and implementation of entity programs and controls to address the risk of fraud. These programs and controls may include

    a.   identifying and measuring fraud risks.

    b.   taking steps to mitigate identified risks.

    c.   implementing and monitoring appropriate preventive and detective internal controls and other deterrent measures.

Table 4-5 summarizes items management may consider in the design of the company's antifraud programs. Appendix D, "Exhibit—Management Antifraud Programs and Controls," of this guide discusses these items in more detail.

Table 4-5
Elements of an Antifraud Program

Element of the Antifraud Program	Design and Implementation of the Entity's Program Should Consider
Identification and measurement of fraud risks	• Vulnerability of the entity to fraudulent activity. • Whether any exposures to fraud could result in a material misstatement of the financial statements or material loss to the organization. • Characteristics that influence the risk of fraud that is specific to the entity, its industry, and country.

Steps to mitigate identified risks	• Changes to the entity's activities and processes, for example
	   — to cease doing business in certain locations.
	   — to reorganize business process.
	   — to monitor or supervise high risk areas more closely.

Implementation and monitoring of appropriate preventive and detective internal controls	• Well-developed control environment, including a strong value system and culture of ethical financial reporting. • Effective and secure information system. • Appropriate monitoring activities. • Control activities over areas identified as high risk. • Controls over interim financial reporting. • Communication procedures to report any requests to commit wrongdoing. • Appropriate oversight by those charged with governance.

IT General Controls

4.63 You should consider whether the entity has responded adequately to the risk arising from IT by establishing effective controls, including effective general controls upon which application controls depend. From the auditor's perspective, controls over IT systems are effective when they maintain the integrity of information and the security of the data such systems process. (AU-C sec. 315 par. .22)

As with all other relevant controls, on all audits you should evaluate the design of IT general controls and determine whether they have been implemented in order to assess the risks of material misstatement. You should test IT general controls when you plan to rely on IT application controls to modify the nature, timing, and extent of your substantive procedures.

Observations and Suggestions

The way in which smaller entities implement IT general controls may be different from the way in which larger entities achieve the same goal. However, even smaller entities will want to implement IT general controls such as the following:

- Secure logical access to critical applications, databases, operating systems, and networks.
- Develop controls related to significant upgrades to the IT operating system or to significant packaged applications. For example, significant upgrades should be tested before they are put into production.
- Back up critical data and programs.
- Restrict physical access to critical hardware items such as the server, telephone lines, and power supply equipment.

Controls Over Nonroutine Transactions, Judgmental Matters, and the Selection and Application of Significant Accounting Policies

4.64 As described in paragraph 3.91, controls related to *significant risks* are relevant to your audit. Frequently, at the financial statement level, *significant risks* often relate to nonroutine transactions and judgmental matters. As such, you will need to evaluate the design of the controls related to nonroutine transactions and judgmental matters and determine whether they have been implemented:

- Nonroutine transactions
- Judgmental matters such as estimates or management's future plans
- The selection and application of significant accounting policies

The sections that follow summarize examples of control policies and procedures for each of these items. Chapter 5, "Risk Assessment and the Design of Further Audit Procedures," of this guide provides guidance on identifying *significant risks*.

4.65 *Controls related to non-routine transactions.* Paragraphs .32c and .A54 of AU-C section 240 direct the auditor to gain an understanding of the business rationale for significant unusual transactions. Indicators that may suggest that significant transactions that are outside the normal course of business for the entity, or that otherwise appear to be unusual, may have been entered into to engage in fraudulent financial reporting or to conceal misappropriation of assets include the following:

- Whether the form of such transactions is overly complex
- Whether management has discussed the nature of and accounting for such transactions with those charged with governance
- Whether management is placing more emphasis on the need for a particular accounting treatment than on the underlying economics of the transaction
- Whether transactions that involve unconsolidated related parties, including variable interest entities, have been properly reviewed and approved by those charged with governance
- Whether transactions involve previously unidentified related parties, or parties unable to support the transaction without assistance from the entity being audited

4.66 *Controls related to accounting estimates*. AU-C section 540, *Auditing Accounting Estimates, Including Fair Value Accounting Estimates, and Related Disclosures* (AICPA, *Professional Standards*), describes the following as examples of controls related to accounting estimates:

- Management communication of the need for proper accounting estimates.
- Accumulation of relevant, sufficient, and reliable data on which to base an accounting estimate.
- Preparation of the accounting estimate by qualified personnel.
- Adequate review and approval of the accounting estimate by appropriate levels of authority, including
  - review of sources of relevant factors.
  - review of development of assumptions.
  - review of reasonableness of assumptions and resulting estimates.
  - consideration of the need to use the work of specialists.
  - consideration of changes in previously established methods to arrive at accounting estimates.
- Comparison of prior accounting estimates with subsequent results to assess the reliability of the process used to develop estimates.
- Consideration by management of whether the resulting accounting estimate is consistent with the operational plans of the entity.

AU-C section 540 addresses the procedures that are appropriate when auditing these estimates.

4.67 AU-C section 240 directs auditors to perform certain procedures to address the risks of material misstatement due to fraud for each of the items listed in paragraph 4.64:

- *Non-routine transactions.* You should gain an understanding of the business rationale for significant transactions that are outside the normal course of business. (AU-C sec. 240 par. .32c)
- *Judgmental matters.* You should perform a retrospective review of significant accounting estimates. (AU-C sec. 240 par. .32bii)
- *Selection and application of accounting policies.* You evaluate management's selection and application of significant accounting principles, particularly those related to subjective measurements and complex transactions. (AU-C sec. 240 par. .29b)

These procedures you perform to assess the risks of material misstatement due to fraud also may help you assess the risks of material misstatement due to error.

Observations and Suggestions

Smaller entities may not have established formal controls over non-routine transactions, judgmental matters, or the selection and application of accounting policies. This lack of formality may be appropriate given the nature of the entity and the relative infrequency with which management addresses these matters. Nevertheless, many smaller entities do have procedures that either serve as a control or as a monitoring control that partially mitigates the severity of any deficiency in internal control, such as a periodic management review of these transactions.

However, a lack of formality does not relieve you of your responsibility to understand controls in these areas. In fact, the lack of formal controls over non-routine transactions, judgmental matters, and accounting policies is quite relevant to your assessment of the *risks of material misstatement*. The lack of a control is not excused due to an entity's size or lack of attention to control issues.

The overreliance by management on the company's external auditors to identify non-routine transactions or situations that require an accounting estimate may be a control deficiency. Under COSO, the independent auditor is not considered a part of the internal control of an entity.

Controls Over the Selection and Application of Significant Accounting Policies

4.68 Management is responsible for adopting appropriate accounting policies. *Risks of material misstatement* of the financial statement arise if management's selection or application of its accounting policies is inappropriate.

4.69 You should obtain an understanding of your client's selection and application of accounting policies, and you should evaluate whether they are appropriate for the client's business and consistent with GAAP and accounting policies used in the relevant industry, or with a comprehensive basis of accounting other than GAAP. Your understanding encompasses

a. the methods the client uses to account for significant and unusual transactions.

b. the effect of significant accounting policies in controversial or emerging areas for which there is a lack of authoritative guidance or consensus.

      c. changes in the selection or application of accounting policies. If such a change has occurred, you should obtain an understanding of the reasons for the change and whether it is appropriate and consistent with GAAP.

      d. when and how the entity will adopt financial reporting standards and regulations that are new to it.

(AU-C sec. 315 par. .12c and .A35)

    4.70   AU-C section 260, *The Auditor's Communication With Those Charged With Governance* (AICPA, *Professional Standards*), addresses the oversight role of those charged with governance relating to the entity's selection and application of its accounting policies. Table 4-6 summarizes that guidance.

Table 4-6
Controls Over the Selection and Application of Accounting Policies

Management has the primary role for the selection and application of accounting policies. However, the oversight of those charged with governance is important for the client to achieve its financial reporting objectives. Controls that ordinarily are relevant to the audit together with examples of circumstances where those charged with governance should exercise their oversight are presented in the following table. In the following examples, if a company does not have an audit committee, those charged with governance should be substituted.

Control Procedure	*Examples*

Informing the audit committee about the initial selection of and subsequent changes to significant accounting policies or their application	The audit committee should be informed of
	
	  a. the initial selection and application of significant accounting policies.
	
	  b. subsequent changes to significant accounting policies.
	
	  c. subsequent changes to the application of significant accounting policies.

Informing the audit committee about the methods used to account for significant unusual transactions	Example transactions include
	
	  • bill-and-hold transactions.
	  • self-insurance.
	  • multielement arrangements contemporaneously negotiated.
	  • sales of assets or licensing arrangements with continuing involvement of the enterprise.

(continued)

©2016, AICPA

Control Procedure	*Examples*
Informing the audit committee about the effect of significant accounting policies in controversial or emerging areas for which there is a lack of authoritative accounting guidance or consensus	Examples of controversial or emerging areas of accounting include • revenue recognition. • off-balance-sheet financing. • accounting for equity investments. • research and development activities. • special purpose financing structures that affect ownership rights (such as leveraged recapitalizations, joint ventures, and preferred stock subsidiaries).

Observations and Suggestions

With regard to a client's selection and application of accounting policies, the auditor has two responsibilities: (1) to assess the client's controls over the selection and application process and (2) to evaluate whether the selection and application of the policies are appropriate. That your client has chosen and applied its accounting policies in an appropriate manner may not provide evidence that the controls over that process are designed and operating effectively. That is, your client may apply its accounting policies properly and still have a control deficiency.

A best practice that has developed is for companies with less experienced accounting personnel to engage a consultant on accounting matters with whom they can periodically discuss issues, before having these issues aired solely with the independent auditor. Reliance on the independent auditor to be the sole source of guidance on accounting issues indicates a deficiency in internal control as defined by the COSO framework and generally accepted auditing standards. Of course, the independent auditor can, and should be, a party to the discussions on accounting matters, but reliance solely on the independent auditor for such matters is a deficiency, significant deficiency, or a material weakness, as determined in the circumstances.

The Responsibilities of Those Charged With Governance

4.71 The responsibilities of those charged with governance are of considerable importance. Their participation in the financial reporting process affects your client's overall control consciousness. In evaluating the quality of that participation, you may consider matters such as

- the independence of the directors.

- their ability to evaluate the actions of management.

- their ability to understand the client's business transactions.

- their understanding of the financial reporting process.

- their ability to evaluate whether the financial statements are fairly presented.

4.72 *Like many companies its size, Young Fashions has difficulty in finding and retaining high-quality independent directors. Company officers constitute four of the seven current members of the board. In spite of the challenges it faces, the co-CEOs of the company have taken steps to upgrade its board of directors, including the following:*

- *The company has contacted the Financial Executives Institute, local universities, and local CPA firms to identify candidates from business, academia, and public accounting who may be available to serve as board members.*
- *The board has formally added to its agenda several items related to the oversight of the financial reporting process, including emerging risks to financial reporting, identified control deficiencies, accounting estimates, and other judgmental matters (including key assumptions), and the review of the financial statements prior to their release.*
- *The board also allocates a portion of every meeting for discussions of issues with the auditors without management present.*

Observations and Suggestions

Not-for-profit organizations may face unique challenges in involving their board of directors in the financial reporting process and serving in an oversight capacity. For example, board members at a not-for-profit organization are often most interested in helping the organization fulfill its mission. These members may lack a strong business background and therefore the ability to evaluate the financial reporting process or whether the financial statements are presented fairly.

In other not-for-profit organizations, board members may be chosen by the executive director or chief executive of the organization, which may impair the board's ability to act independently from management and evaluate their actions. Some boards may not meet outside of the presence of the executive director.

In circumstances such as these, you will need to consider whether the board is capable of fulfilling its oversight responsibilities and whether the circumstances indicate a potential control deficiency.

Evaluating Activity-Level Controls

Information Systems

4.73 As described in chapter 3 of this guide, you should obtain an understanding of the client's information system for significant transactions and transaction streams. This information system consists of the procedures and records established to initiate, record, process, and report these transactions, as well as the related accounting records, supporting information, and specific accounts. (AU-C sec. 315 par. .19)

Understanding Business Processes

4.74 Your client's business processes are inextricably united with the entity's information system. For example, when goods are purchased or sold, information about that transaction is recorded. To the extent that the information is relevant to the financial statements, an understanding of the underlying business process is relevant to the audit. Thus, as part of obtaining an understanding of the design and implementation of your client's information system, you should obtain a sufficient understanding of the underlying business processes. (AU-C sec. 315 par. .19)

Controls Related to the Use of Spreadsheets

4.75 As described in paragraph 2.76, your client's information system includes the use of spreadsheets and other ad hoc processing of information used in the financial reporting process. Thus, your understanding of the information system is not restricted to the formal accounting processing system but encompasses an understanding of how the company uses spreadsheets in its financial reporting process.

4.76 When gaining an understanding of how your client's use of spreadsheets may affect the audit, the following factors may be helpful:

- *Significance of the spreadsheet to the financial information processing stream.* Spreadsheets that are used to process or prepare amounts or disclosures that are material and reported directly in the financial statements are more significant to the financial information system than spreadsheets that process immaterial amounts or disclosures or that affect the financial statements only indirectly. The more significant the spreadsheet is to the financial information system, the greater the risks of material misstatement of the financial statements.

- *Complexity of the spreadsheet.* Spreadsheets that use macros or that link to other spreadsheets are more complex than those that use simple calculations or formulas. As the complexity of the spreadsheet increases, so does the risk of misstatement.

- *Number of spreadsheet users.* Spreadsheets frequently are developed without the controls normally found in more formal, purchased software. For example, the spreadsheet may not have edit checks related to the input of data, or access to the cells containing formulas may not be restricted appropriately. For these reasons, the more people who use the spreadsheet, the greater the risk that it will be used or modified inappropriately, leading to misstatement.

- *Experience and expertise of the individual who developed the spreadsheet.* When spreadsheets are developed by less qualified individuals, the risk of misstatement increases.

Control Activities

4.77 Control activities relevant to the audit are those for which you consider it necessary to obtain an understanding to assess risks of material misstatement and to design and perform further audit procedures. In addition to those control activities described in chapter 3 of this guide that ordinarily are relevant to your audit, which include those related to significant risks, you may determine that an understanding of other control activities is necessary. This determination is a matter of judgment. Chapter 5 of this guide provides additional guidance on identifying significant risks. (AU-C sec. 315 par. .21)

Evaluating Design and Implementation

4.78 Effectively designed control activities are those that are capable—either individually or in combination with other control activities—of satisfying control objectives. Control objectives should be related to the specific risks of "what can go wrong." Thus, the effectiveness of the design of control activities ultimately depends on the degree to which they mitigate the financial reporting risk at the assertion level.

4.79 Assertions are helpful in identifying what can go wrong in the preparation of the financial statements. For example, if you were to consider what can go wrong in the processing of sales transactions, you would consider the completeness assertion and the risk that not all valid sales transactions were captured by the client's information system. You might then identify ways in which the system might not capture all transactions and see whether that risk is being controlled.

4.80 In describing "what can go wrong," it is helpful to describe the risk in a way that is specific to your client's business processes. By necessity, assertions are described in broad terms; however, to be most useful in your audit, the description of risk should reflect the unique circumstances of your client. For example, a description of "what can go wrong" related to the completeness assertion for revenue at a cash business such as a convenience store will be different from a specific description of risk related to the same completeness assertion for a computer software company.

The Identification of Control Deficiencies

4.81 The primary objective of your evaluation of the design and implementation of internal control is to provide evidence to support your assessment of the risks of material misstatement. However, during the course of obtaining this understanding of internal control, you may become aware of deficiencies in the design of controls at either the entity or activity level.

Entity-Level Control Deficiencies

4.82 During the course of evaluating the design and implementation of entity-level controls, you may become aware of control deficiencies, such as the following:

- Inadequate design of internal control over the preparation of the financial statements being audited.

- Inadequate documentation of the components of internal control.

- Insufficient control consciousness within the organization.

- Flaws in the design of IT general controls that prevent the information system from providing complete and accurate information consistent with financial reporting objectives and current needs. See appendix G, "Assessing the Severity of Identified Deficiencies in Internal Control," of this guide (for example, deficiencies 3 and 4) for examples of evaluating IT general control deficiencies.

- Employees or management who lack the qualifications and training to fulfill their assigned functions, for example, the corporate controller is unable to apply GAAP in recording the entity's financial transactions or preparing its financial statements.

- Inadequate design of monitoring controls that assess effectiveness of the entity's internal control over time.

Chapter 7, "Evaluating Audit Findings, Audit Evidence, and Deficiencies in Internal Control," of this guide discusses the identification, evaluation, and reporting of control deficiencies in more detail.

Activity-Level Control Deficiencies

4.83 During the course of evaluating the design and implementation of activity-level controls, you may become aware of control deficiencies, such as the following:

- Inadequate design of internal control over a significant account or process.

- Inadequate documentation of the activity-level components of internal control.

- Absent or inadequate segregation of duties within a significant account or process.

- Absent or inadequate controls over the safeguarding of assets needed for internal control over financial reporting.

- Flaws in the design of IT application controls that prevent the information system from providing complete and accurate information consistent with financial reporting objectives and current needs.

Chapter 7 of this guide discusses the identification, evaluation, and reporting of control deficiencies in more detail.

Audit Documentation

4.84 This chapter provides guidance on certain matters relating to the planning of the audit, including the determination of planning materiality and performance materiality. It also describes how you perform risk assessment procedures to gather an understanding of the client and how you should plan for the performance of those procedures. With regard to these matters, you should document

- a. the key elements of your understanding of the client, including each of the aspects of the client and its environment identified in paragraph 4.02.

- b. with regard to internal control, your documentation should include each of the five elements of internal control.

- c. the risk assessment procedures you performed to gather information about the client.

- d. the sources you used to gather information about the client.

Paragraphs 1.39–.41 provide additional, more general guidance on the preparation of audit documentation.

(AU-C sec. 315 par. .33b)

Summary

4.85 This chapter described the breadth and depth of the understanding of your client that is necessary for you to assess the risks of material misstatement, beginning with your understanding of the client and its environment. This understanding will help you identify the broad business risks facing the company, which is important to your audit because many business risks give rise to risk affecting the preparation of the financial statements.

4.86 Your client's internal control is an integral part of its operations, and obtaining an understanding of internal control is critical if you are to assess properly the risks of material misstatement. Your understanding of internal control involves

- evaluating the design of internal control to determine whether this design has the ability to prevent or to detect and correct material misstatements.
- determining whether the client has implemented the controls, that is, that client personnel are using them.

4.87 You will evaluate internal control and determine their implementation at both the entity level and activity level. By understanding these two levels of control, you will be better able to assess risk at both the financial-statement and the relevant-assertion level.

4.88 The next chapter of this guide discusses how you use your understanding of the client, which includes its internal control, as a basis for assessing the risks of material misstatement.

4.89

Appendix—Answers to Frequently Asked Questions About Understanding the Client, Its Environment, and Its Internal Control

Question	See Paragraphs
What should I understand about my client's industry and other external factors? How will this knowledge help me in my audit?	4.04–.05
What should I understand about my client's business, including sales transactions and IT systems? How will this knowledge help me in my audit?	4.06–.14
Why do I need to understand my client's business risk? How will this understanding help me in my audit?	4.15–.20
Why do I need to understand how my client measures and reviews the company's financial performance? How will this understanding help me in my audit?	4.23–.25
What does it mean to "evaluate the design" of internal control? How do I do this?	4.27–.29
How do I determine if a control has been implemented?	4.30–.32
What is the difference between evaluating control design and testing controls?	4.33–.35
How can I evaluate the design and implementation of internal control if my client does not have extensive documentation?	4.36–.38
How do you evaluate the design and implementation of • the control environment? • the client's risk assessment process? • information and communication? • monitoring? • other entity-level controls?	4.39–.72
How do I evaluate the design and implementation of activity-level controls?	4.77–.80
What information about my understanding of the client should I document?	4.84

Chapter 5

Risk Assessment and the Design of Further Audit Procedures

TABLE OF CONTENTS

Observations and Suggestions

Illustration 5-1
Risk Assessment and the Design of Further Audit Procedures

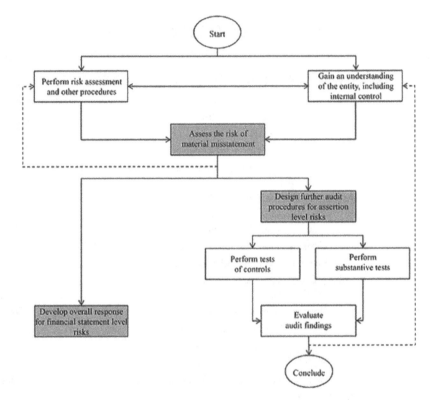

This chapter provides guidance on incorporating your understanding of the entity, its environment, and its internal control into your assessment of the risks of material misstatement and the design of further audit procedures.

Broad Business Risks and Financial Reporting Risks

Your knowledge of the client and the results of your risk assessment procedures should allow you to identify the broad business risks facing the client. This is an important first step in your assessment of the risks of material misstatement of the financial statements because financial reporting risks are derived from these broad business risks. With a working knowledge of your client's business risks, you will be better able to identify financial reporting risks.

Financial Statement Versus Assertion Level Risk. You should assess risk at both the financial statement level and the relevant assertion level. In many cases, you will assess financial statement level risk and relate it to what *can* go wrong at the assertion level. Some financial statement level risks are so pervasive that they cannot be related to a finite set of assertions, and for these risks you may often develop an overall audit response.

Design Further Audit Procedures. Further audit procedures should be responsive to our assessment of the risks of material misstatement. To design these procedures you will choose their nature, timing, and extent.

Your risk assessment procedures allow you to gather the information necessary to obtain an understanding of your client. This knowledge provides a basis for assessing *risks of material misstatement* of the financial statements. These risk assessments are then used to design further audit procedures, such as tests of controls, substantive procedures, or both.

This chapter describes the process for assessing risk at both the financial statement level and relevant assertion level and how to design further audit procedures that effectively address this risk.

Introduction

5.01 Chapters 3, "Planning and Performing Risk Assessment Procedures," and 4, "Understanding the Client, Its Environment, and Its Internal Control," of this guide emphasized that you should obtain an understanding of the client and its environment. This understanding about your client encompasses a broad range of information, including

- industry, regulatory, and other external factors affecting the client, including the applicable financial reporting framework.

- the nature of the entity, including its operations, its ownership and governance structure, the types of investments that the entity is making and plans to make, including investments in entities formed to accomplish specific objectives, and the way that the entity is structured and how it is financed.

- the entity's selection and application of accounting policies, including the reasons for changes thereto. The auditor should evaluate whether the entity's accounting policies are appropriate for its business and consistent with the applicable financial reporting framework and accounting policies used in the relevant industry.

● the entity's objectives and strategies and those related business risks that may result in risks of material misstatement.

● the measurement and review of the entity's financial performance.

● internal control relevant to the audit.

(AU-C sec. 315 par. .12–.13)

This knowledge gained of your client from your understanding forms the basis for identifying risks and evaluating how these risks could give rise to financial material statement misstatements.

5.02 The term *risk assessment procedures* describes a *process* in which you identify and assess the risks of material misstatement, whether due to fraud or error, at the financial statement level and relevant assertion level. Based on risk identified and your assessment you

a. develop an overall response to financial statement level risks, and

b. design further audit procedures in response to assertion level risks.

Observations and Suggestions

Risk assessment in an audit is not a single activity or circumstance but a series of actions. As part of your audit, you may assign a value or relative term (for example, "high" or "low") to the risk of material misstatement (RMM) for a given assertion, but that assignment of value is only a step of the risk assessment process—it is not the entire process.

To assign a value, you often will first identify the risks that could affect the financial statements at the assertion level. You will then analyze these risks as well as the design of the client's controls that address the risks. Only after performing these steps will you be able to make an appropriate assessment of risks at the assertion level and therefore design appropriate audit procedures.

Key steps in the risk assessment process should be documented. This documentation is necessary to support your conclusions about risk at the assertion level and to indicate the evidence supporting your assessment. Under the auditing standards you would not "default" to concluding that risk is "high" without providing some basis for your conclusion. What could go wrong and why is the risk that it might happen "high"? A risk assessment will guide you to setting the appropriate nature, timing, and extent of audit procedures to address the risks that exist.

Finally, your assessment of risk at the assertion level provides support for the decisions you make about the nature, timing, and extent of your substantive procedures and, in some cases, your tests of controls. Because of this direct link between risk assessment and the design and performance of further audit procedures, your risk assessment procedures ultimately support your opinion on the financial statements.

5.03 To provide a proper basis for the design of further audit procedures, your assessment of risk should be expressed for the relevant assertions related to significant classes of transactions, account balances, and disclosures. You relate identified risks to "what can go wrong" at the assertion level in the preparation of the financial statements. For example, "because sales personnel are able to make changes to standard sales contracts and this information is not always communicated to accounting, there is a high risk that changes with accounting implications will not be considered properly, and revenue could be recorded in the wrong accounting period (cut-off)." By expressing your risk assessment at this level of detail, you will be able to design further audit procedures that are directly related to the risk. In this case, by addressing the lack of communication between the sales department and accounting relating to nonstandard contract terms. (AU-C sec. 315 par. .26*b*)

5.04 You should design further audit procedures whose nature, timing, and extent are based on, and are responsive to, your assessed *risks of material misstatement* at the relevant assertion level. The risk assessment reflects your judgment about inherent risk and control risk. The higher you assess the risk, the more persuasive audit evidence you should obtain should provide a high level of assurance about whether the financial statements are stated fairly. (AU-C sec. 330 par. .07)

5.05 To gauge the relative significance of identified risks, you should consider the following:

  a. *Magnitude*, that is, whether the risks are of a magnitude (size) that could result in a material misstatement of the financial statements, and

  b. *Likelihood*, that is, the chance of the material misstatement happening.

(AU-C sec. 315 par. .27*d*)

5.06 By definition, a high likelihood of a misstatement that is material to the financial statements results in a high RMM. Conversely, if you determine that an identified risk would have a lower chance to result in a misstatement and any misstatement that would result would be immaterial, you would assess the risks of material misstatement to be relatively low for that assertion. Illustration 5-2 describes this relationship between magnitude and likelihood when assessing risks of material misstatement.

Illustration 5-2
Relationship Between Magnitude and Likelihood When Assessing Risks of Material Misstatement

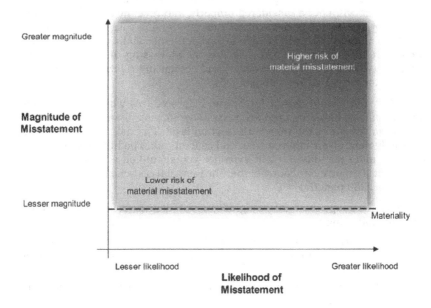

The Committee of Sponsoring Organizations of the Treadway Commission (COSO) framework introduces two additional considerations in assessing risk in addition to likelihood and magnitude: velocity and persistence. These considerations are related to the concept of magnitude. Velocity relates to the speed with which an event might occur. Persistence relates to how long the risk issue might continue and how that might affect the magnitude of the risk. Although the auditing standards do not discuss these additional considerations, velocity and persistence may be useful in assessing risks or may be considered dimensions of magnitude.

The Risks of Material Misstatement

5.07   The risks of material misstatement are the risks that an account or disclosure item contains a material misstatement. Chapter 2, "Key Concepts Underlying the Auditor's Risk Assessment Process," of this guide provides a more detailed discussion of this definition and its implications, including the following:

- The *risks of material misstatement* are defined as a combination of inherent and control risk. (AU-C sec. 200 par. .14)

- The *risks of material misstatement* are the client's risks which exist independently of your audit. (AU-C sec. 200 par. .A41)

- You should assess the *risks of material misstatement* at both the financial statement level and the relevant assertion level. (AU-C sec. 315 par. .26)

Risk Identification

5.08 In a financial statement audit, ultimately you are concerned with the risks related to financial reporting. However, many financial reporting risks are driven by broader business risks, which in turn, stem from the company's business objectives and strategies. (AU-C sec. 315 par. .12*d*)

5.09 *For example:*

- *In an effort to increase profitability (the company's business objective), Young Fashions decides to extend credit to customers to whom it historically has not extended credit (strategy).*

- *As a result of this new strategy, the company is vulnerable to an increase in bad debts and in the time and effort it expends on collections. This could impede its ability to realize its overall objective of increased profitability (business risk).*

- *In regards to financial reporting, there is a risk that those responsible for estimating (or reviewing, as a control) bad debts may not be aware of or properly consider the effects of the new credit policy. Consequently the estimate for the bad debt allowance may be materially misstated (financial reporting risk).*

- *If increased bad debts already have been observed without management consideration of this in the estimation of bad debts, the likelihood issue is moot, and you should go on to assess the magnitude of the possible misstatement.*

Implementation of the COSO framework would likely assess (1) the preceding strategy issue as relates to principle 6 (setting objectives), and (2) the risk as relates to principle 7 (risk of not achieving the objective). If the risk is important to the achievement of objective(s), management should design a control or controls to address this risk (principle 10). The absence of a control over a risk may indicate a control design deficiency of some magnitude. Chapter 7, "Evaluating Audit Findings, Audit Evidence, and Deficiencies in Internal Control," of this guide discusses the assessment of control deficiencies.

5.10 Because financial statement reporting risks are derived from underlying business risks, your identification of the risks of material misstatement begins with an understanding of your client's overall business objectives, their strategies for achieving those objectives, and the risks to their achievement. Chapter 4 of this guide provides additional guidance and examples of the identification of client objectives, strategies, and risks.

5.11 As part of your understanding of internal control, you will gather information about management's risk assessment process. As part of your risk assessment procedures, you also may make inquiries about the risks that management has identified as part of their own risk assessment. The risks that management identifies as part of its risk assessment process should not supplant your own procedures, the results of those procedures, and your professional judgment. However, understanding the risks that management already has identified can facilitate a more efficient and effective audit. (AU-C sec. 315 par. .17)

5.12 It may be helpful to consider a generic set of financial reporting risks. Table 5-1 provides such a list. However to be relevant to your audit, the financial reporting risks you identify and document should be specific to the unique facts and circumstances that exist at your client.

Table 5-1
Types of Misstatement

In general, *risks of material misstatement* may relate to one or more of the following:

  a. An inaccuracy in gathering or processing data from which financial statements are prepared

  b. A difference between the amount, classification, or presentation of a reported financial statement element, account, or item and the amount, classification, or presentation that would have been reported under generally accepted accounting principles (GAAP)

  c. The omission of a financial statement element, account, or item

  d. A financial statement disclosure that is not presented in conformity with GAAP

  e. The omission of information required to be disclosed in conformity with GAAP

  f. An incorrect accounting estimate arising, for example, from an oversight or misinterpretation of facts

  g. Differences between management's and the auditor's judgments concerning accounting estimates, or the selection and application of accounting policies that the auditor considers inappropriate (for example, a departure from GAAP)

Observations and Suggestions

Performing risk assessment procedures and gaining an understanding of your client's business (as described in chapter 3 of this guide) will enable you to identify broad business risks fairly easily. Your challenge will be to analyze these broad business risks—separately and in combination—and to determine the effect, if any, these could have on the financial statements.

In many cases, your understanding of the client will focus on business processes such as sales, purchasing, or cash receipts and disbursements. The risks of material misstatement are focused on accounts and assertions. To properly link your understanding of the client's broad business risks of to the risks of material misstatement, an additional challenge will be to map your understanding of client business processes to specific account balances and their relevant assertions.

Assess Risks at the Financial Statement Level

5.13 Risks of material misstatement at the financial statement level are those risks that relate pervasively to the financial statements and potentially affect many individual assertions. Examples of risks at the financial statement level may relate to the following:

- The process used to prepare the period-end financial statements, including

  — the development of significant accounting estimates.

  — the preparation of the notes to the financial statements.

- The selection and application of significant accounting policies.
- IT general controls.
- The control environment.
- Entity level controls.

Chapter 2 of this guide discusses each of these example financial statement level risks in greater detail.

5.14 *For example, Ownco is a small family-owned business. The company employs a full-time bookkeeper, but this individual performs several incompatible functions. The business owner is actively involved in the business, but this involvement generally is limited to business development and operational issues, not to oversight of the financial reporting process and supervision of the bookkeeper.*

Both the owner-manager and the bookkeeper are qualified and experienced to process or provide oversight to the processing of routine transactions. However, neither is adept at recognizing and applying emerging accounting matters or accounting for other non-routine transactions. This lack of expertise creates a risk that potentially could affect many assertions.

5.15 Your evaluation of the design of the client's control environment will affect your assessment of the risks of material misstatement at the financial statement level. All things being equal, a client with an effectively designed control environment will allow you to have more confidence in the reliability of the evidence you have obtained than a client with an ineffectively designed control environment. Weaknesses may require you to obtain greater quantity and more persuasive evidence or evidence closer to the period end to supplement the evidence of earlier tests.

Whenever your audit strategy goes beyond the *design* of internal control to include an expectation that controls have *operated* effectively throughout the period (that is, you intend to design substantive procedures based on the effective operation of those controls), you should test these controls. (AU-C sec. 330 par. .08*a*)

5.16 *For example, Lee, CPA, audits PQR Corp, which operates in a technology-dependent industry that evolves rapidly. Significant judgment is required to properly apply GAAP, particularly in the areas of revenue recognition and asset valuation. Because of the rapidly evolving nature of the industry, the accounting principles applicable to revenue recognition and asset valuation that are relevant to the company continue to be subject to multiple interpretations and clarifications by the accounting standard setting bodies. These industry conditions create significant financial statement level risks, which affect the valuation assertion for certain assets and relevant assertions related to revenue recognition.*

PQR is headquartered near a town that has experienced a steady decline in population, and for this and other reasons, the company has difficulty in hiring experienced, qualified accounting personnel. The ability of management to hire qualified personnel (its "commitment to competence") is an element of an entity's control environment, and the lack of qualified personnel could be a deficiency in the control environment. However, Garcia, CPA, is the CFO and controller of PQR. She has been with the company since its inception and has worked in the industry her entire 20-year professional career. She keeps herself well-apprised of the evolving business practices and accounting standards that affect the company. Thus, Garcia's strengths may mitigate some of the weaknesses that may exist at the lower levels in the accounting department.

Based on his client acceptance and continuance procedures as well as on information gathered in previous audits, Lee is aware of Garcia's experience, knowledge, and expertise. Intuitively, he feels comfortable relying on her, but intuition alone is not enough to justify this reliance for the audit.

To support his reliance on Garcia, during the current period audit, Lee performs certain risk assessment procedures, which as indicated in chapter 3 of this guide, include more than inquiry. As part of his risk assessment procedures to evaluate control design and confirm their implementation, Lee performs walkthroughs of Garcia's process for monitoring revenue recognition and the valuation of assets, and he observes Garcia's oversight, supervision, and training of accounting personnel.

Based on the design of the financial statement level controls performed by Garcia, the CFO and controller, Lee makes two decisions about the overall approach to the audit.

- *Hanashiro, a well-respected staff auditor with three years' experience, will be responsible for the day-to-day supervision of the audit. Hanashiro has worked on previous audits of PQR in a nonsupervisory capacity, but the other auditors assigned to the engagement have no experience with the client.*

- *The revenue cycle will be tested at an interim date, two months in advance of the period end and be updated to the end of the year.*

Based on his professional judgment, Lee concludes that the information gathered about the design of Garcia's procedures, which was obtained while performing risk assessment procedures, is sufficient and adequate to support his overall approach to staffing the engagement.

5.17 *Assume the same situation as described in paragraph 5.16 except that during the year, Garcia takes a six-week personal leave to care for an aging parent. During her absence, the company does not assign anyone to perform her assigned duties. At the end of her leave, Garcia decides to leave the company and relocate closer to her parents. After a two-week search, the company decides not to hire anyone from the outside to replace Garcia but instead, to promote the most senior person from her staff. This person was quite capable in her former position, but does not have nearly the qualifications, expertise, or experience of Garcia.*

Thus, during the year, the position of CFO and controller was unfilled for two months. At the end of that time, a person who was much less qualified than Garcia filled the position. Under this scenario, the financial statement level risks related to the entity and its business environment remain the same. However, the financial statement level control described in the previous scenario (the oversight and supervision of Garcia) was not operational at the same level of reliability for a good portion of the year. Consequently, the risks of material misstatement at the financial statement level is greater than it was under the previous scenario.

Under this set of facts, Lee, CPA, makes different decisions about the overall approach to the audit.

- Johnson, a five-year staff auditor with a strong reputation for detail, will supervise the audit. The budget for the job will be increased to include more involvement of Karl, a manager with extensive experience auditing technology companies. Karl will become involved immediately in planning the audit.

- Receivables will not be tested at an interim date but will be tested at year end. An additional test will be performed for the two months when there was an unfilled position; adjustments during this period will be carefully reviewed.

These differences in the overall approach to the audit reflect the different risk assessments caused by Garcia's absence.

Overall Responses to Risks at the Financial Statement Level

Observations and Suggestions

Your audit response to financial statement level risks should be responsive to the assessed risk.

The same is true for responses to risk at the account/assertion level. It is critical that your further audit procedures are linked clearly and responsively to your assessment. For example, if you determine that the risks related to the valuation of inventory are significant, the type of substantive procedures you design should provide strong evidence about valuation.

Similarly, your risk assessment at the financial statement level should be clearly aligned to your overall audit strategy, and your overall strategy should be responsive to your risk assessment.

Paragraph .08 of AU-C section 230, *Audit Documentation* (AICPA, *Professional Standards*) states that both your risk assessment and response should be documented to identify the procedures performed, evidence examined, and conclusions reached.

The following paragraph describes some important characteristics of financial statement level risks. The purpose of these descriptions is to help you "bridge" between your assessment of financial statement level risks and your subsequent response.

5.18 Characteristics of financial statement level risks that are relevant for audit purposes include the following:

- *Financial statement level risks can affect many assertions.* By definition, financial statement level risks may result in material misstatements of several accounts or assertions. For example, a lack of controls over journal entries increases the risk that an inappropriate journal entry could be posted to the general ledger at any time during the year or as part of the period-end financial reporting process. The posting of an inappropriate journal entry may not be isolated to one general ledger account but potentially could affect any account. In general, overall audit risk increases when the magnitude or scope of an identified risk of misstatement is not known.

- *Assessing financial statement level risks requires significant judgment.* Ultimately, you should relate identified risks of misstatement to what can go wrong. For example, suppose that while performing risk assessment procedures to gather information about the control environment, you discovered weaknesses relating to the hiring, training, and supervision of entity personnel. These weaknesses result in an increased risk of a misstatement of the financial statements, but it will be a matter of your professional judgment to determine

  - the accounts and relevant assertions that could be affected.
  - the likelihood that a financial statement misstatement will result from the increased risk.
  - the significance of any misstatement.

- *Risks at the financial statement level may not be identifiable with specific assertions.* Control weaknesses at the financial statement level can render well-designed activity-level controls ineffective. For example, a significant risk of management override can potentially negate existing controls and procedures at the activity level in many accounts and for many assertions. Linking such a risk to specific accounts and assertions may be very difficult, and may not even be possible. As another example, your client may have excellent data input controls at the application level. But if poorly designed IT general controls allow many unauthorized personnel the opportunity to access and inappropriately change the data, the well-designed input controls have been rendered ineffective. Also, strengths in financial statement level controls such as an overall culture of ethical behavior may increase the reliability of controls that operate at the activity level. Determining the extent to which financial statement level controls affect the reliability of specific activity level controls (and therefore the assessment of the risks of material misstatement) is subjective and may vary from client to client.

5.19 *For example, Young Fashions does not have a complete, well-designed set of controls relating to accounting estimates, even though estimates are important to the financial statements. More specifically, accounting personnel do a good job making recurring estimates such as the allowance for doubtful accounts and accruals. However, they are much less adept at making estimates related to asset valuation issues, including the impairment of long-lived assets and goodwill. Risks related to accounting estimates may be considered a financial statement level risk because they have the ability to affect many different assertions. But given the circumstances that exist at Young Fashions, these financial statement level risks can be correlated with or mapped to misstatements that can occur in specific accounts and assertions (for example, valuation of long-lived assets and goodwill).*

5.20 However, because of the unique characteristics of financial statement level risks, it may not be possible to correlate all of these risks to a finite set of assertions. For example, a weakness in control environment may affect all or mostly all of the accounts, classes of transactions, or disclosures and the relevant assertions. To respond appropriately to these types of financial statement level risks, you may need to reconsider your overall approach to the engagement. Table 5-2 provides examples of overall responses to risks at the financial statement level that have a pervasive effect on the financial statements and cannot necessarily be mapped to individual assertions.

Table 5-2
Examples of Overall Responses to Risks at the Financial Statement Level

Your overall response to risks at the financial statement level may include

- emphasizing to the audit team the need to maintain professional skepticism in gathering and evaluating audit evidence.
- assigning more experienced staff or those with specialized skills or using specialists.
- providing more supervision.
- incorporating additional elements of unpredictability in the selection of further audit procedures to be performed and in selecting individual items for testing.
- making general changes to the nature, timing, or extent of audit procedures as an overall response, for example, performing substantive procedures at period end instead of at an interim date. One could also focus more time and attention on audit areas more closely associated with the risk.

Observations and Suggestions

Paragraphs .A9–.A10 and .A38–.A42 of AU-C section 240, *Consideration of Fraud in a Financial Statement Audit* (AICPA, *Professional Standards*), describe the overall responses you may take in response to your assessment of the risks of material misstatement due to fraud. When determining your overall audit response, you can consider your assessment of fraud risk concurrently with your assessment of the risks of material misstatement due to error. You may be able to develop one overall response that is appropriate for both kinds of risks.

Assess Risks at the Assertion Level

5.21 Some risks of misstatement relate to a single assertion or a set of assertions for the same business process or class of transactions. For example, the risks associated with the inaccurate counting of inventory at year end may affect the existence and valuation of inventory and the completeness and accuracy of cost of goods sold. Risks associated with the completeness of accounts payable affect payables, purchases, and expenses.

Consideration of the Two Components of the Risks of Material Misstatement

5.22 As described in chapter 2 of this guide, the *risks of material misstatement* are a combination of inherent and control risk, and you can decide whether to assess these two components separately or in combination. Either way, you should assess both components. For example, even if you assess inherent risk as low for a particular assertion, you still should assess control risk.

5.23 *For example, assume you are auditing a payroll account. You believe the payroll is competently prepared and uses a reputable service organization for determining deductions. In addition, you believe the monthly accrual adjustment is relatively easy to calculate. You might be tempted to assess inherent risk as low, partially because of the ease of the calculation, and partially because you have not identified misstatements in this account in prior year audits, and you believe that the bookkeeper is capable of recording the correct monthly amount.*

In this example, your professional judgment concerning the assessment of inherent risk was influenced by your belief that the bookkeeper is competent and has never made an error in prior years in posting the monthly adjustment. It may also reflect confidence in the service organization. As a result, your assessment of inherent risk did not assume that there are no controls because there are some controls in place that are applied in accounting for payroll.

Therefore, you have to be careful when assessing inherent risk as low because you may be assuming that certain basic controls are in place and operating effectively. In such cases, you may actually be making a combined assessment of the risks of material misstatement rather than assessing only inherent risk.

For many auditors, major accounts in the financial statements would not be assessed as low risk because "in the absence of control" the risk of misstatement could be high. Cases of fraud and error have been noted in common accounts such as cash, fixed assets, deferred costs, revenues and payroll.

Consideration of Internal Control in Assessing Risks

5.24 When assessing risks at the assertion level, you may identify the controls that have been implemented (placed in operation) and whose design indicates that the control is capable of effectively preventing or detecting and correcting material misstatements. Determining whether a control is *capable* of effectively preventing or detecting and correcting material misstatements does not require the auditor to obtain evidence about the actual operating effectiveness of the control.

Your assessment of a control may also bring to your attention risks that result from an ineffective or improperly designed control. These additional risks may need to be considered in your audit plan. An important identified risk that is not addressed by a control may be a design deficiency of some magnitude.

5.25 *For example, Young Fashions purchases finished goods from providers located in Asia or Europe. If these goods are not up to specifications provided by Young Fashions, the company has the contractual right to either return finished goods and request a full credit be made to its account or sell the items as "factory seconds" through discount retailers. If they elect to sell the items, the manufacturer will credit Young Fashions for the difference between the profit that would have been made had the company been able to sell the item at full price, and the actual profit made selling the items as factory seconds. In addition, the amount* *of the credit is denominated in foreign currencies, which may fluctuate from the time the goods are initially billed and Young Fashions receives proper credit for unsatisfactory merchandise.*

Because of these complications in determining the proper balance in the payables account, the inherent risk associated with purchases is relatively high. However, the auditor has determined that the company has a highly effective design of the controls related to its return of merchandise. In assessing the risks of material misstatement related to the relevant assertions for purchases, the auditor should consider both the inherent risk of misstatement and the design of the controls being used by the company that can mitigate that risk.

Observations and Suggestions

Evaluating the design of a control and determining whether it has been implemented are vital to properly designing further audit procedures, even if those procedures are expected to consist solely of substantive procedures. For example, consider the design of further audit procedures related to cash balances under three different scenarios.

Scenario one: No interim controls implemented. In gaining an understanding of control design and implementation, you determine that your client only reconciles the bank accounts once a year, when preparing for the audit. That is, this control over cash receipts and disbursements does not exist throughout the year.

Scenario two: Controls exist but are not designed effectively. In this scenario the client prepares monthly bank reconciliations; however, there is inadequate segregation of duties. The person performing the reconciliations also has the ability to post cash receipts and disbursement activity to the general ledger.

Scenario three: Adequately designed controls have been implemented. Your client performs monthly bank reconciliations, and the procedures have been designed effectively, including adequate segregation of duties.

Design of Substantive Procedures

The design of your substantive procedures will vary for each of the previously mentioned scenarios. In scenario one, the client has not implemented what may be an important control over cash receipts and disbursements. Accordingly, you might change the nature of your substantive procedures to include procedures to detect material misstatements caused by fraudulent cash disbursements or activity (such as lapping) related to cash receipts during the year. You note that if the year-end reconciliation is done properly, the financial statements will be correct regarding this item. You may choose to obtain a bank cut-off statement directly and use it to check the reconciliation or to even reperform the year-end reconciliation yourself. You may confirm payment information with client customers as part of your receivables confirmation procedures or you might examine underlying documentation supporting a selection of cash disbursements. You also may extend your planned substantive procedures to examine more cancelled checks or deposits in transit than you otherwise would have. Also, you might check for unusual journal entries, write-offs, or other interim activities that could indicate risks from unreconciled cash.

In scenario three, the client has designed and implemented an effective control procedure. All other circumstances being equal to those of scenario one, under this scenario, you may determine that sufficient relevant audit evidence related to period-end cash balances may be obtained by testing the year-end bank reconciliation. That is, you might not obtain bank cut-off statements, confirm cash, confirm payments received from customers or made to vendors, or perform many of the other procedures that were appropriate for scenario one.

Scenario number two is different from one and three, and could be more troublesome, because there exists a segregation of duties issue that could negate the effectiveness of the reconciliation. You might not perform all the procedures that were appropriate for a situation where virtually no controls have been implemented, but you would have to respond to the fact that the control is not designed effectively (due to a lack of segregation of duties). For example, you may decide to examine reconciliations that were performed by someone else, during the time when the person who typically performed them was on vacation. Or you may perform more detailed tests of certain accounts as a way to detect unauthorized disbursements and scan the nonstandard journal entries for cash account related items. You might also look toward any monitoring procedure that is performed over the reconciliation and its effectiveness. An effective monitoring control can mitigate the severity of this control deficiency to some extent.

Conclusion

Note that each scenario had an effect on the *nature* of the substantive procedures performed. Different procedures were designed to the varying risks presented by the different scenarios.

Absent an evaluation of control design and a determination of whether the controls are being used by the client, the design of your audit procedures may not be an appropriate response to the risks that are present at the client. Without appropriately designed audit procedures, you may fail to gather the sufficient, appropriate audit evidence that is necessary to provide a high level of assurance about whether the financial statements are free of material misstatement.

The deficiency of the lack of segregation of duties in many cases would be a control deficiency of some magnitude to be assessed and considered for reporting under the provisions of AU-C section 265, *Communicating Internal Control Related Matters Identified in an Audit* (AICPA, *Professional Standards*), unless effectively mitigated by other controls.

5.26 Individual control policies and procedures may not address a risk completely in themselves. Often, only multiple control activities, together with other components of internal control (for example, the control environment, risk assessment, information and communication, or monitoring), will be sufficient to address a risk. For this reason, when determining whether identified controls are capable of effectively preventing or detecting and correcting material misstatements, the auditor may consider his or her understanding of control policies and procedures within the context of the processes and systems in which they exist.

5.27 *For example, when processing accounts payable, there may be a risk that the entity processes payments or other debits to the account at the incorrect amount. This error may be introduced at several points within the information processing system. For example, at initiation, if the company writes a manual* *check to the vendor, the amount of the check may be entered incorrectly into the accounting system. At other points in the processing stream, journal entries to adjust payables for billing corrections may be posted inappropriately or at their incorrect amounts. For the audit, to gain a complete understanding of the risks related to the valuation of accounts payable, you may consider both the controls over the initiation of payments and those over the posting of billing adjustments.*

5.28 Controls can be either directly or indirectly related to an assertion. The more indirect the relationship, the less effective the control may be in preventing or detecting and correcting misstatements in that assertion. For example, a sales manager's review of a summary of sales activity for specific stores by region ordinarily is only indirectly related to the completeness assertion for sales revenue. Accordingly, it may be less effective in reducing risk for that assertion than controls more directly related to that assertion, such as matching shipping documents with billing documents. For this reason, when determining whether identified controls are capable of effectively preventing or detecting and correcting material misstatements, it will be helpful to consider whether the identified controls are directly or more indirectly related to a relevant assertion.

5.29 Your audit strategy may include testing controls for the purpose of relying on their operating effectiveness in the design of your substantive procedures. In those circumstances, your initial assessment of the risks of material misstatement will be based on an assumption that controls operated effectively throughout the audit period. However, after performing your tests of controls, you may need to reassess your initial assessment of the risks of material misstatement, for example, if your tests identify deviations in the way the control operated during the period.

Identification of Significant Risks

5.30 As part of your risk assessment, you should identify *significant risks*, one or more of which arise on most audits. *Significant risks* are those that require special audit consideration. This special consideration means that you should

a. obtain an understanding of the controls, including relevant control activities, relevant to the risks and, based on that understanding, evaluate whether such controls are suitably designed and implemented to mitigate such risks. (Paragraphs 4.64–.67 of this guide provide guidance on controls relating to nonroutine transactions and judgmental matters, which often are the source of significant risks.) (AU-C sec. 315 par. .30)

b. perform substantive procedures that are linked clearly and responsively to the risk. Moreover, when your approach to significant risks consists only of substantive procedures, you should perform either

   i. tests of details only, or

   ii. a combination of tests of details and substantive analytical procedures.

That is, the substantive procedures related to *significant risks* should not be limited solely to substantive analytical procedures (when you are not testing the operating effectiveness of controls related to the significant risks).

(AU-C sec. 330 par. .22)

c. if relying on the operating effectiveness of controls intended to mitigate the *significant risk*, you should test controls in the current period and not rely on tests of controls performed in prior years. (AU-C sec. 330 par. .15)

d. document those risks you have identified as *significant*.

5.31 One or more significant risks normally arise on most audits. In exercising professional judgment to determine whether a risk is a significant risk, you should consider

- the nature of the risk.
- the likely magnitude of the potential misstatement, including the possibility that the risk may give rise to multiple misstatements.
- the likelihood of the misstatement occurring.

(AU-C sec. 315 par. .29)

When considering whether an identified risk is a *significant risk*, you should exclude the effect of any controls related to the risk. In other words, your determination of whether a risk is a *significant risk* is based solely on inherent risk. Chapter 2 of this guide provides guidance on the factors that you may consider when assessing inherent risk.

Observations and Suggestions

As stated in paragraph 5.31, the determination of *significant risk* is based solely on inherent risk. It is common for auditors to assess inherent risk as "high," "moderate," or "low." In defining *significant risk* you may think of *significant risk* as one where the inherent risk is higher than the usual "high" and therefore it requires special audit consideration. There may be many audit areas assessed as "high risk" by the auditor, but only a few may be classified as *significant risks* because they require special audit consideration.

For example, in considering the valuation of receivables, you may assess inherent risk to be high because it is based on a subjective estimate. However, suppose that at your specific client

- management has extensive experience in estimating the allowance for doubtful accounts, and there has been little change in the company's products or major customers over the past few years.
- the information used by management to make the estimate is relevant and highly reliable
- the retrospective review of accounting estimates has revealed a good estimation process and not indicated a bias on the part of management. (See paragraph .A52 of AU-C section 240 for a discussion of the retrospective review of accounting estimates.)

Further, suppose that during the current audit period this client

- entered into a transaction with a related party that may be a variable interest entity requiring its consolidation in the financial statements of the client.
- applied for the first time, a relative complex accounting standard relating to leases.

Under these circumstances, the valuation of receivables, the possible consolidation of a variable interest entity, and the new application of an accounting principle may all be judged to be, at a minimum, high inherent risks. But of the three, only the consolidation and lease accounting issues may require special audit consideration. One or both of these two matters might be considered *significant risks*; the valuation of receivables in this case may not be a *significant risk*.

In some companies the valuation of inventories presents an annual challenge that requires careful consideration of the specific facts and circumstances surrounding the valuation assertion. Perhaps the products are highly sensitive to issues relating to a volatile technology, and thus for such a businesses, the valuation of inventory may be a *significant risk* that recurs annually.

In determining whether a risk is a *significant risk*, it is helpful to consider inherent risks not in isolation, but rather, in the context of *all* high inherent risks at the client. As indicated in paragraph 5.29, one or more *significant risks* generally arise on most audits. Thus, significant risks are likely to exist even in those situations where there are no new or unusual circumstances at the client.

Sometimes, comparing all high inherent risks to each other may help you identify which ones are the *significant risks* in those situations.

The unnecessary designation of too many risks as *significant risks* can impair the efficiency of the audit process by requiring special handling of these risks and precluding reliance on controls tested in previous audit periods.

Questions such as the following may help to determine which risks truly require special audit consideration:

- Which of the risks would be most likely to require the immediate, focused attention of the auditor with the final responsibility for the audit? If your firm requires a concurring review of audits, which of the risks would command the initial attention of the concurring reviewer?

- For which risks would you be reluctant to rely on substantive analytical procedures as your only source of audit evidence?

- Which of the risks are atypical for the client and could create a material misstatement?

- Were any of the risks unexpected, given your previous experience with this client?

Nonroutine Transactions and Judgmental Matters

5.32 Nonroutine transactions and judgmental matters may create a *significant risk*. For this reason, you will want to design your risk assessment procedures to identify nonroutine transactions and judgmental matters such as estimates.

5.33 Nonroutine transactions are transactions that are unusual, either due to size or nature, and that therefore occur infrequently. Risks relating to significant nonroutine transactions may arise from matters such as the following:

- Greater management intervention to specify the accounting treatment

- Greater manual intervention for data collection and processing

- Complex calculations or accounting principles
- The nature of nonroutine transactions, which may make it difficult for the entity to implement effective controls over the risks
- Significant related-party transactions

5.34 Judgmental matters may include the development of accounting estimates for which there is significant measurement uncertainty. Risks relating to judgmental matters may arise from matters such as the following:

- Accounting principles for accounting estimates or for revenue recognition may be subject to differing interpretation
- Required judgment may be subjective or complex, or may require assumptions about the effects of future events, for example, judgment about fair value

5.35 *Significant risks* also may arise from management judgments about matters that may affect the recognition, classification, or disclosure of financial statement items. These judgments may include

- the determination of when the company's earnings process is complete, which, in turn, will drive its revenue recognition policies.
- assumptions about intended future actions by management or likely future events. These assumptions may affect the recognition, measurement, or classification of assets and liabilities. For example

  — management's intent with regard to investment securities will determine how those securities are presented and classified in the financial statements.

  — management's projection of expected future cash flows may determine whether the carrying value of an asset has been impaired.

  — management's judgments about the likelihood of a future event occurring (for example, "probable" or "remote") may determine whether a contingent liability should be recognized.

- decisions about the matters to be disclosed in the notes to the financial statements and about the content and language used to describe those matters. These decisions affect the completeness, understandability, and fairness of the company's financial statement disclosures.

Significant Financial Statement Level Risks

5.36 At the financial statement level, significant risks may arise from the following:

- *External circumstances.* External circumstances giving rise to business risks influence your determination of whether the risk requires special audit attention. For example, technological developments might make a particular product obsolete, thereby causing inventory values to be more susceptible to overstatement. Recent significant economic, accounting, or other developments also may require special attention.

- *Factors in the client and its environment.* Factors in the client and its environment that relate to several or all of the classes of transactions, account balances, or disclosures may influence the relative significance of the risk. For example, a lack of sufficient working capital to continue operations or a declining industry characterized by a large number of business failures may have a pervasive effect on risk for several account balances, classes of transactions, or disclosures.

- *Recent developments.* Recent significant economic, accounting, or other developments can affect the relative significance of a risk.

Significant Assertion Level Risks

5.37 At the assertion level, when determining whether an identified risk requires special audit consideration, you may consider a number of matters, including the following:

- *Complex transactions or calculations.* Complex calculations are more likely to be misstated than simple calculations.

- *Risk of fraud or theft.* Revenue recognition is presumed to be a financial reporting fraud risk; cash is more susceptible to misappropriation than inventory of coal.

- *Estimates.* Accounts consisting of amounts derived from accounting estimates that are subject to significant measurement uncertainty pose greater risks than do accounts consisting of relatively routine, factual data.

- *Related party transactions.* Related party transactions may create business risks that can result in a material misstatement of the financial statements.

Observations and Suggestions

To the extent possible, you will want to relate *significant risks* to the relevant assertion level, not simply the account level.

Significant risks may vary between clients in the same industry. At the same client, they may change over time. For example, suppose that your client entered into a hedging transaction. The first time they entered into the transaction you may determine that, due to the complexity of the accounting, there was a *significant risk* that the transaction was accounted for improperly and could materially misstate accounts or disclosures. However, because the transaction was unique and important to the entity, the decision to enter into the transaction was appropriately authorized, the client obtained proper guidance on how to account for the transaction, and the client set up appropriate controls.

Suppose that over time, the company entered into the same type of hedging transactions on a regular basis, as a normal part of its operations. As a routine transaction, determining the proper accounting is no longer considered complex (for this particular client). Additionally, assume the magnitude of potential misstatement is less and now is much less likely to result in a material misstatement. Thus, in later periods you might decide that this is no longer a *significant risk.*

©2016, AICPA

At a similar client, you may discover that the treasurer has the ability to both enter into and approve the transactions.

Under these circumstances, you may determine that a *significant risk* related to hedging transactions still exists related to the authorization of the transaction and whether the company has adequately accounted for and disclosed all obligations and risks that may arise from the transactions.

Linking the Assessed Risks to the Design of Further Audit Procedures

Observations and Suggestions

Paragraphs .30 and .A8 of AU-C section 330, *Performing Audit Procedures in Response to Assessed Risks and Evaluating the Audit Evidence Obtained* (AICPA, *Professional Standards*), requires you to document and establish a "clear linkage" between your assessment of the *risks of material misstatement* and further audit procedures.

Linkage describes the relationship between the assessed risk and your further tests. *Clear linkage* means that the further tests are responsive to the assessed risks and that there is a close correlation between the assertions of the assessed risk and the assertions addressed by the substantive procedure. The test should provide strong evidence about the assertion that is at RMM. A vague correlation between your assessed risks and your further audit procedures may indicate that yet additional audit procedures may need to be performed to address the identified risks.

Although generic audit programs for standard audit areas may be helpful in providing a starting point for determining the nature of the substantive procedures you will perform, it is important to modify generic audit programs as necessary to ensure that your choice of substantive procedures is clearly linked to your assessed risks.

In practice, clear linkages can be made between assessed risks and further audit procedures addressing the assessed risks.

In paperless audits, clear linkage can often be established by creating hyperlinks between the risks identified during risk assessment and the relevant electronic working papers. In manual or electronic working paper environments, cross references can aid in ensuring that all the assessed risks are addressed in the audit.

Failure to provide these linkages

- can make engagement team reviews and quality reviews less efficient.
- can cause a failure to document strategies and important interconnections between tests in different audit areas (for example, sales, cash, and accounts receivable).
- can leave assessed risks unaddressed during the audit.

Please refer also to AU-C section 230.

5.38 Your risk assessment process culminates with the articulation of the account balances, classes of transactions, or disclosures where material misstatements are most likely to occur and—even more specifically—how the misstatements may occur and the assertions that are likely to be misstated. This assessment of the risks of misstatement, which relates identified financial reporting risks to what can go wrong at the assertion level, provides a basis for the design of further audit procedures.

Design of Further Audit Procedures

5.39 Further audit procedures provide important audit evidence to support your audit opinion. These procedures consist of tests of controls and substantive procedures. You may determine that a combined approach using both tests of the operating effectiveness of controls and substantive procedures is an effective approach.

5.40 You should design and perform further audit procedures whose nature, timing, and extent are responsive to the assessed risks of material misstatement at the relevant assertion level. Effectively designed procedures provide a clear linkage between the risk assessments and the nature, timing, and extent of the further audit procedures. (AU-C sec. 330 par. .06–.07)

5.41 In designing further audit procedures, you should consider matters such as

- the significance of the risk and the likelihood that a material misstatement will occur. In general, the more significant (in terms of likelihood and magnitude) the risk, the greater the quality of evidence should be gathered, and the more reliable and relevant your audit evidence should be.

- the characteristics of the class of transactions, account balance, or disclosure involved, which will help determine the nature, timing, and extent of procedures available to you. For example, the gross accounts receivable balance comprises transactions with third parties, which means you can contact these external parties to confirm the transactions or individual account balances. On the other hand, the allowance for doubtful accounts is an estimate prepared internally, which does not lend itself to confirmation but to other substantive procedures, for example performing procedures to test the aging of accounts receivables.

- the nature of the specific controls used by the client, in particular, whether they are manual or automated.

- whether you plan to test controls in order to modify the nature, timing, and extent of substantive procedures.

(AU-C sec. 330 par. .06–.07)

Nature of Further Audit Procedures

5.42 The nature of further audit procedures refers to

a. their purpose, that is, tests of controls or substantive procedures (or dual-purpose tests) and whether they are designed to test for overstatement, understatement, or both.

b. their type, that is

    i. inspection,

    ii. observation,

    iii. inquiry,

    iv. confirmation,

    v. recalculation,

    vi. reperformance, or

    vii. analytical procedures (including scanning).

Table 5-3 and paragraphs 5.43–.54 provide additional guidance on each of these procedures.

Observations and Suggestions

Of the three variables that you consider when you design further audit procedures (nature, timing, and extent), it is your choice of the type of procedures (their nature) that will be most important in determining whether the further audit procedures are responsive to assessed risks.

Table 5-3
Types of Audit Procedures

Type of Procedure	Definition	Additional Guidance
Inspection of Documents	Inspection of documents involves examining records or documents, whether internal or external, in paper form, electronic form, or other media.	• This procedure provides audit evidence of varying degrees of reliability, depending on their nature and source and, in the case of internal documents, on the effectiveness of the controls over their production. • Some documents represent direct audit evidence of the existence of an asset but not necessarily about ownership or value. • Inspecting an executed contract may provide audit evidence relevant to the entity's application of accounting principles, such as revenue recognition. • Some forms of documents are less persuasive than others. For example, faxes and copies may be less reliable than original documents.

Types of Audit Procedures—*continued*

Type of Procedure	Definition	Additional Guidance
Inspection of Tangible Assets	Inspection of tangible assets consists of physical examination of the assets.	• This procedure may provide audit evidence relating to existence, but not necessarily about the entity's rights and obligations or the valuation of the assets. • Inspection of individual inventory items ordinarily accompanies the observation of inventory counting.
Observation	Observation consists of looking at a process or procedure being performed by others.	• This procedure provides audit evidence about the performance of a process or procedure but is limited to the point in time at which the observation takes place and by the fact that the act of being observed may affect how the process or procedure is performed.
Confirmation	Confirmation is the process of obtaining a representation of information or of an existing condition directly from a knowledgeable third party.	This procedure • frequently is used in relation to account balances and their components but need not be restricted to these items. • can be designed to ask if any modifications have been made to an agreement, and if so, what the relevant details are. • also is used to obtain audit evidence about the absence of certain conditions, for example, the absence of an undisclosed agreement that may influence revenue recognition. See AU-C section 505, *External Confirmations* (AICPA, *Professional Standards*), for further guidance on confirmations.

(continued)

Types of Audit Procedures — *continued*

Type of Procedure	Definition	Additional Guidance
Recalculation	Recalculation consists of checking the mathematical accuracy of documents or records.	• This procedure can be performed through the use of information technology, for example, by applying a data extraction application or other computer assisted audit techniques (CAATs).
Reperformance	Reperformance is the auditors independent execution of procedures or controls that were originally performed as part of the entity's internal control.	• This procedure may be performed either manually or through the use of CAATs, for example, reperforming the aging of accounts receivable.

Inquiry

5.43 Inquiry consists of seeking information of knowledgeable individuals. These individuals may be involved in the financial reporting process or outside of that process; they may be internal or external to the company. Inquiry is used extensively throughout the audit and often is complementary to other audit procedures. Inquiries may range from formal written inquiries to informal oral inquiries. Asking questions of knowledgeable individuals is only part of the inquiry process. Evaluating the responses to your inquiries is an equally integral part of the process.

5.44 Inquiry normally involves

- considering the knowledge, objectivity, experience, responsibility, and qualifications of the individual to be questioned.
- asking clear, concise, and relevant questions.
- using open or closed questions appropriately.
- listening actively and effectively.
- considering the reactions and responses and asking follow-up questions.
- evaluating the response.

See appendix I, "Suggestions for Conducting Inquiries," of this guide for further guidance on performing inquiries.

5.45 Responses to inquiries may provide you with information you did not previously possess or with corroborative audit evidence. Alternatively, responses might provide information that differs significantly from other information you have obtained. In those situations, you should resolve any significant inconsistencies in the information obtained. In some cases, responses to inquiries provide a basis for you to modify or perform additional audit procedures. (AU-C sec. 500 par. .10)

5.46 Paragraph .A2 of AU-C section 500, *Audit Evidence* (AICPA, *Professional Standards*), states that although inquiry may provide important audit evidence and may even produce evidence of a misstatement, inquiry alone ordinarily does not provide sufficient appropriate audit evidence to detect a material misstatement. Moreover, inquiry alone is not sufficient to test the operating effectiveness of controls.

5.47 In some instances, you may need to obtain evidence about management's intended actions, for example when obtaining evidence to support management's classification of investments as either trading, available for sale, or hold to maturity. To corroborate management's responses to questions regarding their intended future action, the following may provide relevant information:

- Management's past history of carrying out its stated intentions
- Their stated reasons for choosing a particular course of action
- Their ability to pursue a specific course of action

5.48 In some cases, you may consider it necessary to obtain replies to inquiries in the form of written representations from management. For example, when obtaining oral responses to inquiries, the nature of the response may be so significant that it warrants obtaining written representation from the source. See AU-C section 580, *Written Representations* (AICPA, *Professional Standards*), for further guidance on written representations.

Substantive Analytical Procedures

5.49 Substantive analytical procedures consist of evaluations of financial information made by a study of plausible relationships among both financial and nonfinancial data. Substantive analytical procedures also encompass the investigation of identified fluctuations and relationships that are inconsistent with other relevant information or deviate significantly from predicted amounts. See AU-C section 520, *Analytical Procedures* (AICPA, *Professional Standards*), for further guidance on analytical procedures. (AU-C sec. 520 par. .04)

5.50 *Scanning accounting data.* Scanning is an analytical procedure that includes

- the identification of anomalous individual items within account balances or other data. You may identify these items by reading or analyzing entries in any one of a number of accounting records, including transaction listings, subsidiary ledgers, general ledger control accounts, adjusting entries, suspense accounts, reconciliations, or other detailed reports. Computer assisted audit techniques (CAATs) may help you identify anomalies.

- the search for large or unusual items in the accounting records (for example, nonstandard journal entries), as well as in transaction data (for example, suspense accounts, adjusting journal entries) for indications of misstatements that have occurred.

Your determination of which items in a population are anomalous, large, or unusual is a matter of your informed professional judgment.

5.51 Because you test the items selected by scanning, you obtain audit evidence about those items. Your scanning also may provide some audit evidence about the items not selected because you have used professional judgment to determine that the items not selected are less likely to be misstated.

The Selection of Audit Procedures

5.52   Your risk assessments will have a bearing on your selection of audit procedures. The higher your assessment of risk, the more reliable and relevant (that is, persuasive) the audit evidence you seek from substantive procedures. This determination of the requisite reliability and relevance of audit evidence may affect both the types of audit procedures to be performed and their combination. For example, you may confirm the completeness of the terms of a contract with a third party, in addition to inspecting the document and obtaining management's representation. This combination of several procedures would result in more reliable and relevant audit evidence than you would have obtained by performing only one procedure.

5.53   In determining the audit procedures to be performed, you should consider the underlying reasons for your assessment. These underlying reasons relate to both the inherent and control risks related to the assertion. For example, if you assessed risks of material misstatement to be low that a material misstatement might occur because of low inherent risk, you may determine that substantive analytical procedures alone may provide sufficient appropriate audit evidence. On the other hand, if you expect that there is a lower RMM because the client has effective controls and you intend to design substantive procedures based on relying on the effective operation of those controls, you should perform tests of controls or dual-purpose tests in addition to analytical procedures or other substantive procedures. (AU-C sec. 330 par. .07)

Observations and Suggestions

It is common for auditors to use standardized audit programs as a starting point for determining the nature of their further audit procedures. To develop such a program requires certain assumptions to be made about the risks of material misstatement, your audit strategy, the effectiveness of the design or operation of internal control, and other matters. Accordingly, when starting to tailor your audit program from standardized audit programs, you will want to consider the assumptions underlying the type of procedures to be performed and whether those assumptions are consistent with your knowledge of the client and the audit evidence you have obtained.

For example, a standardized audit program for fixed assets may assume that the area has high inherent risk but low control risk and that the primary risk of material misstatement was incorrectly capitalizing expenditures for repairs and maintenance or other expenses. Because control risk was assumed to be low, the audit strategy underlying the program was one in which the auditor would be testing controls over fixed asset additions. Based on these assumptions, the program calls for you to select fixed asset additions that exceed a certain amount and examine supporting documentation to determine that the item was properly capitalized at an appropriate amount. A sample of other fixed asset additions may also be required. The program also calls on you to scan repairs and maintenance account for any items that should have been capitalized.

Your client may be different. Suppose that your client acquired a great deal of fixed assets during the year and that, due to the nature of the business, the

                                                          ©2016, AICPA

primary RMM was improperly classifying leasehold improvements as furniture and equipment. Further, suppose that the client's IT system shared a great deal of information between systems and that as a result of your audit approach in other areas, you already had planned to test IT general and application controls that were relevant to fixed asset additions. Under this scenario, some of the procedures that appeared in the standard audit program may not be relevant or different procedures may need to be performed to address specific risks. For example, you will want to perform procedures specifically to address the misclassification of fixed assets. Additionally, because of the tests of controls you already will be performing, you may determine that further tests of details are not required and that analytical procedures (combined with your tests of controls) would be sufficient.

Further audit procedures should be linked clearly to the specific risk assessments that exist at your client. Those specific assessments—together with your audit plan, knowledge of the client, and other matters—may or may not be consistent with the assumptions underlying a particular standard audit program. The use of a standard audit program whose underlying assumptions vary from the conditions that exist on your engagement will result in you performing (or not performing) further audit procedures that are linked clearly to your risk assessments. Consequently, you may not be able to provide a high level of assurance about whether the financial statements are free of material misstatement.

Testing Information Produced by the Client's Information System

5.54 You should obtain audit evidence about the accuracy and completeness of information produced by the entity's information system whenever you use that information in performing further audit procedures. For example, the auditors of Young Fashions use nonfinancial production and sales information to perform substantive analytical procedures. To justify relying on this information, paragraph .09 of AU-C section 500 states that the auditor should obtain audit evidence about the accuracy and completeness of such information. This audit evidence may be obtained either by tests of controls or substantive procedures. Relevant evidence may also be gathered while assessing the three principles associated with the Information and Communication component per the COSO framework.

Timing of Further Audit Procedures

5.55 Timing refers to when you perform your audit procedures or to the period or date to which the audit evidence applies. You may perform further audit procedures

- at an interim date,
- at period end, or
- after period end, in those instances where the procedure cannot be performed prior to or at year end (for example, agreeing the financial statements to the accounting records).

5.56 The higher the risks of material misstatement, the more likely it is that you will

- perform substantive procedures nearer to, or at, the period end rather than at an earlier date, or

- perform audit procedures unannounced or at unpredictable times (for example, performing audit procedures at selected locations on an unannounced basis).

Table 5-4 provides a summary of other matters you may consider when determining the timing of your tests.

Table 5-4
Matters to Consider When Determining Timing of Tests

In considering when to perform audit procedures, you may consider matters such as

- your assessed risk of misstatement. In general, the higher the risk, the more likely it is that you will perform procedures nearer to or at the period end.
- the control environment. In general, the more effective the control environment, the more likely it is that you will be able to perform tests as of an interim date.
- when the information necessary to perform your procedures is available (for example, electronic files may subsequently be overwritten, or procedures to be observed may occur only at certain times).
- the nature of the risk (for example, if there is a risk of inflated revenues to meet earnings expectations by subsequent creation of false sales agreements, you may examine contracts available on the date of the period end).
- the period or date to which the audit evidence relates.

Observations and Suggestions

Procedures that you perform at or close to period end will provide more reliable audit evidence on ending balances. On the other hand, performing audit procedures before the period end may help you identify significant matters at an early stage of the audit, thus allowing you to either resolve the issue with the help of the client, or develop an effective audit approach to address the issue.

Performing Procedures at an Interim Date

5.57 If you perform tests before period end, you should cover the remaining period by (a) performing substantive procedures, combined with tests of controls for the intervening period, or (b) if the auditor determines that it is sufficient, further substantive procedures only, which provide a reasonable basis for extending the audit conclusions from the interim date to the period-end. Chapter 6, "Performing Further Audit Procedures," of this guide provides further guidance on updating tests of controls and substantive procedures performed at an interim date.

Extent of Further Audit Procedures

5.58   Extent refers to the quantity of a specific audit procedure to be performed, for example, a sample size or the number of observations of a control activity. You may determine the extent of your audit procedure after considering all of the following:

- Performance materiality
- Your assessed risks of material misstatement
- The degree of assurance you plan to obtain

5.59   As the risks of material misstatement increases, you may increase the extent of audit procedures. However, increasing the extent of an audit procedure is effective only if the procedure itself is both relevant to the specific risk and reliable; therefore, the nature of the audit procedure is the most important consideration.

The AICPA Audit Guide *Audit Sampling* provides additional guidance on sampling for substantive testing.

Determining Whether to Test Controls

Observations and Suggestions

Your determination about whether to test controls to validate your assessment of controls in your *risk of material misstatement* is done at the assertion level on an assertion-by-assertion basis. That is, you do not make a decision about testing controls for the entire audit as a whole, but rather for certain specific accounts and assertions.

The results of your tests of controls may allow you to assess control risk for specific assertions below the maximum, which in turn, would allow you to make appropriate modifications to the nature, timing, and extent of planned substantive procedures that address the same assertion.

You are not required to test controls if you choose an all substantive audit approach even in those situations where you believe that the design and implementation of the client's internal control are capable of preventing or detecting and correcting material misstatements.

5.60   You should perform tests of controls when either

- a. your assessment of *risk of material misstatement* at the assertion level includes an expectation of the operating effectiveness of controls, or
- b. you determine that substantive procedures alone do not provide sufficient appropriate audit evidence at the relevant assertion level.

(AU-C sec. 330 par. .08)

It only makes sense to test controls when you have determined that the controls being used by client personnel have been designed effectively. An ineffectively designed control cannot be proven effective by testing. Substantively testing the accuracy and existence of transactions (and not controls) also is not evidence of the effective operation of controls (and does not confirm that controls even exist).

Observations and Suggestions

The term *expectation of the operating effectiveness of control* means that your understanding of the client's internal control has enabled you to initially assess control risk at less than maximum because you believe that the design and implementation of controls suggests that they are capable of effectively preventing or detecting and correcting material misstatements. This initial assessment of control risk is subject to the satisfactory results of your tests of operating effectiveness of those controls to support that initial control risk assessment.

An Expectation of Control Operating Effectiveness

5.61   As described in paragraph 3.04 and table 3-2 of this guide, your audit strategy as reflected in your audit plan will include a decision about whether you will test the operating effectiveness of internal control. However, as described in paragraph 3.05 of this guide, audit planning is a continuous process— your audit plan will evolve throughout the course of the engagement, as you gather additional information and form a deeper understanding of your client. Thus, your decision about whether to test controls may be revisited periodically over the entire course of the audit, for example, as you evaluate the design of internal control and determine how controls are being used by client personnel.

5.62   Your decision about whether to rely on controls may be considered within a cost-benefit framework. If the benefits of testing control effectiveness— both in terms of audit efficiency and effectiveness—are greater than the cost of testing controls, you would be inclined to adopt an audit strategy (or modify a preliminary strategy) that includes testing controls.

5.63   *The incremental cost of testing controls.* As first described in paragraph 1.19 of this guide, on every audit, you should evaluate the design of internal control and determine whether controls have been implemented. Chapters 3 and 4 of this guide describe the process for obtaining this understanding of internal control, and this process is fairly rigorous. When evaluating the costs of testing controls, in many cases you will only consider the incremental cost of testing controls, compared to the costs already incurred to evaluate their design and implementation.

5.64   *For example, suppose that you inspected several monthly reconciliations between the accounts payable subsidiary ledger and the general ledger account. As a risk assessment procedure, you inspected these reconciliations primarily to determine whether your client had implemented the control. It is unlikely that the mere inspection of these reconciliations would be sufficient to draw a low risk conclusion about their operating effectiveness.*

However, the reperformance of these reconciliations may provide sufficient, appropriate audit evidence of operating effectiveness.

The incremental cost of reperforming the reconciliations you already are inspecting may be fairly minimal, whereas the benefits of being able to rely on the controls to design your substantive procedures may be substantial.

5.65   *Consider costs over a three-year period.* As described in paragraph 6.54 of this guide, if certain conditions are met, the audit evidence gathered from tests of controls may be relevant for a three-year period. Thus, when evaluating the incremental cost of testing controls, consider that these costs may benefit three engagements.

Reminder: this "three-year" guidance does not apply for *significant risks*.

5.66 *Consider costs of testing complementary controls.* As described in paragraphs 2.57–.61 of this guide, the operating effectiveness of controls you want to test may be affected by other, complementary controls. For example, the effective operation of IT application controls over time depends on the effective functioning of IT general controls. Accordingly, when evaluating the costs of testing controls, you will consider the incremental cost of testing *all* controls that are necessary to gather audit evidence about operating effectiveness. Paragraph 6.11 of this guide provides additional guidance on testing the related controls that affect the operating effectiveness of the control activity that is the primary subject of your tests of controls.

Observations and Suggestions

When evaluating the benefits of testing controls, it is common for auditors to consider whether relying on controls can reduce the extent of substantive procedures, for example, by reducing the number of accounts receivable confirmations to send.

However, when your client's internal controls operate effectively, the *nature* of your substantive procedures may also be affected. For example, you may be able to perform substantive analytical procedures rather than tests of details. For accounts such as receivables and inventories where certain substantive procedures (for example, confirmations and inventory count observations) may be expected or required, these procedures may be limited to a minimum. Often, modifying the nature of your substantive procedures will provide as much benefit as or more benefit than increasing the extent of your procedures.

5.67 *The nature of the client's information system may affect the benefit to be derived from testing controls.* As described in paragraph 2.67 of this guide, it is common for IT systems to store data in a database, which is then accessed by a variety of IT "modules," such as procurement, order processing, or inventory management. Testing this system and obtaining audit evidence that the modules operate properly and that the integrity of the data is maintained may allow you to perform different types of tests that improve both audit efficiency and effectiveness. These tests may include

- substantive analytical procedures. As stated in paragraph .A17 of AU-C section 520, the level of assurance you obtain from substantive analytical procedures is influenced by the reliability of your client's information system. By testing controls, you may establish the reliability of the client's system, which will allow you to perform analytical procedures that provide you with a higher level of assurance. In some instances, this level of assurance may be sufficient, thereby eliminating the need for you to perform substantive tests of details.

- computer assisted auditing techniques. The effectiveness of a CAATs application (for example, data extraction) is improved when the client data that serves as the source of the application is accurate. With audit evidence supporting the operating effectiveness of the controls over the electronic processing of data, you will be in a position to more effectively deploy CAATs across a wider variety of transactions and accounts and rely on the quality of the information used in your analysis.

5.68 *The nature of the tests influences your decision about testing controls.* In some instances it may be more effective and efficient to test controls rather than perform substantive procedures. For example, if an entity uses an inventory costing method that creates "layers" of costs (for example, LIFO or FIFO) it may be easier and more efficient to test the operating effectiveness of controls over the entity's inventory costing system and performing analytical procedures instead of performing tests of details over the costing of the entire inventory balance.

Similarly, some financial services firms have excellent controls over the trades and transactions in and out of a customer's account, and it may be very costly and ineffective to rely on extensive confirmation procedures to validate the customer balances or individual transactions, so control reliance may significantly reduce the extent of confirmation procedures required.

5.69 *By relying on controls, you may reduce the sample sizes.* When the client has controls that operate effectively, you may reduce the level of your assessed risks of material misstatement. A reduction in RMM levels generally results in a reduction in sample sizes for substantive testing. Put another way, with a lower level of RMM, you may be able to accept smaller substantive sample sizes (based on lower confidence levels) and still achieve a low audit risk. Even a small reduction in confidence levels can result in a significant reduction in sample sizes.

Observations and Suggestions

For example, suppose you are designing a sample of accounts receivable and you will draw your sample from a population with total recorded amount of $150,000. You desire a substantial amount of audit assurance (that is, you have not tested controls and therefore have a higher assessed level of *risks of material misstatement*, and you have planned no other substantive procedures of receivables for existence). Assume further that tolerable misstatement is $10,000 and that there is no expected misstatement in the population. Using an assurance factor of 3, as provided for in the AICPA Audit Guide *Audit Sampling*, and based on these assumptions, your sample size might be (150,000/10,000) x 3 = 45 sampling units.

Now suppose that you perform some tests of controls, find them to be effective, and therefore require less assurance from your substantive procedures. All other factors being equal (and using the sample size factor provided for in the AICPA Audit Guide *Audit Sampling*), your substantive sample size might be (150,000/10,000) x 2.3 = 35 sampling units. That is, by performing some limited testing of controls, you have reduced the extent of your confirmation and reconciliation effort by 22 percent. More extensive testing of controls (for example, at high assurance) would lead to substantial additional reductions in substantive detail test sample sizes.

Because you are now testing controls, you would need to weigh the cost and time savings of performing the one procedure to save effort in the other.

> You may find additional guidance on applying sampling in substantive tests of details in chapter 4, "Nonstatistical and Statistical Audit Sampling for Substantive Tests of Details," of the AICPA Audit Guide *Audit Sampling*.

Audit Documentation

5.70 In regards to the assessment of risk and design of further audit procedures, you should document

    a. the assessment of the *risks of material misstatement* at both the financial statement level and the relevant assertion level. (AU-C sec. 315 par. .33)

    b. the overall response to address the assessed risks of misstatement at the financial statement level. (AU-C sec. 330 par. .30)

    c. the identified risks and related controls evaluated for

        i. *significant risks.*

        ii. those circumstances where substantive procedures alone will not provide sufficient appropriate audit evidence.

    (AU-C sec. 315 par. .33)

    d. the nature, timing, and extent of the further audit procedures. (AU-C sec. 330 par. .30)

    e. the linkage of those procedures with the assessed risks at the relevant assertion level. (AU-C sec. 330 par. .30)

Paragraphs 1.39–.41 of this guide provide additional, more general guidance on the preparation of audit documentation.

Observations and Suggestions

AU-C section 230 states that documentation should be sufficient such that an experienced auditor, with no prior experience with this client, can understand the procedures performed, evidence examined, and conclusions reached. Your strategy and how you addressed the risks you identified should be "transparent."

As an aid to staff and partner reviewers, many audit firm policies encourage more cross references between risks and audit procedures that address these risks.

In addition, the evidence you considered when making the risk assessment should be evident. For example, suppose you are assessing inherent risk related to debt, and you assess inherent risk to be low. What is the basis for that assessment? Is it because the client has variable rate debt but interest rates are not expected to change? Or is it because the client has only fixed rate debt? Or is the client simply not exposed to interest rate risk?

Paragraph 5.70 discusses the documentation of the basis for that inherent risk assessment.

Documenting the basis for your risk assessment also helps you in future audits. If documented well in year one, it will be easier for you to update your risk assessment and identify relevant changes in the business environment in subsequent years.

©2016, AICPA

Summary

5.71 This chapter described a process for assessing the *risks of material misstatement* of the client's financial statements. The results of your risk assessment procedures and your knowledge of the client and its environment, which were described in chapter 4 of this guide, provide the primary inputs into this process.

5.72 Many of the *risks of material misstatement* of the financial statements are driven by broad business risks, so your assessment process begins by identifying these broad business risks facing the client. Once you identify these, you will analyze them to determine how they affect the financial reporting process, if at all.

5.73 After identifying financial reporting risk, you will assess the relative significance of the risk by considering the magnitude of the risk and the likelihood that it will occur. Risk should be assessed at both the financial statement level and relevant assertion level. If possible, financial statement risk should be related to what can go wrong at the assertion level. If the financial reporting risk is so pervasive that its effect cannot be isolated to a finite set of assertions, you will develop an overall response to this risk.

5.74 Your risk assessments will drive the design of further audit procedures, which consist of tests of controls (when controls reliance is planned) and substantive procedures. These further audit procedures should be clearly linked and responsive to the assessed risk. The design of further audit procedures includes determining their nature, timing, and extent. Of these elements, it is the nature of the tests that is of most importance.

5.75 Chapter 6 of this guide discusses how you will perform the audit procedures that have been designed.

                                                            ©2016, AICPA

5.76

Appendix—Answers to Frequently Asked Questions About Risk Assessment and the Design of Further Audit Procedures

Question	See Paragraphs
What is meant by *risk assessment* and *risks of material misstatement*?	5.02–.07
What risk might exist at the financial statement level? How should I design my audit to be responsive to that risk?	5.13–.20
What does it mean to assess risk at the assertion level?	5.21–.23
What is the relationship between inherent risk and control risk? Should I assess these two risks separately or together? What issues may arise if I make separate inherent and control risk assessments?	5.21–.29
What are *significant risks*? Will I always have *significant risks* on my audits? What are the implications of identifying a risk as a *significant risk*?	5.30–.37
What is meant by the term *linkage*? Why is it important to *link* further audit procedures to risk?	5.38
What is meant by the term *further audit procedures*?	5.39–.42
How can I select appropriate audit procedures to perform? How can I justify modifying standardized audit programs?	5.52–.53
Under what circumstances should I test controls?	5.60–.69
What risk assessment matters should I document?	5.70

Chapter 6

Performing Further Audit Procedures

TABLE OF CONTENTS

Observations and Suggestions

Illustration 6-1
Overview of Performing Further Audit Procedures

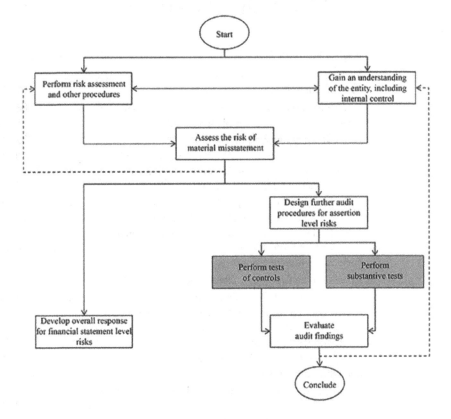

> *Further audit procedures consist of tests of controls and substantive procedures. The previous chapter provided guidance on how to design the nature, timing, and extent of these audit procedures, with an emphasis on linking your response to your assessed risks. This chapter provides guidance on performing planned procedures.*
>
> ***Tests of the Operating Effectiveness of Controls.*** *On all engagements, you are required to evaluate the design of the client's internal control and to determine that the controls have been implemented. In some situations, your audit strategy may involve relying on the operating effectiveness of the controls for some assertions in the design of your substantive procedures. In those instances, you will design and perform tests of the operating effectiveness of controls, in addition to the procedures you perform to evaluate design. This chapter provides guidance on how to evaluate the operating effectiveness of controls.*
>
> ***Substantive Procedures.*** *Most likely, you will perform a variety of substantive procedures on a number of account balances, classes of transactions, disclosures, and the overall presentation of the financial statements and should perform substantive procedures as defined in chapter 5, "Risk Assessment and the Design of Further Audit Procedures," of this guide. In many cases, several procedures may be necessary to address an assessed risk. This chapter focuses on guidance related to the performance of these substantive procedures.*

The previous chapter described how to design further audit procedures in a way that is responsive to and clearly linked with your assessment of the risks of material misstatement. This chapter provides guidance on how to perform the further audit procedures you have designed.

This chapter focuses only on those audit procedures you perform at the assertion level. Paragraphs 5.18–.20 of this guide describe how to develop an overall response to risk at the financial statement level.

Introduction

6.01 Further audit procedures consist of tests of the operating effectiveness of controls and substantive procedures.

Tests of Controls

6.02 Tests of controls provide evidence about the effectiveness of the operation of a control in preventing or detecting material misstatements in a financial statement assertion. In tests of controls, you often are concerned about the rates of any deviation from a prescribed control procedure. Tests of controls are necessary when your audit strategy involves relying on the operating effectiveness of the controls for some assertions in the design of your substantive procedures.

6.03 When performing tests of controls, you should obtain audit evidence that controls operate effectively. This includes obtaining audit evidence about

    a. how controls were applied at relevant times during the period under audit.

    b. the consistency with which they were applied.

    c. by whom they were applied, or in the case of IT controls, the means by which they are applied.

(AU-C sec. 330 par. .10)

©2016, AICPA

6.04 When evaluating the operating effectiveness of controls, you also should evaluate the misstatements you detect when performing substantive procedures. For example, suppose that, through the confirmation of accounts receivable, you identify several billing errors where the client failed to bill its customers at the proper amount, and the error went undetected until the customer contacted the company. Your detection of these errors is relevant, reliable audit evidence about the relative ineffectiveness of the related controls. Your detection of a material misstatement that indicates that such misstatement would not have been detected by the entity's internal control is an indicator of a material weakness. (AU-C sec. 330 par. .16)

Observations and Suggestions

Beginning with illustration 1-1, this guide has described auditing as an iterative, nonlinear process. You form a preliminary audit strategy and plan and obtain an understanding of the client and its environment to assess the risks of material misstatement. That understanding or the resulting assessment may cause you to re-examine and possibly revise your initial audit strategy and plan, which in turn may cause you to obtain additional information about the client.

Paragraph 6.04 describes another example of this iterative process, in which you make an assessment of control risk and then discover misstatements that were not prevented or detected and corrected by the company's internal control. This discovery will often cause you to re-examine your initial assessment of internal control, which may cause a revision to the audit strategy, and so on.

Many audits proceed in this dynamic, ever-changing fashion in which the results of audit procedures result in a revision of earlier judgments, which result in new or revised audit procedures. Because of this interconnectedness, it is helpful for auditors to consider the results of audit procedures not in isolation, but rather, in terms of how they affect the audit as a whole.

6.05 The absence of misstatements detected by a substantive procedure does not provide audit evidence about the operating effectiveness of related controls (or whether controls even exist). For example, if you found no differences or exceptions noted by customers during the confirmation of receivables, it would be inappropriate for you to draw any conclusion about the effectiveness of any related controls. (AU-C sec. 330 par. .16)

General Considerations When Testing Controls

Sources of Audit Evidence About Internal Control Effectiveness

6.06 The audit evidence used to provide support for your conclusion about the operating effectiveness of controls during the audit period may come from a variety of sources, including

- tests of controls performed during the current period.
- risk assessment procedures performed during the current period.
- evidence provided in a type 2 SOC 1 report under AU-C section 402, *Audit Considerations Relating to an Entity Using a Service Organization* (AICPA, *Professional Standards*).

- evidence obtained from the performance of procedures in previous audits.

- the information gathered and conclusions reached as part of your quality control procedures for client acceptance and continuance. For example, client acceptance procedures may include inquiries of attorneys, bankers, or others in the business community about client management that provide insight into their

    — competence,

    — integrity,

    — operating philosophy, and

    — ethical values.

Risk Assessment Procedures Versus Tests of Controls

6.07 Risk assessment procedures allow you to evaluate the *design effectiveness* of internal control for the purpose of assessing risks of material misstatement. Tests of controls build on your evaluation of design effectiveness and allow you to assess the operating effectiveness of controls during the operating period. The results of your tests of controls are used to design substantive procedures.

6.08 In some instances, risk assessment procedures, although not specifically designed as tests of controls, may nevertheless provide evidence about their operating effectiveness. For example, a walkthrough or the observation of the performance of a control may provide evidence about the operating effectiveness of controls. The sufficiency of that audit evidence depends on those factors described in table 7-3, as well as on the nature of the control itself. For example, your observation of the client's physical inventory count, which is performed only once a year, may provide you with sufficient evidence about their operation. On the other hand, the observation of the performance of an edit check, performed on every transaction entered into the IT system, is much less likely to provide sufficient evidence about the operating effectiveness of the control throughout the audit period.

Evidence of Operating Effectiveness of Controls at a Service Organization

6.09 As described in paragraph 3.128 of this guide, a type 2 SOC 1 service auditor's report may provide evidence about the operating effectiveness of controls at a service organization. However, controls over the information provided to the service organization may still need to be assessed.

Evaluating the Effectiveness of Indirect Controls

6.10 When designing tests of controls, you may focus first on testing control activities because the control activities component of internal control is the one most directly related to the assertion. For example, physically counting goods that have been received and comparing the quantity and description to the vendor's packing slip is directly related to the existence and perhaps the valuation of inventory.

6.11 In some circumstances, in addition to testing the controls that relate directly to assertions, it may be necessary for you to obtain audit evidence supporting the effective operation of indirect controls upon which the effectiveness of the direct control depends. (AU-C sec. 330 par. .10*b*) For example, assume you decide to test the effectiveness of a user review of exception reports detailing sales in excess of authorized credit limits. The user review combined with the related follow up is the control that is of direct relevance to you. In many cases, the controls over the accuracy of the information in the reports are described as indirect controls.

Because of the inherent consistency of IT processing, audit evidence about the implementation of an automated application control, when considered in combination with audit evidence about the operating effectiveness of the entity's general IT controls, also may provide substantial audit evidence about its operating effectiveness.

When considering the need to test indirect controls, you may consider the following:

a. *The significance of the indirect control to the effective functioning of the direct control.* As the effectiveness of the direct control becomes more dependent on the indirect control, your need to test the indirect control ordinarily increases.

b. *The relative significance of the audit evidence of the indirect control to the auditor's conclusion on the effectiveness of the direct control.* Your conclusion about the operating effectiveness of a control activity is supported by a combination of evidence about (i) the operating effectiveness of the direct control activity itself and (ii) the operating effectiveness of other, indirect controls upon which the effectiveness of the direct control depends. In some instances, you may be able to support a conclusion based primarily on tests of the direct control, with little evidence about the operating effectiveness of the related indirect controls. In other instances (for example, IT application controls), your conclusion may be based primarily on tests of the indirect controls and less so on tests of the direct control. In those situations where you rely significantly on the operating effectiveness of the indirect control, you should obtain more sufficient and adequate audit evidence to support the conclusion on the operating effectiveness of the indirect control, for example, the monitoring of the performance of the reconciliation.

c. *The degree of reliability required of the audit evidence obtained about internal control operating effectiveness.* Testing the indirect control increases the reliability of the audit evidence obtained about the operating effectiveness of the direct control. For example, you may test four month-end reconciliations and draw a conclusion about the effectiveness of those reconciliations for an entire 12-month period. If you have tested the operating effectiveness of the indirect controls related to the reconciliation, the conclusion about the effectiveness of the reconciliation during the period you did not test will be more reliable than if you did not test the indirect controls.

d. *Evidence of operating effectiveness that may have been obtained as part of obtaining an understanding of the design and implementation of the indirect controls.* When performing risk assessment procedures to obtain an understanding of internal control, you may obtain some information about the operating effectiveness of the indirect controls as they relate to an assertion. For example, risk assessment procedures may provide you with some evidence about the operating effectiveness of portions of the control environment. This information about operating effectiveness may be limited, but nevertheless, it may be sufficient for the purpose of drawing a conclusion about the operating effectiveness of the direct control.

Observations and Suggestions

You will need to exercise your judgment to determine when or whether and how to test indirect controls. Common examples of indirect controls upon which the effective operation of other controls often include

- IT general controls,
- segregation of duties, and
- the effective communication of control responsibilities when the employee responsible for performing the control changed during the period.

The Committee of Sponsoring Organizations of the Treadway Commission (COSO) framework specifies, under the control activities component, principles and associated points of focus addressing the selection and development of IT general control activities over technology (principle 11).

6.12 When testing indirect controls, you may choose not to test the operating effectiveness of the entire component to which the indirect control pertains, but may limit the tests to those elements of the component that have an immediate bearing on the effectiveness of the direct control.

For example, when testing controls over purchasing to place moderate reliance on them, you may consider the need to test the control environment or IT general controls relating to the entire entity beyond the required (minimum) design and implementation assessment procedures you already have performed. If practical, you may limit your tests to those aspects of the control environment or IT general controls that have a direct bearing on the financial statement assertions related to purchasing. To place high reliance on the controls, you may often need to gather additional evidence concerning the IT general controls and overall control environment to support high reliance on the purchasing controls.

6.13 Consider the following situation:

Young Fashions receives all its goods from overseas suppliers. Some of its finished garments in the JY Sport line are similar in design to garments in the more expensive Couture line. The primary difference between the two is in the composition and quality of the fabric—a silk garment in the Couture line may be similar to a garment in the JY Sport line that is made from a blend of synthetic fibers.

To the untrained eye, these similar garments are indistinguishable from each other. The packaging containers label the garments, but for quality control purposes, the company examines each shipment of material received prior to stocking them. This operational control also serves as an important financial reporting control because the information about the materials (for example, the identification of the material, its weight, and quality) are compared to the shipping document and vendor invoice.

©2016, AICPA

The company's review of its finished goods shipments has a direct effect on the existence and valuation of inventory. However, for this control procedure to be effective, the individuals performing the procedure must be properly trained, and they must operate in an environment where the proper performance of the procedure is emphasized appropriately. The auditor considers training and the "tone at the top" (both of which are elements of the control environment) to have an immediate bearing on the effectiveness of the inspection of finished goods, but only an indirect effect on preventing or detecting and correcting misstatements related to the valuation and existence of inventory.

After considering the factors listed in paragraph 6.11, the auditor determines that he or she wants to obtain audit evidence about the operating effectiveness of these indirect controls. In this example, the auditor may design tests of controls related to training and tone at the top for the personnel charged with performing the inspection. The auditor may not need to extensively test control environment components that do not have an immediate bearing on the performance of the control (for example, compensation policies, the alignment of authority and responsibility, or the oversight of the board of directors).

The auditor may also decide not to determine whether the components of the control environment that have an immediate bearing on the performance of the raw materials test are operating effectively throughout the organization. When testing indirect controls, the auditor may limit those tests to controls or elements of control components that have an immediate bearing on the effectiveness of the direct control.

Observations and Suggestions

Testing the control environment can be challenging because the control environment comprises primarily subjective matters such as "tone at the top" or management's philosophy and operating style, for which empirical evidence about operating effectiveness may not exist. Nevertheless, in many cases it is possible to design procedures that, if performed properly, may provide you with persuasive evidence about the operating effectiveness of the control environment.

Procedures that may be useful for testing the control environment include

- inquiries of management, appropriate individuals in the internal audit function (if such function exists), and others within the entity about specific *actions* management has taken that illustrate the tone at the top, operating style, or other elements of the control environment.
- surveys of employees asking for their observations about management's actions and the control environment at the entity.
- reading and evaluating documentation related to control environment elements. For example, personnel policies, training materials, budgets, codes of conduct, job descriptions, and other documents that may provide some evidence about the design of control environment policies and procedures.
- observations made by the audit engagement team members related to the other procedures mentioned previously. Useful information and data may be obtained by the collective observations and the documentation thereof by all audit team members.

                                        ©2016, AICPA

When evaluating "tone at the top" and other subjective matters such as management's attitude toward financial reporting and internal control, it may be helpful to focus on management's actions and how they responded to issues you raise during your audit. For example, you may consider management's response to matter, such as

- internal control deficiencies.
- misstatements.
- their responsibility for preparing the financial statements.
- allegations of fraud or suspected fraud.
- the presence of fraud risk factors under their control, such as compensation policies, that may increase the company's vulnerability to fraud.
- violations of the company's code of conduct.

Management's response to the identification of these aforementioned types of issues is addressed in principles 5 and 17 in the COSO framework.

The Relationship Between Tests of Controls and Substantive Procedures

6.14 There is often an inverse relationship between the persuasiveness of the audit evidence to be obtained from substantive procedures and that obtained from tests of controls. As the persuasiveness of the audit evidence obtained from tests of controls increases, the sufficiency and adequacy of the audit evidence required from substantive procedures likely decreases. For example, in circumstances when you adopt a strategy at the assertion level that consists primarily of tests of controls, you should perform tests of controls to obtain more persuasive audit evidence about their operating effectiveness. (AU-C sec. 330 par. .09)

6.15 On the other hand, the more audit evidence from substantive procedures, the less audit evidence from tests of controls would be necessary. In many instances, the nature and extent of substantive procedures alone may provide sufficient, appropriate evidence at the assertion level, which would make the testing of control effectiveness (beyond assessing their design and implementation) unnecessary. (The risk model discussion in the Audit Guide *Audit Sampling* provides a framework for assessing how controls testing can influence other substantive procedures.)

A Financial Statement Audit Versus an Examination of Internal Control

6.16 Testing the operating effectiveness of internal control to support an opinion on the financial statements is different from testing controls to support an opinion on the effectiveness of the internal control system.

6.17 In an attestation engagement to examine the effectiveness of internal control, the audit evidence obtained from the tests of internal control may be the principal evidence you have to support your opinion. In contrast, when performing an audit of the financial statements, you often perform both tests of controls and substantive procedures. The objective of the tests of controls in a financial statement audit is to assess the operating effectiveness of controls and incorporate this assessment into the design of the nature, timing, and extent of substantive procedures. Thus, when testing controls in a financial statement audit, you have more flexibility in determining not only whether to test the operating effectiveness of controls, and if so which controls to test, but also the level of effectiveness of those controls that is necessary to provide the desired level of support for an opinion on the financial statements.

Determining the Nature of the Tests of Controls

Observations and Suggestions

Determining the nature of your tests of controls means deciding on what type of test you will perform. For example, to obtain audit evidence about the effectiveness of a control, what will you do? Will you make inquiries? Observe activities? Reperform procedures? Will you select a sample of transactions for detail testing? What population will you draw your sample from?

Your choice of the type of procedure you will perform is the critical element of performing an effective audit.

6.18 The nature of the procedures you perform to test controls has a direct bearing on the relevance and reliability of your audit evidence. When responding to assessed risks of material misstatement, the nature of the audit procedures is of most importance. Performing more tests or conducting the tests closer to the period end will not compensate for a poorly designed test that produces information that lacks relevance or reliability about the effectiveness of a control.

6.19 The types of audit procedures available for obtaining audit evidence about the effectiveness of controls can include

- inquiries of appropriate entity personnel.
- inspection of documents, reports, or electronic files indicating performance of the control.
- observation of the application of the control.
- reperformance of the application of the control by the auditor.

6.20 The nature of the particular control influences the type of audit procedure necessary to obtain audit evidence about operating effectiveness. Documentation may provide evidence about the performance of some controls, and in these situations, you may inspect this documentation to obtain evidence about the operating effectiveness of the control.

6.21 For other controls, documentation may not be available or relevant. For example, documentation of the operation may not exist for some factors in the control environment, such as assignment of authority and responsibility, or for some types of control activities, such as control activities performed automatically by the client's IT system. In these circumstances, audit evidence about operating effectiveness may be obtained through inquiry in combination with other audit procedures such as observation of the performance of the control or the use of computer assisted audit techniques (CAATs). Under AU-C section 265, *Communicating Internal Control Related Matters Identified in an Audit* (AICPA, *Professional Standards*), entities should be encouraged to improve weak documentation.

6.22 Paragraphs 3.112–.113 and 3.116–.117 of this guide describe the limits of inquiry and observation when obtaining evidence about the design and implementation of internal control. When choosing the audit procedures you will perform to gather evidence about the operating effectiveness of controls, these same limitations may apply for tests of controls.

6.23 Because of the limits of inquiry and observation, inquiry combined with inspection or reperformance may provide more relevant and reliable audit evidence than a combination of only inquiry and observation. For example, you may inquire about and observe the entity's procedures for opening the mail and processing cash receipts to test the operating effectiveness of controls over cash receipts. Because an observation is pertinent only at the point in time at which it is made, you might find it necessary to supplement the observation with other observations or inquiries of entity personnel, and you may also inspect documentation about the operation of such controls at other times during the audit period.

Tests of IT Controls

6.24 Because of the inherent consistency of IT processing, audit evidence about the implementation of an automated control, combined with audit evidence about the operating effectiveness of IT general controls (and in particular, security and change controls) may provide you substantial audit evidence about the operating effectiveness of the control during the entire audit period. That is, once you have determined that an IT application control has been implemented (placed in operation), you may be able to draw a conclusion about the operating effectiveness of the IT portion of the control activity, so long as you have determined that relevant IT general controls are operating effectively.

Observations and Suggestions

IT application controls often consist of an automated portion and a manual portion, both of which operate effectively together. For example, the IT system may create an exception report of transactions that do not meet certain criteria. By itself, the production of such a report is not sufficient to prevent or detect a material misstatement. To be effective, someone at the client reviews the exception report and then follows up and properly resolves the items listed.

Determining that the automated portion of an IT application control has been implemented and that relevant IT general controls have operated effectively provides you with evidence about the operating effectiveness only for the automated portion of the control. To properly evaluate the entire control, you also will have to gather evidence about the operation of the manual component of the control—in our example, the manual follow up of items included on the exception report.

6.25 *For example, the processing of sales on account at Ownco includes a control to ensure that credit sales to a wholesale customer do not exceed that customer's authorized credit limit. This control is programmed into the entity's IT system, which generates an exception report of credit sales over a customer's authorized credit limit. The system does not allow processing of the transaction to continue until the exception has been acted on and properly resolved.*

During the performance of the risk assessment procedures, the auditor identified this control and determined that it was suitably designed and implemented (placed in operation). To obtain audit evidence about the operating effectiveness of the control, the auditor may test the application control directly, for example, through the offline processing of a sample of transactions to determine if the programmed control functions as designed. In addition, the auditor may choose to test the IT general controls (especially security and change controls) that clearly and directly relate to the operating effectiveness of the application control to ensure the continuing operating effectiveness of the control throughout the period.

In determining the nature of the procedures to test the operating effectiveness of IT general controls, the auditor may consider the limited evidence provided by the procedures performed to simply confirm the control was implemented (placed in operation). Because the auditor's conclusion about the operating effectiveness of the IT application control throughout the period is based primarily on the operating effectiveness of the IT general controls (that is, the auditor has only assessed the design of the application control and determined that it has been placed in operation) the auditor should test the IT general control in a manner that results in sufficient audit evidence. (AU-C sec. 330 par. .11)

The follow up of exceptions generated by the performance of the IT application control is a separate manual control that is necessary to achieving the control objective. Testing the ability of the IT system to generate an accurate exception report provides no evidence relating to the user's ability to properly resolve the identified exceptions. Evidence regarding the manual component of the control might need to be obtained through a separate audit procedure.

6.26 Factors that the IT professional may consider in determining the extent of tests of controls include the following:

- General controls

  — The frequency of the event(s) occurring to which the control applies would determine the relevant population for sample or test selection.

  — The auditor should select tests that cover the entire period relevant for operational effectiveness.

  — When multiple general controls affect one or more financially relevant applications, the auditor may need to determine if some combination of general controls needs to be tested.

- Applications controls considerations

  — Normally, a test of one specific instance of an automated application control is a relevant basis for concluding on that control's effectiveness. However, the auditor would also need to confirm the deployment and operational effectiveness of general controls over access and program changes that help ensure the integrity of application controls.

  — When considering whether to use audit evidence for automated control testing from prior audits, the auditor should consider the effectiveness of general controls that help ensure the integrity of application controls. Evidence of highly effective general controls, especially change management, will provide a basis for the auditor to reduce, but not eliminate, tests of automated controls.

Tests of Spreadsheets

6.27 Spreadsheets in many cases lack the controls that usually are present for formal, purchased software. Absent audit evidence indicating that appropriate controls over spreadsheets have been implemented, you may continue to need to test spreadsheet controls even after their implementation.

Dual Purpose Tests

6.28 Some audit procedures may simultaneously provide audit evidence that both

- supports the relevant assertion or detects material misstatement, and

- supports a conclusion about the operating effectiveness of related controls.

Tests that achieve both of these objectives concurrently on the same transaction are usually referred to as dual-purpose tests. For example, you may examine an invoice to determine whether it has been approved and also to provide substantive audit evidence about the existence and amount of the transaction.

6.29 When performing a dual purpose test, you may consider whether the design and evaluation of such tests can accomplish both objectives. For example, the population for purposes of testing controls and applying substantive procedures relating to a class of transactions, such as payroll, are the same. However, for an account balance such as accounts receivable, the population for substantive procedures would be the period-end balances, whereas the population for tests of controls would encompass the period during which the period-end balances were generated through sales, cash receipts, and other transactions.

6.30 Furthermore, when performing such tests, you may consider how the outcome of the tests of controls may affect your determination about the extent of substantive procedures to be performed. For example, if controls are found to be ineffective, you would consider whether the sample size you designed for the dual purpose test was adequate or whether the sample size for substantive procedures should be increased from that originally planned.

6.31 You can find additional guidance on the use of dual-purpose tests in paragraphs 2.12–.14 of the AICPA Audit Guide *Audit Sampling*.

Audit Sampling in Tests of Controls

Observations and Suggestions

The guidance in this section applies to the use of audit sampling. However, many of the ideas and concepts presented here may be applicable to tests of controls when sampling is not applicable.

Sampling in the context of controls is discussed in more detail in chapter 3, "Nonstatistical and Statistical Audit Sampling in Tests of Controls, of the AICPA Audit Guide *Audit Sampling*.

6.32   Audit sampling for tests of controls is in many cases appropriate when application of the control leaves documentary evidence of performance and the performance of the control takes place too many times to be able to examine each operation. Audit sampling for tests of controls that do not leave such evidence (such as some automated controls or other controls that can only be observed) might be appropriate, however, when you are able to plan the audit sampling procedures early in the engagement. For example, you might wish to observe the performance of prescribed control activities for bridge toll collections. In that case, a sample of days and locations for observation of actual activities would be selected. You need to plan the sampling procedure to allow for observation of the performance of such activities on days selected from the period under audit.

Some Tests of Controls May Not Involve Audit Sampling

6.33   Sampling concepts do not apply for some tests of controls. For example

- tests of automated application controls are often tested only once or a few times when effective IT general controls are present.

- sampling may not be applicable to analyses of controls for determining the appropriate segregation of duties (unless you are testing the client's documented analysis of the segregation of duties or a documented schedule of password permissions in an IT environment) or other analyses that do not yield documentary evidence of performance.

- sampling may not apply to tests of certain documented controls or to analyses of the effectiveness of security and access controls (unless examining a client's schedule of password permissions).

- sampling may not apply to some tests directed toward obtaining audit evidence about the operating effectiveness of the control environment or the accounting system. Some examples are the inquiry or observation of the effectiveness of the actions of those charged with governance or assessing the competence of key accounting personnel.

6.34   In addition, when the performance of a control is not documented or evidenced, such as the performance of an automated control where no record of the control performance is retained, the concept of sampling such a control in the conventional sense may not be meaningful. For example, such a test may be performed contemporaneously with its occurrence or tested with a *test deck* of data with known properties that are designed to test the programming of the automated controls. The extent of testing and the periods included in the test are determined based on the quality of the related IT general controls. Such tests often do not involve audit sampling.

General Considerations When Audit Sampling Is Used in Tests of Controls

6.35   This section provides a brief summary of the matters to consider when you plan to use audit sampling in your tests of controls. Chapter 3 of the AICPA Audit Guide *Audit Sampling* provides more detailed guidance.

                                                    ©2016, AICPA

Defining the Deviation Conditions

6.36 Based on your understanding of internal control, you may often identify the characteristics that would indicate performance of the control you plan to test. You then may define the possible deviation conditions. For tests of controls, a deviation is a departure from the expected performance of the prescribed control. Performance of a control consists of all the steps you believe are necessary to support your assessed level of control risk.

Considering the Population

6.37 You should consider the purpose of the audit procedure and the characteristics of the population from which the sample will be drawn to determine that the population from which the sample will be drawn is appropriate for the specified audit objective. For example, if you wish to test the operating effectiveness of a control designed to ensure that all shipments are billed, it would be ineffective to sample items that have already been billed. Rather, you would sample the population of shipped items to determine whether selected shipments were billed. Similarly, you cannot identify unrecorded liabilities from the population of recorded liabilities. Instead you would examine support for liabilities entered and disbursements made after year end. (AU-C sec. 530 par. .06)

6.38 You will often select sampling units from a physical representation of the population. For example, if you define the population as all approved vendors as of a specific date, the physical representation might be the printout of the approved vendor list as of that date or an electronic file purportedly containing the list of approved vendors.

6.39 You should select items for the sample in such a way that you can reasonably expect the sample to be representative of the relevant population. If the physical representation and the desired population differ, you might make erroneous conclusions about the population. For example, if you wish to perform a test of controls for the vouchers issued in 20XX, such vouchers are the population. If you physically select the vouchers from a filing cabinet, the vouchers in the filing cabinet are the physical representation. If the vouchers in the cabinet represent all the vouchers issued in 20XX, the physical representation and the population are the same. If they are not the same because vouchers have been removed or vouchers issued in other years have been added, the conclusion applies only to the vouchers in the cabinet. (AU-C sec. 530 par. .08)

6.40 Making selections from a controlled source minimizes differences between the physical representation and the population. For example, you might make selections from a cash disbursements journal that has been reconciled with issued checks through a bank reconciliation. You might test the footing to obtain reasonable assurance that the source of selection contains the same transactions as the population.

6.41 If you determine that items are missing from the physical representation, you would select a new physical representation or perform alternate procedures on the missing items. You ordinarily will inquire about the reason that items are missing.

Defining the Sampling Unit

6.42 The individual items constituting a population are sampling units. (AU-C sec. 530 par. .05) A sampling unit for tests of controls may be, for example, a document, an entry, or a line item where examination of the sampling unit provides evidence of the operation of the control. Each sampling unit constitutes one item in the population. You may define the sampling unit in light of the control being tested. For example, if the test objective is to determine whether disbursements have been authorized and the prescribed control requires an authorized signature on the voucher before processing, the sampling unit might be defined as the voucher. On the other hand, if one voucher pays several invoices and the prescribed control requires each invoice to be authorized individually, the line item on the voucher representing the invoice might be defined as the sampling unit. Note that each sampling unit may provide evidence of the application of more than one control. For example, support for recording a receivable may indicate that the billed service was rendered or product shipped, the amounts were checked for accuracy, and the customer is listed on the approved customer list.

Observations and Suggestions

An overly broad definition of the sampling unit might not be efficient. For example, if you are testing a control over the pricing of invoices and each invoice contains up to 10 items, you could define the sampling unit as an individual invoice or as a line item on the invoice. If you define the invoice as the sampling unit, you would test all the line items on the invoice. If you define the line items as the sampling unit, only the selected line items need be tested. If either sampling unit definition is appropriate to achieve the test objective, it is commonly more efficient to define the sampling unit as the more detailed alternative (in this case, a line item).

An important efficiency consideration in selecting a sampling unit is the manner in which the documents are filed and cross-referenced. For example, if a test of purchases starts from the purchase order, it might not be possible to locate the voucher and canceled check in some accounting systems because the systems have been designed to provide an audit trail from voucher to purchase order but not necessarily vice versa.

Determining the Method of Selecting the Sample

6.43 Sample items should be selected in such a way so the sample can be expected to be representative of the population and thus the results can be projected to the population. Therefore, all items in the population should have an opportunity to be selected. Paragraphs 3.30–.36 of the AICPA Audit Guide *Audit Sampling* provide additional guidance on selecting a sample. (AU-C sec. 530 par. .08)

Determining the Timing of Tests of Controls

6.44 The timing of your tests of controls affects the relevance and reliability of the resulting audit evidence. In general, the relevance and reliability of the audit evidence obtained diminishes as time passes between the testing of the controls and the end of the period under audit. For this reason, when tests of controls are performed during an interim period or carried forward from a previous audit, you should determine what additional audit evidence should be obtained to support a conclusion on the current operating effectiveness of those controls.

6.45 The timing of your tests of controls depends on your objective:

    a. When controls are tested as of a point in time, you have obtained audit evidence that the controls operated effectively only at that time.

    b. If you test controls throughout a period, you obtain audit evidence of the effectiveness of the operation of the control during that period.

(AU-C sec. 330 par. .11)

6.46 Audit evidence pertaining only to a point in time may be sufficient for your purpose, for example, when testing controls over the client's physical inventory counting at the period end. If, on the other hand, you need audit evidence of the effectiveness of a control over a period, audit evidence pertaining only to a point in time may be insufficient, and you may find it necessary to supplement your tests with others that provide audit evidence that the control operated effectively during the period under audit. For example, for an automated control, you may test the operation of the control at a particular point in time. You then may perform tests of controls to determine whether the control operated consistently during the audit period, or you may test with the intention of relying on general controls pertaining to the modification and use of that computer program during the audit period. (AU-C sec. 330 par. .11)

6.47 The tests you perform to supplement tests of controls at a point of time may be part of your tests of controls over your client's monitoring of controls.

6.48 *For example, suppose that the auditor tested Ownco's reconciliation of the accounts receivable trial balance to the general ledger account total for one month. That test provides evidence that the control operated effectively at that point in time, and so to draw a conclusion about the operating effectiveness of the control for the entire period, the auditor would have to supplement the one test. The auditor's test of Ownco's monitoring of this reconciliation may provide some additional audit evidence needed. Suppose that the controller monitors the performance of the control by making a timely review of each monthly reconciliation. If the auditor obtains evidence that the controller's review operated effectively during the period, the auditor may have sufficient audit evidence from his tests, including from the monitoring control to conclude that the reconciliation also operated effectively during the period.*

Updating Tests of Controls Performed During an Interim Period

6.49 You may test controls as of or for a period that ends prior to the balance sheet date. This date often is referred to as the "interim date" or "interim period." The period of time between the interim date or period and the balance sheet date often is referred to as the "remaining period."

6.50 When you test controls during an interim period or as of an interim date, you should

    a. obtain audit evidence about the nature and extent of any significant changes in internal control that occurred during the remaining period, and

    b. determine what additional audit evidence should be obtained for the remaining period. Table 6-1 summarizes the factors you should consider when making this determination.

(AU-C sec. 330 par. .12)

Table 6-1
Updating Tests of Controls From an Interim Date
to the Balance Sheet Date

To determine what additional audit evidence you should obtain to update tests of controls performed in advance of the balance sheet date, you may consider

a. the significance of the assessed *risks of material misstatement* at the relevant assertion level.

b. the specific controls that were tested during the interim period.

c. the degree to which audit evidence about the operating effectiveness of those controls was obtained.

d. the length of the remaining period.

e. the extent to which the auditor intends to reduce further substantive procedures based on the reliance of controls.

f. the control environment.

g. the volume or value of transactions processed in the remaining period.

6.51 When you test controls as of or during an interim period, you should obtain evidence about the nature and extent of any significant changes in internal control, including personnel performing the control, that occur during the remaining period. If significant changes do occur, you may consider the effects on the audit strategy and audit plan, and you may revise your understanding of internal control and consider testing the changed controls. Alternatively, you may consider performing substantive analytical procedures or tests of details covering the remaining period. (AU-C sec. 330 par. .12)

6.52 You may obtain additional evidence about the operating effectiveness of controls during the remaining period by performing procedures such as

a. extending the testing of the operating effectiveness of controls over the remaining period, or

b. testing the client's monitoring of controls.

6.53 Procedures you may perform during the remaining period include

- inquiries and observations related to the performance of the control, the monitoring of the control, or any changes to the control during the remaining period.

- a walkthrough covering the period between the interim date and the period end.

- the same procedures you performed at interim, but directed to the period from interim to period end.

Observations and Suggestions

If you use audit sampling to test controls, you consider how your sampling plan will be affected by your decision to test controls as of an interim date. For example, if you define the population to include transactions from the entire period under audit, you can allocate your sample between transactions that occurred during the interim period and those that are expected to occur during the remaining period.

For example, if in the first 10 months of the year the client issued invoices numbered from 1 to 10,000, you might estimate that another 2,500 invoices will be issued during the remaining 2 months and use 1 to 12,500 as the numerical sequence for selecting the desired sample. Invoices with numbers 1 to 10,000 would be subjected to possible selection during the interim work, and the remaining 2,500 invoices would be subject to sampling during the completion of the audit.

Use of Audit Evidence Obtained in Prior Audits

6.54 If certain conditions are met, you may use audit evidence obtained in prior audits to support your conclusion about the operating effectiveness of controls in the current audit. (This approach is not available for *significant risks*.) If you plan to use evidence obtained in prior periods, you should consider

- a. whether the use of this evidence is appropriate and, if so,
- b. the length of the time period that may elapse before retesting the control.

(AU-C sec. 330 par. .13)

Table 6-2 summarizes the factors you may consider when determining whether to use audit evidence about the operating effectiveness you obtained in a prior audit.

Table 6-2

Considerations When Determining Whether to Use Audit Evidence From Prior Audits

	Appropriateness of Using Evidence From Prior Audit		Length of Time Before Retesting Control	
	May Be Appropriate	May Not Be Appropriate	Longer	Shorter
Effectiveness of control environment, the client's risk assessment, monitoring, and IT general controls	Effective design and operation	Evidence of poor design or operation	Effective design and operation	Evidence of poor design or operation
Risk arising from characteristics of the control	Largely automated control	Significant manual or judgmental component to control	Largely automated control	Significant manual or judgmental component to control
Changes in circumstances at the client that may require changes in controls, including personnel changes that affect application of the control	Minor changes in client circumstances, including personnel	Significant changes in client circumstances, including personnel	Minor changes in client circumstances, including personnel	Significant changes in client circumstances, including personnel
Operating effectiveness of the control	Control operated effectively in prior audit	Control did not operate effectively in prior audit	Control operated effectively in prior audit	Control did not operate effectively in prior audit
Risks of material misstatement	Low risk of material misstatement for relevant assertion	High risk of material misstatement for relevant assertion	Low risk of material misstatement for relevant assertion	High risk of material misstatement for relevant assertion
Extent of reliance on the control to design substantive procedures	Low reliance on the control	High reliance on the control	Low reliance on the control	High reliance on the control

6.55 If you plan to use audit evidence about the operating effectiveness of controls obtained in prior audits, you should

    a. obtain audit evidence about whether changes in those specific controls have occurred subsequent to the prior audit, and

    b. perform audit procedures to establish the continuing relevance of audit evidence obtained in the prior audit.

(AU-C sec. 330 par. .14)

6.56 Even when you use audit evidence about the operating effectiveness of controls obtained in prior periods, you still should evaluate the design effectiveness and implementation of controls in the current period. The procedures performed as described in paragraph 6.55 may help you to fulfill this responsibility; however, you may have to supplement these procedures with others. For example, if the controls have not changed from the previous period but the client's business process have changed, you will need to determine whether the design of controls remains effective in light of the changed business processes.

6.57 You may not rely on audit evidence about the operating effectiveness of controls obtained in prior audits for controls that

    a. have changed significantly since the prior audit,

    b. pertain to business processes that have changed significantly since the prior audit, or

    c. mitigate significant risks. (Paragraphs 5.30–.37 of this guide describe the designation of certain risks as *significant risks*.)

For any control that meets one of the previously mentioned criteria, you should test operating effectiveness in the current audit.

(AU-C sec. 330 par. .14*a*)

6.58 For example, changes in a system that enable an entity to receive a new report from the system probably is not a significant change and therefore is unlikely to affect the relevance of prior-period audit evidence. On the other hand, a change that causes data to be accumulated or calculated differently probably is significant and therefore does affect the relevance of audit evidence obtained in the prior period, in which case the operating effectiveness of the control should be tested in the current period.

Rotating Emphasis on Tests of Controls

6.59 When you plan to rely on controls that have not changed since they were last tested, you should test the operating effectiveness of these controls at least once every third audit. There also may be some controls, such as over revenue recognition or inventories that, due to their importance to the client financial statements, might be subject to testing every two years or every year, depending on the risks, even when there are purported to be no changes in controls. (AU-C sec. 330 par. .14*b*)

6.60 When there are a number of controls for which you plan to use audit evidence obtained in prior audits, you may wish to test the operating effectiveness of *some* controls each audit. However, when you are testing controls for only one or two key classes of transactions in an entity, rotating the testing of these controls may not be warranted.

6.61 *For example, the auditors of Young Fashion tested controls related to certain assertions for revenue recognition, receivables, and inventory. All of these* *tests were performed in Year 1. Assuming that none of the controls changed, the auditor should test them again at least once every third audit, in this case, Year 4. However, the auditor also should test some controls each audit. Therefore, the auditor may test all three groups of controls in Year 4 but might test some of them in Years 2 and 3 as well.*

Furthermore, even when controls are not being tested between testing years, you should have a basis for asserting that the controls have not changed, such as through inquiries, walkthroughs, or other evidence.

Determining the Extent of Tests of Controls

6.62   The extent of your tests of controls affects the sufficiency of the audit evidence you obtain to support the auditor's assessment of the operating effectiveness of controls. You should obtain more persuasive audit evidence the greater your reliance placed on the effectiveness of a control. (AU-C sec. 330 par. .09) As such, you may increase the extent of testing the controls to obtain the desired level of assurance that the controls are operating effectively

   a.   at the relevant assertion level, and

   b.   either throughout the period, or as of the point in time when you plan to rely on the control.

Table 6-3 summarizes the factors you may consider in determining the extent of your tests of controls.

Table 6-3
Factors to Consider When Determining the Extent of Tests of Controls

Factors you may consider in determining the extent of tests of controls include the following:

   a. The frequency of the performance of the control by the entity during the period.

   b. The length of time during the audit period that the auditor is relying on the operating effectiveness of the control.

   c. The relevance and reliability of the audit evidence to be obtained in supporting that the control prevents, or detects and corrects, material misstatements at the relevant assertion level.

   d. The extent to which audit evidence is obtained from tests of other controls that meet the same audit objective.

   e. The extent to which the auditor plans to rely on the operating effectiveness of the control in the assessment of risk (and thereby reduce substantive procedures based on the reliance of such control). The more the auditor relies on the operating effectiveness of controls in the assessment of risk, the greater is the extent of the auditor's tests of controls.

   f. The expected deviation from the control. (See paragraph 6.75.)

Sampling Considerations

6.63   You may consider using an audit sampling technique to determine the extent of tests whenever the control is applied on a transaction basis (for example, matching approved purchase orders to supplier invoices) and it is applied frequently. When a control is applied periodically (for example, monthly reconciliations of accounts receivable subsidiary ledger to the general ledger), you might consider guidance appropriate for testing smaller populations (for example, testing the control application for two months and reviewing evidence the control operated in other months or reviewing other months for unusual items). AU-C section 530, *Audit Sampling* (AICPA, *Professional Standards*), and paragraphs 3.37–.63 of the AICPA Audit Guide *Audit Sampling* provide further guidance on the application of sampling techniques to determine the extent of testing of controls. The AICPA Audit Guide *Audit Sampling* also provides guidance for testing in smaller populations.

6.64 As indicated in table 6-3, you may consider the expected deviation from the control when determining the extent of tests. As the rate of expected deviation from a control increases, the extent of testing of the control will increase. However, if the rate of expected deviation is expected to be too high, you may determine that tests of controls for a particular assertion may not be effective. In this case you may conclude that a control deficiency exists and you should consider its severity and whether it should be communicated to those charged with governance or management. A control deficiency exists when the observed rate of deviation exceeds the expected rate of deviation used in designing the controls test.

The Use of Walkthroughs as a Test of Controls

6.65 As described in paragraphs 3.122–.125 of this guide, a walkthrough of a transaction process does not involve audit sampling. However, it may be one observation that is part of evidence gathering. A walkthrough may be designed to provide evidence regarding just the design and implementation of controls. However, a walkthrough may be designed to include procedures that are also tests of the operating effectiveness of relevant controls (for instance, inquiry combined with observation, inspection of documents, or reperformance). If such procedures are performed in the context of a walkthrough, you may consider whether the procedures have been performed at an adequate level to obtain some evidence regarding the operating effectiveness of the control. Such a determination would depend on

- the nature of the control (for example, automated versus manual), and
- the nature of your procedures to test the control (for example, inquiry about the entire year and observation versus examination of documents or reperformance).

6.66 For example, when a walkthrough includes inquiry and observation of the people involved in executing a control and where you are satisfied that a strong control environment and adequate monitoring are in place, you may conclude that the process provides some evidence about operating effectiveness. You use professional judgment to evaluate the extent of evidence obtained. In some cases, the procedures performed during the walkthrough may provide sufficient evidence of operating effectiveness (for example, for a fully automated control procedure in a system with effective IT general controls). In other cases, you may conclude that the procedures performed during the walkthrough provide evidence to reduce but not eliminate other control testing.

6.67 If you perform procedures that are a test of operating effectiveness of a control as part of a walkthrough, you may consider whether additional instances of the operation of the control need to be examined to support a conclusion regarding the control's operating effectiveness.

6.68 If an audit sample of repeated occurrences of a control is deemed necessary (for example, examining documentation relating to a manual control), the test of controls performed in the context of the walkthrough may be considered to yield the evidence regarding operating effectiveness that comes from a sample size of one for each item and control point walked through the system. In such circumstances, you may want to select an audit sample to gather evidence relating to additional instances of the operation of the control in order to obtain a sufficient level of evidence relating to operating effectiveness. When repeated instances of a control's execution are required to draw a conclusion regarding operating effectiveness, the evidence obtained in the context of the walkthrough is in many cases insufficient to conclude that the control is operating effectively.

Extent of Testing IT Controls

6.69 IT processing is, in many cases, consistent. An automated control should function consistently unless the program (including the tables, files, or other permanent data used by the program) is changed. Therefore, you may be able to limit the testing of an IT application control to one or a few instances of the control operation, provided that you determine that related IT general controls operated effectively during the period of reliance.

Evaluating the Operating Effectiveness of Controls at a Service Organization

6.70 When the user auditor's risk assessment includes an expectation that controls at the service organization are operating effectively, the user auditor should obtain audit evidence about the operating effectiveness of those controls from one or more of the following procedures:

  a. Obtaining and reading a type 2 SOC 1 report, if available

  b. Performing appropriate tests of controls at the service organization

  c. Using another auditor to perform tests of controls at the service organization on behalf of the user auditor

Service Organization Controls

6.71 If the user auditor plans to use a type 2 SOC 1 report as audit evidence that controls at the service organization (including subservicers, as applicable) are operating effectively, the user auditor should determine whether the service auditor's report provides sufficient appropriate audit evidence about the effectiveness of the controls to support the user auditor's risk assessment by

  a. evaluating whether the type 2 SOC 1 report is for a period that is appropriate for the user auditor's purposes;

  b. determining whether complementary user entity controls identified by the service organization are relevant in addressing the *risks of material misstatement* relating to the relevant assertions in the user entity's financial statements and, if so, obtaining an understanding of whether the user entity has designed and implemented such controls and, if so, testing their operating effectiveness;

    c. evaluating the adequacy of the time period covered by the tests of controls and the time elapsed since the performance of the tests of controls; and

    d. evaluating whether the tests of controls performed by the service auditor and the results thereof, as described in the service auditor's report, are relevant to the assertions in the user entity's financial statements and provide sufficient appropriate audit evidence to support the user auditor's risk assessment.

(AU-C sec. 402 par. .16–.17)

Fraud, Noncompliance With Laws and Regulations, and Uncorrected Misstatements Related to Activities at the Service Organization

6.72 The user auditor should inquire of management of the user entity about whether the service organization has reported to the user entity, or whether the user entity is otherwise aware of, any fraud, noncompliance with laws and regulations, or uncorrected misstatements affecting the financial statements of the user entity. The user auditor should evaluate how such matters, if any, affect the nature, timing, and extent of the user auditor's further audit procedures, including the effect on the user auditor's conclusions and user auditor's report.

The COSO framework specifies the expectation that the entity will communicate to its service organization the entity's standards of conduct and seek to confirm the service organization understands and is in compliance with the entity's policies.

This may require amendments to working agreements between the entity and the service organization.

Performing Tests of Controls

6.73 After you have planned the nature, timing, and extent of your tests of controls, you will often select the items to be tested to determine whether they contain deviations from the prescribed control. When making those determinations, you may encounter the following circumstances:

- *Voided or unused documents.* You might select a voided item to be tested. For example, you might be performing a test of controls related to the client's vouchers in which you match random numbers with voucher numbers. However, a random number might match with a voucher that has been voided. If you obtain evidence that the voucher has been properly voided and does not represent a deviation from the proscribed control, you may replace the voided voucher.

- *Mistakes in estimating population sequences.* In some circumstances, you will need to estimate your population size and numbering sequence before the transactions have occurred. The most common example of this situation occurs when you perform tests of controls as of an interim date. If you overestimate the population size and numbering sequence, any numbers that are selected as part of the sample and that exceed the actual numbering sequence used are treated as unused documents. If you underestimate the population size and numbering sequence, you may design additional audit procedures to apply to the items not included in your population.

- *Stopping the test before completion.* Occasionally you might find a number of unexpected deviations in auditing the first part of a sample. As a result, you might believe that even if no additional deviations were to be discovered in the remainder of the sample, the results of the sample would not support the planned assessed level of control risk or any reliance on the control being tested. Under these circumstances, you reassess the level of control risk and consider whether it is appropriate to continue the test.

- *Inability to examine selected items.* In some instances you might not be able to examine a selected item (for example, if the document cannot be found). If possible, you should perform alternative procedures to test whether the control was applied as prescribed. If it is not possible to perform alternative procedures, you should consider selected items to be deviations from the controls. Missing documentation is commonly encountered in certain types of fraud as a means to avoid or thwart discovery.

6.74 Paragraphs 3.64–.70 of the AICPA Audit Guide *Audit Sampling* provide more detailed guidance on performing tests of controls.

Assessing the Operating Effectiveness of Controls

Evidence About Operating Effectiveness

6.75 The concept of effectiveness of the operation of controls recognizes that some deviations in the way your client applies the controls may occur. Deviations from prescribed controls may be caused by factors such as changes in key personnel, significant seasonal fluctuations in volume of transactions, and human error.

6.76 When you encounter deviations in the operation of controls, those deviations will have an effect on your assessment of operating effectiveness. A control with an observed non-negligible deviation rate is not an effective control. For example, if you design a test in which you select a sample of, say, 25 items and expect no deviations, the finding of one deviation would be considered a non-negligible deviation because, based on the results of your test of the sample, the desired level of confidence of the test has not been obtained.

6.77 Paragraphs 3.72–.77 of the AICPA Audit Guide *Audit Sampling* provide detailed guidance on how to calculate the deviation rate and options to consider when unexpected deviations appear in the sample.

6.78 There are sources of audit evidence beyond your tests of controls that contribute to your assessment of the operating effectiveness of controls. The extent of misstatements you detect by performing substantive procedures also may alter your judgment about the effectiveness of controls in a negative direction (as described in paragraph 6.04). However, misstatement-free results of substantive procedures do not indicate that a lower assessment of control risk should be substituted for the one supported by the procedures you used to assess control risk. (AU-C sec. 330 par. .16)

Investigating Additional Implications of Identified Deviations

6.79 When you detect control deviations during the performance of tests of controls, you should make specific inquiries to understand these matters and their potential consequences, for example, by inquiring about the timing of personnel changes in key internal control functions. (AU-C sec. 330 par. .17)

6.80 Qualitative aspects of deviations from controls include (1) the nature and cause of the deviations, such as whether they result from fraud or errors, which may arise from misunderstanding of instructions or carelessness, and (2) the possible relationship of the deviations to other phases of the audit. The discovery of fraud ordinarily requires a broader consideration of the possible implications than does the discovery of an error, and it may elevate the severity of the related deficiency in internal control and the importance of the misstatements to designing other audit procedures. The reason for deficiencies in controls may reveal issues related to different COSO principles. For example, a control deficiency arising from a test of the operating effectiveness of the control activities deployed by the entity (principle 12) may be due to ineffective training or hiring practices. This, may affect the conclusions with respect to commitment to competence (principle 4).

6.81 Deviations in the application of control activities may be caused by the ineffective operation of indirect controls such as IT general controls, the control environment, or other components of internal control. To gain an understanding of the deviations in control, you may wish to make inquiries and perform other tests to identify possible weaknesses in the control environment or other indirect controls.

6.82 For example, suppose that one of your client's primary controls related to the existence of inventory—periodic test counts—had several instances where the number of items counted by the count teams did not agree to the actual physical count of the items on hand. When gaining a further understanding of the nature of these deviations, you determine that the underlying cause is poor training of the test count teams and a lack of written instructions. Training and written instructions are indirect controls that may affect the operating effectiveness of controls other than those related to existence. For example, the lack of training and instruction could result in the count teams reporting the wrong product number or description, which also could affect the valuation of inventory. This finding could cause the company and auditor to conclude that a re-count is necessary once the teams are properly trained. Such findings could affect your assessment of the control risk.

Assessing Effectiveness

6.83 After considering the results of tests of controls and any misstatements detected from the performance of substantive procedures, you should determine whether the audit evidence obtained provides an appropriate basis for reliance on the controls. If the reliance on the controls is not warranted, you should determine whether

- the tests provide a basis for reliance on the controls,

- additional tests of controls are necessary, or

- how the potential risks of misstatement will be addressed using substantive procedures.

If you conclude that reliance on certain controls is not warranted, it is unnecessary to perform further tests of those controls.

(AU-C sec. 330 par. .17)

Deficiencies in the Operation of Controls

6.84 You may consider whether deviations in the operation of controls have been caused by an underlying control deficiency. When evaluating the reason for a control deviation, you may consider

- whether the control is automated (in the presence of effective information technology general controls, an automated application control is expected to perform as designed),
- the degree of intervention by entity personnel contributing to the deviation (for example, was the deviation evidence of a possible override), and,
- if management was aware of the deviation, its actions in response to the matter.

If you identify one or more deficiencies in internal control, you should evaluate each deficiency to determine whether, individually or in combination, they constitute significant deficiencies or material weaknesses.

(AU-C sec. 265 par. .09)

6.85 Regardless of the reason for the deviation, numerous or repeated instances of the deviation may constitute a significant deficiency or material weakness. Table 6-4 provides examples of control deficiencies related to deviations you may identify as a result of performing tests of controls. Chapter 7, "Evaluating Audit Findings, Audit Evidence, and Deficiencies in Internal Control," of this guide focuses in more detail on the identification and severity assessment of control deficiencies.

Sampling Considerations

6.86 When you identify control deviations and the deviation rate in the sample exceeds the expected deviation rate used in planning, deficiencies in the design or operating effectiveness of the control are implied. After you gain an understanding of the nature and cause of the deviations (as described in paragraphs 6.84–.87), you then may apply the following approaches:

- Consider whether other indirect controls exist that fully or partially mitigate the deficiency found in the tested control; if so, understand and test those controls to determine the extent to which the control objective is achieved.
- Assess the likelihood and magnitude of the deficiency, as discussed in chapter 7 of this guide.

To apply both approaches at the same time to evaluate a deficiency is ordinarily not appropriate because it would likely understate the severity of the deficiency. However, you could apply the first approach and if not successful in limiting the severity of the deficiency, you could apply the upper limit approach (the second approach) as described in paragraphs 3.84–.91 of the AICPA Audit Guide *Audit Sampling*.

Table 6-4
Example Control Deficiencies From Failures in the Operation of Controls

The following are examples of circumstances that may be control deficiencies of some magnitude:

- Failure in the operation of properly designed controls within a significant account or process, for example, the failure of a control such as dual authorization for significant disbursements within the purchasing process.

- Failure of the information and communication component of internal control to provide complete and accurate output because of deficiencies in timeliness, completeness, or accuracy, for example, the failure to obtain timely and accurate consolidating information from remote locations that is needed to prepare the financial statements.

- Failure of controls designed to safeguard assets from loss, damage, or misappropriation. For example, a company uses security devices to safeguard its inventory (preventive controls) and also performs periodic physical inventory counts (detective control) timely in relation to its financial reporting. However, a preventive control failure may be mitigated by an effective detective control that prevents the misstatement of the financial statements. Suppose the inventory security control fails. Although the physical inventory count does not safeguard the inventory from theft or loss, it prevents a material misstatement to the financial statements if performed effectively and timely (near or at the reporting date). In the absence of a timely count, a deficient preventive control may be a deficiency in internal control of some magnitude.

- Failure to perform reconciliations of significant accounts, for example, accounts receivable subsidiary ledgers are not reconciled to the general ledger account in a timely or accurate manner.

- Undue bias or lack of objectivity by those responsible for accounting decisions, for example, consistent under accruals of expenses or overstatement of allowances at the direction of management.

- Misrepresentation by client personnel to the auditor (an indicator of fraud).

- Management override of controls that would enable the entity to prepare financial statements in accordance with generally accepted accounting principles (GAAP).

- Failure of an application control caused by a deficiency in the design or operation of an IT general control.

- An observed deviation rate that exceeds the number of deviations you expected when you designed a test of the operating effectiveness of a control. For example, if you design a test in which you select a sample and expect no deviations, the finding of one deviation is a nonnegligible deviation rate because, based on the results of your test of the sample, the desired level of confidence was not obtained.

6.87 Illustration 6-2 summarizes your considerations related to tests of controls.

Illustration 6-2
Considerations Relating to Tests of Controls

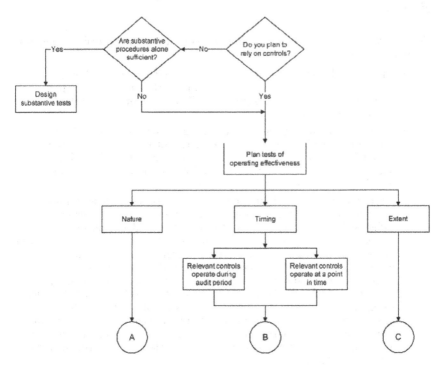

                                    ©2016, AICPA

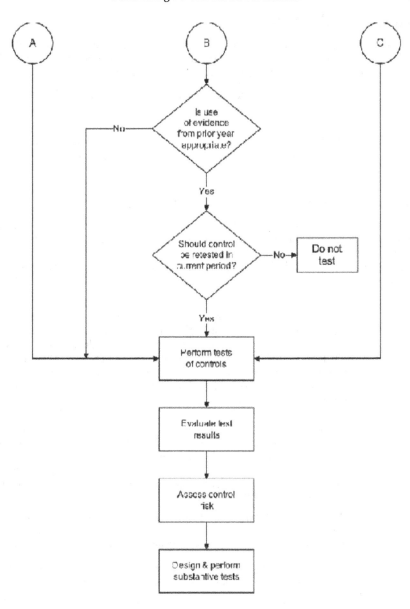

Substantive Procedures

6.88 The objective of your substantive procedures is to detect individual misstatements that alone or in the aggregate cause material misstatements at the assertion level. Substantive procedures include the following:

- Tests of details of classes of transactions, account balances, and disclosures.

- Analytical procedures. AU-C section 520, *Analytical Procedures* (AICPA, *Professional Standards*), provides guidance on the application of analytical procedures as substantive procedures.

(AU-C sec. 330 par. .04)

Substantive Procedures You Should Perform on Every Audit

6.89 Your substantive procedures[1] should be responsive to your assessed risks of material misstatement. However, you should design and perform substantive procedures for all relevant assertions related to each material class of transactions, account balances, or disclosures regardless of your risk assessment because your risk assessment may not identify all risks. (AU-C sec. 330 par. .06–.07 and .18)

- *Substantive procedures of material items.* You should perform substantive procedures for all relevant assertions for each material class of transactions, account balance, and disclosure. For example, if you determine that long-term debt is a material account, you should perform substantive procedures for all assertions that are relevant to long-term debt, even if you have determined that it is unlikely that the assertion could contain a material misstatement. You may determine that the risk of the entity not having the obligation to repay the debt is low, but nevertheless, you should perform a substantive procedure (for example, confirming the terms of the debt with the lender) to address the risk. Because the account is material, you are precluded from relying solely on risk assessment procedures or tests of controls to support your conclusion. (AU-C sec. 330 par. .18)

- *Substantive procedures related to the financial statement closing process.* On all your engagements you should include audit procedures related to the financial statement closing process, such as

  - agreeing the financial statements, including their accompanying notes, to the underlying accounting records.

  - examining material journal entries and other adjustments made during the course of preparing the financial statements.

The nature and extent of your examination of journal entries and other adjustments depend on the nature and complexity of the client's financial reporting system and the associated risks of material misstatement.

(AU-C sec. 330 par. .21)

---

[1] Substantive procedures include both substantive analytical procedures and substantive tests of detail.

                                                      ©2016, AICPA

Observations and Suggestions

Coordination With AU-C section 240

AU-C section 240, *Consideration of Fraud in a Financial Statement Audit* (AICPA, *Professional Standards*), directs the auditor to test the appropriateness of journal entries and other adjustments (for example, entries posted directly to financial statement drafts) in order to identify misstatements due to fraud.

The guidance provided by AU-C section 240 may help you design the nature, timing, and extent of testing of journal entries required by AU-C section 330, *Performing Audit Procedures in Response to Assessed Risks and Evaluating the Audit Evidence Obtained* (AICPA, *Professional Standards*). In addition, the tests of journal entries and adjustments you perform to meet the requirements of AU-C section 240 may be done concurrently with the tests of journal entries required by AU-C section 330. However, the nature, timing, and extent of procedures required under AU-C section 240 are different from those required under AU-C section 330. Therefore, the tests performed solely for one standard will not necessarily satisfy all requirements of the other. Care needs to be taken that the designed procedures can satisfy both purposes. For example,

- AU-C section 330 directs you to examine material journal entries and other adjustments made during the course of preparing the financial statements. Although AU-C section 240 acknowledges that your tests of journal entries might focus on year-end entries and adjustments, you may also consider testing journal entries that were made throughout the period under audit.
- AU-C section 330 directs you to examine all material journal en-tries and other adjustments. AU-C section 240 requires you to consider materiality and additional factors when determining which journal entries to examine.

Supporting Documentation

Your client may use a spreadsheet application to provide the information supporting their journal entries and adjustments. As previously indicated, the controls related to spreadsheet applications in many cases are not designed effectively, and so you may often want to perform other tests of the information produced by the spreadsheet to determine that journal entries, adjustments, and disclosures are proper.

Substantive Procedures Related to Significant Risks

6.90 Paragraphs 5.30–.37 of this guide define and describe *significant risks*, which arise on most audits and which require special audit consideration. When your audit approach to significant risks consists only of substantive procedure, your substantive procedures should include tests of details.

Audit evidence in the form of external confirmations received directly by you from appropriate confirming parties may assist you in obtaining audit evidence with the high level of reliability that you require to respond to *significant risks* of material misstatement.

(AU-C sec. 330 par. .22)

Nature of Substantive Procedures

6.91 To address any given assertion, your substantive procedures to detect material misstatements may consist of either tests of details or substantive analytical procedures, or both. In general, substantive analytical procedures are more applicable to large volumes of transactions that tend to be predictable over time.

6.92 Determining the mix of substantive procedures to perform depends on the *risks of material misstatement*. As the *risks of material misstatement* for a given assertion increase, the reliability of the audit evidence needed also increase. For example, you may determine that there is a relatively high risk of material misstatement related to the valuation of goodwill but a relatively low risk related to valuation of fixed assets. As such, the substantive procedures you perform to address the valuation of goodwill should provide more reliable audit evidence than those performed related to the valuation of fixed assets. (AU-C sec. 330 par. .07)

6.93 In designing substantive procedures related to the existence or occurrence assertion, you may select from items contained in a financial statement amount and should obtain the relevant audit evidence. On the other hand, in designing audit procedures related to the completeness assertion, you may select from audit evidence indicating that an item should be included in the relevant financial statement amount and should investigate whether that item is so included. A common example is examining subsequent cash disbursements to determine that accrued liabilities were complete as of year-end. The knowledge you gained by understanding the client's business and its environment may be helpful in selecting the nature, timing, and extent of audit procedures related to the completeness assertion.

Tests of Details

6.94 *Reliability of tests of details.* Table 2-7 and other text in chapter 2, "Key Concepts Underlying the Auditor's Risk Assessment Process," of this guide provide guidance on assessing the reliability of various types of audit evidence. Reviewing this guidance can help you determine the nature of your substantive procedure.

6.95 *For example, Ownco is involved in a dispute with a former employee who was terminated for cause and who now is seeking unemployment compensation. The outcome of the matter will affect the company's liability relating to employer's portion of accrued unemployment tax.*

To gather evidence relating to the matter, the auditor may perform tests of details, including making inquiries of management or requesting an opinion from the company's legal counsel. An inquiry of management will produce audit evidence that is based on an oral statement by someone inside the company—which many times is less reliable than a document prepared by a knowledgeable source outside the entity (which is the evidence the auditor would obtain if the auditor requested and received a letter from the company's legal counsel).

Either one of these substantive procedures may be appropriate, depending on the auditor's assessment of the risks of material misstatement relating to the accuracy of the unemployment tax accrual. If the auditor assesses that risk and exposure to be relatively high, more reliable audit evidence is needed (the letter from the attorney). If the assessed risk and exposure is low, less reliable audit evidence is needed.

                                                    ©2016, AICPA

Substantive Analytical Procedures

6.96 When designing substantive analytical procedures, you may consider matters such as

- the suitability of using substantive analytical procedures, given the assertions. Analytical procedures may not be suitable for all assertions. For example, transactions subject to management discretion (such as a decision to delay advertising expenses) may lack the predictability between periods or financial statement accounts that is necessary to perform and effective analytical procedure.
- the reliability of the data, whether internal or external, from which the expectation of recorded amounts or ratios is developed. To assess the reliability of the data used in a substantive analytical procedure, you may consider its source and the conditions under which it was gathered.
- whether the expectation is sufficiently precise to identify the possibility of a material misstatement at the desired level of assurance. The precision of your expectation depends on (among other things)
  - your identification and consideration of factors that significantly affect the amount being audited (for example, contributions to an employee 401(k) plan depends on compensation expense and the percentage of the employer contribution committed to by management).
  - the level of data used to develop your expectation. In many cases, expectations developed at a detailed level may have a greater chance of detecting a material misstatement than do broad comparisons.
- the amount of any difference in recorded amounts from expected values that is acceptable. The smaller the difference between your expected amount and the recorded amount that you can accept, the more precise your expectation should be.
- the risk of management override of controls. Management override of controls might result in adjustments to the financial statements outside of the normal financial reporting process, which may result in artificial changes to the financial statement relationships being analyzed. These artificial relationships may result in you drawing erroneous conclusions about your substantive analytical procedures.

Paragraphs .A47–.A54 of AU-C section 240 direct you to perform certain procedures to assess the risk of management override of controls.

The AICPA publication *Management Override of Controls: The Achilles Heel of Fraud Prevention* is available at www.aicpa.org/ForThePublic/Audit CommitteeEffectiveness/DownloadableDocuments/achilles_heel.pdf.

The Reliability of Data Used in Analytical Procedures

6.97 Ultimately, the reliability of your substantive analytical procedures depends on the reliability of the data used in your analysis. Even if all other relevant factors indicate that your analytical procedures are reliable, the ultimate reliability of your procedure will be compromised if the underlying data is not reliable. Table 6-5 summarizes factors that affect the reliability of data used for analytical procedures.

Table 6-5
Factors That Affect the Reliability of Data Used in Analytical Procedures

The following factors may influence your consideration of the reliability of data for performing analytical procedures:

- Whether the data was obtained from independent sources outside the entity or from sources within the entity
- If data was obtained from sources outside the entity, the credibility of those sources, for example, whether data obtained from Internet sources is reliable
- Whether the sources within the entity were independent of those who are responsible for the amount being audited
- Whether the data was developed under a reliable system with effectively designed (and, for high reliance on analytical procedures, operating) controls
- Whether the data was subjected to audit testing in the current or prior year
- Whether the expectations were developed using data from a variety of sources

(AU-C sec. 540, par. .A17–.A20.)

6.98   You may consider testing the controls over your client's preparation of information you use in applying analytical procedures. Frequently, it is more efficient for you to test controls rather than establish the reliability of the data by performing other audit tests over individual reports.

6.99   *For example, Young Fashions stores all data related to production, shipping, and sales, in a central database. This database is then accessed to produce a wide variety of reports of both financial and nonfinancial data. The auditors use these reports to perform analytical procedures on a number of items, including revenue, cost of sales, sales commissions, inventory obsolescence, sales returns, and bad debt allowance.*

Testing controls over the information processing system allows the auditor to establish the reliability of the data for all reports used in their analytical procedures, which is more efficient than performing tests to determine the reliability of each and every report.

6.100   Paragraphs .A7–.A9 of AU-C section 520 provide additional guidance on the design of substantive analytical procedures.

The Use of Computer Assisted Audit Techniques in Substantive Procedures

6.101   CAATs may be used to facilitate tests of details of classes of transactions, account balances, and disclosures. When using CAATs, you will want to have comfort that the data has integrity and that there are controls over that data. Once those conditions have been met, CAATs allow you to use the client's data files to assess transactional and supporting data. CAATs allow you to take vast amounts of normalized data and integrate and analyze that data, allowing you to

- identify data that is potentially an outlier or anomaly and
- perform sample size determination, selections, and results projections.

6.102 The following are examples of substantive procedures you may perform using CAATs:

- Recalculation including the use of CAATs to recalculate report balance
- Reperformance
- Analytical procedures including using CAATs to test journal entry files for unusual entries (for example, Benford's Law test for suspicious digital frequencies or numerical sequences)

Observations and Suggestions

CAATs enable you to expand the extent of your substantive procedures. For instance, when testing an entity's transactions, of which there may be thousands or more, CAATs allow you to test across the entire population for specific characteristics as opposed to being limited to a sample of items. In general, the use of CAATs can provide you more flexibility and evidence than more traditional substantive procedures, perhaps at a lower cost. Once they are established, updating CAATs can be done with relative ease because it involves gaining access to current data (transactional information) and performing the same audit procedures as before to cover the remaining time period.

Timing of Substantive Procedures

Substantive Procedures Performed at an Interim Date

6.103 In some circumstances, you may choose to perform substantive procedures at an interim date. When you perform procedures as of a date before year end, you increase the risk that you will fail to detect a material misstatement that may exist at year end. This risk increases as the length of the period between your interim tests and year end increases and as the contents of an account change. Table 6-6 summarizes factors you may consider when determining whether to perform substantive procedures at an interim date.

Table 6-6
Matters to Consider in Determining Whether to Perform Substantive Procedures at an Interim Date

Factor to Consider	Likelihood of Performing Substantive Procedures at an Interim Date	
	More Likely	Less Likely
Control environment and other relevant controls	Effectively designed or operating controls, including the control environment	Ineffectively designed or operating controls, including the control environment
The availability of information for the remaining period	Information is available that will allow you to perform procedures related to the remaining period.	Lack of information necessary to perform procedures related to the remaining period
Assessed risk	Lower risk of material misstatement for the relevant assertion	Higher risk of material misstatement for the relevant assertion
Nature of transactions or account balances and relevant assertions	Year-end balances are reasonably predictable with respect to amount, relative significance, and composition.	Year-end balances can fluctuate significantly from interim balances, for example, due to rapidly changing business conditions, seasonality of business, transactions that are subject to management's discretion, or volume of transactions naturally passing through an account.
Ability to perform audit procedures to cover remaining period	You will be able to perform all necessary procedures to cover the remaining period.	Your ability to perform procedures relating to the remaining period is limited, for example, by a lack of available information.

6.104 The objective of some of the tests may make the results of the tests irrelevant if performed at an interim date. For example, tests related to the preparation of the financial statements or the client's compliance with debt covenants in many cases provide relevant audit evidence only if performed at the period end.

6.105 In addition to those items described in table 6-6, the circumstances of the engagement may result in you performing certain tests at an interim date. For example, your client may require you to identify all material misstatements shortly after year end (which is common for companies that wish to issue a press release of their earnings for the period). In that situation, you may decide to confirm receivables prior to year end because the time period between the end of the period and the release of earnings is too short to allow you to send and receive confirmations of customers and to complete your test work.

6.106 Your ability to perform audit procedures relating to the remaining period depends a great deal on whether the client's accounting system is able to provide the information you need to perform your procedures. That information should be sufficient to allow you to investigate

    a. significant unusual transactions or entries (including those at or near the period end).

    b. other causes of significant fluctuations or fluctuations that did not occur.

    c. changes in the composition of the classes of transactions or account balances.

6.107 In addition to those items listed in table 6-2, when performing substantive procedures at an interim date, you also may consider whether related audit procedures are coordinated properly. This consideration includes, for example

- coordinating the audit procedures applied to related-party transactions and balances.
- coordinating the testing of interrelated accounts and accounting cutoffs.
- maintaining temporary audit control over assets that are readily negotiable and simultaneously testing such assets and cash on hand and in banks, bank loans, and other related items.

6.108 When you perform substantive procedures at an interim date, you should cover the remaining period by performing

    a. substantive procedures, combined with tests of controls for the intervening period, or

    b. if you determine that it is sufficient, further substantive procedures only, that provide a reasonable basis for extending the audit conclusion from the interim date to the period end.

(AU-C sec. 330 par. .23)

6.109 When you perform substantive procedures at an interim date, you may reconcile the account balance at the interim date to the balance in the same account at year end. The reconciliation may allow you to

- identify amounts that appear unusual.
- investigate these amounts.
- perform substantive analytical procedures or tests of details to test the intervening period.

6.110 If you detect misstatements in classes of transactions or account balances at an interim date that you did not expect when assessing the risks of material misstatement you should evaluate whether

- your assessment of risk and the
- nature, timing or extent of your planned substantive procedures covering the remaining period need to be modified.

(AU-C sec. 330 par. .24)

Observations and Suggestions

Paragraph 6.110 describes the matters you should evaluate when you detect misstatements in a class of transactions or account balance at an interim date. To comply with this guidance, it will help if you consider the underlying cause or causes of the misstatement. For example, suppose that you confirm accounts receivable as of October 31, and as a result of that procedure, discover that your client recorded the same sale twice. Both revenue and accounts receivable will be overstated and inventory will be understated as a result of this error.

To determine whether your initial assessment of risk remains appropriate and your planned substantive procedures for the remaining period are adequate, you will want to consider the reason the client billed its customer twice. Was it due to poorly designed controls over sales or to some other factor? The answer to that question will help you determine the most appropriate procedures to perform during the remaining period. For example, if poorly designed controls were the cause of the misstatement, the audit evidence you obtain from substantive analytical procedures for the remaining period may not be as reliable as it would be if controls were designed effectively.

When you detect misstatements at interim, you also will want to consider how the misstatement, if uncorrected, will affect year-end balances. In the example just discussed, a sale that is recorded twice, if left uncorrected by the client, will affect the account balance for sales and receivables at year end. As such, you will have to evaluate the matter when determining whether the financial statements are materially misstated. (See chapter 7 of this guide for guidance on evaluating audit findings.) On the other hand, the misstatement of inventory may not have any effect on year-end inventory account balance. If the client performed a physical inventory count subsequent to October 31, the misstatement of inventory and cost of sales caused by relieving inventory twice for the same sale most likely would have been detected and corrected through the client's book-to-physical inventory adjustment.

However, even in those circumstances where the known misstatement is corrected by year end (in our example, through the book-to-physical adjustment), it would be important that you should consider whether there might be other misstatements in the December 31 balance that are similar to those you detected at interim. This consideration will affect your judgments about likely misstatement at year end. You may calculate a likely misstatement based on further tests of the year-end balance.

Thus, in determining the effect that misstatements detected as of an interim date have on the final account balances, you will have to consider carefully how the client addressed those misstatements, if at all, during the remaining period as well as how your detection of the known misstatement at interim affects your year-end audit conclusions.

Substantive Procedures Performed in Previous Audits

6.111 In most cases, audit evidence from substantive procedures you performed in a prior audit provides little or no audit evidence for the current period, since balances often change in composition from period to period. However, you may use audit evidence obtained during a prior period in the current period audit, provided both the audit evidence and the related subject matter are fundamentally the same. For example, a legal opinion would continue to be relevant audit evidence if it were received in a prior period related to the structure of a securitization transaction and no changes have occurred during the current period. Whenever you use audit evidence from a prior period in the current audit, you should determine whether changes have occurred since the previous audit that may affect its relevance to the current audit. (AU-C sec. 315 par. .10)

Extent of the Performance of Substantive Procedures

6.112 The greater the risks of material misstatement, the greater the extent of your substantive procedures. However, the nature of your audit procedures is of most importance in responding to assessed risks. Increasing the extent of an audit procedure is appropriate only if the procedure itself is relevant to the specified risk.

6.113 *Considerations for designing tests of details.* When determining the extent of your tests of details, you ordinarily think in terms of sample size. However, you also may consider other matters, including whether it is more effective to use other methods of selecting items for testing, such as selecting large or unusual items from a population, rather than performing sampling or stratifying the population into homogeneous sub-populations for sampling. AU-C section 530 and the AICPA Audit Guide *Audit Sampling* provide guidance on the use of sampling and other means of selecting items for testing.

Adequacy of Presentation and Disclosure

6.114 You should perform audit procedures to evaluate whether the overall presentation of the financial statements—including disclosures—is in accordance with GAAP. The procedures you perform to make this evaluation should be designed after considering the assessed risks of material misstatement. (AU-C sec. 330 par. .26)

6.115 Your evaluation of the financial statements includes consideration of both the individual financial statements and the financial statement disclosures. Your evaluation of disclosures includes matters such as

- the terminology used,
- the amount of detail provided, and
- the bases of amounts reported.

6.116 *Additional considerations.* With regard to individual financial statements, as discussed in paragraph 6.115, it is important that you should evaluate whether they are presented in a manner that reflects the appropriate classification and description of financial information. For disclosures, it is important that you consider whether management disclosed a particular matter in light of the circumstances and facts of which you are aware at the time. You also may consider whether information in disclosures is expressed clearly.

Performing Procedures to Address the Risks of Material Misstatement Due to Fraud

6.117 AU-C section 240 directs you to perform auditing procedures in response to assessed risks of material misstatement due to fraud. In many circumstances, these audit procedures also provide audit evidence related to material misstatements caused by error. For example, suggested audit procedures relating to revenue recognition, inventory quantities, management estimates, and responses to risks of misstatements arising from misappropriations of assets may be appropriate responses to your assessment of the risks of material misstatement described in chapter 4, "Understanding the Client, Its Environment, and Its Internal Control," of this guide.

Audit Documentation

6.118 With regard to the performance of further audit procedures, you should document

> *a.* the overall responses to address the assessed *risks of material misstatement* at the financial statement level and the nature, timing, and extent of the further audit procedures performed;
>
> *b.* the linkage of those procedures with the assessed risks at the relevant assertion level; and
>
> *c.* the results of the audit procedures, including conclusions when such conclusions are not otherwise clear.

(AU-C sec. 330 par. .30)

> *d.* if you plan to use audit evidence about the operating effectiveness of controls obtained in previous audits, you should include in the audit documentation the conclusions reached about relying on such controls that were tested in a previous audit.

Paragraphs 1.39–.41 of this guide provide additional, more general, guidance on the preparation of audit documentation.

(AU-C sec. 330 par. .31)

Summary

6.119 In response to your assessment of the *risks of material misstatement*, you will develop an overall response to financial statement level risks and design further audit procedures, which consist of tests of controls and substantive procedures. This chapter focused on performing these further audit procedures, which include tests of controls and substantive procedures.

6.120 Your assessment of the *risks of material misstatement*, adjusted for results of your tests of controls will affect the nature, timing, and extent of your substantive procedures. If certain conditions are met, you may use the results of tests of controls performed in prior periods as audit evidence for your conclusion about control operating effectiveness in the current audit period.

6.121 During your tests of controls, you may identify deviations in the application of the control. These deviations may be indicative of one or more control deficiencies, the severity of which you will need to assess. If your tests of controls indicate that they may not be operating effectively, you will need to consider whether the nature, timing, and extent of your planned substantive procedures should be modified.

6.122 Substantive procedures include substantive analytical procedures and tests of details. Substantive procedures should be performed on each engagement.

6.123 Performing substantive procedures may lead to the identification of misstatements, which you will need to evaluate and communicate to management.

6.124 Chapter 7 of this guide provides guidance on the evaluation of the audit findings from your substantive procedures and of any identified control deficiencies.

Appendix—Answers to Frequently Asked Questions About Performing Further Audit Procedures

Question	See Paragraphs
What are the objectives of tests of controls?	6.02–.03
What factors should I consider when designing tests of controls?	6.06–.17
What procedures can I perform to test controls?	6.18–.43
Should I be testing controls as of a single point in time or throughout a period?	6.44–.48
What should I do to update tests of controls performed at an interim date?	6.49–.53
Can I use audit evidence obtained in prior periods to support a conclusion about control operating effectiveness in the current period?	6.54–.61
How many tests of controls should I perform?	6.62–.69
How do I test the operating effectiveness of controls when the client uses a service organization to process certain transactions?	6.70–.72
Once I have completed my tests of controls, how do I evaluate the results?	6.75–.87
What substantive procedures should I perform on every audit?	6.88–.90
How do I determine the proper mix of substantive procedures to perform?	6.92
In what circumstances should I consider performing substantive procedures at an interim date? If I do perform substantive procedures at an interim date, what should I do to test the roll-forward period?	6.103–.110
How should I evaluate the adequacy of the financial statement presentation and disclosures?	6.114–.116

Chapter 7

Evaluating Audit Findings, Audit Evidence, and Deficiencies in Internal Control

TABLE OF CONTENTS

Observations and Suggestions

Illustration 7-1
Overview of Evaluating Audit Findings and Audit Evidence

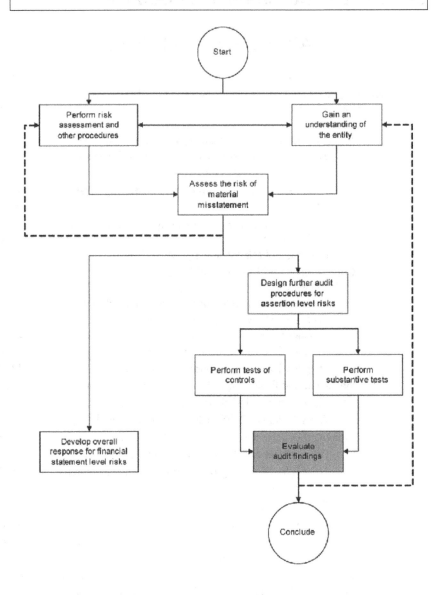

As you perform your further audit procedures, you should evaluate the resulting audit evidence. That audit evidence may either confirm your risk assessments or cause you to reevaluate those risk assessments and design and perform additional audit procedures.

This chapter describes how you evaluate the results of your audit procedures.

You also may become aware of deficiencies either in the design or operation of your client's internal control. This chapter also describes how you evaluate and communicate internal control findings.

Evaluating Misstatements. *The results of your substantive procedures may lead you to identify misstatements in amounts, classification, presentation, or disclosures in the financial statements. You should determine whether these misstatements, both individually and in the aggregate, are material. The auditor should accumulate all misstatements identified during the audit, other than those that the auditor believes are trivial, and communicate them to the appropriate level of management. This communication should occur on a timely basis. You should also request management to correct all misstatements. In evaluating the aggregate effect of the misstatements, you also should consider the effect on the current period of the aggregate uncorrected misstatements from prior periods. Uncorrected misstatements should be included in the management representation letter and communicated to those charged with governance.*

Evaluating Audit Evidence. *At the end of the audit, you should conclude whether you have obtained sufficient appropriate audit evidence to support your opinion on the financial statements at a low level of audit risk. Thus, you should evaluate whether your audit was performed at a level that allows you to conclude at a high level of assurance that the financial statements, as a whole, are free of material misstatement.*

Identification of Deficiencies in Internal Control. *You may become aware of deficiencies in internal control at any point during your audit, including during the performance of risk assessment procedures, the evaluation of control design and implementation, or the testing of internal control operating effectiveness. The results of your substantive procedures may cause you to reevaluate your earlier assessment of internal controls, and that reevaluation also may lead you to identify deficiencies in internal control.*

Evaluation and Communication of Deficiencies in Internal Control *. You should evaluate the severity of identified deficiencies in internal control. Some deficiencies may be considered significant deficiencies. The most severe deficiencies are material weaknesses. You should communicate in writing to management and those charged with governance all significant deficiencies and material weaknesses of which you become aware during the audit.*

As the audit proceeds, and as misstatements and control deficiencies are identified, you may need to reassess the risk assessments you initially made and consider whether the audit plan is sufficient to be able to conclude at a low risk that the financial statements contain a material misstatement.

As you perform further audit procedures, you will need to evaluate the results of your tests. If you identify misstatements, you should communicate them to management and those charged with governance, and request management to correct all misstatements. At the conclusion of the audit, you should evaluate your audit evidence to determine whether it supports your opinion and allows you to conclude at a low level of risk that the financial statements are free of material misstatement.

This chapter provides guidance on evaluating the results of your audit procedures, communicating your findings to management, and ultimately evaluating the audit evidence you obtained. Throughout your audit you may identify deficiencies in internal control. These too should be evaluated and, if necessary, communicated to management and those charged with governance.

Introduction

7.01 The results of further audit procedures may lead you to identify

 a. misstatements of amounts, classification, presentation, or disclosures in the financial statements, as a result of your substantive procedures, or

 b. deficiencies in internal control, as a result of tests of controls or performing substantive procedures.

This chapter describes how you evaluate and, if necessary, communicate both misstatements and deficiencies.

Evaluating Misstatements of Amounts, Classification, Presentation, or Disclosures in the Financial Statements

7.02 When you identify misstatements in amounts, classification, presentation, or disclosures in the financial statements, you should

 a. evaluate the misstatements, both individually and in the aggregate, and

 b. communicate these misstatements, unless trivial, to management and those charged with governance.

Reevaluation of Your Risk Assessments

7.03 Based on the audit evidence you obtain from your audit procedures, you should reevaluate your assessment of the risks of material misstatement at the relevant assertion level to determine whether they remain appropriate. (AU-C sec. 330 par. .27)

7.04 *For example, the auditors of ABC Company, Inc. determined that there was a relatively low risk that the company would fail to record year-end sales in the proper accounting period (cut-off assertion). The nature, timing, and extent of the auditor's substantives procedures relating to this assertion were designed based on this assessment.*

However, because December 31 fell on a Sunday, there was some confusion among warehouse and accounting personnel about how to record certain orders that were not picked up by the shipping service even though ABC Company had finished preparing the items for shipment.

A comment received on an accounts receivable confirmation led a staff auditor to investigate the discrepancy reported by the customer, which ultimately resulted in the identification of the underlying cause of the misstatement.

This misstatement of revenues and accounts receivable caused the auditors to reevaluate their initial risk assessment relating to shipping cut-off, including the risks relating to the effective design of controls. As a result of this reevaluation, the team increased the extent of their tests of details over shipping cut-off to obtain a higher level of assurance that they had identified all material misstatements relating to cut-off errors. Further, a deficiency in internal control was noted to exist underlying the finding.

Observations and Suggestions

Your audit is a cumulative and iterative process. As you perform planned audit procedures, information may come to your attention that differs significantly from the information on which the risk assessments were based.

The identification of a misstatement of an account or a note to the financial statements is one example of new, unexpected information that you uncover during your audit. When you identify a misstatement, the communication of that misstatement to management and their correction of that misstatement is only a part of your responsibilities. In addition, you may

- determine whether the misstatement indicates the existence of a deficiency in internal control, and
- analyze the effect, if any, the new information has on your previous risk assessments. The results of this reevaluation may result in you performing additional procedures that you had not previously planned to perform.

In this way, a reevaluation of audit risk also may involve an update of your audit strategy and your audit plan.

Finally, you cannot simply assume that an instance of fraud or error is an isolated occurrence. To properly reevaluate your *risks of material misstatement*, the overall audit strategy and audit plan, you may need to perform audit procedures to gain an understanding of the underlying cause of the misstatement, as illustrated in the example in paragraph 7.04.

(AU-C sec. 450 par. .06)

Materiality Considerations as Your Audit Progresses

7.05 Paragraph 3.06 of this guide describes how you should determine a materiality level for the financial statements as a whole to help you plan your audit. However, while planning the audit, it is not feasible for you to anticipate *all* the circumstances that may ultimately influence judgments about materiality in evaluating the audit findings at the completion of your audit. You should revise materiality for the financial statements as a whole in the event you become aware of information that would have caused you to have determined a different amount initially. (AU-C sec. 320 par. .12)

Observations and Suggestions

You should obtain a high level of assurance about whether the client's financial statements are free of material misstatement. The performance of risk assessment and further audit procedures help you gather the audit evidence required to obtain a high level of assurance, but ultimately, your ability to meet your overall responsibility depends on your judgment about what is "material" to the financial statements.

If you err in your judgment about materiality and set it at a level that is higher than appropriate, your audit procedures may be insufficient to provide reasonable assurance of detecting misstatements at the appropriate materiality level.

For example, during planning, you set materiality based on income; since the company had projected income before tax of $100,000 at the beginning of the audit, you set materiality at $5,000 because you judged that aggregate misstatements affecting the company's income are not material. But suppose that information comes to your attention that income before tax will be half of what was projected, and thus you determine that the appropriate materiality should have been $2,500.

Unless you adjust your audit procedures to take into account this revised, lower level of materiality, you will not be able to conclude with a high level of assurance that you have detected all misstatements that truly are material. In this case, this could require you to greatly increase (for example, double) the extent of testing.

7.06 If you become aware of information during the audit that would have caused you to have determined a different (lower) amount of materiality than initially determined, you should revise materiality for the financial statements as a whole. Further, you should also revise the performance materiality level or levels for particular classes of transactions, account balances, or disclosures. If you conclude that a lower materiality amount is appropriate, you should also determine whether it is necessary to revise performance materiality and whether the nature, timing, and extent of planned further audit procedures remain appropriate. (AU-C sec. 320 par. .12–.13)

Qualitative Aspects of Materiality

7.07 As indicated in paragraph 3.08 of this guide, judgments about materiality include both quantitative and qualitative information. However, judgments about materiality used for planning purposes are primarily determined using quantitative considerations.

7.08 For the purposes of evaluating misstatements, your judgments about materiality should consider qualitative factors. Table 7-1 summarizes qualitative factors that you may consider when determining whether misstatements are material. These circumstances presented in table 7-1 are only examples. Not all of these examples are likely to be present in all audits, nor is the list complete. The existence of any circumstances such as these does not necessarily lead to a conclusion that the misstatement is material.

Table 7-1
Qualitative Factors That May Influence the Determination of Materiality

Qualitative considerations influence your determination about whether misstatements are material. Qualitative factors that you may consider when making judgments about materiality include the following:

- The potential effect of the misstatement on trends, especially trends in profitability.
- A misstatement that changes a loss into income or vice versa.
- The potential effect of the misstatement on the entity's compliance with loan covenants, other contractual agreements, and regulatory provisions.
- The existence of statutory or regulatory reporting requirements that affect materiality thresholds.
- A change masked in earnings or other trends, especially in the context of general economic and industry conditions.
- A misstatement that has the effect of increasing management's compensation, for example, by satisfying the requirements for the award of bonuses or other forms of incentive compensation.
- The sensitivity of the circumstances surrounding the misstatement, for example, the implications of misstatements involving fraud and possible illegal acts, violations of contractual provisions such as debt covenants, and conflicts of interest.
- The significance of the financial statement element affected by the misstatement, for example, a misstatement affecting recurring earnings as contrasted to one involving a nonrecurring charge or credit, such as an extraordinary item.
- The effects of misclassifications, for example, misclassification between operating and nonoperating income or recurring and nonrecurring income items or a misclassification between fund-raising costs and program activity costs in a not-for-profit organization.
- The significance of the misstatement relative to reasonable user needs, for example
  - earnings to investors and the equity or cash flow amounts to creditors.
  - the magnifying effects of a misstatement on the calculation of purchase price in a transfer of interests (buy-sell agreement).
  - the effect of misstatements of earnings when contrasted with expectations.
  - the views and expectations of those charged with governance and management, which may be helpful in gaining or corroborating an understanding of user needs.

(continued)

Qualitative Factors That May Influence the Determination of Materiality—*continued*

- The definitive character of the misstatement, for example, the precision of an error that is objectively determinable as contrasted with a misstatement that unavoidably involves a degree of subjectivity through estimation, allocation, or uncertainty.
- The motivation of management with respect to the misstatement, for example, (1) an indication of a possible pattern of bias by management when developing and accumulating accounting estimates, (2) a misstatement precipitated by management's continued unwillingness to correct weaknesses in the financial reporting process, or (3) an intentional decision not to follow generally accepted accounting principles.
- The existence of offsetting effects of individually significant but different misstatements.
- The likelihood that a misstatement that is currently immaterial may have a material effect in future periods because of a cumulative effect, for example, that builds over several periods.
- The cost of making the correction. It may not be cost-beneficial for the client to develop a system to calculate a basis to record the effect of an immaterial misstatement. On the other hand, if management appears to have developed a system to calculate an amount that represents an immaterial misstatement, it may reflect a motivation of management.
- The risk that possible additional undetected misstatements would affect the auditor's evaluation.

Misstatements

7.09 *Misstatements* are defined as a difference between the amount, classification, presentation, or disclosure of a reported financial statement item and the amount, classification, presentation, or disclosure that is required for the item to be presented fairly in accordance with the applicable financial reporting framework. (AU-C sec. 450 par. .04)

You may find it useful to distinguish among factual misstatements, judgmental misstatements, and projected misstatements as follows:

    a. *Factual misstatements* are misstatements about which there is no doubt.

    b. *Judgmental misstatements* are differences between your judgments and management's judgments concerning accounting estimates that you consider unreasonable or the selection or application of accounting policies by the client that you consider inappropriate.

    c. *Projected misstatements* are your best estimate of misstatements in populations, involving the projection of misstatements identified in audit samples to the entire population from which the samples were drawn. Projected misstatements may include factual misstatements identified in specific items from which the projections are made.

7.10 You should accumulate misstatements (factual, judgmental, and projected) identified during the audit. (AU-C sec. 450 par. .05) You should determine whether uncorrected misstatements are material, individually or in the aggregate, for purposes of determining whether the financial statements are free of material misstatement. (AU-C sec. 450 par. .11) You should also communicate misstatements to the appropriate level of management. (AU-C sec. 450 par. .07)

The Possibility of Undetected Misstatements

7.11 In most cases, you do not test 100 percent of the transactions your client entered into during the year, nor do you identify and test all other events or circumstances that could affect the financial statements and related disclosures. As such, a sampling risk exists that, after performing your audit procedures, some misstatements in the financial statements may remain undetected. Also, an identified misstatement may not be an isolate occurrence but rather indicative of a breakdown in internal control or the use of inappropriate assumptions or valuation methods. Further, if the aggregate of misstatements accumulated approaches materiality, a greater than acceptably low level of risk may exist for possible undetected misstatements. You may find it necessary to consider the possibility of these undetected misstatements when evaluating audit findings.

Evaluating Results From Different Types of Substantive Procedures

Substantive Analytical Procedures

7.12 Substantive analytical procedures normally would not specifically identify a misstatement. Rather, the results of these procedures would provide you with only an indication of whether a misstatement might exist in the account or class of transactions. (AU-C sec. 520 par. .05c)

7.13 If the difference between an amount recorded in the financial statements and the expectation you developed as part of your substantive analytical procedures is significant, that difference should be investigated. (AU-C sec. 520 par. .07)

7.14 This investigation may involve

- making inquiries of management and obtaining appropriate audit evidence relevant to management's response; and

- performing other audit procedures as necessary in the circumstances.

(AU-C sec. 520 par. .07)

7.15 If the amount of the difference is not determinable from the procedures performed, you may request management to investigate, and you may need to expand your procedures to determine if a misstatement might exist.

Observations and Suggestions

Paragraph 7.13 describes your evaluation of the difference between your expectation and the recorded amount as one that requires a consideration of whether that difference is "significant." As used in this context, the "significance" of a difference in many cases is determined by comparing it to performance materiality. As the amount of the difference approaches performance materiality, the risk that a misstatement greater than performance materiality exists in the account increases.

"Significant" for analytical procedures is in many cases less than material, and may be an amount the auditor determines based on performance materiality.

Results of Audit Sampling

7.16   When you use audit sampling to test an assertion, you should project the results of audit sampling to the population. (AU-C sec. 530 par. .13) That latter misstatement is considered a projected misstatement and evaluated as such. Paragraphs 4.71–.92 of the AICPA Audit Guide *Audit Sampling* provide more detailed guidance on projecting misstatements identified in the sample to the population.

Differences in Estimates

7.17   In many cases, financial statements include one or more accounting estimates. You should obtain an understanding of the requirements of the applicable financial reporting framework relevant to accounting for estimates; how the client identifies transactions, events and conditions that may give rise to the need to recognize and disclose estimates; and how the client makes estimates and the data used. (AU-C sec. 540 par. .08)

7.18   No one accounting estimate can be considered accurate with certainty. Therefore, you may determine that a difference between an estimated amount best supported by your audit evidence and management's estimate included in the financial statements may not be significant. Such a difference would not be considered to be a misstatement. However, if you believe that the client's estimated amount included in the financial statements is unreasonable, you may treat the difference at least between that estimate and the nearest reasonable estimate as a judgmental misstatement.

7.19   The nearest reasonable estimate may be a point estimate or a range of acceptable amounts as follows:

   a. *Point estimate*. If your estimate is a point estimate, the difference between that point estimate and management's estimate included in the financial statements constitutes a judgmental misstatement.

   b. *Range of acceptable amounts*. If your analysis of an accounting estimate results in a range of acceptable amounts, management's estimate will fall either inside or outside of that acceptable range. For example, if your analysis leads you to conclude that the client's allowance for doubtful accounts is between $130,000 and $160,000, the client's estimate will either be inside or outside of that range.

    i. If management's recorded estimate falls within your range of acceptable amounts, you would conclude that management's estimate is reasonable.

    ii. If management's recorded estimate falls outside your range of acceptable amounts, the difference between the recorded amount and the amount at the nearest end of your range would be considered a judgmental misstatement.

Observations and Suggestions

Using a range of acceptable amounts is effective only if the range is relatively narrow—the spread of the range is less than performance materiality. In the example in paragraph 7.19, if the range was from $130,000 to $1,000,000, and performance materiality was $50,000, you may not have sufficient appropriate evidence about the estimate, so you would want to perform additional tests to narrow the estimate so the spread is less than performance materiality.

Consideration of Possible Bias

7.20 You should review the judgments and decisions made by management in the making of accounting estimates to identify whether indicators of possible management bias exist. For example, if each accounting estimate included in the financial statements was individually reasonable, but the effect of the difference between management's estimate and your estimate was to increase income, you may find it necessary to reconsider whether other recorded estimates reflect a similar bias. If so, you may perform additional audit procedures to address those estimates. (AU-C sec. 540 par. .21)

7.21 In some instances, management's recorded estimates may be clustered at one end of the range of acceptable amounts in one year and clustered at the other end of the range of acceptable amounts in the subsequent year. Such a circumstance indicates the possibility that management is using swings in accounting estimates to offset higher- or lower-than-expected earnings. If you believe that management is making estimates in this fashion, you may consider communicating this matter to those charged with governance. (AU-C sec. 540 par. .21)

7.22 AU-C section 240, *Consideration of Fraud in a Financial Statement Audit* (AICPA, *Professional Standards*), directs you to perform a retrospective review of management's accounting estimates to identify indications of possible bias and, if identified, to respond appropriately.

Communication of Misstatements to Management

7.23 You should accumulate all misstatements you identify during the audit—except those you believe are trivial—and communicate them to management. In complying with this requirement

    a. matters that are "trivial" are amounts you determine below which misstatements need not be accumulated. This amount is set so that any such misstatements, either individually or when aggregated with other such misstatements, would not be material to the financial statements, after the possibility of further undetected misstatements is considered. (AU-C sec. 450 par. .05)

b. the communication to management *should* occur on a timely basis, which enables management to evaluate the items and either to tell you that they disagree with you and why or to concur that the items are misstatements and to take action as necessary. (AU-C sec. 450 par. .07)

c. determining which level of management to communicate the misstatements to is a matter of judgment that depends on factors such as

    i. the nature, size, and frequency of the misstatement.

    ii. the level of management that can take the necessary action.

7.24 The nature of your communication and the related request you make of management depends on whether the misstatement is a factual, projected, or judgmental misstatement. In addition, you may find it necessary to

- discuss with management the effect on the auditor's report if management does not examine the class of transactions, account balance, or disclosure to identify and correct misstatements found.

- perform further audit procedure to reevaluate the reasonableness of the estimate after management has reconsidered its assumptions and methods, and corrected any misstatements found.

7.25 If management decides not to correct some or all of the misstatements, you should obtain an understanding of the reasons for not making the corrections and take those reasons into account when considering the qualitative aspects of the entity's accounting practices and the implications for the auditor's report. (AU-C sec. 450 par. .09)

7.26 *For example, the auditors of Ownco identified the following items when performing their substantive procedures:*

- *The company over-accrued office expenses by $325 because accounting personnel failed to consider a credit granted by the supplier for returned office supplies. This was based on the auditor's 100 percent examination of all accruals.*

- *At year end, the company had written checks totaling approximately $5,000 that it did not mail until 2 weeks of the new year had elapsed. This failure to mail the checks prior to year end was done intentionally so the bookkeeper could review the payments after he returned from vacation. The held checks were incorrectly recorded as a reduction of cash and accounts payable at year end.*

- *The company erred in pricing certain finished goods. The auditor detected the misstatements by examining the supporting documentation for a sample of inventory items and projecting an identified misstatement to the entire population from which it was drawn. The amount of the projected misstatement was approximately $12,000.*

The auditor responded to these items in the following ways:

- *The over-accrued office expenses fell below the amount the auditor considered trivial. That is, even a significant number of misstatements of $325, when aggregated, would not be material to the financial statements. As a trivial item, it was not accumulated by the auditor for further consideration and was not communicated to client management. Had this been based on a sample, the auditor would first calculate the projected misstatement and then determine whether the projected misstatement was trivial.*

- *The $5,000 of held checks was considered to be a factual misstatement, a specific misstatement arising from mistakes in overlooking facts and processing information. As such, the auditors communicated the matter to management and asked them to correct the financial statements.*

- *The $12,000 inventory pricing misstatement is a projected misstatement because the amount was identified in a sample that was extrapolated to the entire population. As a projected misstatement, the auditor did not request that the client correct the financial statements for the extrapolated amount. Rather, the auditor requested that the client investigate the pricing of inventory further to identify and correct any misstatements.*

The client did so and identified misstatements of $13,500. These were corrected. Because the auditor's estimate was based on an adequate sample, and management adjusted to an amount close to the auditor's estimate, no further testing was performed.

Consideration and Evaluation of Uncorrected Misstatements

7.27 Prior to evaluating the effect on uncorrected misstatements you should reassess materiality to confirm whether it remains appropriate in the context of the client's actual financial results. (AU-C sec. 450 par. .10) You should then determine whether the uncorrected misstatements are material, either individually or in the aggregate. (AU-C sec. 450 par. .11) To make this determination you should consider

    a.   the size and nature of the misstatements, both in relation to particular classes of transactions, account balances, or disclosures and the financial statements as a whole, and the particular circumstances of their occurrence (AU-C sec. 450 par. .11) and

    b.   the effect of uncorrected misstatements related to prior periods on the relevant classes of transactions, account balances, or disclosures and the financial statements as a whole. (AU-C sec. 450 par. .11)

7.28 When applying the concept of materiality to the evaluation of audit findings you may consider

- both the quantitative (size) and qualitative (nature) aspects of the misstatements.

- the effect of the misstatements on both the financial statements taken as a whole and on particular classes of transactions, account balances, and disclosures.

- the particular circumstances related to the occurrence of the misstatements.

7.29 When evaluating misstatements in relation to individual classes of transactions, account balances, or disclosures, you should consider whether that misstatement has exceeded the materiality level for that particular class of transactions, account balances, or disclosures. Thus, you may use a relevant lower misstatement threshold in evaluating individual misstatements. Paragraph 3.14 of this guide provides guidance on reducing financial statement materiality for particular items.

Evaluating Uncorrected Misstatements Individually

7.30 You should consider separately each uncorrected misstatement before considering them in the aggregate. When considering a misstatement separately, you may consider

    a. its effect on the relevant individual classes of transactions, account balances, or disclosures.

    b. whether, the materiality level for that particular class of transactions, account balances, or disclosure has been exceeded.

If an individual misstatement is judged to be material, it is unlikely that it can be offset by other misstatements. (AU-C sec. 450 par. .A21) However, it is appropriate to offset misstatements when they are disclosed together in the financial statements.

For example, suppose your client failed to accrue for a purchase of office supplies. It also overestimated the accrual of contingent rent expense due for the year. If office supplies and rent expense are combined for the financial statements (for example, as "occupancy costs") and the accruals for both of these items are combined as accrued expenses, it may be appropriate to offset the two misstatements and evaluate only the net difference between them.

Evaluating Uncorrected Misstatements in the Aggregate

7.31 Uncorrected misstatements are aggregated in a way that enables you to consider whether they materially misstate the particular classes of transactions, account balances, or disclosures and financial statements taken as a whole. (AU-C sec. 450 par. .11*a*) This aggregation allows you to compare the misstatements to both the financial statements and to individual amounts, subtotals, or totals.

7.32 Your evaluation of aggregated misstatements includes the consideration of the risk of undetected misstatements as described in paragraph 7.11.

As the aggregate of the misstatements approaches the materiality level, the risk increases that those misstatements (in combination with undetected misstatements) exceed materiality. Accordingly, you determine whether your audit plan (nature, timing and extent) needs to be revised. (AU-C sec. 450 par. .06*b*)

Observations and Suggestions

In some instances it has been noted that management may deliberately immaterially misstate financial statement amounts in order to achieve objectives that might not be obvious. For example, a slight understatement of

---

liabilities might have the effect of meeting a required debt covenant ratio, where the ratio would not be acceptable, but for the misstatement. In other situations a profit sharing or bonus award may be predicated on meeting certain benchmarks. When the financial metrics appear to be close to those benchmarks, there may be a motivation to meet the threshold by misstatement.

Thus, when waiving adjustments that may not be material, the auditor may consider other metrics and benchmarks before being satisfied that the misstatements do not require correction.

7.33 *For example, at the end of your audit, you had factual misstatements of $50,000 and judgmental misstatements of $200,000. The client investigated and corrected all the factual misstatements and $150,000 of the judgment misstatements; this left $50,000 of uncorrected judgmental misstatement. Materiality for the financial statement was $500,000. You need to consider whether there could be $450,000 of undetected misstatements given all the procedures you performed and the misstatements you detected. You made a judgment that you had a high level of assurance that this was unlikely, given the nature, timing, and extent of procedures performed.*

However, if materiality were $60,000, you might believe that it is possible that you could have missed $10,000 of misstatement in the audit process, given the nature, timing, and extent of your audit procedures and the audit findings. Thus, you might not be able to conclude at a low risk that the financial statements are free of material misstatement. In that case you might request the client to investigate and resolve some of the remaining potential misstatement or perform further audit procedures to reduce the potential misstatement amount and reduce audit risk to an appropriately low level.

Consideration of Prior Year's Uncorrected Misstatements

7.34 You should consider the effect on uncorrected misstatements related to prior periods on the relevant classes of transactions, account balances, or disclosures and the financial statements as a whole for the current period. (AU-C sec. 450 par. .11*b*)

7.35 *For example, suppose that your client inappropriately applies accounting principles relating to the capitalization of fixed assets. As a result, expenditures that should be capitalized are expensed. In year 1, the total amount of expenditures that should have been capitalized was $15,000. Expenses for the year are overstated by $15,000 and fixed assets are understated by the same amount. The auditor should ask the client to adjust the financial statements for the misstatement. If not adjusted, the auditor should determine whether the $15,000 is considered immaterial individually and in the aggregate to both the income statement and the balance sheet. Assume no adjustment is made, although the item is included in the representation letter and those charged with governance are informed.*

In year 2, the company follows the same policy, and $18,000 is inappropriately expensed. For the year, expenses are overstated by $18,000. But the cumulative effect of the incorrect application of an accounting principle is different for the balance sheet. At the end of year 2, fixed assets are understated by the amount that was not capitalized during year 2 ($18,000) plus the amount that was not capitalized in year 1, less depreciation ($15,000 less, say $1,000). That is, the balance sheet is misstated by $32,000. The auditor should ask the client to adjust for the misstatement of $32,000. If not, the auditor should evaluate whether *the $32,000 is considered immaterial individually and in the aggregate to both the income statement and the balance sheet. Assume no adjustment is made, although the item is included in the representation letter and those charged with governance are informed.*

In year 3 the policy continues. Additional expenditures are expensed rather than capitalized. In any given year, the amount that is expensed is not material to the income statement, but over time, the cumulative effect of the misstatements on the balance sheet continues to grow. And every year you need to ask management and those charged with governance to adjust both the balance sheet and the income statement. Management also needs to include their view that these amounts are not material in the management representation letter.

This example provides one perspective on how to assess such misstatements that relate to current and prior periods. A fuller discussion of this issue is provided in appendix F, "Consideration of Prior Year Uncorrected Misstatements" of this guide.

7.36 You should determine whether uncorrected misstatements are material, individually or in the aggregate. In connection therewith you should consider

- the size and nature of the misstatements, both in relation to particular classes of transactions, account balances, or disclosures and the financial statements as a whole, and the particular circumstances of their occurrence and

- the effect of uncorrected misstatements related to prior periods on the relevant classes of transactions, account balances, or disclosures and the financial statements as a whole.

Observations and Suggestions

The guidance related to misstatements from a prior period pertains only to *uncorrected* misstatements. If your client corrects all the misstatements you identify, there is nothing left that may affect subsequent periods.

7.37 Appendix H, "Examples of Circumstances That May Be Deficiencies, Significant Deficiencies, or Material Weaknesses," of this guide provides additional discussion, guidance, and examples of how to consider uncorrected misstatements from a prior period.

Evaluating the Financial Statements as a Whole

7.38 You should evaluate whether the financial statements as a whole are free of material misstatement. In making this evaluation, you should evaluate the uncorrected misstatements and reassess materiality under paragraph .12 of AU-C section 320, *Materiality in Planning and Performing an Audit* (AICPA, *Professional Standards*). (AU-C sec. 450 par. .10–.11)

7.39 When determining whether the effect of uncorrected misstatements, individually or in the aggregate, is material, you should consider the nature and size of the misstatements in relation to the nature and size of items in the financial statements. For example,

- an amount that is material to the financial statements of one entity may not be material to another entity of a different size or nature.

- an amount that is material to the financial statements of an entity in one year may not be material to that same entity in a different year.

(AU-C sec. 450 par. .11*a*)

7.40 If you believe that the financial statements as a whole are materially misstated and management refuses to make the necessary corrections, you should determine the implications for your audit report under AU-C section 700, *Forming an Opinion and Reporting on Financial Statements* (AICPA, *Professional Standards*).

7.41 If you conclude that the effects of uncorrected misstatements do not cause the financial statements to be materially misstated, you should consider the effect of undetected misstatements, which are described in paragraph 7.11. Because of the possibility of undetected misstatements, as the aggregate uncorrected misstatements approach materiality, the risk that the financial statements may be materially misstated also increases. As such, you should determine whether the audit plan needs to be revised if the aggregate of misstatements accumulated during the audit approaches materiality. (AU-C sec. 450 par. .06)

Evaluating the Sufficiency of Audit Evidence

7.42 You should conclude whether you have obtained sufficient appropriate audit evidence. In forming your conclusion, you should consider all relevant audit evidence, regardless of whether it appears to corroborate or to contradict the financial statement assertions. (AU-C sec. 330 par. .28) Table 7-2 summarizes some of the factors that influence your consideration of whether the audit evidence you obtained during your audit was sufficient and appropriate.

7.43 If you determine that you have not obtained sufficient appropriate audit evidence about a relevant assertion, you should attempt to obtain further evidence. If you are unable to obtain sufficient appropriate audit evidence, you would express a qualified opinion or a disclaimer of opinion on the financial statements. (AU-C sec. 330 par. .29)

Table 7-2
Sufficient Appropriate Audit Evidence

The sufficiency and appropriateness of audit evidence to support your conclusions throughout the audit are a matter of professional judgment. This judgment regarding what constitutes sufficient appropriate audit evidence is influenced by such factors as the

- significance of the potential misstatement in the relevant assertion and the likelihood of its having a material effect, individually or aggregated with other potential misstatements, on the financial statements.
- effectiveness of management's responses and controls to address the risks.

(continued)

Sufficient Appropriate Audit Evidence—*continued*

- experience gained during previous audits with respect to similar potential misstatements.
- results of audit procedures performed, including whether such audit procedures identified specific instances of fraud or error.
- source and reliability of available information.
- persuasiveness of the audit evidence.
- understanding of the entity and its environment, including its internal control.

Identifying and Evaluating Deficiencies in Internal Control

7.44 AU-C section 265, *Communicating Internal Control Related Matters Identified in an Audit* (AICPA, *Professional Standards*), requires you to communicate to management and those charged with governance significant deficiencies and material weaknesses identified in your audit. Chapter 2, "Key Concepts Underlying the Auditor's Risk Assessment Process," of this guide provides definitions of

- *deficiency in internal control,*
- *significant deficiency,* and
- *material weakness.*

AU-C section 265 is not applicable if the auditor is engaged to report on the effectiveness of an entity's internal control over financial reporting under Statement on Auditing Standards No. 130, *An Audit of Internal Control Over Financial Reporting That Is Integrated With an Audit of Financial Statements* (AICPA, *Professional Standards*, AU-C sec. 940).

7.45 Deficiencies in internal control may involve one or more of the five internal control components described in this guide that affect an entity's internal control over financial reporting.

Identification of Deficiencies in Internal Control

7.46 In an audit, you are not required to perform procedures to identify deficiencies in internal control. However, during the risk assessment process (for example, obtaining an understanding of the entity and its environment) and during other stages of the audit process (for example, performing further audit procedures to respond to assessed risk), you may become aware of deficiencies in internal control. (AU-C sec. 265 par. .02)

Classification of Deficiencies in Internal Control

7.47 You should determine whether you have identified one or more deficiencies in internal control. (AU-C sec. 265 par. .08) If you have identified such deficiencies you should evaluate each deficiency to determine whether the deficiencies, individually or in combination, are significant deficiencies or material weaknesses. (AU-C sec. 265 par. .09)

> **Material weakness.** A material weakness is a deficiency, or combination of deficiencies in internal control over financial reporting,

such that there is a reasonable possibility that a material misstatement of the financial statements will not be prevented or detected and corrected on a timely basis.

Significant deficiency. A significant deficiency is a deficiency, or combination of deficiencies, in internal control over financial reporting, that is less severe than a material weakness yet important enough to merit attention by those charged with governance.

(AU-C sec. 265 par. .07)

Appendix G, "Assessing the Severity of Identified Deficiencies in Internal Control," of this guide contains additional examples to assist auditors in evaluating the severity of an identified deficiency in internal control.

Appendix H of this guide is reproduced here from AU-C section 265.

Practice Considerations for Auditors of Entities Using the COSO Framework

The Committee of Sponsoring Organizations of the Treadway Commission (COSO) framework contains guidance for assessing the severity of deficiencies. However, the guidance for assessing the severity of deficiencies and communicating deficiencies to management and governance in AU-C section 265 (as illustrated in this guide) should be followed by auditors. Entities wishing to synchronize their assessments with those of their auditors may similarly look to generally accepted auditing standards regarding the classification of deficiencies as deficiencies, significant deficiencies, and material weaknesses.

The COSO framework does not use the term *material weakness* or *significant deficiency*. Rather, the COSO framework uses the term *major deficiency*, which is defined as an internal control deficiency or combination of deficiencies that severely reduces the likelihood that the entity can achieve its objectives. Further, according to the COSO framework, a major deficiency in one component cannot be mitigated to an acceptable level by the presence and functioning of another component, nor can a major deficiency in a relevant principle be mitigated to an acceptable level by the presence and functioning of other principles.

Evaluating Deficiencies in Internal Control

7.48 You are required to evaluate each deficiency in internal control identified during the audit to determine, whether such deficiency individually or in combination with others, constitute significant deficiencies or material weaknesses. (AU-C sec. 265 par. .09) A deficiency in internal control over financial reporting exists when the design or operation of a control does not allow management or employees, in the normal course of performing their assigned functions, to prevent or detect and correct a misstatement of the financial statements on a timely basis. (AU-C sec. 265 par. .07) The severity of a deficiency or combination of deficiencies, considers not only whether a misstatement has actually occurred but also

- the magnitude of the potential misstatement that could result from the deficiency or deficiencies and

- whether there is a reasonable possibility that the client's controls would fail to prevent, or detect and correct, a misstatement of an account balance or disclosure. A reasonable possibility exists when the chance of the future event or events occurring is more than remote.[1]

Observations and Suggestions

To be clear, a control deficiency does not need to cause a misstatement in order for it to be a material weakness, a significant deficiency, or just a deficiency. Likelihood of occurrence and potential materiality help classify the severity of a deficiency. However, a misstatement often implies that an internal control has failed, either in design or operating effectiveness. Similarly, the severity of a deficiency is not measured by the size of any associated misstatement, but by the likelihood and magnitude criteria. However, it would be difficult to see how the severity of a deficiency might be less than its observed magnitude, thus a material misstatement is an indicator of a material weakness in controls.

7.49 That a misstatement of the financial statements did not occur is not relevant to your identification of a deficiency or your evaluation and does not provide evidence that identified deficiencies are not significant deficiencies or material weaknesses. Your evaluation of the severity of deficiencies depends on the potential for misstatement during the period under audit, not on whether a misstatement actually has occurred. Chapter 2 of this guide provides more guidance on the definition of *deficiency in internal control, significant deficiency*, and *material weakness*.

7.50 Professional judgment is required to evaluate the severity of deficiencies in internal control, either individually or in combination. In making this judgment, factors that may affect the likelihood that a control could fail to prevent or detect and correct a misstatement, include, but are not limited to, the following:

- The nature of the financial statement, classes of transactions, account balances, disclosures, and assertions involved. (For example, suspense accounts and related party transactions involve greater risk)
- The cause and frequency of the exceptions detected as a result of the deficiency or deficiencies
- The susceptibility of the related assets or liabilities to loss or fraud
- The subjectivity and complexity or extent of judgment required to determine the amount involved
- The interaction or relationship of the control with other controls
- The interaction among the deficiencies
- The possible future consequences of the deficiency
- The importance of controls to the financial reporting process

---

[1] A reasonable possibility exists when the likelihood of an event occurring is either reasonably possible or probable as defined as follows:

Reasonably possible. The chance of the future event or events occurring is more than remote but less than likely.

Probable. The future event or events are likely to occur. (Paragraph .A154 of Statement on Auditing Standards No. 130, *An Audit of Internal Control Over Financial Reporting That Is Integrated With an Audit of Financial Statements* [AICPA, *Professional Standards*, AU-C sec. 940] modified paragraph .07 of AU-C section 265, *Communicating Internal Control Related Matters Identified in an Audit* [AICPA, *Professional Standards*]).

7.51 Factors affect the magnitude of a misstatement that might result from a deficiency or deficiencies in controls include, but are not limited to, the following:

- The financial statement amounts or total of transactions exposed to the deficiency
- The volume of activity (in the current period or expected future periods) in the class of transactions or account balance exposed to the deficiency

The maximum amount by which an account balance or total of transactions can be overstated in many cases is the recorded amount, whereas understatements could be larger than the recorded amount.

Table 7-3 provides examples of how you might consider likelihood and magnitude when evaluating the severity of a deficiency in internal control.

Table 7-3
Consideration of Likelihood and Magnitude

Factor to Consider	Examples
Likelihood of Misstatement	The following are examples of deficiencies in internal control and how their likelihood might be considered: • Failure to obtain required authorization for a valid disbursement. (In this case, you consider the likelihood of a misstatement resulting from recording an unauthorized disbursement.) • A deficiency identified as a result of a financial statement misstatement. (In this case, there is at least a reasonable possibility that a misstatement could occur because it did occur.)
Magnitude of Misstatement	When evaluating the magnitude of a potential misstatement resulting from a deficiency in internal control, you may consider the volume of activity in the account balance or class of transactions that would be exposed to the deficiency. You also may consider any effective compensating controls. A compensating control is a control that limits the severity of a deficiency and prevents it from rising to the level of a significant deficiency or, in some cases, a material weakness. Its precision is determined by the effectiveness of the procedure. The following is an example of a deficiency and how its magnitude might be considered when there is a compensating control: An owner-managed entity does not segregate duties within the accounts payable function. As a compensating control, the owner reviews the supporting documentation for all disbursements exceeding $1,000. You would evaluate the effect of this compensating control and determine whether it operates effectively for the purpose of mitigating the effects of the deficiency in the accounts payable function (the lack of segregation of duties).

Deviations in the Operations of Controls

7.52 A deficiency in operation exists when a properly designed control does not operate as designed or when the person performing the control does not possess the necessary authority or competence to perform the control effectively. (AU-C sec. 265 par. .07) When you test the operating effectiveness of controls, you may encounter deviations in their operation, for example, the control was not performed properly. When you identify control deviations and the deviation rate in the sample exceeds the expected deviation rate, you would conclude that a deficiency in the control exists. To evaluate the severity of a deficiency in internal control identified in your tests of controls, you will want to assess the potential magnitude of the related financial statement misstatement as discussed previously. Paragraphs 3.84–.91 of the AICPA Audit Guide *Audit Sampling* provide detailed guidance on assessing the potential magnitude of a deficiency.

7.53 When you obtain evidence that a control does not operate effectively, you may become aware of indirect or compensating controls that, if effective, may limit the severity of the deficiency and prevent it from being a significant deficiency or a material weakness. In these circumstances, although you are not required to consider the effects of these compensating controls for the purpose of evaluating the severity of the deficiency; you may choose to do so.

7.54 To consider the effects of an indirect (for example, compensating) control when evaluating the severity of a deficiency in a control that does not operate effectively, you would evaluate the design and test the compensating control for operating effectiveness as part of your financial statement audit. Compensating controls can limit the severity of the deficiency, but they do not eliminate the deficiency.

7.55 Identified deficiencies in internal control that individually are not significant deficiencies may—when aggregated with other deficiencies in internal control—constitute a significant deficiency or material weakness. As such, you should evaluate each deficiency to determine whether individually or in combination they constitute significant deficiencies or material weaknesses. (AU-C sec. 265 par. .09) Multiple deficiencies that affect the same significant financial statement account, or disclosure, relevant assertion, or component of internal control may increase the risks of material misstatement to such an extent to give rise to a significant deficiency or material weakness, even though such deficiencies, when evaluated individually, may be less severe.

Observations and Suggestions

You may determine that management failed to identify a material misstatement that your audit eventually uncovered. Even if management corrects the financial statements to properly account for example, a sale-leaseback, your identification of the matter, combined with their lack of identification of the matter, may lead you to determine that a significant deficiency (and probably a material weakness) exists in the controls relating to nonroutine transactions and possibly in other areas (for example, the control environment or the oversight of the financial reporting process by those charged with governance).

To help the client strengthen its internal control and eliminate the need for you to communicate a significant deficiency or material weakness, you and your client will need to

- have a clear understanding of your respective responsibilities relative to the preparation of the financial statements and the implementation and maintenance of internal control.

- establish a clear understanding of the status of the financial information that is being presented to the auditor (for example, an incomplete draft of the financial statements) and what is expected of the auditor.

7.56 If you initially determine that a deficiency, or a combination of deficiencies, is not a material weakness, you should consider whether prudent officials, having knowledge of the same facts and circumstances, would likely reach the same conclusion. (AU-C sec. 265 par. .10)

Process for Evaluating Deficiencies in Internal Control

7.57 When evaluating the severity of a deficiency in internal control, the first step is to determine whether the control deficiency is a material weakness. Some questions to consider when making this determination include the following:

- Is it reasonably possible that a misstatement of any magnitude could occur and not be prevented or detected and corrected on a timely basis by the client's internal control?

- Is the magnitude of a potential misstatement material to the financial statements? A misstatement is material, either individually or when aggregated with other misstatements, if it would cause the entity's financial statements to be materially misstated.

If the answer to both questions is *yes*, then the deficiency is a material weakness.

If an auditor concludes that the entity does not have an effective system of internal control (for example, due to a principle or component not being present or not functioning, or due to the five components not operating together in an integrated manner), a material weakness exists.

7.58 Deficiencies considered less severe than material weaknesses, but important enough to merit the attention of those charged with governance are classified as significant deficiencies. Appendix H of this guide contains additional information that may be useful in making this determination.

Communication of Internal Control Matters

Observations and Suggestions

Before you communicate the existence of any significant deficiencies or material weaknesses, you may need to clarify for your clients the role you can play with respect to their internal control. An auditor cannot be a part of their client's internal control.

How you respond to your client's deficiencies in internal control, in terms of designing and performing further auditing procedures, does not affect or mitigate the client's deficiencies in internal control. Just as an auditor's response

> to detection risk is independent of the client's control risk, so too the auditor's response to a deficiency in internal control does not change the deficiency.

Form

7.59 Deficiencies identified during the audit and evaluated as significant deficiencies or material weaknesses should be communicated in writing to those charged with governance on a timely basis. Such significant deficiencies or material weaknesses include those that were remediated during the audit. (AU-C sec. 265 par. .11)

Observations and Suggestions

Management may already know of the existence of significant deficiencies or material weaknesses, and the existence of these deficiencies may represent a conscious decision by management, those charged with governance, or both, to accept that degree of risk because of cost or other considerations. Management is responsible for making decisions concerning costs to be incurred and related benefits. You are responsible for communicating significant deficiencies and material weaknesses, regardless of management's decisions.

7.60 Nothing precludes you from communicating to management and those charged with governance other matters related to the client's internal control. For example, you may communicate

- matters you believe to be of potential benefit to the client, such as recommendations for operational or administrative efficiency, or for improving controls.
- deficiencies that are not significant deficiencies or material weaknesses.

You need not communicate these matters in writing.

Content

7.61 The written communication of significant deficiencies and material weaknesses should include

- the definition of the term *material weakness* and, where relevant, *significant deficiency.*
- a description of the significant deficiencies and material weaknesses and an explanation of their potential effects.
- sufficient information to enable those charged with governance and management to understand the context of the communication.
- a restriction regarding the use of the communication to management, those charged with governance, and others within the organization, and any governmental authority to which the auditor is required to report.

To enable those charged with governance and management to understand the context and implications of the communication you should also include the following elements:

- The purpose of the audit was for the auditor to express an opinion on the financial statements.

- The audit included consideration of internal control over financial reporting in order to design audit procedures that are appropriate in the circumstances but not for the purpose of expressing an opinion on the effectiveness of internal control.

- The auditor is not expressing an opinion of the effectiveness of internal control.

- The auditor's consideration of internal control was not designed to identity all deficiencies in internal control that might be material weaknesses or significant deficiencies, and therefore, material weaknesses or significant deficiencies may exist that were not identified.

(AU-C sec. 265 par. .14)

7.62 In some circumstances, you may include additional statements in your communication regarding

- the general inherent limitations of internal control, including management override of controls, or

- the specific nature and extent of your consideration of internal control during the audit.

7.63 A client may ask you to issue a written communication indicating that no material weaknesses were identified during the audit of the financial statements. You are not precluded from issuing such a communication, provided it includes the matters required under paragraph .15 of AU-C section 265. Exhibit B, "Illustrative No Material Weakness Communication," of AU-C section 265 provides an illustrative communication indicating that no material weaknesses were identified during the audit.

7.64 Exhibit B of AU-C section 265 includes, if one or more significant deficiencies have been identified, an additional fourth paragraph that may be added as follows:

> *Our audit was also not designed to identify deficiencies in internal control that might be significant deficiencies. A significant deficiency is a deficiency, or a combination of deficiencies, in internal control that is less severe than a material weakness, yet important enough to merit attention by those charged with governance. We communicated the significant deficiencies identified during our audit in a separate communication dated [date].*

7.65 You should not issue a written representation stating that no significant deficiencies were identified during the audit. (AU-C sec. 265 par. .16)

7.66 Management may wish to, or may be required by a regulator to, prepare a written response to the auditor's communication regarding significant deficiencies or material weaknesses identified during the audit. Such management communications may include a description of corrective actions taken by the entity, the entity's plans to implement new controls, or a statement indicating that management believes the cost of correcting a significant deficiency or material weakness would exceed the benefits to be derived from doing so.

7.67 If such a written response is included in a document containing the auditor's written communication to management and those charged with governance concerning identified significant deficiencies or material weaknesses, you may add a paragraph to your written communication disclaiming an opinion on such information. The following is an example of such a paragraph:

> *ABC Company's written response to the significant deficiencies [and material weaknesses] identified in our audit has not been subjected to the auditing procedures applied in the audit of the financial statements and, accordingly, we express no opinion on it.*

Timing

7.68 Your written communication of significant deficiencies and material weaknesses is best made by the report release date (which is the date you grant the client permission to use your auditor's report in connection with the financial statements), but should be made no later than 60 days following the report release date. (AU-C sec. 265 par. .13)

7.69 For some matters, early communication to management or those charged with governance may be important because of their relative significance and the urgency for corrective follow-up action. Accordingly, you may decide to communicate certain matters during the audit. These matters need not be communicated in writing during the audit, but significant deficiencies and material weaknesses should ultimately be included in a written communication, even if they were remediated during the audit. (AU-C sec. 265 par. .11)

Observations and Suggestions

Your client may ask how it is possible to express an unqualified opinion on the financial statements when material weaknesses in internal control were present.

You may wish to explain that your audit was designed to provide reasonable assurance that the financial statements are free from material misstatements. Internal control should be designed to prevent or detect and correct material misstatements. The auditor is not part of the client's internal control.

You can express an unqualified opinion on the financial statements even though material weaknesses in internal control are present, by performing sufficient procedures and obtaining appropriate audit evidence to afford reasonable assurance that the financial statements are free from material misstatement. However, these procedures do not *correct* deficiencies in internal control; the deficiencies in internal control could still result in a material misstatement not being prevented or detected and corrected on a timely basis by the client's internal control.

Audit Documentation for Misstatements

7.70 With respect to misstatements, you should document

    a. the amount below which misstatements would be regarded as clearly trivial, *b.* all misstatements accumulated during the audit and whether they have been corrected, and

  c. your conclusion regarding whether uncorrected misstatements, individually or in the aggregate, are material and the basis for that conclusion.

(AU-C sec. 450 par. .12)

Chapter 1, "Overview of Applying the Audit Risk Standards," of this guide provides additional, more general guidance on the preparation of audit documentation.

Summary

7.71 As a result of performing your substantive procedures, you may identify misstatements and you should accumulate all misstatements (except those that are trivial) that you identify during the audit. Those misstatements may be categorized as factual, judgmental, or projected.

7.72 *Factual misstatements* are misstatements about which there is no doubt. *Judgment misstatements* are differences arising from the judgments of management concerning accounting estimates that the auditor considers unreasonable or the selection or application of accounting policies that the auditor considers inappropriate. *Projected misstatements* are the auditor's best estimate of misstatements in populations, involving the projection of misstatements identified in auditing a sample to the entire population from which the sample was drawn.

7.73 You should communicate on a timely basis with the appropriate level of management all misstatements accumulated, and you should request management to correct those misstatements.

7.74 You should evaluate uncorrected misstatements to determine whether they are material, either individually or in the aggregate. This evaluation of uncorrected misstatements should include a consideration of uncorrected misstatements from previous periods that continue to effect the current year's financial statements. Further, such evaluation of uncorrected misstatements should also consider possible undetected misstatements, which are discussed in paragraph 7.11.

7.75 If you evaluate the uncorrected misstatements as not material, you may conclude that the financial statements are free of material misstatement. If you evaluate the uncorrected misstatements as material then the financial statements contain a material misstatement, and you should modify your auditor's report accordingly.

7.76 In the course of performing your audit, you may identify deficiencies in internal control, which you will need to evaluate and communicate to management.

7.77 Deficiencies in internal control may range in severity from inconsequential to significant deficiencies to material weaknesses. Some deficiencies may be considered significant deficiencies; others may be considered to be at least significant deficiencies and a strong indicator of material weaknesses.

7.78 For deficiencies in internal control not specifically identified as significant deficiencies, you determine their severity by considering the likelihood and significance of any misstatement that could result from the deficiency. That process notwithstanding, once you have made an initial evaluation of the severity of a deficiency in internal control, you should consider whether prudent officials, in the conduct of their own affairs, would agree with your conclusion about the deficiency.

                                         ©2016, AICPA

Appendix—Answers to Frequently Asked Questions About Evaluating Audit Findings, Audit Evidence, and Deficiencies in Internal Control

Question	See Paragraphs
How is materiality used at the end of the audit to evaluate misstatements?	7.05–.08
What is the distinction among factual, judgmental, and projected misstatements? How are these types of misstatements considered when determining whether the financial statements are free of material misstatements?	7.09–.10
How do I evaluate the results from substantive analytical procedures, sampling, and differences in estimates?	7.12–.22
What misstatements should I communicate to management? What requests should I make of management with regard to these misstatements?	7.23–.26
How do I evaluate uncorrected misstatements to determine whether the financial statements are *presented fairly in all material respects*?	7.27–.33
How do prior year's uncorrected misstatements affect my determination of whether the current year's financial statements are presented fairly?	7.34–.37 and appendix H of this guide
How do I know if I have obtained enough audit evidence to support my audit opinion?	7.42–.43
What is the difference between a material weakness and a significant deficiency?	7.47
What steps should I follow to evaluate deficiencies in internal control?	7.57
What is the *prudent official test*?	7.56
If I identify deficiencies in internal control, what should I communicate to management? When should I make this communication?	7.59–.69
What matters regarding the evaluation of audit findings should I document?	7.70

Part II

Additional Resources

Appendix A

Considerations in Establishing the Overall Audit Strategy[1]

This appendix is nonauthoritative and is included for informational purposes only.

A.01 This appendix provides examples of matters the auditor may consider in establishing the overall audit strategy. Many of these matters also will influence the auditor's detailed audit plan. The examples provided cover a broad range of matters applicable to many engagements. Although some of the following matters may be required by other AU-C sections, not all matters are relevant to every audit engagement, and the list is not necessarily complete.

Characteristics of the Engagement

A.02 The following are some examples of characteristics of the engagement:

- The financial reporting framework on which the financial information to be audited has been prepared, including any need for reconciliations to another financial reporting framework
- Industry specific reporting requirements, such as reports mandated by industry regulators
- The expected audit coverage, including the number and locations of components to be included
- The nature of the control relationships between a parent and its components that determine how the group is to be consolidated
- The extent to which components are audited by other auditors
- The nature of the business divisions to be audited, including the need for specialized knowledge
- The reporting currency to be used, including any need for currency translation for the audited financial information
- The need for statutory or regulatory audit requirements (for example, the Office of Management and Budget Circular A-133, *Audits of States, Local Governments, and Non-Profit Organizations*)
- Whether the entity has an internal audit function and, if so, whether (in which areas and to what extent) the work of the internal audit function can be used in obtaining audit evidence or whether internal auditors can be used to provide direct assistance
- The entity's use of service organizations and how the auditor may obtain evidence concerning the design or operation of controls performed by them
- The expected use of audit evidence obtained in previous audits (for example, audit evidence related to risk assessment procedures and tests of controls)

---

[1] This section is reprinted from paragraph .A25 of AU-C section 300, *Planning an Audit* (AICPA, *Professional Standards*).

- The effect of IT on the audit procedures, including the availability of data and the expected use of computer assisted audit techniques
- The coordination of the expected coverage and timing of the audit work with any reviews of interim financial information and the effect on the audit of the information obtained during such reviews
- The availability of client personnel and data

Reporting Objectives, Timing of the Audit, and Nature of Communications

A.03 The following examples illustrate reporting objectives, timing of the audit, and nature of communications:

- The entity's timetable for reporting, including interim periods
- The organization of meetings with management and those charged with governance to discuss the nature, timing, and extent of the audit work
- The discussion with management and those charged with governance regarding the expected type and timing of reports to be issued and other communications, both written and oral, including the auditor's report, management letters, and communications to those charged with governance
- The discussion with management regarding the expected communications on the status of audit work throughout the engagement
- Communication with auditors of components regarding the expected types and timing of reports to be issued and other communications in connection with the audit of components
- The expected nature and timing of communications among engagement team members, including the nature and timing of team meetings and timing of the review of work performed
- Whether there are any other expected communications with third parties, including any statutory or contractual reporting responsibilities arising from the audit

Significant Factors, Preliminary Engagement Activities, and Knowledge Gained on Other Engagements

A.04 The following examples illustrate significant factors, preliminary engagement activities, and knowledge gained on other engagements:

- The determination of materiality, in accordance with AU-C section 320, *Materiality in Planning and Performing an Audit* (AICPA, *Professional Standards*), and, when applicable, the following:
  - The determination of materiality for components and communication thereof to component auditors in accordance with AU-C section 600, *Special Considerations—Audits of Group Financial Statements (Including the Work of Component Auditors)* (AICPA, *Professional Standards*)

— The preliminary identification of significant components and material classes of transactions, account balances, and disclosures

- Preliminary identification of areas in which there may be a higher risk of material misstatement
- The effect of the assessed risk of material misstatement at the overall financial statement level on direction, supervision, and review
- The manner in which the auditor emphasizes to engagement team members the need to maintain a questioning mind and exercise professional skepticism in gathering and evaluating audit evidence
- Results of previous audits that involved evaluating the operating effectiveness of internal control, including the nature of identified deficiencies and action taken to address them
- The discussion of matters that may affect the audit with firm personnel responsible for performing other services to the entity
- Evidence of management's commitment to the design, implementation, and maintenance of sound internal control, including evidence of appropriate documentation of such internal control
- Volume of transactions, which may determine whether it is more efficient for the auditor to rely on internal control
- Importance attached to internal control throughout the entity to the successful operation of the business
- Significant business developments affecting the entity, including changes in IT and business processes, changes in key management, and acquisitions, mergers, and divestments
- Significant industry developments, such as changes in industry regulations and new reporting requirements
- Significant changes in the financial reporting framework, such as changes in accounting standards
- Other significant relevant developments, such as changes in the legal environment affecting the entity

Nature, Timing, and Extent of Resources

A.05 The following examples illustrate the nature, timing, and extent of resources:

- The selection of the engagement team (including, when necessary, the engagement quality control reviewer [see AU-C section 220, *Quality Control for an Engagement Conducted in Accordance With Generally Accepted Auditing Standards* (AICPA, *Professional Standards*)]) and the assignment of audit work to the team members, including the assignment of appropriately experienced team members to areas in which there may be higher risks of material misstatement
- Engagement budgeting, including considering the appropriate amount of time to set aside for areas in which there may be higher risks of material misstatement

Appendix B

Understanding the Entity and Its Environment[1]

This appendix is nonauthoritative and is included for informational purposes only.

B.01 This appendix provides additional guidance on matters the auditor may consider when obtaining an understanding of the industry, regulatory, and other external factors that affect the entity; the nature of the entity; objectives and strategies and related business risks; and measurement and review of the entity's financial performance. The examples provided cover a broad range of matters applicable to many engagements; however, not all matters are relevant to every engagement and the list of examples is not necessarily complete. Additional guidance on internal control is contained in paragraph .A157 of AU-C section 315, *Understanding the Entity and Its Environment and Assessing the Risks of Material Misstatement* (AICPA, *Professional Standards*).

Industry, Regulatory, and Other External Factors

B.02 Examples of matters an auditor may consider include the following:

- Industry conditions, such as the following:
  - The market and competition, including demand, capacity, and price competition
  - Cyclical or seasonal activity
  - Product technology relating to the entity's products
  - Supply availability and cost

- Regulatory environment, such as the following:
  - Accounting principles and industry-specific practices
  - Regulatory framework for a regulated industry
  - Legislation and regulation that significantly affect the entity's operations
    - Regulatory requirements
    - Direct supervisory activities
  - Taxation (corporate and other)
  - Government policies currently affecting the conduct of the entity's business, such as the following:
    - Monetary, including foreign exchange controls
    - Fiscal

---

[1] This section is reprinted from paragraph .A156 of AU-C section 315, *Understanding the Entity and Its Environment and Assessing the Risks of Material Misstatement* (AICPA, *Professional Standards*).

- Financial incentives (for example, government aid programs)
- Tariffs and trade restrictions
  - Environmental requirements affecting the industry and the entity's business
- Other external factors currently affecting the entity's business, such as the following:
  - General level of economic activity (for example, recession, growth)
  - Interest rates and availability of financing
  - Inflation and currency revaluation

Nature of the Entity

B.03   Examples of matters an auditor may consider include the following:

- Business operations, such as the following:
  - Nature of revenue sources (for example, manufacturer; wholesaler; banking, insurance, or other financial services; import-export trading, utility, transportation, and technology products and services)
  - Products or services and markets (for example, major customers and contracts, terms of payment, profit margins, market share, competitors, exports, pricing policies, reputation of products, warranties, backlog, trends, marketing strategy and objectives, and manufacturing processes)
  - Conduct of operations (for example, stages and methods of production, subsidiaries or divisions, delivery of products and services, and details of declining or expanding operations)
  - Alliances, joint ventures, and outsourcing activities
  - Involvement in e-commerce, including Internet sales and marketing activities
  - Geographic dispersion and industry segmentation
  - Location of production facilities, warehouses, and offices
  - Key customers
  - Important suppliers of goods and services (for example, long-term contracts, stability of supply, terms of payment, imports, and methods of delivery, such as "just-in-time")
  - Employment (for example, by location, supply, wage levels, union contracts, pension and other postemployment benefits, stock option or incentive bonus arrangements, and government regulation related to employment matters)
  - Research and development activities and expenditures
  - Transactions with related parties

- Investments, such as the following:
    - Acquisitions, mergers, or disposals of business activities (planned or recently executed)
    - Investments and dispositions of securities and loans
    - Capital investment activities, including investments in plant and equipment and technology, and any recent or planned changes
    - Investments in nonconsolidated entities, including partnerships, joint ventures, and special-purpose entities
    - Life cycle stage of enterprise (start-up, growing, mature, declining)
- Financing, such as the following:
    - Group structure—major subsidiaries and associated entities, including consolidated and nonconsolidated structures
    - Debt structure, including covenants, restrictions, guarantees, and off-balance-sheet financing arrangements
    - Leasing of property, plant, or equipment for use in the business
    - Beneficial owners (local and foreign business reputation and experience)
    - Related parties
    - Use of derivative financial instruments
- Financial reporting, such as the following:
    - Accounting principles and industry-specific practices
    - Revenue recognition practices
    - Accounting for fair values
    - Inventories (for example, locations and quantities)
    - Foreign currency assets, liabilities, and transactions
    - Industry-specific significant categories (for example, loans and investments for banks, accounts receivable and inventory for manufacturers, research and development for pharmaceuticals)
    - Accounting for unusual or complex transactions including those in controversial or emerging areas (for example, accounting for stock-based compensation)
    - Financial statement presentation and disclosure

Observations and Suggestions

The characteristics of multiple locations and significant investments may indicate the applicability of AU-C section 600, *Special Considerations—Audits of Group Financial Statements (Including the Work of Component Auditors)* (AICPA, *Professional Standards*), which governs many planning and performance considerations when it applies.

Objectives and Strategies and Related Business Risks

B.04 Examples of matters an auditor may consider include the following matters:

- Existence of objectives (that is, how the entity addresses industry, regulatory, and other external factors) relating to, for example, the following:
  - Industry developments (a potential related business risk might be, for example, that the entity does not have the personnel or expertise to deal with the changes in the industry)
  - New products and services (a potential related business risk might be, for example, that there is increased product liability)
  - Expansion of the business (a potential related business risk might be, for example, that the demand has not been accurately estimated)
  - New accounting requirements (a potential related business risk might be, for example, incomplete or improper implementation, or increased costs)
  - Regulatory requirements (a potential related business risk might be, for example, that there is increased legal exposure)
  - Current and prospective financing requirements (a potential related business risk might be, for example, the loss of financing due to the entity's inability to meet requirements)
  - IT (a potential related business risk might be, for example, that systems and processes are not compatible)
  - Risk appetite of managers and stakeholders
- Effects of implementing a strategy, particularly any effects that will lead to new accounting requirements (a potential related business risk might be, for example, incomplete or improper implementation)

Measurement and Review of the Entity's Financial Performance

B.05 Examples of matters an auditor may consider include the following:

- Key ratios and operating statistics
- Key performance indicators
- Employee performance measures and incentive compensation policies
- Trends
- Use of forecasts, budgets, and variance analysis

- Analyst reports and credit rating reports
- Competitor analysis
- Period-on-period financial performance (revenue growth, profitability, and leverage)

Appendix C
Internal Control Components

This appendix is nonauthoritative and is included for informational purposes only.

C.01 This appendix further explains the components of internal control as set out in paragraphs .04, .15–.25, and .A78–.A121 of AU-C section 315, *Understanding the Entity and Its Environment and Assessing the Risks of Material Misstatement* (AICPA, *Professional Standards*), as they relate to a financial statement audit. This appendix also explains how the concepts in AU-C section 315 correspond to the Committee of Sponsoring Organizations of the Treadway Commission's (COSO) *Internal Control—Integrated Framework* as updated in 2013 (COSO framework).

Control Environment

C.02 The control environment encompasses the following elements:

    a. *Communication and enforcement of integrity and ethical values.* The effectiveness of controls cannot rise above the integrity and ethical values of the people who create, administer, and monitor them. Integrity and ethical values are essential elements of the control environment that influence the effectiveness of the design, administration, and monitoring of other components of internal control. Integrity and ethical behavior are the product of the entity's ethical and behavioral standards, how they are communicated, and how they are reinforced in practice. They include management's actions to remove or reduce incentives and temptations that might prompt personnel to engage in dishonest, illegal, or unethical acts. They also include the communication of entity values and behavioral standards to personnel through policy statements and codes of conduct and by example.

    b. *Commitment to competence.* Competence is the knowledge and skills necessary to accomplish tasks that define the individual's job. Commitment to competence includes management's consideration of the competence levels for particular jobs and how those levels translate into requisite skills and knowledge.

    c. *Participation of those charged with governance.* An entity's control consciousness is significantly influenced by those charged with governance. Attributes include those charged with governance's independence from management, the experience and stature of its members, the extent of its involvement and scrutiny of activities, the appropriateness of its actions, the information it receives, the degree to which difficult questions are raised and pursued with management, and its interaction with the internal audit function (if any) and external auditors. The importance of responsibilities of those charged with governance is recognized in codes of practice and other regulations or guidance produced for the benefit of those charged with governance. Other responsibilities of those charged with governance include oversight of the design and effective operation of whistle-blower procedures and of the process for reviewing the effectiveness of the entity's internal control.

d. *Management's philosophy and operating style.* Management's philosophy and operating style encompass a broad range of characteristics. For example, management's attitudes and actions toward financial reporting may manifest themselves through conservative or aggressive selection from available alternative accounting principles or conscientiousness and conservatism with which accounting estimates are developed.

e. *Organizational structure.* An entity's organizational structure provides the framework within which its activities for achieving entity-wide objectives are planned, executed, controlled, and reviewed. Establishing a relevant organizational structure includes considering key areas of authority and responsibility and appropriate lines of reporting. An entity develops an organizational structure suited to its needs. The appropriateness of an entity's organizational structure depends in part on its size and the nature of its activities.

f. *Assignment of authority and responsibility.* The assignment of authority and responsibility may include policies relating to appropriate business practices, knowledge and experience of key personnel, and resources provided for carrying out duties. In addition, it may include policies and communications directed at ensuring that all personnel understand the entity's objectives, know how their individual actions interrelate and contribute to those objectives, and recognize how and for what they will be held accountable.

g. *Human resource policies and practices.* Human resource policies and practices often demonstrate important matters regarding the control consciousness of an entity. For example, standards for recruiting the most qualified individuals, with an emphasis on educational background, prior work experience, past accomplishments, and evidence of integrity and ethical behavior, demonstrate an entity's commitment to competent and trustworthy people. Training policies that communicate prospective roles and responsibilities and include practices such as training schools and seminars illustrate expected levels of performance and behavior. Promotions driven by periodic performance appraisals demonstrate the entity's commitment to the advancement of qualified personnel to higher levels of responsibility.

Application to Small and Midsized Entities

C.03   Small and midsized entities may implement the control environment elements differently than larger entities. For example, smaller entities might not have a written code of conduct but, instead, develop a culture that emphasizes the importance of integrity and ethical behavior through oral communication and by management example. Similarly, those charged with governance in smaller entities may not include independent or outside members. However, the absence of documentation can also make it difficult to identify and test controls and assess changes in the controls over time.

The COSO framework accepts that certain controls may still exist even though they are not documented. However, the COSO framework, as revised in 2013, notes that regulators may require documentation.

Practice Considerations for Auditors of Entities Using the COSO Framework

There are five principles relating to the control environment component specified in the COSO framework:

- Principle 1. The organization demonstrates a commitment to integrity and ethical values.
- Principle 2. The board of directors demonstrates independence from management and exercises oversight of the development and performance of internal control.
- Principle 3. Management establishes, with board oversight, structures, reporting lines, and appropriate authorities and responsibilities in the pursuit of objectives.
- Principle 4. The organization demonstrates a commitment to attract, develop, and retain competent individuals in alignment with objectives.
- Principle 5. The organization holds individuals accountable for their internal control responsibilities in the pursuit of objectives.

The following elements in paragraph C.02 correspond as follows to the principles of the control environment component specified in the COSO framework:

- Element (*a*) corresponds to principle 1
- Elements (*b*) and (*g*) correspond largely to principle 4
- Element (*c*) corresponds to principle 2 (and also is relevant for principle 3)
- Elements (*e*) and (*f*) correspond largely to principle 3 (and also principle 5)

Element (*d*) does not correspond directly to a separate COSO framework principle, but deficiencies related to this element may correlate to the principle most closely reflecting the nature of the deficiency.

The Entity's Risk Assessment Process

C.04 For financial reporting purposes, the entity's risk assessment process includes how management identifies business risks relevant to the preparation and fair presentation of financial statements in accordance with the entity's applicable financial reporting framework, estimates their significance, assesses the likelihood of their occurrence, and decides upon actions to respond to and manage them and the results thereof. For example, the entity's risk assessment process may address how the entity considers the possibility of unrecorded transactions or identifies and analyzes significant estimates recorded in the financial statements.

©2016, AICPA

Risks relevant to reliable financial reporting include external and internal events, as well as transactions or circumstances that may occur and adversely affect an entity's ability to initiate, authorize, record, process, and report financial data consistent with the assertions of management in the financial statements. Management may initiate plans, programs, or actions to address specific risks or it may decide to accept a risk because of cost or other considerations. Risks can arise or change due to circumstances such as the following:

- *Changes in operating environment.* Changes in the regulatory or operating environment can result in changes in competitive pressures and significantly different risks.

- *New personnel.* New personnel may have a different focus on, or understanding of, internal control.

- *New or revamped information systems.* Significant and rapid changes in information systems can change the risk relating to internal control.

- *Rapid growth.* Significant and rapid expansion of operations can strain controls and increase the risk of a breakdown in controls.

- *New technology.* Incorporating new technologies into production processes or information systems may change the risk associated with internal control.

- *New business models, products, or activities.* Entering into business areas or transactions with which an entity has little experience may introduce new risks associated with internal control.

- *Corporate restructurings.* Restructurings may be accompanied by staff reductions and changes in supervision and segregation of duties that may change the risk associated with internal control.

- *Expanded foreign operations.* The expansion or acquisition of foreign operations carries new and often unique risks that may affect internal control (for example, additional or changed risks from foreign currency transactions).

- *New accounting pronouncements.* Adoption of new accounting principles or changing accounting principles may affect risks in preparing financial statements.

Practice Considerations for Auditors of Entities Using the COSO Framework

There are four principles relating to the risk assessment component specified in the COSO framework:

- Principle 6. The organization specifies objectives with sufficient clarity to enable the identification and assessment of risks relating to objectives.
- Principle 7. The organization identifies risks to the achievement of its objectives across the entity and analyzes risks as a basis for determining how the risks should be managed.
- Principle 8. The organization considers the potential for fraud in assessing risks to the achievement of objectives.

- Principle 9. The organization identifies and assesses changes that could significantly impact the system of internal control.

The many considerations listed in paragraph C.04 are embodied in principle 9 in the COSO framework. The COSO framework emphasizes the importance of specifying objectives (principle 6) in identifying risks (principle 7). In the COSO framework, assessing fraud risk is a separate principle (principle 8). Appendix D, "Exhibit—Management Antifraud Programs and Controls," in this guide addresses entity considerations relevant to this principle.

The Information System, Including the Related Business Processes Relevant to Financial Reporting, and Communication

C.05 An information system consists of infrastructure (physical and hardware components), software, people, procedures, and data. Many information systems rely extensively on IT.

C.06 The information system relevant to financial reporting objectives, which includes the accounting system, consists of the procedures, whether IT or manual, and records established to initiate, authorize, record, process, and report entity transactions (as well as events and conditions) and to maintain accountability for the related assets, liabilities, and equity. Transactions may be initiated manually or automatically by programmed procedures. Authorization includes the process of approving transactions by the appropriate level of management. Recording includes identifying and capturing the relevant information for transactions or events. Processing includes functions such as edit and validation, calculation, measurement, valuation, summarization, and reconciliation, whether performed by IT or manual procedures. Reporting relates to the preparation of financial reports as well as other information, in electronic or printed format, that the entity uses in measuring and reviewing the entity's financial performance and in other functions. The quality of system-generated information affects management's ability to make appropriate decisions in managing and controlling the entity's activities and to prepare reliable financial reports.

C.07 The information system relevant to financial reporting objectives, which includes the financial reporting system, encompasses methods and records that

- identify and record all valid transactions.
- describe on a timely basis the transactions in sufficient detail to permit proper classification of transactions for financial reporting.
- measure the value of transactions in a manner that permits recording their proper monetary value in the financial statements.
- determine the time period in which transactions occurred to permit recording of transactions in the proper accounting period.
- present properly the transactions and related disclosures in the financial statements.

Communication, which involves providing an understanding of individual roles and responsibilities pertaining to internal control over financial reporting, may take such forms as policy manuals, accounting and financial reporting manuals, and memoranda. Communication also can be made electronically, orally, and through the actions of management.

> **Practice Considerations for Auditors of Entities Using the COSO Framework**
>
> There are three principles relating to the information and communication component specified in the COSO framework:
>
> - Principle 13. The organization obtains or generates and uses relevant, quality information to support the functioning of internal control.
> - Principle 14. The organization internally communicates information, including objectives and responsibilities for internal control, necessary to support the functioning of internal control.
> - Principle 15. The organization communicates with external parties regarding matters affecting the functioning of internal control.
>
> Largely, the factors of information and communication listed in paragraphs C.06–C.07 are embodied in principles 13, 14, and 15 in the COSO framework. However, the COSO framework explicitly reflects external communication as a separate principle (principle 15).
>
> In the COSO framework, information technology general controls (ITGC) is a component within a separate principle (principle 11) as part of the control activities component. This aligns more closely the ITGC assessment with the underlying computer application controls which are usually assessed in conjunction with transaction processing. ITGC deficiencies could have a direct effect on any information processing relating to the entity, including principles 14 and 15, and also in the monitoring component (which usually relies heavily on information provided by the system).

Control Activities

C.08   Generally, control activities that may be relevant to an audit may be categorized as policies and procedures that pertain to the following:

- *Performance reviews.* These control activities include reviews and analyses of actual performance versus budgets, forecasts, and prior-period performance; relating different sets of data (operating or financial) to one another, together with analyses of the relationships and investigative and corrective actions; comparing internal data with external sources of information; and review of functional or activity performance.

- *Information processing.* The two broad groupings of information systems control activities are application controls, which apply to the processing of individual applications, and general IT controls, which are policies and procedures that relate to many applications and support the effective functioning of application controls by helping to ensure the continued proper operation of information systems. Examples of application controls include checking the arithmetical accuracy of records; maintaining and reviewing accounts and trial balances; automated controls, such as edit checks of input data and numerical sequence checks; and manual follow-up of exception reports. Examples of general IT controls are program change controls; controls that restrict access to programs or data; controls over the implementation of new releases of packaged software applications; and controls over system software that restrict access to, or monitor the use of, system utilities that could change financial data or records without leaving an audit trail.

- *Physical controls.* This includes controls that encompass the

    — physical security of assets, including adequate safeguards, such as secured facilities over access to assets and records.

    — authorization for access to computer programs and data files.

    — periodic counting and comparison with amounts shown on control records (for example comparing the results of cash, security, and inventory counts with accounting records).

    The extent to which physical controls intended to prevent theft of assets are relevant to the reliability of financial statement preparation and, therefore, the audit, depends on circumstances such as when assets are highly susceptible to misappropriation.

- *Segregation of duties.* Assigning different people the responsibilities of authorizing transactions, recording transactions, and maintaining custody of assets. Segregation of duties is intended to reduce the opportunities to allow any person to be in a position to both perpetrate and conceal errors or fraud in the normal course of the person's duties.

Certain control activities may depend on the existence of appropriate higher level policies established by management or those charged with governance. For example, authorization controls may be delegated under established guidelines, such as investment criteria set by those charged with governance; alternatively, nonroutine transactions, such as major acquisitions or divestments, may require specific high level approval, including, in some cases, that of shareholders.

Application to Small and Midsized Entities

C.09 The concepts underlying control activities in small or midsized organizations are likely to be similar to those in larger entities, but the formality with which they operate varies. Further, smaller entities may find that certain types of control activities are not relevant because of controls applied by management. For example, management's retention of authority for approving credit sales, significant purchases, and draw-downs on lines of credit can provide strong control over those activities, lessening or removing the need for more detailed control activities. An appropriate segregation of duties often appears to present difficulties in smaller organizations. Even companies that have only a few employees, however, may be able to assign responsibilities to achieve appropriate segregation or, if that is not possible, to use management oversight of the incompatible activities to achieve control objectives.

Practice Considerations for Auditors of Entities Using the COSO Framework

There are three principles relating to the control activities component specified in the COSO framework. In the COSO framework, the control activities component follows the risk assessment component and precedes the information and communication component (while in AU-C section 315, control activities follows information and communication):

- Principle 10. The organization selects and develops control activities that contribute to the mitigation of risks to the achievement of objectives to acceptable levels.
- Principle 11. The organization selects and develops general control activities over technology to support the achievement of objectives.
- Principle 12. The organization deploys control activities through policies that establish what is expected and procedures that put policies into action.

The first of these principles (principle 10) corresponds with the objectives and risk sequence of principles in the risk assessment component. Gaps in controls design can be more easily discerned when objectives and risks are clearly articulated. Computer IT general controls are set out as a separate principle (principle 11) in the COSO framework. Principle 12 is where most transaction process controls (including computer application controls) are addressed.

Monitoring of Controls

C.10   An important management responsibility is to establish and maintain internal control on an ongoing basis. Management's monitoring of controls includes considering whether they are operating as intended and that they are modified as appropriate for changes in conditions. Monitoring of controls may include activities such as management's review of whether bank reconciliations are being prepared on a timely basis, the internal audit function's evaluation of sales personnel's compliance with the entity's policies on terms of sales contracts, and a legal department's oversight of compliance with the entity's ethical or business practice policies. Monitoring also is done to ensure that controls continue to operate effectively over time. For example, if the timeliness and accuracy of bank reconciliations are not monitored, personnel are likely to stop preparing them.

C.11   The internal audit function or personnel performing similar functions may contribute to the monitoring of an entity's controls through separate evaluations. Ordinarily, they regularly provide information about the functioning of internal control, focusing considerable attention on evaluating the effectiveness of internal control; communicate information about strengths and deficiencies in internal control; and provide recommendations for improving internal control.

C.12   Monitoring activities may include using information from communications from external parties that may indicate problems or highlight areas in need of improvement. Customers implicitly corroborate billing data by paying their invoices or complaining about their charges. In addition, regulators may communicate with the entity concerning matters that affect the functioning of internal control (for example, communications concerning examinations by bank regulatory agencies). Also, management may consider communications relating to internal control from external auditors in performing monitoring activities.

Application to Small and Midsized Entities

C.13 Ongoing monitoring activities of small and midsized entities are more likely to be informal and are typically performed as a part of the overall management of the entity's operations. Management's close involvement in operations often will identify significant variances from expectations and inaccuracies in financial data.

Practice Considerations for Auditors of Entities Using the COSO Framework

There are two principles specified in the COSO framework relating to the monitoring activities component:

- Principle 16. The organization selects, develops, and performs ongoing and/or separate evaluations to ascertain whether the components of internal control are present and functioning.

- Principle 17. The organization evaluates and communicates internal control deficiencies in a timely manner to those parties responsible for taking corrective action, including senior management and the board of directors, as appropriate.

These two principles relate to the concepts discussed in paragraphs C.10–C.12.

Appendix D

Exhibit—Management Antifraud Programs and Controls

This appendix is nonauthoritative and is included for informational purposes only.

Guidance to Help Prevent, Deter, and Detect Fraud

This document is being issued jointly by the following organizations:

> American Institute of Certified Public Accountants (AICPA)
>
> Association of Certified Fraud Examiners (ACFE)
>
> Financial Executives International (FEI)
>
> Information Systems Audit and Control Association (ISACA)
>
> The Institute of Internal Auditors (IIA)
>
> Institute of Management Accountants (IMA)
>
> Society for Human Resource Management (SHRM)

In addition, we would also like to acknowledge the American Accounting Association, the Defense Industry Initiative, and the National Association of Corporate Directors for their review of the document and helpful comments and materials.

We gratefully acknowledge the valuable contribution provided by the Anti-Fraud Detection Subgroup:

Daniel D. Montgomery, *Chair*
Toby J.F. Bishop
Dennis H. Chookaszian
Susan A. Finn
Dana Hermanson
David L. Landsittel
Carol A. Langelier
Joseph T. Wells
Janice Wilkins

Finally, we thank the staff of the AICPA for their support on this project:

Charles E. Landes
Director
Audit and Attest Standards

Richard Lanza
Senior Program Manager
Chief Operating Office

Kim M. Gibson
Senior Technical Manager
Audit and Attest Standards

Hugh Kelsey
Program Manager
Knowledge Management

©2016, AICPA

This document was commissioned by the Fraud Task Force of the AICPA's Auditing Standards Board. This document has not been adopted, approved, disapproved, or otherwise acted upon by a board, committee, governing body, or membership of the issuing organizations.

Preface

Some organizations have significantly lower levels of misappropriation of assets and are less susceptible to fraudulent financial reporting than other organizations because these organizations take proactive steps to prevent or deter fraud. It is only those organizations that seriously consider fraud risks and take proactive steps to create the right kind of climate to reduce its occurrence that have success in preventing fraud. This document identifies the key participants in this antifraud effort, including the board of directors, management, internal and independent auditors, and certified fraud examiners.

Management may develop and implement some of these programs and controls in response to specific identified risks of material misstatement of financial statements due to fraud. In other cases, these programs and controls may be a part of the entity's enterprise-wide risk management activities.

Management is responsible for designing and implementing systems and procedures for the prevention and detection of fraud and, along with the board of directors, for ensuring a culture and environment that promotes honesty and ethical behavior. However, because of the characteristics of fraud, a material misstatement of financial statements due to fraud may occur notwithstanding the presence of programs and controls such as those described in this document.

Introduction

Fraud can range from minor employee theft and unproductive behavior to misappropriation of assets and fraudulent financial reporting. Material financial statement fraud can have a significant adverse effect on an entity's market value, reputation, and ability to achieve its strategic objectives. A number of highly publicized cases have heightened the awareness of the effects of fraudulent financial reporting and have led many organizations to be more proactive in taking steps to prevent or deter its occurrence. Misappropriation of assets, though often not material to the financial statements, can nonetheless result in substantial losses to an entity if a dishonest employee has the incentive and opportunity to commit fraud.

The risk of fraud can be reduced through a combination of prevention, deterrence, and detection measures. However, fraud can be difficult to detect because it often involves concealment through falsification of documents or collusion among management, employees, or third parties. Therefore, it is important to place a strong emphasis on fraud prevention, which may reduce opportunities for fraud to take place, and fraud deterrence, which could persuade individuals that they should not commit fraud because of the likelihood of detection and punishment. Moreover, prevention and deterrence measures are much less costly than the time and expense required for fraud detection and investigation.

An entity's management has both the responsibility and the means to implement measures to reduce the incidence of fraud. The measures an organization takes to prevent and deter fraud also can help create a positive workplace environment that can enhance the entity's ability to recruit and retain high-quality employees.

Research suggests that the most effective way to implement measures to reduce wrongdoing is to base them on a set of core values that are embraced by the entity. These values provide an overarching message about the key principles guiding all employees' actions. This provides a platform upon which a more detailed code of conduct can be constructed, giving more specific guidance about permitted and prohibited behavior, based on applicable laws and the organization's values. Management needs to clearly articulate that all employees will be held accountable to act within the organization's code of conduct.

This document identifies measures entities can implement to prevent, deter, and detect fraud. It discusses these measures in the context of three fundamental elements. Broadly stated, these fundamental elements are (1) create and maintain a *culture* of honesty and high ethics; (2) *evaluate* the risks of fraud and implement the processes, procedures, and controls needed to mitigate the risks and reduce the opportunities for fraud; and (3) develop an appropriate *oversight* process. Although the entire management team shares the responsibility for implementing and monitoring these activities, with oversight from the board of directors, the entity's chief executive officer (CEO) should initiate and support such measures. Without the CEO's active support, these measures are less likely to be effective.

The information presented in this document generally is applicable to entities of all sizes. However, the degree to which certain programs and controls are applied in smaller, less-complex entities and the formality of their application are likely to differ from larger organizations. For example, management of a smaller entity (or the owner of an owner-managed entity), along with those charged with governance of the financial reporting process, are responsible for creating a culture of honesty and high ethics. Management also is responsible for implementing a system of internal control commensurate with the nature and size of the organization, but smaller entities may find that certain types of control activities are not relevant because of the involvement of and controls applied by management. However, all entities must make it clear that unethical or dishonest behavior will not be tolerated.

Creating a Culture of Honesty and High Ethics

It is the organization's responsibility to create a culture of honesty and high ethics and to clearly communicate acceptable behavior and expectations of each employee. Such a culture is rooted in a strong set of core values (or value system) that provides the foundation for employees concerning how the organization conducts its business. It also allows an entity to develop an ethical framework that covers (1) fraudulent financial reporting, (2) misappropriation of assets, and (3) corruption as well as other issues.[1]

Creating a culture of honesty and high ethics should include the following.

Setting the Tone at the Top

Directors and officers of corporations set the "tone at the top" for ethical behavior within any organization. Research in moral development strongly suggests that honesty can best be reinforced when a proper example is set—sometimes

---

[1] Corruption includes bribery and other illegal acts.

referred to as the tone at the top. The management of an entity cannot act one way and expect others in the entity to behave differently.

In many cases, particularly in larger organizations, it is necessary for management to both behave ethically and openly communicate its expectations for ethical behavior because most employees are not in a position to observe management's actions. Management must show employees through its words and actions that dishonest or unethical behavior will not be tolerated, even if the result of the action benefits the entity. Moreover, it should be evident that all employees will be treated equally, regardless of their position.

For example, statements by management regarding the absolute need to meet operating and financial targets can create undue pressures that may lead employees to commit fraud to achieve them. Setting unachievable goals for employees can give them two unattractive choices: fail or cheat. In contrast, a statement from management that says, "We are aggressive in pursuing our targets, while requiring truthful financial reporting at all times," clearly indicates to employees that integrity is a requirement. This message also conveys that the entity has "zero tolerance" for unethical behavior, including fraudulent financial reporting.

The cornerstone of an effective antifraud environment is a culture with a strong value system founded on integrity. This value system often is reflected in a code of conduct.[2] The code of conduct should reflect the core values of the entity and guide employees in making appropriate decisions during their workday. The code of conduct might include such topics as ethics, confidentiality, conflicts of interest, intellectual property, sexual harassment, and fraud.[3] For a code of conduct to be effective, it should be communicated to all personnel in an understandable fashion. It also should be developed in a participatory and positive manner that will result in both management and employees taking ownership of its content. Finally, the code of conduct should be included in an employee handbook or policy manual, or in some other formal document or location (for example, the entity's intranet) so it can be referred to when needed.

Senior financial officers hold an important and elevated role in corporate governance. Although members of the management team, they are uniquely capable and empowered to ensure that all stakeholders' interests are appropriately balanced, protected, and preserved. For examples of codes of conduct, see Attachment 1, "AICPA 'CPA's Handbook of Fraud and Commercial Crime Prevention,' An Organizational Code of Conduct," and Attachment 2, "Financial Executives International Code of Ethics Statement" provided by FEI. In addition, visit the Institute of Management Accountant's Ethics Center at www.imanet.org for their members' standards of ethical conduct.

Creating a Positive Workplace Environment

Research results indicate that wrongdoing occurs less frequently when employees have positive feelings about an entity than when they feel abused,

---

[2] An entity's value system also could be reflected in an ethics policy, a statement of business principles, or some other concise summary of guiding principles.

[3] Although the discussion in this document focuses on fraud, the subject of fraud often is considered in the context of a broader set of principles that govern an organization. Some organizations, however, may elect to develop a fraud policy separate from an ethics policy. Specific examples of topics in a fraud policy might include a requirement to comply with all laws and regulations and explicit guidance regarding making payments to obtain contracts, holding pricing discussions with competitors, environmental discharges, relationships with vendors, and maintenance of accurate books and records.

threatened, or ignored. Without a positive workplace environment, there are more opportunities for poor employee morale, which can affect an employee's attitude about committing fraud against an entity. Factors that detract from a positive work environment and may increase the risk of fraud include

- top management that does not seem to care about or reward appropriate behavior.
- negative feedback and lack of recognition for job performance.
- perceived inequities in the organization.
- autocratic rather than participative management.
- low organizational loyalty or feelings of ownership.
- unreasonable budget expectations or other financial targets.
- fear of delivering "bad news" to supervisors and/or management.
- less-than-competitive compensation.
- poor training and promotion opportunities.
- lack of clear organizational responsibilities.
- poor communication practices or methods within the organization.

The entity's human resources department often is instrumental in helping to build a corporate culture and a positive work environment. Human resource professionals are responsible for implementing specific programs and initiatives, consistent with management's strategies, that can help to mitigate many of the detractors mentioned previously. Mitigating factors that help create a positive work environment and reduce the risk of fraud may include

- recognition and reward systems that are in tandem with goals and results.
- equal employment opportunities.
- team-oriented, collaborative decision-making policies.
- professionally administered compensation programs.
- professionally administered training programs and an organizational priority of career development.

Employees should be empowered to help create a positive workplace environment and support the entity's values and code of conduct. They should be given the opportunity to provide input to the development and updating of the entity's code of conduct, to ensure that it is relevant, clear, and fair. Involving employees in this fashion also may effectively contribute to the oversight of the entity's code of conduct and an environment of ethical behavior (see the section titled "Developing an Appropriate Oversight Process").

Employees should be given the means to obtain advice internally before making decisions that appear to have significant legal or ethical implications. They should also be encouraged and given the means to communicate concerns, anonymously if preferred, about potential violations of the entity's code of conduct, without fear of retribution. Many organizations have implemented a process for employees to report on a confidential basis any actual or suspected wrongdoing, or potential violations of the code of conduct or ethics policy. For example, some organizations use a telephone "hotline" that is directed to or monitored by an ethics officer, fraud officer, general counsel, internal audit director, or another trusted individual responsible for investigating and reporting incidents of fraud or illegal acts.

Hiring and Promoting Appropriate Employees

Each employee has a unique set of values and personal code of ethics. When faced with sufficient pressure and a perceived opportunity, some employees will behave dishonestly rather than face the negative consequences of honest behavior. The threshold at which dishonest behavior starts, however, will vary among individuals. If an entity is to be successful in preventing fraud, it must have effective policies that minimize the chance of hiring or promoting individuals with low levels of honesty, especially for positions of trust.

Proactive hiring and promotion procedures may include

- conducting background investigations on individuals being considered for employment or for promotion to a position of trust.[4]
- thoroughly checking a candidate's education, employment history, and personal references.
- periodic training of all employees about the entity's values and code of conduct, (training is addressed in the following section).
- incorporating into regular performance reviews an evaluation of how each individual has contributed to creating an appropriate workplace environment in line with the entity's values and code of conduct.
- continuous objective evaluation of compliance with the entity's values and code of conduct, with violations being addressed immediately.

Training

New employees should be trained at the time of hiring about the entity's values and its code of conduct. This training should explicitly cover expectations of all employees regarding (1) their duty to communicate certain matters; (2) a list of the types of matters, including actual or suspected fraud, to be communicated along with specific examples; and (3) information on how to communicate those matters. There also should be an affirmation from senior management regarding employee expectations and communication responsibilities. Such training should include an element of "fraud awareness," the tone of which should be positive but nonetheless stress that fraud can be costly (and detrimental in other ways) to the entity and its employees.

In addition to training at the time of hiring, employees should receive refresher training periodically thereafter. Some organizations may consider ongoing training for certain positions, such as purchasing agents or employees with financial reporting responsibilities. Training should be specific to an employee's level within the organization, geographic location, and assigned responsibilities. For example, training for senior manager level personnel would normally be different from that of nonsupervisory employees, and training for purchasing agents would be different from that of sales representatives.

Confirmation

Management needs to clearly articulate that all employees will be held accountable to act within the entity's code of conduct. All employees within senior management and the finance function, as well as other employees in areas that

---

[4] Some organizations also have considered follow-up investigations, particularly for employees in positions of trust, on a periodic basis (for example, every five years) or as circumstances dictate.

might be exposed to unethical behavior (for example, procurement, sales and marketing) should be required to sign a code of conduct statement annually, at a minimum.

Requiring periodic confirmation by employees of their responsibilities will not only reinforce the policy but may also deter individuals from committing fraud and other violations and might identify problems before they become significant. Such confirmation may include statements that the individual understands the entity's expectations, has complied with the code of conduct, and is not aware of any violations of the code of conduct other than those the individual lists in his or her response. Although people with low integrity may not hesitate to sign a false confirmation, most people will want to avoid making a false statement in writing. Honest individuals are more likely to return their confirmations and to disclose what they know (including any conflicts of interest or other personal exceptions to the code of conduct). Thorough follow-up by internal auditors or others regarding nonreplies may uncover significant issues.

Discipline

The way an entity reacts to incidents of alleged or suspected fraud will send a strong deterrent message throughout the entity, helping to reduce the number of future occurrences. The following actions should be taken in response to an alleged incident of fraud:

- A thorough investigation of the incident should be conducted.[5]
- Appropriate and consistent actions should be taken against violators.
- Relevant controls should be assessed and improved.
- Communication and training should occur to reinforce the entity's values, code of conduct, and expectations.

Expectations about the consequences of committing fraud must be clearly communicated throughout the entity. For example, a strong statement from management that dishonest actions will not be tolerated, and that violators may be terminated and referred to the appropriate authorities, clearly establishes consequences and can be a valuable deterrent to wrongdoing. If wrongdoing occurs and an employee is disciplined, it can be helpful to communicate that fact, on a no-name basis, in an employee newsletter or other regular communication to employees. Seeing that other people have been disciplined for wrongdoing can be an effective deterrent, increasing the perceived likelihood of violators being caught and punished. It also can demonstrate that the entity is committed to an environment of high ethical standards and integrity.

Evaluating Antifraud Processes and Controls

Neither fraudulent financial reporting nor misappropriation of assets can occur without a perceived opportunity to commit and conceal the act. Organizations

---

[5] Many entities of sufficient size are employing antifraud professionals, such as certified fraud examiners, who are responsible for resolving allegations of fraud within the organization and who also assist in the detection and deterrence of fraud. These individuals typically report their findings internally to the corporate security, legal, or internal audit departments. In other instances, such individuals may be empowered directly by the board of directors or its audit committee.

should be proactive in reducing fraud opportunities by (1) identifying and measuring fraud risks, (2) taking steps to mitigate identified risks, and (3) implementing and monitoring appropriate preventive and detective internal controls and other deterrent measures.

Identifying and Measuring Fraud Risks

Management has primary responsibility for establishing and monitoring all aspects of the entity's fraud risk-assessment and prevention activities.[6] Fraud risks often are considered as part of an enterprise-wide risk management program, though they may be addressed separately.[7] The fraud risk-assessment process should consider the vulnerability of the entity to fraudulent activity (fraudulent financial reporting, misappropriation of assets, and corruption) and whether any of those exposures could result in a material misstatement of the financial statements or material loss to the organization. In identifying fraud risks, organizations should consider organizational, industry, and country-specific characteristics that influence the risk of fraud.

The nature and extent of management's risk assessment activities should be commensurate with the size of the entity and complexity of its operations. For example, the risk assessment process is likely to be less formal and less structured in smaller entities. However, management should recognize that fraud can occur in organizations of any size or type, and that almost any employee may be capable of committing fraud given the right set of circumstances. Accordingly, management should develop a heightened "fraud awareness" and an appropriate fraud risk-management program, with oversight from the board of directors or audit committee.

Mitigating Fraud Risks

It may be possible to reduce or eliminate certain fraud risks by making changes to the entity's activities and processes. An entity may choose to sell certain segments of its operations, cease doing business in certain locations, or reorganize its business processes to eliminate unacceptable risks. For example, the risk of misappropriation of funds may be reduced by implementing a central lockbox at a bank to receive payments instead of receiving money at the entity's various locations. The risk of corruption may be reduced by closely monitoring the entity's procurement process. The risk of financial statement fraud may be reduced by implementing shared services centers to provide accounting services to multiple segments, affiliates, or geographic locations of an entity's operations. A shared services center may be less vulnerable to influence by local operations managers and may be able to implement more extensive fraud detection measures cost-effectively.

---

[6] Management may elect to have internal audit play an active role in the development, monitoring, and ongoing assessment of the entity's fraud risk-management program. This may include an active role in the development and communication of the entity's code of conduct or ethics policy, as well as in investigating actual or alleged instances of noncompliance.

[7] Some organizations may perform a periodic self-assessment using questionnaires or other techniques to identify and measure risks. Self-assessment may be less reliable in identifying the risk of fraud due to a lack of experience with fraud (although many organizations experience some form of fraud and abuse, material financial statement fraud or misappropriation of assets is a rare event for most) and because management may be unwilling to acknowledge openly that they might commit fraud given sufficient pressure and opportunity.

Implementing and Monitoring Appropriate Internal Controls

Some risks are inherent in the environment of the entity, but most can be addressed with an appropriate system of internal control. Once fraud risk assessment has taken place, the entity can identify the processes, controls, and other procedures that are needed to mitigate the identified risks. Effective internal control will include a well-developed control environment, an effective and secure information system, and appropriate control and monitoring activities.[8] Because of the importance of information technology in supporting operations and the processing of transactions, management also needs to implement and maintain appropriate controls, whether automated or manual, over computer-generated information.

In particular, management should evaluate whether appropriate internal controls have been implemented in any areas management has identified as posing a higher risk of fraudulent activity, as well as controls over the entity's financial reporting process. Because fraudulent financial reporting may begin in an interim period, management also should evaluate the appropriateness of internal controls over interim financial reporting.

Fraudulent financial reporting by upper-level management typically involves override of internal controls within the financial reporting process. Because management has the ability to override controls, or to influence others to perpetrate or conceal fraud, the need for a strong value system and a culture of ethical financial reporting becomes increasingly important. This helps create an environment in which other employees will decline to participate in committing a fraud and will use established communication procedures to report any requests to commit wrongdoing. The potential for management override also increases the need for appropriate oversight measures by the board of directors or audit committee, as discussed in the following section.

Fraudulent financial reporting by lower levels of management and employees may be deterred or detected by appropriate monitoring controls, such as having higher-level managers review and evaluate the financial results reported by individual operating units or subsidiaries. Unusual fluctuations in results of particular reporting units, or the lack of expected fluctuations, may indicate potential manipulation by departmental or operating unit managers or staff.

Developing an Appropriate Oversight Process

To effectively prevent or deter fraud, an entity should have an appropriate oversight function in place. Oversight can take many forms and can be performed by many within and outside the entity, under the overall oversight of the audit committee (or board of directors where no audit committee exists).

Audit Committee or Board of Directors

The audit committee (or the board of directors where no audit committee exists) should evaluate management's identification of fraud risks, implementation of antifraud measures, and creation of the appropriate "tone at the top." Active oversight by the audit committee can help to reinforce management's commitment to creating a culture with "zero tolerance" for fraud. An entity's

---

[8] The report of the Committee of Sponsoring Organizations of the Treadway Commission, *Internal Control—Integrated Framework*, provides reasonable criteria for management to use in evaluating the effectiveness of the entity's system of internal control.

audit committee also should ensure that senior management (in particular, the CEO) implements appropriate fraud deterrence and prevention measures to better protect investors, employees, and other stakeholders. The audit committee's evaluation and oversight not only helps make sure that senior management fulfills its responsibility, but also can serve as a deterrent to senior management engaging in fraudulent activity (that is, by ensuring an environment is created whereby any attempt by senior management to involve employees in committing or concealing fraud would lead promptly to reports from such employees to appropriate persons, including the audit committee).

The audit committee also plays an important role in helping the board of directors fulfill its oversight responsibilities with respect to the entity's financial reporting process and the system of internal control.[9] In exercising this oversight responsibility, the audit committee should consider the potential for management override of controls or other inappropriate influence over the financial reporting process. For example, the audit committee may obtain from the internal auditors and independent auditors their views on management's involvement in the financial reporting process and, in particular, the ability of management to override information processed by the entity's financial reporting system (for example, the ability for management or others to initiate or record nonstandard journal entries). The audit committee also may consider reviewing the entity's reported information for reasonableness compared with prior or forecasted results, as well as with peers or industry averages. In addition, information received in communications from the independent auditors[10] can assist the audit committee in assessing the strength of the entity's internal control and the potential for fraudulent financial reporting.

As part of its oversight responsibilities, the audit committee should encourage management to provide a mechanism for employees to report concerns about unethical behavior, actual or suspected fraud, or violations of the entity's code of conduct or ethics policy. The committee should then receive periodic reports describing the nature, status, and eventual disposition of any fraud or unethical conduct. A summary of the activity, follow-up and disposition also should be provided to the full board of directors.

If senior management is involved in fraud, the next layer of management may be the most likely to be aware of it. As a result, the audit committee (and other directors) should consider establishing an open line of communication with members of management one or two levels below senior management to assist in identifying fraud at the highest levels of the organization or investigating any fraudulent activity that might occur.[11] The audit committee typically has the ability and authority to investigate any alleged or suspected wrongdoing brought to its attention. Most audit committee charters empower the committee to investigate any matters within the scope of its responsibilities, and to retain legal, accounting, and other professional advisers as needed to advise the committee and assist in its investigation.

---

[9] See the report of the National Association of Corporate Directors (NACD) Blue Ribbon Commission on the Audit Committee, (Washington, D.C.: National Association of Corporate Directors, 2000). For the board's role in the oversight of risk management, see report of the NACD Blue Ribbon Commission on Risk Oversight, (Washington, D.C.: National Association of Corporate Directors, 2002).

[10] See AU-C section 265, *Communicating Internal Control Matters Identified in an Audit*, and AU-C section 260, *The Auditor's Communication With Those Charged With Governance* (AICPA, *Professional Standards*).

[11] The *Report of the NACD Best Practices Council: Coping with Fraud and Other Illegal Activity, A Guide for Directors, CEOs, and Senior Managers* (1998) sets forth "basic principles" and "implementation approaches" for dealing with fraud and other illegal activity.

All audit committee members should be financially literate, and each committee should have at least one financial expert. The financial expert should possess

- an understanding of generally accepted accounting principles and audits of financial statements prepared under those principles. Such understanding may have been obtained either through education or experience. It is important for someone on the audit committee to have a working knowledge of those principles and standards.

- experience in the preparation and/or the auditing of financial statements of an entity of similar size, scope and complexity as the entity on whose board the committee member serves. The experience would generally be as a chief financial officer, chief accounting officer, controller, or auditor of a similar entity. This background will provide a necessary understanding of the transactional and operational environment that produces the issuer's financial statements. It will also bring an understanding of what is involved in, for example, appropriate accounting estimates, accruals, and reserve provisions, and an appreciation of what is necessary to maintain a good internal control environment.

- experience in internal governance and procedures of audit committees, obtained either as an audit committee member, a senior corporate manager responsible for answering to the audit committee, or an external auditor responsible for reporting on the execution and results of annual audits.

Management

Management is responsible for overseeing the activities carried out by employees, and typically does so by implementing and monitoring processes and controls such as those discussed previously. However, management also may initiate, participate in, or direct the commission and concealment of a fraudulent act. Accordingly, the audit committee (or the board of directors where no audit committee exists) has the responsibility to oversee the activities of senior management and to consider the risk of fraudulent financial reporting involving the override of internal controls or collusion (see discussion on the audit committee and board of directors).

Public companies should include a statement in the annual report acknowledging management's responsibility for the preparation of the financial statements and for establishing and maintaining an effective system of internal control. This will help improve the public's understanding of the respective roles of management and the auditor. This statement has also been generally referred to as a *Management Report* or *Management Certificate*. Such a statement can provide a convenient vehicle for management to describe the nature and manner of preparation of the financial information and the adequacy of the internal accounting controls. Logically, the statement should be presented in close proximity to the formal financial statements. For example, it could appear near the independent auditor's report, or in the financial review or management analysis section.

Internal Auditors

An effective internal audit team can be extremely helpful in performing aspects of the oversight function. Their knowledge about the entity may enable them to identify indicators that suggest fraud has been committed. The *Standards for the Professional Practice of Internal Auditing* (IIA Standards), issued by IIA, state, "The internal auditor should have sufficient knowledge to identify the indicators of fraud but is not expected to have the expertise of a person whose primary responsibility is detecting and investigating fraud." Internal auditors also have the opportunity to evaluate fraud risks and controls and to recommend action to mitigate risks and improve controls. Specifically, the IIA Standards require internal auditors to assess risks facing their organizations. This risk assessment is to serve as the basis from which audit plans are devised and against which internal controls are tested. The IIA Standards require the audit plan to be presented to and approved by the audit committee (or board of directors where no audit committee exists). The work completed as a result of the audit plan provides assurance on which management's assertion about controls can be made.

Internal audits can be both a detection and a deterrence measure. Internal auditors can assist in the deterrence of fraud by examining and evaluating the adequacy and the effectiveness of the system of internal control, commensurate with the extent of the potential exposure or risk in the various segments of the organization's operations. In carrying out this responsibility, internal auditors should, for example, determine whether

- the organizational environment fosters control consciousness.
- realistic organizational goals and objectives are set.
- written policies (for example, a code of conduct) exist that describe prohibited activities and the action required whenever violations are discovered.
- appropriate authorization policies for transactions are established and maintained.
- policies, practices, procedures, reports, and other mechanisms are developed to monitor activities and safeguard assets, particularly in high-risk areas.
- communication channels provide management with adequate and reliable information.
- recommendations need to be made for the establishment or enhancement of cost-effective controls to help deter fraud.

Internal auditors may conduct proactive auditing to search for corruption, misappropriation of assets, and financial statement fraud. This may include the use of computer-assisted audit techniques to detect particular types of fraud. Internal auditors also can employ analytical and other procedures to isolate anomalies and perform detailed reviews of high-risk accounts and transactions to identify potential financial statement fraud. The internal auditors should have an independent reporting line directly to the audit committee, to enable them to express any concerns about management's commitment to appropriate internal controls or to report suspicions or allegations of fraud involving senior management.

Independent Auditors

Independent auditors can assist management and the board of directors (or audit committee) by providing an assessment of the entity's process for identifying, assessing, and responding to the risks of fraud. The board of directors (or audit committee) should have an open and candid dialogue with the independent auditors regarding management's risk assessment process and the system of internal control. Such a dialogue should include a discussion of the susceptibility of the entity to fraudulent financial reporting and the entity's exposure to misappropriation of assets.

Certified Fraud Examiners

Certified fraud examiners may assist the audit committee and board of directors with aspects of the oversight process either directly or as part of a team of internal auditors or independent auditors. Certified fraud examiners can provide extensive knowledge and experience about fraud that may not be available within a corporation. They can provide more objective input into management's evaluation of the risk of fraud (especially fraud involving senior management, such as financial statement fraud) and the development of appropriate antifraud controls that are less vulnerable to management override. They can assist the audit committee and board of directors in evaluating the fraud risk assessment and fraud prevention measures implemented by management. Certified fraud examiners also conduct examinations to resolve allegations or suspicions of fraud, reporting either to an appropriate level of management or to the audit committee or board of directors, depending upon the nature of the issue and the level of personnel involved.

Other Information

To obtain more information on fraud and implementing antifraud programs and controls, please go to the following websites where additional materials, guidance, and tools can be found.

American Institute of Certified Public Accountants	www.aicpa.org
Association of Certified Fraud Examiners	www.acfe.com/
Financial Executives International	www.fei.org
Information Systems Audit and Control Association	www.isaca.org
The Institute of Internal Auditors	www.theiia.org
Institute of Management Accountants	www.imanet.org
National Association of Corporate Directors	www.nacdonline.org
Society for Human Resource Management	www.shrm.org

Attachment 1: AICPA "CPA's Handbook of Fraud and Commercial Crime Prevention," An Organizational Code of Conduct

The following is an example of an organizational code of conduct, which includes definitions of what is considered unacceptable, and the consequences of any breaches thereof. The specific content and areas addressed in an entity's code of conduct should be specific to that entity.

Organizational Code of Conduct

The Organization and its employees must, at all times, comply with all applicable laws and regulations. The Organization will not condone the activities of employees who achieve results through violation of the law or unethical business dealings. This includes any payments for illegal acts, indirect contributions, rebates, and bribery. The Organization does not permit any activity that fails to stand the closest possible public scrutiny.

All business conduct should be well above the minimum standards required by law. Accordingly, employees must ensure that their actions cannot be interpreted as being, in any way, in contravention of the laws and regulations governing the Organization's worldwide operations.

Employees uncertain about the application or interpretation of any legal requirements should refer the matter to their superior, who, if necessary, should seek the advice of the legal department.

General Employee Conduct

The Organization expects its employees to conduct themselves in a businesslike manner. Drinking, gambling, fighting, swearing, and similar unprofessional activities are strictly prohibited while on the job.

Employees must not engage in sexual harassment, or conduct themselves in a way that could be construed as such, for example, by using inappropriate language, keeping or posting inappropriate materials in their work area, or accessing inappropriate materials on their computer.

Conflicts of Interest

The Organization expects that employees will perform their duties conscientiously, honestly, and in accordance with the best interests of the Organization. Employees must not use their position or the knowledge gained as a result of their position for private or personal advantage. Regardless of the circumstances, if employees sense that a course of action they have pursued, are presently pursuing, or are contemplating pursuing may involve them in a conflict of interest with their employer, they should immediately communicate all the facts to their superior.

Outside Activities, Employment, and Directorships

All employees share a serious responsibility for the Organization's good public relations, especially at the community level. Their readiness to help with religious, charitable, educational, and civic activities brings credit to the Organization and is encouraged. Employees must, however, avoid acquiring any business interest or participating in any other activity outside the Organization that would, or would appear to

- create an excessive demand upon their time and attention, thus depriving the Organization of their best efforts on the job.

- create a conflict of interest—an obligation, interest, or distraction—that may interfere with the independent exercise of judgment in the Organization's best interest.

Relationships With Clients and Suppliers

Employees should avoid investing in or acquiring a financial interest for their own accounts in any business organization that has a contractual relationship with the Organization, or that provides goods or services, or both to the Organization, if such investment or interest could influence or create the impression of influencing their decisions in the performance of their duties on behalf of the Organization.

Gifts, Entertainment, and Favors

Employees must not accept entertainment, gifts, or personal favors that could, in any way, influence, or appear to influence, business decisions in favor of any person or organization with whom or with which the Organization has, or is likely to have, business dealings. Similarly, employees must not accept any other preferential treatment under these circumstances because their position with the Organization might be inclined to, or be perceived to, place them under obligation.

Kickbacks and Secret Commissions

Regarding the Organization's business activities, employees may not receive payment or compensation of any kind, except as authorized under the Organization's remuneration policies. In particular, the Organization strictly prohibits the acceptance of kickbacks and secret commissions from suppliers or others. Any breach of this rule will result in immediate termination and prosecution to the fullest extent of the law.

Organization Funds and Other Assets

Employees who have access to Organization funds in any form must follow the prescribed procedures for recording, handling, and protecting money as detailed in the Organization's instructional manuals or other explanatory materials, or both. The Organization imposes strict standards to prevent fraud and dishonesty. If employees become aware of any evidence of fraud and dishonesty, they should immediately advise their superior or the Law Department so that the Organization can promptly investigate further.

When an employee's position requires spending Organization funds or incurring any reimbursable personal expenses, that individual must use good judgment on the Organization's behalf to ensure that good value is received for every expenditure.

Organization funds and all other assets of the Organization are for Organization purposes only and not for personal benefit. This includes the personal use of organizational assets, such as computers.

Organization Records and Communications

Accurate and reliable records of many kinds are necessary to meet the Organization's legal and financial obligations and to manage the affairs of the Organization. The Organization's books and records must reflect in an accurate and timely manner all business transactions. The employees responsible for accounting and recordkeeping must fully disclose and record all assets, liabilities, or both, and must exercise diligence in enforcing these requirements.

Employees must not make or engage in any false record or communication of any kind, whether internal or external, including but not limited to

- false expense, attendance, production, financial, or similar reports and statements.

- false advertising, deceptive marketing practices, or other misleading representations.

Dealing With Outside People and Organizations

Employees must take care to separate their personal roles from their Organization positions when communicating on matters not involving Organization business. Employees must not use organization identification, stationery, supplies, and equipment for personal or political matters.

When communicating publicly on matters that involve Organization business, employees must not presume to speak for the Organization on any topic, unless they are certain that the views they express are those of the Organization, and it is the Organization's desire that such views be publicly disseminated.

When dealing with anyone outside the Organization, including public officials, employees must take care not to compromise the integrity or damage the reputation of either the Organization, or any outside individual, business, or government body.

Prompt Communications

In all matters relevant to customers, suppliers, government authorities, the public and others in the Organization, all employees must make every effort to achieve complete, accurate, and timely communications—responding promptly and courteously to all proper requests for information and to all complaints.

Privacy and Confidentiality

When handling financial and personal information about customers or others with whom the Organization has dealings, observe the following principles:

a. Collect, use, and retain only the personal information necessary for the Organization's business. Whenever possible, obtain any relevant information directly from the person concerned. Use only reputable and reliable sources to supplement this information.

b. Retain information only for as long as necessary or as required by law. Protect the physical security of this information.

c. Limit internal access to personal information to those with a legitimate business reason for seeking that information. Use only personal information for the purposes for which it was originally obtained. Obtain the consent of the person concerned before externally disclosing any personal information, unless legal process or contractual obligation provides otherwise.

Attachment 2: Financial Executives International Code of Ethics Statement

The mission of FEI includes significant efforts to promote ethical conduct in the practice of financial management throughout the world. Senior financial officers hold an important and elevated role in corporate governance. Although members of the management team, they are uniquely capable and empowered to ensure that all stakeholders' interests are appropriately balanced, protected, and preserved. This code provides principles that members are expected to adhere to and advocate. They embody rules regarding individual and peer responsibilities, as well as responsibilities to employers, the public, and other stakeholders.

All members of FEI will

 a. act with honesty and integrity, avoiding actual or apparent conflicts of interest in personal and professional relationships.

 b. provide constituents with information that is accurate, complete, objective, relevant, timely, and understandable.

 c. comply with rules and regulations of federal, state, provincial, and local governments, and other appropriate private and public regulatory agencies.

 d. act in good faith; responsibly; and with due care, competence, and diligence, without misrepresenting material facts or allowing one's independent judgment to be subordinated.

 e. respect the confidentiality of information acquired in the course of one's work except when authorized or otherwise legally obligated to disclose. Confidential information acquired in the course of one's work will not be used for personal advantage.

 f. share knowledge and maintain skills important and relevant to constituents' needs.

 g. proactively promote ethical behavior as a responsible partner among peers, in the work environment, and in the community.

 h. achieve responsible use of and control over all assets and resources employed or entrusted.

Appendix E

Illustrative Financial Statement Assertions and Examples of Substantive Procedures Illustrations for Inventories of a Manufacturing Company

This appendix is nonauthoritative and is included for informational purposes only.

E.01 This appendix illustrates the use of assertions in designing substantive procedures and does not illustrate tests of controls. The following examples of substantive procedures are not intended to be all-inclusive, nor is it expected that all of the procedures would be applied in an audit. The particular substantive procedures to be used in each circumstance depend on the auditor's risk assessments and tests of controls.

Illustrative Assertions About Account Balances	*Examples of Substantive Procedures*
Existence	
Inventories included in the balance sheet physically exist.	• Physical examination of inventory items • Obtaining confirmation of inventories at locations outside the entity • Inspection of documents relating to inventory transactions between a physical inventory date and the balance sheet date
Inventories represent items held for sale or use in the normal course of business.	• Inspecting perpetual inventory records, production records, and purchasing records for indications of current activity • Reconciling items in the inventory listing to a current computer-maintained sales catalog and subsequent sales and delivery reports using computer assisted audit techniques (CAATs) • Inquiry of production and sales personnel • Using the work of specialists to corroborate the nature of specialized products

(continued)

Illustrative Assertions About Account Balances	Examples of Substantive Procedures
Rights and Obligations	
The entity has legal title or similar rights of ownership to the inventories.	• Examining paid vendors' invoices, consignment agreements, and contracts • Obtaining confirmation of inventories at locations outside the entity
Inventories exclude items billed to customers or owned by others.	• Examining paid vendors' invoices, consignment agreements, and contracts • Inspecting shipping and receiving transactions near year end for recording in the proper period
Completeness	
Inventory quantities include all products, materials, and supplies on hand.	• Observing physical inventory counts • Analytically comparing the relationship of inventory balances to recent purchasing, production, and sales activities • Inspecting shipping and receiving transactions near year end for recording in the proper period
Inventory quantities include all products, materials, and supplies owned by the company that are in transit or stored at outside locations.	• Obtaining confirmation of inventories at locations outside the entity • Analytically comparing the relationship of inventory balances to recent purchasing, production, and sales activities
Inventory listings are accurately compiled and the totals are properly included in the inventory accounts.	• Inspecting shipping and receiving transactions near year end for recording in the proper period • Examining the inventory listing for inclusion of test counts recorded during the physical inventory observation • Reconciliation of all inventory tags and count sheets used in recording the physical inventory counts using CAATs • Recalculation of inventory listing for clerical accuracy using CAATs • Reconciling physical counts to perpetual records and general ledger balances and investigating significant fluctuations using CAATs

Illustrative Assertions About Account Balances	*Examples of Substantive Procedures*
Valuation and Allocation	
Inventories are properly stated at cost (except when market is lower).	• Examining paid vendors' invoices and comparing product prices to standard cost build-ups • Analytically comparing direct labor rates to production records • Recalculation of the computation of standard overhead rates • Examining analyses of purchasing and manufacturing standard cost variances
Slow-moving, excess, defective, and obsolete items included in inventories are properly identified.	• Examining an analysis of inventory turnover • Analyzing industry experience and trends • Analytically comparing the relationship of inventory balances to anticipated sales volume • Walk-through of the plant for indications of products not being used • Inquiring of production and sales personnel concerning possible excess, or defective or obsolete inventory items • Logistic and distribution business process (for example, cycle time, volume of returns, or problems with suppliers)
Inventories are reduced, when appropriate, to replacement cost or net realizable value.	• Inspecting sales catalogs or industry publications for current market value quotations • Recalculation of inventory valuation reserves • Analyzing current production costs • Examining sales after year end and open purchase order commitments

(continued)

Illustrative Assertions About Presentation and Disclosure	Examples of Substantive Procedures
Rights and Obligations	
The pledge or assignment of any inventories is appropriately disclosed.	• Obtaining confirmation of inventories pledged under loan agreements
Completeness	
The financial statements include all disclosures related to inventories specified by generally accepted accounting principles.	• Using a disclosure checklist to determine whether the disclosures included in generally accepted accounting principles were made
Understandability	
Inventories are properly classified in the balance sheet as current assets.	• Examining drafts of the financial statements for appropriate balance sheet classification
Disclosures related to inventories are understandable.	• Reading disclosures for clarity
Accuracy and Valuation	
The major categories of inventories and their bases of valuation are accurately disclosed in the financial statements.	• Examining drafts of the financial statements for appropriate disclosures • Reconciling the categories of inventories disclosed in the draft financial statements to the categories recorded during the physical inventory observation

---

Appendix F

Consideration of Prior Year Uncorrected Misstatements

This appendix is nonauthoritative and is included for informational purposes only.

F.01 At the final stage of the audit, the auditor assesses uncorrected misstatements that affect the current year financial statements to determine whether they are material, individually or in the aggregate.

F.02 Misstatements affecting the current financial statements include those arising in the current period and those that arose in a prior period that were not corrected, but still have an effect on the current financial statements. The cumulative effect of uncorrected misstatements related to prior periods may have a material effect on the current period's financial statements.

F.03 Management may decide not to correct some misstatements remaining in the financial statements at the end of a period when they are not material. Unadjusted misstatements can arise from a variety of circumstances. For example, management may be willing to adjust for factual misstatements, but more reluctant to adjust some or all judgmental misstatements related to estimates, or projected misstatements, especially when the client disagrees with them. In addition, a projected likely misstatement from a small audit sample may not be sufficient to determine an amount to be recorded. Another example is that an insignificant accrual might not be recorded because it would have an immaterial effect on income in the current period. The balance sheet accrual misstatement will remain until it is deliberately corrected in some future period. Some misstatements may arise in one period and then correct themselves over time. For example, inventory overstatement misstatements in one period increase income in the period in which they occur, then flow through earnings of the next period (via the cost of sales) and reduce income in the next period when final inventories are "trued-up" at the end of the second period. The effects of this misstatement only affected these two periods. Similarly, over the depreciable life of an asset, mistakes in computing annual depreciation amounts will be corrected.

F.04 Over the years, several approaches to assessing the effect of current and prior year misstatements have evolved. Management and those charged with governance decide how to correct for misstatements.

- *The income-focused approach.* One approach to assessing the effect of uncorrected misstatements is to focus on the combined income statement effects of current and prior year misstatements affecting current income to determine that the combined effect of these misstatements does not materially misstate current period income. An adjustment is required when the effect of the misstatements on current period income is greater than materiality.

- *The balance sheet-focused approach.* Another approach followed by some companies and their auditors is to assess the aggregate misstatements remaining uncorrected in the year-end balance sheet and determine that misstatements that could affect future periods when they correct themselves or are corrected do not materially misstate income in future periods. An adjustment is considered to be required when the cumulative misstatements on the balance sheet exceed materiality.

- *Applying both approaches.* Other companies and their auditors apply both approaches and require an adjustment if either approach indicates an adjustment is necessary. Applying both approaches consistently over time retains the benefits of each approach and overcomes the weaknesses of each approach.

F.05   The intent of AU-C section 450, *Evaluation of Misstatements Identified During the Audit* (AICPA, *Professional Standards*), is not to prescribe the use of a specific approach, but to allow existing practice, which recognizes all of the approaches previously discussed. If past accumulated misstatements are corrected, accounting standards provide guidance on the correction of prior period misstatements.

F.06   Following are simple, but commonly encountered, examples of applying the approaches to a specific situation.

Example 1: Accrued Sick Pay

F.07   Under generally accepted accounting principles, sick pay that is earned but not taken, and can be carried forward until paid out or taken at retirement, should be accrued. This scenario is found in some municipal school districts. Suppose that materiality for the entity was $100,000, and that in the initial year of operation, $25,000 of accrued sick pay should have been accrued, but was not corrected as it was not material. Net receipts over expenditures would be overstated by $25,000 and liabilities would be understated by $25,000. Neither the income-focused approach nor the balance sheet-focused approach would require an adjustment because neither financial statement is materially misstated under this fact pattern.

F.08   However, assume this fact pattern reoccurs annually. After 5 years, the cumulative liability would be understated by $125,000. However, because the annual misstatement of net receipts is still immaterial ($25,000), a strict application of the income-focused approach would ignore the growing balance sheet problem. If, at some point in time, the balance sheet liability account were partially or fully corrected, there would be an effect on current income (or a restatement of prior periods, or both) from the correction of the past uncorrected amounts.

F.09   From the balance sheet-focused approach perspective, and only considering this 1 issue, the balance sheet misstatement after the fourth year would be capped at materiality, and in year 5 an accrual would need to be recognized and expense recorded for at least $25,000, as after that point, any further understatement of the liability would exceed materiality (for example, $100,000).

F.10   When there are multiple accounts and misstatements, the net aggregate of the misstatements flowing through the income statement (income statement-focused approach) or remaining in various balance sheet accounts (balance sheet-focused approach) would to be compared to materiality.

Example 2: Inventory

F.11 Another example illustrates the case where prior year waived adjustments reverse through income in later periods. Although both approaches consider the implications of the reversal of any prior year waived adjustments, they do so from a different perspective. Suppose inventory was, based on sample evidence, possibly overstated by $25,000 in year 1. The amount was assessed as immaterial. The inventory account and income in year 1 would be overstated by $25,000. Neither approach to waived adjustments would require an adjustment to be made. If the inventory amount is correct in the ending balance sheet in year 2, the income-focused approach would recognize that income in year 2 was *understated* by $25,000 (an immaterial amount) because the prior year unadjusted misstatement flowed through income (via increasing cost of sales and the opening inventory balance) in year 2. Under a balance sheet-focused approach, "all has become right in the world," because the ending balance sheet in year 2 would be correct. The income statement effect of the prior year misstatement would not be considered in year 2.

F.12 Applying one approach or the other can sometimes result in different auditor actions because potential adjustments are aggregated at year end, and the potential income and balance sheet effects will differ between the two approaches. This may result in situations where one approach may indicate an adjustment is required, but the other may not.

F.13 To continue the illustration, suppose further that in year 2, instead of correcting the ending inventory, the ending inventory was again overstated, but this time by $50,000. The income-focused approach would recognize the $25,000 net effect of the current and prior period misstatement on income ($50,000 year 2 overstatement minus $25,000 year 1 overstatements that reverse, create a net $25,000 overstatement of income). Under the pure income-focused approach, the misstatement of the balance sheet would be ignored.

F.14 Some companies and their auditors may follow a hybrid approach that suggests that balance sheet misstatements might be considered if they breach balance sheet materiality.

F.15 The balance sheet-focused approach would focus on the $50,000 overstatement in ending inventory. However, the balance sheet-focused approach would cap any cumulative balance sheet misstatement at materiality ($100,000), if the cumulative balance sheet account misstatement ever increased to that level.

Strengths and Weaknesses of the Two Approaches

Income Statement-focused Approach

F.16 The strengths of the income statement-focused approach (sometimes referred to as the *rollover method*) are that it considers the income effect of netting current period and prior period misstatements that are flowing through income and it is designed to determine that current income is not materially misstated. The weakness of this approach is that, if strictly applied with no consideration of the balance sheet, immaterial misstatements could accumulate over time on the balance sheet to more than material amounts. Correcting some or all of these amounts in some future period could have a significant effect on current income or force a restatement. These balance sheet misstatements also create prime opportunities for earnings management, as it can later be difficult for auditors to argue that companies should not correct amounts that auditors and companies both believe to be misstated.

F.17 The maximum exposure on balance sheet misstatement created by applying solely the income-focused approach is potentially unlimited because cumulative balance sheet misstatements are not considered by this approach.

F.18 However, many companies and their auditors intuitively recognize this practical issue and may indeed cap the balance sheet misstatement at some point, but they may not have a formalized approach to deciding when and how to do this.

Balance Sheet-focused Approach

F.19 The strength of the balance sheet-focused approach (sometimes referred to as the *iron curtain method*) is that aggregate misstatements in the balance sheet are capped at materiality. The weakness of this approach is that in an unusual circumstance, it could allow income in a particular year to be misstated by more than a material amount if there were a swing in the misstatements affecting income of greater than a material amount (for example, a swing between overstated and understated amounts on the balance sheet).

F.20 For example, using an inventory example, if in year 1 a $90,000 potential inventory overstatement was unadjusted, and the next year a potential $90,000 inventory understatement was unadjusted based on the balance sheet not being materially misstated, the income effect of the 2 misstatements would not be considered under the pure balance sheet-focused approach. However, we know that the net income effect of the misstatements was a $180,000 understatement in year 2 because the year 1 $90,000 overstatement flowed through cost of sales to reduce income in year 2 and the $90,000 understatement in ending inventory in year 2 also worked to reduce income that year (assuming purchases were properly accounted for as a component of cost of sales). This combined effect on income exceeds materiality, even though the balance sheet at the end of year 2 is not materially misstated. The maximum exposure on income created by applying solely the balance sheet approach is nearly twice materiality (a swing between a marginally material overstatement and a marginally material understatement). It is considered rare that such an issue would arise due to 1 account, but it may be more common and less visible when multiple account misstatements aggregate to near-material amounts.

F.21 In this latter example, the income-focused approach would recognize the net $180,000 understatement of income, and require at least an $80,000 adjustment of the income statement and inventory account (income and inventory would be adjusted upward) to determine that income is not materially misstated.

Applying Both Approaches

F.22 Some companies and their auditors, to avoid the potential weaknesses of the income or balance sheet approaches, consider the misstatements in the ending balance sheet *and* also the misstatements flowing through income in the current period, and require an adjustment to determine that neither income nor the balance sheet is materially misstated. When this approach is followed from the inception of the business, cumulative material balance sheet misstatements are unlikely to ever occur (unless materiality levels decline significantly between periods). Auditors that advocate this approach also point out that this approach provides more accurate periodic financial information to users.

F.23 The correction of all factual misstatements on an annual basis will contribute to fewer instances where balance sheet misstatements will accumulate and become troublesome in future periods.

AU-C Section 450 Is Not Prescriptive

F.24 Paragraph .11 of AU-C section 450 states

The auditor should determine whether uncorrected misstatements are material, individually or in the aggregate. In making this determination, the auditor should consider

a. the size and nature of the misstatements, both in relation to particular classes of transactions, account balances, or disclosures and the financial statements as a whole, and the particular circumstances of their occurrence and

b. the effect of uncorrected misstatements related to prior periods on the relevant classes of transactions, account balances, or disclosures and the financial statements as a whole.

F.25 Because the application of the income statement-focused or the balance sheet-focused or both approaches together would consider the effects of uncorrected misstatements, albeit from different perspectives, any of these approaches could be used to satisfy the requirements of AU-C section 450.

F.26 In recent years, companies have been more open to adjusting for all factual and some portion of judgmental or projected misstatement, so the overall differences in outcome from applying one approach versus another may be less today than in prior years. Indeed, paragraph .A10 of AU-C section 450 encourages the recording of all factual misstatements:

The auditor should request management to record the adjustment needed to correct all factual misstatements, including the effect of prior period misstatement (see paragraph .A10), other than those that the auditor believes are trivial.

Furthermore, if understatements in some accounts and overstatements in other accounts can be validly netted, the effects of any differences in the approaches may also be mitigated.

F.27 When selecting an appropriate approach for an engagement, auditors can consider the strengths and weaknesses of the various approaches and the risks that a selected approach might have for the client and the auditor.

F.28 If the approach selected is not followed consistently from year to year, current and prior period misstatements can have an erratic effect on the reported amounts. Changing approaches might also raise the issue of whether a prior period adjustment is necessary when correcting prior period balance sheet misstatements.

Appendix G

Assessing the Severity of Identified Deficiencies in Internal Control

This appendix is nonauthoritative and is included for informational purposes only.

Practice Considerations for Auditors of Entities Using the COSO Framework

The Committee of Sponsoring Organizations of the Treadway Commission's (COSO) *Internal Control—Integrated Framework* (COSO framework) contains guidance for assessing the severity of deficiencies. However, the guidance for assessing the severity of deficiencies and communicating deficiencies to management and governance in AU-C section 265, *Communicating Internal Control Related Matters Identified in an Audit* (AICPA, *Professional Standards*) (as illustrated in this guide and its appendixes), should be followed by auditors. Entities wishing to synchronize their assessments with those of their auditors may similarly look to the auditing standards regarding the classification of deficiencies as deficiencies, significant deficiencies, and material weaknesses.

G.01 This appendix contains examples to help you evaluate the severity of a control deficiency identified during a financial statement audit. Like all examples, this appendix should supplement and not sup-plant auditor judgment. Use of the examples and analyses may result in more consistent judgments be-tween engagements and across individual audit practices.

G.02 Additional examples of circumstances that may be classified as deficiencies of some magnitude are listed in paragraph .A37 of AU-C section 265. That appendix is reproduced as appendix H, "Examples of Circumstances That May Be Deficiencies, Significant Deficiencies, or Material Weaknesses," of this guide. Additional guidance on assessing the severity of some types of deficiencies is contained within that standard. The definitions used in this appendix of deficiency, significant deficiency and material weakness are also taken from that standard.

G.03 The examples in this appendix illustrate deficiencies in internal control identified during a financial statement audit. Different conclusions may be reached for deficiencies in internal control identified during an engagement performed under AT section 501, *An Examination of an Entity's Internal Control Over Financial Reporting That Is Integrated With an Audit of Its Financial Statements* (AICPA, *Professional Standards*). AT section 501 is designed to report on controls "as of" a specific reporting date, and for audit purposes the effectiveness of controls are assessed over the reporting period. Consequently, deficiencies in general controls such as access and security, controls over program changes and new program development and controls over computer operations may have an effect on the auditor's ability to rely on the underlying application controls throughout the period the deficiency existed. AU-C section 315, *Understanding the Entity and Its Environment and Assessing the Risks of Material Misstatement*, and AU-C section 330, *Performing Audit Procedures in Response* *to Assessed Risks and Evaluating the Audit Evidence Obtained* (AICPA, *Professional Standards*), provide guidance on the role of general controls relative to application controls during an audit.

Examples of Evaluating the Significance of Deficiencies in Internal Control in Various Situations

G.04   The following examples illustrate a thought process for evaluating the significance of deficiencies in internal control in various situations. These examples are for illustrative purposes only.

Deficiency 1: Reconciliations of Interentity Accounts Are Not Performed on a Timely Basis

Situation 1A: Significant Deficiency

G.05   The entity processes a significant number of routine interentity transactions on a monthly basis. Individual interentity transactions are not material and primarily relate to balance sheet activity, for example, cash transfers between business units to finance normal operations.

G.06   A formal management policy requires monthly reconciliations of interentity accounts and confirmation of balances between business units. However, the entity does not have a process in place to ensure that these procedures are performed. As a result, detailed reconciliations of interentity accounts are not performed on a timely basis. Management performs monthly procedures to investigate selected large-dollar inter entity account differences. In addition, management prepares a detailed monthly variance analysis of operating expenses to assess their reasonableness.

G.07   Based on only these facts, the auditor might determine that this deficiency represents a significant deficiency. The magnitude of a financial statement misstatement resulting from this deficiency is probably less than material, because individual interentity transactions are not material, and the compensating controls operating monthly are sufficient in the auditor's judgment to detect a material misstatement. Furthermore, the transactions are primarily restricted to balance sheet accounts. However, the compensating detective controls are designed to detect only material misstatements. Because the stated control policies have not been implemented effectively and the combination of controls that are in place do not address the detection of misstatements that are less than material. The matter is important enough to warrant the attention of those charged with governance.

Further Analysis of Situation 1A

G.08   Because the entity does not have a process in place to ensure that the monthly procedures are performed, these controls were not operating, so the likelihood test has been met and the auditor proceeds to assess the potential magnitude of the deficiency.

G.09   The auditor then considers whether the exposure is more than material. Because it is not, the auditor would apply the "prudent official" test before concluding that the deficiency is a significant deficiency.

G.10 When applying the deficiency evaluation framework, the auditor may quantify the gross exposure and assumed effectiveness of the compensating controls based on an analysis of the facts and circumstances. This may facilitate the documentation of the judgments and decisions leading to the auditor's final conclusions.

Situation 1B: Material Weakness

G.11 The entity processes a significant number of inter entity transactions on a monthly basis. Inter entity transactions relate to a wide range of activities, including transfers of inventory between business units involving inter entity profit, allocation of research and development costs to business units, and allocation of central corporate charges. Individual inter entity transactions frequently are material.

G.12 A formal management policy requires monthly reconciliation of inter entity accounts and confirmation of balances between business units. However, the entity does not have a process in place to ensure that these procedures are performed on a consistent basis. As a result, reconciliations of inter entity accounts are not performed on a timely basis, and differences in inter entity accounts are frequent and significant. Management does not implement any other controls to investigate significant inter entity account differences.

G.13 Based on only these facts, the auditor may determine that this deficiency represents a material weakness. The magnitude of a financial statement misstatement resulting from this deficiency could reasonably be expected to be material because individual inter entity transactions frequently are material and relate to a wide range of activities. Additionally, actual unreconciled differences in inter entity accounts have been, and are, material. The likelihood of a material misstatement is clearly reasonably possible because such misstatements have frequently occurred and compensating controls are ineffective, either because they were not properly designed or are not operating effectively. Taken together, the magnitude and likelihood of misstatement of the financial statements resulting from this internal control deficiency meet the criteria in the definition of a material weakness.

Further Analysis of Situation 1B

G.14 The description of situation 1B indicates that there is no process in place to ensure that this monthly control is performed on a consistent basis. Therefore, the control is not operating, and the "likelihood" test has been met. The auditor proceeds to assess the magnitude.

G.15 The description notes that the gross exposure is material. The description also notes that there are no complementary or compensating controls. Because the exposure is material, the assessment would continue and the auditor would consider whether other factors might limit the deficiency to a significant deficiency. Factors such as the following are considered in making this evaluation:

- The pervasiveness of the deficiency across the entity
- The relative significance of the deficient control to the component
- An indication of increased risks of error, evidenced by a history of misstatement
- An increased susceptibility to fraud, including the risk of management override

- The cause and frequency of known or detected exceptions in the operating effectiveness of a control
- The possible future consequences of the deficiency

G.16 When assessing the severity of the deficiency, the auditor may quantify the exposure and assumed effectiveness of compensating controls based on an analysis of the facts and circumstances. This may facilitate the documentation of the judgments and the decisions leading to the auditor's final assessment.

Deficiency 2: Modifications of Standard Sales Contract Terms Are Not Reviewed to Evaluate Their Effect on the Timing and Amount of Revenue Recognition

Situation 2A: Significant Deficiency

G.17 The entity uses a standard sales contract for most transactions. Individual sales transactions are not material to the entity. Sales personnel are permitted to modify sales contract terms. Personnel in the entity's accounting group review significant or unusual modifications of the sales contract terms but do not review changes in the standard shipping terms. The changes in the standard shipping terms could cause a delay in the timing of revenue recognition. Management reviews gross margins on a monthly basis and investigates any significant or unusual relationships. In addition, management reviews the reasonableness of inventory levels at the end of each accounting period. There have been a limited number of instances in which revenue was inappropriately recorded in advance of shipment, but the related amounts have not been material.

G.18 Based on only these facts, the auditor might determine that this deficiency represents a significant deficiency. The magnitude of a financial statement misstatement resulting from this deficiency could reasonably be expected to be less than material, because individual sales transactions are not material and the compensating detective controls, which operate monthly and at the end of each financial reporting period, are assessed as sufficient to limit a misstatement to less than a material amount. Furthermore, the risk of material misstatement is limited to revenue recognition misstatements related to shipping terms, as opposed to broader sources of misstatement in revenue recognition. However, the compensating detective controls are designed to detect only material misstatements. These compensating controls do not effectively address the detection of misstatements that are less than material, as evidenced by situations in which transactions were improperly recorded. Therefore, it would seem that this situation is important enough to merit attention of those charged with governance.

Further Analysis of Situation 2A

G.19 The description of situation 2A indicates that the entity does not have a control to review changes in shipping terms, which is an identified risk for this business. Analysis of this design weakness meets the likelihood criteria and is then evaluated regarding the potential magnitude of the deficiency when assessing its severity.

G.20 Management's review of gross margins and period-end inventories are noted as compensating controls.

G.21 The gross dollar exposure of transactions exposed to the deficiency is noted as less than material. The effectiveness of the compensating controls is not specifically quantified, but the description of the preceding situation states that these controls were designed to detect only material misstatement, thus they probably would not be useful in limiting the deficiency to inconsequential.

G.22 The severity of the deficiency may be limited to a significant deficiency based on the compensating controls.

G.23 The auditor might further consider the reasonableness of the assertion that the compensating controls would limit misstatements to less than a material amount by considering the tests management performed and the threshold that management used for investigating differences, and noting evidence that the review was performed. This assessment would serve as a basis for the auditor's judgment that the likelihood of a material misstatement as a result of this deficiency is remote.

G.24 The deficiency needs to be further considered relative to the "prudent official" consideration before concluding that the deficiency is limited to a significant deficiency.

G.25 Even though misstatements related to this issue were not detected in the past, this is not evidence that an effective control is in place. The focus should be on the *potential* misstatement due to the design deficiency.

G.26 When assessing the severity of the deficiency, the auditor may quantify the exposure and assumed effectiveness of compensating controls based on an analysis of the facts and circumstances. This may facilitate the documentation of the judgments and decisions leading to the auditor's final assessment.

Situation 2B: Material Weakness

G.27 The entity has a standard sales contract, but sales personnel frequently modify the terms of the contract. Certain modifications can affect the timing and amount of revenue recognized. Individual sales transactions frequently are material to the entity, and the gross margin can vary significantly for each transaction.

G.28 The entity does not have procedures in place for accounting personnel to regularly review modifications of sales contract terms. Although management reviews gross margins on a monthly basis, the significant differences in gross margins for individual transactions make it difficult for management to identify potential misstatements. Improper revenue recognition has occurred in the past, and the amounts have been material.

G.29 From these facts, the auditor may determine that this deficiency represents a material weakness. The magnitude of a financial statement misstatement resulting from this deficiency could reasonably be expected to be material because individual sales transactions are frequently material, and gross margin can vary significantly with each transaction (which would make compensating detective controls based on a reasonableness review ineffective). Additionally, improper revenue recognition has occurred in the past, and the amounts have been material. Therefore, a reasonable possibility exists that the control will not prevent or detect and correct a material misstatement. Taken together, the magnitude and likelihood of misstatement of the financial statements resulting from this internal control deficiency meet the definition of a material weakness.

Further Analysis of Situation 2B

G.30 The description of situation 2B indicates that the entity does not have procedures in place for accounting personnel to regularly review modifications of sales contract terms, an identified risk for this business. Analysis of design weaknesses meets the likelihood criteria for a deficiency, and weaknesses are evaluated regarding potential magnitude.

G.31 Management's review of gross margins and period-end inventories are noted as compensating controls, but in the auditor's judgment the variations in gross margin due to changes in contract terms may render them ineffective in detecting material misstatement.

G.32 The gross dollar exposure of the missing control is noted as material. The effectiveness of the compensating controls is not specifically quantified, but the preceding description indicates that they probably would not be effective in detecting material misstatement.

G.33 The entity's past experience with this issue provides evidence that the exposure resulting from the absence of a control is material. Although the focus of the assessment of the control weakness should be on the *potential* misstatement resulting from the absence of this control, that potential can rarely, if ever, be limited to less than the observed exposure based on past, actual misstatement.

G.34 When assessing the severity of the deficiency, the auditor may quantify the exposure and assumed effectiveness of compensating controls based on an analysis of the facts and circumstances. This may facilitate the documentation of the judgments and decisions leading to the auditor's final assessment.

Situation 2C: Material Weakness

G.35 The entity has a standard sales contract; however, sales personnel frequently modify the terms of the contract. Sales personnel frequently grant unauthorized and unrecorded sales discounts to customers without the authorization of management or the knowledge of the accounting department. These discounts are taken by customers, deducted from the amount paid, and recorded as outstanding balances in the accounts receivable aging. Although the amounts of these discounts are individually insignificant, they are material in the aggregate and have arisen consistently during the past few years.

G.36 Based on only these facts, the auditor may determine that this deficiency represents a material weakness. The magnitude of a financial statement misstatement resulting from this deficiency would reasonably be expected to be material, because the frequency of occurrence allows insignificant amounts to become material in the aggregate. The likelihood of a material misstatement of the financial statements resulting from this internal control deficiency is reasonably possible (even if the entity reserved for uncollectible accounts) due to the likelihood of material misstatement of the gross accounts receivable balance. Therefore, this internal control deficiency meets the definition of a material weakness.

Further Analysis of Situation 2C

G.37 Because of the missing controls, there is a reasonable possibility of a material misstatement of the financial statements resulting from this internal control deficiency and the analysis of the deficiency rests on its magnitude to assess its severity.

G.38 The gross exposure is noted as material in the aggregate, and no redundant, or compensating controls are noted.

G.39 The auditor may quantify the exposure and assumed effectiveness of compensating controls based on an analysis of the facts and circumstances when applying the deficiency evaluation framework. This may facilitate the documentation of the judgments and decisions leading to the auditor's final assessment.

Deficiency 3: Information Technology General Control Deficiency—Security and Access [Principle 11]

G.40 The entity has an Internet connection that enables sales personnel to communicate sales information back to the company on a timely basis, and use selected entity applications, such as time and expense reporting. Access through the Internet is restricted to selected applications that are necessary for the users' purpose. An assessment of the password and firewall protection indicates an effective design to prevent unauthorized third-party access.

G.41 The entity provides a standard software platform image[1] on the workstations of all employees connected to its internal network. There is password protection at the network level. The image includes all of the accounting software packages used.

G.42 No issues have been reported relating to Internet or internal network security or access controls.

Situation 3A: Not a Deficiency

G.43 The entity uses an effective application-level password system that permits access to application level programs and data only to authorized individuals. Based on an analysis of personnel duties and their access, the auditor assesses, supported by observation, inquiry, and an examination of evidence, that the access and security control design is appropriate to achieve both segregation of duties and effective security and access control.

Further Analysis of Situation 3A

G.44 Neither management nor the auditor has identified any design or operating deficiencies related to the Internet access of sales personnel.

G.45 The use of a standard software platform image that lists all accounting applications and data sources (rather than only the applications and data available to the specified user) is a potential security and access IT general control deficiency. However, the implementation of effective application and data level security that restricts access to only authorized persons is considered a sufficiently strong control to achieve the control objective.

Situation 3B: Material Weakness

G.46 Neither management nor the auditor have identified any design or operating deficiencies related to the Internet access of certain software packages by sales personnel.

---

[1] Every computer lists all the software application options.

G.47   However, in this situation, the network does not control access to various applications once the user has logged in. Access to all accounting software and data is available to all employees from all employee office workstations. The honesty of employees and the perceived lack of competence of unauthorized individuals to initiate and authorize transactions or change data in the system (because they have not received training) has been the chief source of comfort to management regarding the risk of fraud or loss. Management also has taken comfort from the lack of any detected problems to date.

Further Analysis of Situation 3B

G.48   Based on the fact pattern, from an IT general controls perspective, this situation would be considered a material weakness because control over access to the internal network system is ineffective in preventing unauthorized persons from creating a material misstatement or fraud. Also, there is no application level security to prevent any individual who is logged into the system from initiating and processing a transaction within the system. Thus, application level controls are not able to detect that unauthorized transactions might have been posted to the various accounts, a significant fraud risk. Redundant or compensating controls that achieve the same control objective were not identified.

G.49   Even if specific deficiencies at the application level were not identified, the deficiency at the IT general control level might preclude reliance on the underlying application controls over the period of time the deficiency existed. Paragraph .A108 of AU-C section 315 states:

> Although ineffective general IT controls do not by themselves cause misstatements, they may permit application controls to operate improperly and allow misstatements to occur and not be detected. For example, if deficiencies in the general IT controls over access security exist and applications are relying on these general controls to prevent unauthorized transactions from being processed, such general IT control deficiencies may have a more severe effect on the effective design and operation of the application control. General IT controls are assessed with regard to their effect on applications and data that become part of the financial statements.

G.50   Thus, IT general deficiencies in internal control may therefore have a greater significance in an audit of the financial statements than in an attestation regarding internal controls under Statement on Auditing Standards No. 130, *An Audit of Internal Control Over Financial Reporting That Is Integrated With an Audit of Financial Statements* (AICPA, *Professional Standards*, AU-C sec. 940) when the attestation is set up to report on controls "as of" a specific date. In such an examination, the underlying application controls can be tested at or near the "as of" reporting date to mitigate the severity of IT general deficiencies in internal control at a point in time; however, this mitigation approach may not be relevant to an audit of the financial statements that covers a period of time.

Further, paragraph .13 of AU-C section 330 reminds us that weak IT general controls are one of the conditions that would preclude reliance in the current period on controls tests performed in a prior period.

G.51   In this situation the entity did not identify any compensating controls that would limit the severity of the weakness to less than materiality.

G.52 The fact that no issues have been identified regarding this matter is not relevant in its potential classification for audit purposes as a material weakness. The "could" factor would indicate its appropriate classification as a material weakness.

G.53 This weakness might preclude the auditor from concluding that the security and access component of IT general controls was effective for purposes of relying on the continued operation of application controls during the period. Even if the auditor did not wish to rely extensively on application controls, the ineffective design of the security and access controls provides easy access for fraud or error to be introduced into the financial statements. Furthermore, ineffective security and access controls could permit an individual to modify accounting applications or data and then also disguise the changes to escape detection.

Deficiency 4: Information Technology General Controls—Lack of a Formal Process for Changes in Application Controls

G.54 The entity lacks a formal documented process to ensure that changes in programs that relate to accounting application packages are authorized and implemented effectively, including appropriate testing of the changes. The entity does not rely on any spreadsheets for accounting functions, and all transactions are processed directly through the accounting software.

Situation 4A: Not a Deficiency

G.55 The entity uses only packaged software applications, as its accounting needs are very simple. The packaged software systems used do not have functions that enable the entity to modify the operation of the software. No new versions of the software were installed during the year.

Further Analysis of Situation 4A

G.56 The "change control" element within the IT general control environment is not relevant to this entity because the software cannot be modified. Thus, the lack of a formal change control function is not currently considered an IT general control deficiency for this company in this period.

G.57 This conclusion is analogous to the example given in paragraph .A108 of AU-C section 315, which states:

> For example, if no new systems are implemented during the period of the financial statements, deficiencies in the general IT controls over application system acquisition and development may not be relevant to the financial statements being audited.

Situation 4B: A Potential Significant Deficiency

G.58 The entity's accounting and financial reporting related application software is relatively sophisticated and permits customization by the entity. Each year, a number of changes are made to the software to improve performance or respond to the changing business needs of the entity. Although change control procedures and controls do exist, and qualified programmers seem to be used, tests and past experience indicate that these controls are not working at a highest level of reliability, and several inconsequential errors were detected in the current year that were traced back to change control procedures.

Further Analysis of Situation 4B

G.59 The existence of issues arising from the change control procedures indicates a deficiency of some magnitude. The facts of the situation do not indicate that there are compensating controls that achieve the same control objective. Further analysis of the potential severity of the deficiency indicates that there *are* compensating controls at the user and monitoring levels that are effective in limiting the severity of the deficiency to less than materiality. These controls were assessed as effective in limiting the severity of the deficiency to less than a material weakness based on their ability to detect certain issues in the current period.

G.60 Even though the identified deficiencies were inconsequential, the auditor may conclude that inconsequential misstatements might not always be detectable on a timely basis by the compensating controls and therefore would merit the attention of those charged with governance.

Deficiency 5: Aggregation of Several Deficiencies

Situation 5A: Material Weakness

G.61 The auditor of XYZ entity agrees that based on the context in which the following deficiencies occurred:

- Inadequate segregation of duties over certain information-system access controls relating to revenue recognition.
- Several instances of revenue transactions that were not properly recorded in subsidiary ledgers. The transactions were not material, either individually or in the aggregate.
- A lack of timely reconciliation of the account balances related to the improperly recorded transactions.

G.62 Based on only these facts, the auditor may determine that the combination of these significant deficiencies in a very significant account represents a material weakness. Individually, these deficiencies might not be a material weakness. However, each of these significant deficiencies affects the same account. Taken together, there is a reasonable possibility that a material misstatement could occur and not be prevented or detected. Therefore, in combination, these deficiencies may represent a material weakness.

G.63 The auditor uses judgment to assess whether significant deficiencies aggregate to a material weakness based on the facts and circumstances of each case. The assessment of whether deficiencies aggregate to a material weakness is not a simple quantitative matter, but involves significant judgment. This example should not be interpreted to imply that a specific number of deficiencies always results in a material weakness.

Situation 5B: Material Weakness

G.64 During its assessment of internal control over financial reporting, management of a financial institution identified deficiencies in the design of controls over the estimation of credit losses (a critical accounting estimate); the operating effectiveness of controls for initiating, processing, and reviewing adjustments to the allowance for credit losses; and the operating effectiveness of controls designed to prevent and detect the improper recognition of interest income. The auditor believes that, in the overall context, each of these deficiencies individually represents a significant deficiency.

G.65 In addition, during the past year, the entity experienced a significant level of growth in its loan balances that were subjected to controls governing credit-loss estimation and revenue recognition, and further growth is expected in the upcoming year.

G.66 Based only on these facts, the auditor may conclude that the combination of these significant deficiencies represents a material weakness because

- the balances in the loan accounts affected by these significant deficiencies have increased over the past year and are expected to increase in the future.
- this growth in loan balances, coupled with the combined effect of the aforementioned significant deficiencies, results in a reasonable possibility that a material misstatement of the allowance for credit losses or interest income could occur.

G.67 Deficiencies may be aggregated by account and by component of internal control.

G.68 In this case, because multiple significant deficiencies relate to control activities in the same account and include a critical accounting estimate, the auditor may conclude that, in the aggregate, they constitute a material weakness. Growth in the account increases the likelihood that the deficiencies could cause a material misstatement.

G.69 The auditor uses judgment to assess whether deficiencies aggregate to a material weakness based on the facts and circumstances of each case. This example is not meant to imply that any specific number of deficiencies always results in a material weakness.

Appendix H

Examples of Circumstances That May Be Deficiencies, Significant Deficiencies, or Material Weaknesses[1]

This appendix is nonauthoritative and is included for informational purposes only.

Paragraph .A11 of AU-C section 265, *Communicating Internal Control Related Matters Identified in an Audit* (AICPA, *Professional Standards*), identifies indicators of material weaknesses in internal control.

Practice Considerations for Auditors of Entities Using the COSO Framework

The Committee of Sponsoring Organizations of the Treadway Commission's updated *Internal Control—Integrated Framework* (COSO framework) contains guidance for assessing the severity of deficiencies. However, the guidance for assessing the severity of deficiencies and communicating deficiencies to management and governance in AU-C section 265 (as illustrated in this guide and its appendixes) should be followed by auditors. Entities wishing to synchronize their assessments with those of their auditors may similarly look to the auditing standards regarding the classification of deficiencies as deficiencies, significant deficiencies, and material weaknesses.

Deficiencies in the Design of Controls

The following are examples of circumstances that may be deficiencies, significant deficiencies, or material weaknesses related to the design of controls:

- Inadequate design of internal control over the preparation of the financial statements being audited.
- Inadequate design of internal control over a significant account or process.
- Inadequate documentation of the components of internal control.
- Insufficient control consciousness within the organization (for example, the tone at the top and the control environment).
- Evidence of ineffective aspects of the control environment, such as indications that significant transactions in which management is financially interested are not being appropriately scrutinized by those charged with governance.
- Evidence of an ineffective entity risk assessment process, such as management's failure to identify a risk of material misstatement that the auditor would expect the entity's risk assessment process to have identified.

---

[1] This section is reprinted from paragraph .A37 of AU-C section 265, *Communicating Internal Control Related Matters Identified in an Audit* (AICPA, *Professional Standards*).

- Evidence of an ineffective response to identified significant risks (for example, absence of controls over such a risk).
- Absent or inadequate segregation of duties within a significant account or process.
- Absent or inadequate controls over the safeguarding of assets (this applies to controls that the auditor determines would be necessary for effective internal control over financial reporting).
- Inadequate design of IT general and application controls that prevent the information system from providing complete and accurate information consistent with financial reporting objectives and current needs.
- Employees or management who lack the qualifications and training to fulfill their assigned functions. For example, in an entity that prepares financial statements in accordance with generally accepted accounting principles (GAAP), the person responsible for the accounting and reporting function lacks the skills and knowledge to apply GAAP in recording the entity's financial transactions or preparing its financial statements.
- Inadequate design of monitoring controls used to assess the design and operating effectiveness of the entity's internal control over time.
- Absence of an internal process to report deficiencies in internal control to management on a timely basis.
- Absence of a risk assessment process within the entity when such a process would ordinarily be expected to have been established.

Failures in the Operation of Internal Control

- Failure in the operation of effectively designed controls over a significant account or process (for example, the failure of a control such as dual authorization for significant disbursements within the purchasing process).
- Failure of the information and communication component of internal control to provide complete and accurate output because of deficiencies in timeliness, completeness, or accuracy (for example, the failure to obtain timely and accurate consolidating information from remote locations that is needed to prepare the financial statements).
- Failure of controls designed to safeguard assets from loss, damage, or misappropriation. This circumstance may need careful consideration before it is evaluated as a significant deficiency or material weakness. For example, assume that a company uses security devices to safeguard its inventory (preventive controls) and also performs periodic physical inventory counts (detective control) timely in relation to its financial reporting. Although the physical inventory count does not safeguard the inventory from theft or loss, it prevents a material misstatement of the financial statements if performed effectively and timely. Therefore, given that the definitions of *material weakness* and *significant deficiency* relate to

likelihood of misstatement of the financial statements, the failure of a preventive control such as inventory tags will not result in a significant deficiency or material weakness if the detective control (physical inventory) prevents a misstatement of the financial statements. Material weaknesses relating to controls over the safeguarding of assets would only exist if the company does not have effective controls (considering both safeguarding and other controls) to prevent or detect and correct a material misstatement of the financial statements.

- Failure to perform reconciliations of significant accounts. For example, accounts receivable subsidiary ledgers are not reconciled to the general ledger account in a timely or accurate manner.
- Undue bias or lack of objectivity by those responsible for accounting decisions (for example, consistent understatement of expenses or overstatement of allowances at the direction of management).
- Misrepresentation by client personnel to the auditor (an indicator of fraud).
- Management override of controls.
- Failure of an application control caused by a deficiency in the design or operation of an IT general control.
- An observed deviation rate that exceeds the deviation rate expected by the auditor in a test of the operating effectiveness of a control. For example, if the auditor designs a test in which he or she selects a sample and expects no deviations, the finding of one deviation is a nonnegligible deviation rate because, based on the results of auditor's test of the sample, the desired level of confidence was not obtained.

Appendix I

Suggestions for Conducting Inquiries

This appendix is nonauthoritative and is included for informational purposes only.

I.01 Inquiry alone is not sufficient to determine whether a control has been implemented. However, for some tasks inquiry will provide a principal source of evidence regarding the implementation of some areas relating to internal control. For example, inquiry may be a principal source of evidence in evaluating the design of the communication of antifraud programs or ethics policies as part of evaluating the design of the control environment.

I.02 A common companion procedure will be observation. Regardless of what is said, your observations when on-site will provide confirming or disconfirming evidence that should be documented as a source of evidence.

I.03 This guidance was developed to assist you in conducting a successful inquiry. However, the skill of inquiring is an art, and your experience and continuing attention to building interviewing skills will help you conduct more effective inquiries.

Relevant Areas and Tasks

I.04 Some of the areas where inquiries will be used to gather evidence include

- walkthroughs—confirming documented procedures;
- "tone at the top";
- antifraud programs;
- ethics policies;
- personnel policies;
- management override;
- password and security;
- information systems; and
- monitoring and supervision.

I.05 Inquiries are also required procedures in completing your responsibilities regarding considerations of fraud in the conduct of the financial statement audit under AU-C section 240, *Consideration of Fraud in a Financial Statement Audit* (AICPA, *Professional Standards*).

I.06 Wherever possible, identify and review objective evidence that will help you formulate your assessment. For example, when assessing the effectiveness of corporate ethics and code of conduct policies, read them first as a basis for the interview. Consider their effectiveness as written. Inquire of human resources whether records are kept of employees completing any required ethics courses or refresher courses, and if so, examine these records for completeness and inquire about how exceptions are handled. Are the records, the policy, and interview results consistent? If so, document this. Together, your various procedures contribute to the evidence supporting your overall determination of whether a control policy or procedure is being used by company personnel.

Planning and Strategy

I.07 Like all areas of the audit, planning is essential. Consider upfront when and where inquiries will be needed to gather audit evidence. When visiting remote locations and it is appropriate to do so, gather the relevant information when on-site for other purposes so separate trips are not necessary for each phase of the audit process. When procedures are performed in advance of the "as of" reporting date, consider how you will update or confirm your earlier understanding.

I.08 Corporate and country cultures can be important considerations in evaluating responses during an inquiry. In certain cultures, one might be very reluctant to question a person in authority, even in the face of overwhelming evidence of a problem. In other cultures, nonverbal cues can be confusing, as a head movement back and forth that would ordinarily indicate "no," actually could indicate "yes," or that the listener is following the conversation closely. Be alert to such situations and factor this into your strategy. Some corporate cultures are more relaxed and conversation is encouraged, and in others, formal memos (and e-mails between persons in adjoining cubicles) are the primary means of communication. These factors can affect the information that is communicated and the way it is communicated in an interview.

Tips for an Effective and Efficient Inquiry

I.09 Do your homework before beginning the inquiry. Know the information you wish to gather and the related policy regarding the topic.

I.10 Make sure the inquiry is conducted by the right auditor. When the interviewee is the Chief Executive Officer, a partner or manager will often conduct the inquiry.

I.11 Recognize we all have relative comfort zones in performing certain tasks. If the interview could be conducted by a number of individuals, important tasks should be handled in the initial year by those most comfortable with the inquiry process.

The Inquiry Itself

I.12 Start the inquiry by introducing yourself and the relating the purpose of the inquiry.

I.13 Early in the inquiry, ask short factual questions and open-ended questions to put the respondent at ease, for example:

- How long have you been with the company?
- How long have you been in your current position?
- Describe for me some of your daily responsibilities.

I.14 Pay attention to nonverbal cues. Follow up a few questions later, following the previous line of questioning if something comes to your attention due to an obvious shift in demeanor or attitude.

I.15 With nonaccounting personnel, avoid technical terms that relate to auditing (for example, defalcation, "Financial Accounting Standards Board") and alarming wording ("Our firm is required make inquiries of certain individuals regarding fraud"). Sometimes respondents will not understand the context in which the question is being asked. Be prepared to detect this and clarify.

I.16 Whenever possible make the questions personal (Have *you* ever become aware of an instance where... How do *you* think the company would respond if they became aware of an instance...). Respondents often have a difficult time speaking for the company (How would the company respond if...).

I.17 Be prepared for the unexpected. Follow up, and gather enough information so that matter can be pursued later if necessary ("Sure, I was asked to override the normal procedures...lots of times...but I refused..."). Listen carefully, and do not become focused on your note-taking while the interviewee is speaking.

I.18 Ask for information rather than provide the answer.

- "Do you do anything to show you have performed the reconciliation?" versus "Do you then initial the invoice?"

- Start with "Are you aware of whether the company has an antifraud policy?" versus "Did you take the required refresher course this year on the company's antifraud policy?"

I.19 Extensive note-taking or the use of recording devices can unnerve the respondent and diminish the effectiveness of the inquiry. Trying to type notes on a portable computer during the inquiry can also be distracting. Often it will be best to take notes on a manual form or on a small note pad during the inquiry, and type up the formal notes immediately after the inquiry.

I.20 When the inquiry is completed, thank the participant for his or her time and ask if you can follow up if there are further questions.

I.21 Collaborate with others on the engagement team working in this area to identify issues or inconsistencies in responses.

Scope

I.22 Consider the nature of the inquiry and identify relevant participants. When the scope of the inquiry includes the company as a whole (for example, awareness of the corporate ethics policy), evidence should be gathered from a variety of personnel groups, including production and sales personnel, administrative personnel, and management. Although not necessarily covering all groups in any one year, the sample should include a variety of personnel groups.

Following Up

I.23 There will be instances when follow-up will be necessary. Often, issues and comments can be clarified by a simple phone call, but if significant additional information is needed or in a high-risk situation such as a risk of fraud, the auditor may need to meet further with the employee to gather information.

I.24 Remember that a *strong* suspicion of fraud or evidence of fraud should be communicated first to the engagement manager or partner, as it may call for timely communication to those charged with governance. The audit committee or board may engage other independent, trained, forensic investigators to examine the situation more closely. Auditors are not generally trained as fraud examiners, and much evidence can be altered or destroyed in a short time if employees believe that they have been targeted for investigation. Time is of the essence if fraud is suspected.

Appendix J

Matters to Consider in Determining Performance Materiality

This appendix is nonauthoritative and is included for informational purposes only.

J.01 You should determine an amount lower than the materiality level for the financial statements as a whole for purposes of designing further audit procedures to respond to risks of material misstatement and significant risks. This lower amount is called *performance materiality*. Establishing performance materiality creates an allowance for the possibility that individually immaterial misstatements could, in the aggregate, be significant or material, and it allows for the possibility that undetected misstatements may exist after the auditor applies procedures to the populations. Both the consideration of possible aggregate misstatements and creating an allowance for possible undetected misstatements are considerations when planning any audit. The factors identified in table J-1 help you make a proper allowance for undetected misstatements in particular engagement circumstances by setting performance materiality and tolerable misstatement.

J.02 Some auditors may use a fixed proportion of materiality to establish performance materiality, which is then applied to all accounts. Auditors that align tolerable misstatement and performance materiality (that is, set them at the same amount) may a use a range for setting performance materiality and tolerable misstatement of between 50 and 75 percent depending on the risk of material misstatement associated with the particular class of transaction, account balance, or disclosure item. Using a fixed dollar amount (or fixed proportion of materiality) may not be an effective or efficient approach to use in every engagement. When tolerable misstatement is set separately for testing within an account, it should not be more than the performance materiality amount. When tolerable misstatement is set using the benchmark percentages, then performance materiality can be set higher than tolerable misstatement. Unfortunately, precise calculations of the optimal relation between materiality and performance materiality would have to be worked out on an engagement-by-engagement and perhaps an account-by-account basis using a statistical framework, and might also consider the relative costs of auditing various accounts. In most cases, making such a precise determination is impractical. Thus, the use of a generally conservative rule of thumb is a commonly applied approach and does simplify the judgment process.

J.03 Although in some cases performance materiality may appropriately be set closer to materiality, in other cases a greater cushion is needed to ensure that when the overall audit results are aggregated, an adequate allowance for undetected misstatement (further possible misstatement in addition to factual, judgmental, and projected misstatements) has been made, thus supporting an overall "low risk" audit conclusion.

J.04 Performance materiality need not be set at the same amount for each account. The objective is to set the performance materiality amounts at the planning stage so that after aggregating the audit results there remains a sufficient allowance for undetected misstatement to support the conclusion that a low risk audit has been performed. For example, at the end of an audit, aggregate misstatements consisting of factual, judgmental, and projected misstatement totals $85,000 and materiality is $100,000, the auditor should consider if the nature, timing, and extent of the aggregate procedures performed indicate that there is a low risk that $15,000 or more of undetected misstatement remains in the remaining untested populations. If not, additional procedures or an adjustment of some of the misstatements may need to be performed for the auditor to conclude at a low risk that the financial statements are not materially misstated or additional adjustments need to be made to reduce potential undetected misstatements.

J.05 For example, if only one account balance or stream of transactions is significant to the financial statements and the primary source of assurance for that account is derived from a single substantive procedure of details, and other accounts will be able to be tested with relative certainty, then performance materiality might be set closer to materiality. When there are numerous accounts where uncertainty exists or results of numerous tests at various locations, performance materiality/tolerable misstatement might be set at, for example, 50 percent or less of materiality. Although some auditors set a single relationship for all accounts, others may vary the relationship somewhat to reflect risk and characteristics. Whether the relationship between performance materiality/tolerable misstatement and materiality is varied between accounts, the audit risk and allowance for sampling risk is still to be determined for the aggregate of samples.

When performing multiple tests on an account, balance, or class of transactions, the concept of tolerable misstatement is applied to each test. In the same way performance materiality "steps down" from materiality for the aggregation of account results, tolerable misstatement can "step down" from performance materiality when tolerable misstatement is set to consider factors at the testing level not reflected in the performance materiality determination. Additionally, if only a portion of the total population is involved in the test, tolerable misstatement might be set lower then performance materiality. Tolerable misstatement is established to allow for expected misstatement at the sample level and when multiple estimation or sampling results will need to be combined in reaching conclusions on an account, balance or class of transactions. Performance materiality is used when setting the scope and evaluating/summarizing results for the account, balance or class of transactions. Chapter 4, "Nonstatistical and Statistical Audit Sampling for Substantive Tests of Details," of the AICPA Guide *Audit Sampling* provides further discussion of the purpose and setting of performance materiality and tolerable misstatement and refines table J-1 to distinguish between those factors that might be more closely associated with one measure or the other.

J.06 Additional considerations in setting performance materiality are discussed in appendix L, "The Effect of Group Audits on Planning and Determining Materiality," when applying AU-C section 600, *Special Considerations—Audits of Group Financial Statements (Including the Work of Component Auditors)* (AICPA, *Professional Standards*).

Table J-1
Factors to Consider in Setting Performance Materiality

Factor to Consider in Setting Performance Materiality	Conditions Leading to a Performance Materiality Much Lower Than Materiality	Conditions Leading to a Performance Materiality Closer to Materiality	Comments
Expected total amount of factual and judgmental and projected misstatements (based on past significant misstatements and other factors).	A greater number of misstatements.	A lesser number of misstatements.	The allowance for undetected misstatements is typically greater when more misstatements are identified.
Management's attitude toward proposed adjustments.	Management is generally resistant to adjustments.	Management is open to considering adjustments and usually corrects all known misstatements and many likely misstatements.	More adjustments of factual and judgmental and projected misstatements will lessen the amount needed to allow for undetected misstatements.
Number of accounts where amounts will be subject to estimation and will not be able to be determined with precision.	A significant number of accounts.	One or a few accounts.	A greater allowance for undetected misstatements is needed when there are more accounts that are subject to estimation procedures.
Locations, subsidiaries, or samples within an account where separate procedures are applied for each location but that will be aggregated in reaching audit conclusions.	A significant number of locations, subsidiaries, or samples within an account.	One or a few locations, subsidiaries, or samples within an account.	A greater allowance for undetected misstatements is needed for the imprecision of many samples.

Note: In any sample, the projected misstatement is not "the amount" that corrects the financial statements. This is because of the inherent limitations of a sample in providing precise results. The statistical precision of the result (in many cases, unknown for nonstatistical samples) provides reliable limits (upper and/or lower) on the misstatement of population amounts at a specified confidence (assurance) level. Consequently there is a high probability that *some* of the projected misstatement is indeed misstated and could, with confidence, be proposed as an adjustment to the financial statements. The projected amount is the best (most likely) estimate of the misstatement.

Part III

Illustrative Audit Documentation Case Study

Appendix K

Illustrative Audit Documentation Case Study: Young Fashions, Inc.

This appendix is nonauthoritative and is included for informational purposes only.

Practice Considerations for Auditors of Entities Using the COSO Framework

This case study has appeared in previous editions of this guide. It is updated in this edition to indicate in brackets where the principles established in the Committee of Sponsoring Organizations of the Treadway Commission's updated *Internal Control—Integrated Framework* (COSO framework) might apply (for example, "[principle 1]"). Further discussion of the principles is provided in appendix C, "Internal Control Components."

Although it may be efficient to reconsider documentation approaches to streamline documentation based on the COSO framework updated in 2013, existing documentation may still allow an entity to demonstrate that the principles and components are present and functioning and that the components are operating in an integrated manner.

Objective of the Illustrative Audit Documentation Case Study

The purpose of the following group of appendixes is to illustrate the types of audit documentation an auditor might prepare to apply some of the guidance provided in this guide. The exhibits are not a full set of illustrated audit documentation. The auditor would include documentation of other account balance or class of transaction information.

This documentation illustrates only one of many ways that an auditor might document the procedures, findings, judgments, conclusions, and other matters described in the guide. The example documentation may not represent the most efficient ways to comply with the audit documentation requirements. In some instances, the form of the example documentation was dictated by the need to present a paper-based example (rather than computer-based version) and the space limitations imposed by page size. Sample computer-based documentation may be presented differently.

Summary of Documentation Requirements

You should document matters pertaining to each step in the risk assessment process to demonstrate that the risk assessment requirements were satisfied. Your audit documentation should enable an experienced auditor, having no previous connection to the audit, to understand

- the work performed,
- the evidence examined and the source of the information, and
- the conclusions reached.

The form and extent of audit documentation is for you to determine using professional judgment. AU-C section 230, *Audit Documentation* (AICPA, *Professional Standards*), provides general guidance regarding the purpose, content, ownership, and confidentiality of audit documentation. Examples of common documentation techniques include narrative descriptions, questionnaires, checklists, and flowcharts. These techniques may be used alone or in combination.

The form and extent of your documentation is influenced by the following:

- The nature, size, and complexity of the entity and its environment.
- The availability of information from the entity.
- The specific audit methodology and technology used in the course of the audit.

Chapters 1, "Overview of Applying the Audit Risk Standards," and 3–6 of this guide describe the documentation requirements related to the application of the audit risk standards in practice.

The following table summarizes those documentation requirements and provides a reference to where this guide discusses those requirements. The table also provides a cross-reference to the appendix where you can find illustrative documentation that meets the requirement.

Table K-1

Documentation Requirement	Ref.
The level of materiality for the financial statements as a whole, which you used to plan your risk assessment procedures.	K-1-1
Performance materiality.	K-1-1
A description of the nature, timing, and extent of risk assessment procedures, as well as any changes to those plans as the audit progresses.	K-1-1
Audit strategy.	K-1-1
Audit plan.	Not included

The discussion among the audit team regarding the clients financial statements and the risk of material misstatement due to error or fraud. This documentation should include, at a minimum, the following matters:
 	
   a. How and when the discussion occurred
   b. The subject matter discussed
   c. The audit team members who participated in the discussion and
   d. Significant decisions reached about the teams planned responses, both at the financial statement and the assertion level
	K-5

The sources of information from which the understanding of the client was obtained.	K-1, K-2-1, K-3, K-4

Documentation Requirement	Ref.
The risk assessment procedures performed to gather the information used to obtain an understanding of the client.	K-1, K-2-1, K-3, K-4
The key elements of your understanding of the client and its environment identified.	K-1, K-2, K-3, K-4
With regard to internal control, your understanding of the controls relevant to the audit, including (a) an evaluation of whether the design of the control, individually or in combination, is capable of effectively preventing or detecting and correcting material misstatements, and (b) a determination of whether the control exists and the entity is using it.	K-2, K-3, K-4
Entity-Level Risks The assessment of the risks of material misstatement at the financial statement level.	K-5
The overall response to address the assessed risks of misstatement at the financial statement level.	K-5
Activity-Level Risks The assessment of the risks of material misstatement at the relevant assertion level.	K-5
The basis for the assessed risks of material misstatement.	K-5

The identified risks and related controls evaluated to identify
 	
    a. significant risks.
    b. those circumstances where substantive procedures alone will not provide sufficient appropriate audit evidence.
	K-5 K-5

The nature, timing, and extent of the further audit procedures.	K-5
The linkage of those procedures with the assessed risks at the relevant assertion level.	K-5
The results of further audit procedures.	Not included
The conclusions reached with regard to the use in the current audit of audit evidence about the operating effectiveness of controls that was obtained in a prior audit.	Not included
A summary of uncorrected misstatements, other than those that are trivial, related to factual and projected misstatements. This summary documentation allows you to	K-6

(continued)

Documentation Requirement	Ref.
a. separately consider the effects of factual, judgmental, and projected misstatements, b. consider the aggregate effect of misstatements on the financial statements, and c. consider the qualitative factors that are relevant to your consideration of whether the misstatements are material.	
Your communication of factual, judgmental, and projected misstatements and proposed adjustments to management and those charged with governance.	K-6
Your conclusion as to whether uncorrected misstatements, individually or in the aggregate, do or do not cause the financial statements to be materially misstated.	K-6
The basis for your conclusion.	K-6
Your conclusion as to the severity of control deficiencies.	K-6

How the Case Study Is Organized

The following diagram describes how the appendixes are organized.

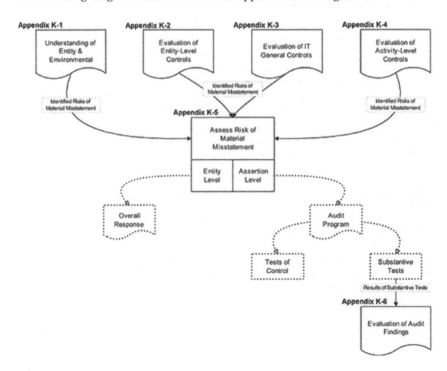

This case study has four information-gathering appendixes:

- K-1, "Understanding of Entity and Its Environment." This appendix includes example documentation of the auditors understanding of the client and its environment, except for internal controls, but including inherent risk.

- K-2, "Evaluation of Entity-Level Controls." This appendix provides example documentation of the auditor's evaluation of entity-level controls, except for IT general controls. [Principles 1–5, 10, and 12]

- K-3, "Understanding of Internal Control—IT General Controls." This appendix provides example documentation of the auditor's evaluation of IT general controls. In this case study we did not rely on IT controls because (1) IT controls were not adequate in the prior year and (2) we found IT general controls were not adequate for the first nine months. [Principle 11]

- K-4, "Evaluation of Activity-Level Controls—Wholesale Sales." This appendix provides example documentation of an evaluation of activity-level controls. In this case study we have presented only one class of transactions, sales. In practice, the auditor would evaluate activity-level controls for each significant class of transactions. [Principles 10, 12]

The performance of risk assessment procedures may identify *risks of material misstatement*. For example, in this case study, the auditor identifies risks related to

- possible management override of controls.

- reduced margins and higher inventory levels, which may result in over-valuing inventory (K-1).

- the determination of sales commissions, which are calculated using spreadsheets without adequate controls (K-2).

- a lack of logical access controls over all databases during a portion of the year (K-3).

- the potential loss or corruption of data during the upgrade of the company's order management system to a newer version (K-4).

All identified risks of material misstatement were evaluated to determine an overall response (financial statement-level risks) or to design further audit procedures (relevant assertion level risks). Appendix K-5 illustrates an example of how you might document your assessment of the *risks of material misstatement*.

This case study does not include example documentation of the auditors overall response, or the complete design of further audit procedures, as documented in an audit program. However, appendix K-5 does provide a summary of the auditors response to the assessed *risks of material misstatement*, which is an example of how you might provide a clear link between assessed *risks of material misstatement* and the design of further audit procedures.

This case study does not include examples of audit documentation of tests of controls or substantive procedures. The results of substantive procedures may result in the identification of misstatements. You must consider the effect of these misstatements. Appendix K-6 illustrates how an auditor might document this evaluation.

Also note that the performance of risk assessment procedures documented in appendixes K-1, K-2, K-3, and K-4 also may lead the auditor to identify control deficiencies, the significance of which also should be evaluated. This case study provides examples of how the auditor might document the identification of control deficiencies.

Summary of Company Included in the Illustrative Documentation

The company that serves as the basis of this case study is Young Fashions, Inc., a privately held company that designs and sells men's and women's apparel. The garments are manufactured by third party suppliers located in Asia and Europe. The company is owned by the Young family and is run by the children of its founder. Annual revenues are $110 million to $115 million; total assets are approximately $100 million.

The following summarizes some of the key features of the entity. This information was carried forward from prior audits and updated during planning.

Company Description	Young Fashions, Inc.
Nature of business	Apparel manufacturer
Most significant business processes	• Purchasing of finished goods or piece goods from third-party manufacturers • Sales and distribution • Apparel design
Number of locations	3
Corporate structure	Single entity
Year end	December 31
Ownership	Nonpublic and closely held ownership
Trading of common stock	None
Number of personnel	
Top management	4
Accounting dept.	6
Staff	190
Total	200
Financial information (estimated)	
Current year revenues	$114 million
Current year net income	$8.2 million
Current year total assets	$98 million

Company Description	Young Fashions, Inc.
Volumes	
Sales invoices	50,000
Purchase transactions	2,000
Inventory items	1,000
Customers	200
Vendors	50
Control Structure	
History of adjustments	Typically relate to estimates and cutoff
Client control documentation	Partial
Audit committee	None
Those charged with governance	Board of directors
Internal audit function	None
Segregation of duties	Good
Accounting System	
Computer hardware	Networked personal computers with dedicated server and AS 400 mid-range
Accounting software	Unmodified mid-level accounting software
Number of nonaccounting systems	2
IT processing	Distributed
Number of IT personnel	2, full-time, reporting to CFO
Revenue system	Online, real-time capture of transactions through server; daily batch processing by AS 400
Use of spreadsheets to process information outside the accounting application	Depreciation schedules, accruals, sales commissions, and support for some disclosures maintained on spreadsheets
Electronic commerce capabilities	EDI is used for • customer orders. • order of component parts, tracking of inventory and payments to vendors.
Key electronic files	Master-price file Customer file Outstanding transactions file Accounts receivable master file General ledger master file

(continued)

Company Description	Young Fashions, Inc.
Controls over financial reporting process	Limited
Revenue Transactions [1]	
How is transaction initiated?	Sales order submitted by customer electronically based on standing purchase order. Computer-generated exception report is prepared for manual follow-up.
Sales order	Electronic, entered by customer. Company IT system automatically generates an order confirmation, which is sent electronically to customer.
Shipping report, bill of lading, packing slip	Manual, enter quantities in computer when shipment is prepared. Computer-generated packing slip, manual bill of lading. Upon shipment, system generates shipping confirmation and sends electronic notification to customers.
Sales invoice	Customer and quantity data from packing slip. Prices in master file. Computer-generated sales invoice submitted electronically to customer.

[1] Revenue is excerpted as an illustration. All major classes of transactions and transaction streams might be included here in a full case study.

Appendix K-1

Young Fashions: Understanding of Entity and Its Environment

This appendix is nonauthoritative and is included for informational purposes only.

Observations and Suggestions

You are required to obtain an understanding of your client and its environment. Not only does this understanding allow you to identify and assess risks of material misstatement, it also allows you to exercise informed judgment about other audit matters such as

- materiality, performance materiality, and tolerable misstatement.
- whether the client's selection and application of accounting policies are appropriate and financial statement disclosures are adequate.
- areas where special audit consideration may be necessary, for example, related party transactions.
- the expectation of recorded amounts that you develop for performing analytical procedures.
- the design and performance of further audit procedures.
- the evaluation of audit evidence.

Your understanding of the client encompasses the following aspects of the clients business:

- External factors
- The nature of the client, such as its operations and organizational structure
- The clients objectives and strategies and resulting business risks
- How management measures and reviews the entity's financial performance
- The clients internal control

This appendix illustrates an example form and the documentation of your understanding of all of these elements, *except for* internal control. Appendixes K-2, K-2-1, K-3, and K-4 illustrate the documentation of the understanding of internal control at both the entity and activity level, including an understanding of IT controls.

This example assumes that the auditor will carry forward audit evidence regarding controls that was obtained in previous audits. When audit evidence is carried forward in this manner, you should perform procedures to determine that the audit evidence remains relevant for the current audit. This example illustrates how you might document the procedures performed to update audit evidence from a prior period as well as the results of those procedures.

©2016, AICPA   AAG-ARR APP K-1

Some of the procedures performed to update the understanding of the entity involve inquiries of company management. As a matter of audit efficiency, you may wish to make inquiries of management about the risks of fraud (as required by AU-C section 240, *Consideration of Fraud in a Financial Statement Audit* [AICPA, *Professional Standards*]) when making inquiries to update your understanding of the entity and its environment.

One of the primary objectives of obtaining an understanding of the entity and its environment, including internal control, is to identify *risks of material misstatement*. This example illustrates how you might document identified risks of material misstatement. These risks of material misstatement have been cross-referenced to appendix K-5, which illustrates how you might document your assessment of the risk of material misstatement

All information that appears in this font style illustrates information completed by the auditor.

Instructions for Preparation

This form documents the procedures performed and understanding obtained about the following aspects of your client's business:

- External factors
- The nature of the client
- The client's objectives and strategies and resulting business risks [principle 6 and principle 7]
- How management measures and reviews the entity's financial performance

Part I of this form is divided into four segments, which correspond to these items. Within each segment are three parts:

- *Understanding obtained in prior engagements.* This part presents your understanding of the client that has been carried forward from previous engagements
- *Procedures performed.* This part documents the risk assessment and other procedures you performed to determine that your understanding from the prior period remains relevant in the current period.
- *Changes in the current period.* This part documents changes at the client or in its environment that you identified while updating our understanding. [principle 9]

Part II of the form is the documentation of planning analytical procedures. These procedures also provide audit evidence supporting your understanding of the client and its environment.

Your understanding of the client and its environment may lead you to identify risks of material misstatement. Part III of this form summarizes the risks of material misstatement identified in other parts of the form.

Part I—Understanding the Entity and Its Environment

Overview of the Client

As part of our client acceptance and continuance procedures, we updated the general understanding of the client obtained in prior years.

Understanding Obtained in Prior Engagements

Young Fashions is a privately held company that designs and sells men's and women's apparel. The company has two distinct brands: J Young Couture, which is a high-end, fashion forward line, and JY Sport, which provides more casual wear. The company sells it lines through department stores and clothing stores and also operates a small chain of its own retail outlets.

The company does not manufacture its own garments, but instead outsources the manufacturing to third-party suppliers located in Asia and Europe. In most cases, Young owns the goods at the manufacturer. See inventory system documentation [not included in this illustration]. The company is owned by the Young family and is run by the children of its founder.

In the prior year the Company recorded all adjustments proposed by the auditor. In prior periods the auditor communicated the lack of IT security and the need for an IT director as material weaknesses. The company indicated these issues would be addressed in the current period.

Written Understanding.

See Engagement Letter [not included].

Procedures Performed to Update our Understanding

We performed the following procedures to assess the continued relevance of the audit evidence obtained in previous engagements and to identify changes in the nature of the client's overall business. This included a review of the client's assessment of changes in risks as well as our independent assessment of this factor. [principle 9]

See Client Continuance Form (also includes procedures performed) [not included].

Changes to Our Understanding in the Current Period

As a result of performing the procedures indicated, we noted the following changes in the company's overall business that have occurred since the prior engagement and that may affect the current period audit.

The company hired an IT director during the year and security controls have been strengthened over the year, although they may not have been effective for the entire year. For further detail, see the Internal Controls documentation (reference).

Observations and Suggestions

The remaining part of this appendix is divided into four segments, each one relating to different aspects of the company and its environment (for example, external factors, nature of the client, and so on).

Each of these segments is further divided into the following parts:

- Understanding obtained in prior engagements
- Procedures performed to update the understanding obtained in the prior engagement
- Changes to the understanding of the client's business from the prior engagement

This organization scheme follows the process for updating your understanding of the client's business from prior engagements, which is discussed in more detail in paragraphs 3.130–.142 of this guide.

External Factors

In obtaining our understanding of *the apparel* industry and other external factors affecting the client, we considered the following matters:

- Industry conditions
- Regulatory environment
- Government policies affecting the conduct of the client's business
- Other external factors that affect the client's business

Understanding Obtained in Prior Engagements

The men's and women's apparel industry is extremely competitive, and no one brand dominates market share. J Young Couture and JY Sport are smaller players in the industry and are considered a niche brand. The competition for market share, together with the constant availability of discounted garments available over the Internet (for example, e-Bay and a variety of discount retailers) create a consistent downward pressure on prices.

The industry is quite seasonal, tracking with the four seasons. Most designers release two collections per year, spring / summer and fall / winter. The end of each season is marked by significant markdowns by the company's customers in order to move inventory and prepare for the new season. Within the retail industry, these end-of-season markdowns are partially paid for by the supplier (Young Fashions). Once the amount of the markdown is determined, an allowance is calculated which is used to offset the amounts due the supplier (Young Fashions).

The company's year end is December 31. By that date, all winter merchandise has been shipped and most has been paid for, although markdowns will still be coming in January, February, and March (see working paper XXX for the audit of this estimate). The December 31 year end means there will be lower inherent risk for the year-end shipping and sales cutoff, since the winter line has mostly been shipped and the spring line is not yet ready to be shipped. There is some production of spring season merchandise at December 31, and there might be shipments between the vendor and the manufacturer or between the manufacturer and the company warehouse. These are not extensive since many of the vendors and manufacturers close the last week of the year.

Since the early 19X0s, very few U.S. apparel companies have manufactured their own garments, and Young Fashions is no different. Suppliers generally are located in Europe (predominately Italy) and Southeast Asia (Malaysia, Hong Kong, and China).

Technology and IT systems play an important part in the industry. Customers may stock out of items and need new shipments; raw materials must be shipped to third-party manufacturers; finished goods must be shipped to the company warehouse or direct to customers; and customer orders must be managed. To remain competitive, companies in this industry have IT systems capable of managing all aspects of operations. Larger retailers also require their suppliers (for example, Young Fashions) to meet certain guidelines, which include supplier IT systems that integrate with the retailer's inventory and purchasing functions. Among other things, this integration provides the supplier with information about inventory balances and sales by product, which is important for estimating end-of-season markdowns.

The use of off-shore suppliers is regulated and subjects the company to certain laws and taxes. Changes in the regulations, such as tariffs, can have a significant effect on company business. Off-shore suppliers also subject the company to a variety of federal and state taxes.

Some business practices that are standard in Europe or Southeast Asia may be viewed as exploitive or unethical in the United States. Issues such as employee working conditions may cast the company in an unfavorable light and hurt its brand.

Procedures Performed

We performed the following procedures to assess the continued relevance of the audit evidence obtained in previous engagements and to identify changes in external factors affecting the client:

- *Discussion with Jane Young Ching (8/15), Josh Young (8/15), and Bob Maguire, Operations Manager (8/22)*
- *Read memo dated February 10, 20X4 from Bob Maguire, Operations Manager, and Barry Gregg, Sales Manager, to Young Fashions' customers, "Current Weather Problems in Malaysia"*
- *Read article "Begnini Makes Good on Promises to Labor," The Economist, April 8, 20X4*
- *Tracked monthly conversion rate of euro vs. U.S. dollar (see working paper X-X)* [not included in this guide]
- *Reviewed the Young fashion website*
- *Searched on Internet for relevant articles in Apparel News*
- *Read report of CS Inc. (stockbroker) on apparel industry*
- *Read annual reports for key customers*

Changes to Our Understanding in the Current Period

As a result of performing the procedures indicated, we noted the following changes in external matters that have occurred since the prior engagement and that may affect the current period audit:

- *Decline in the dollar versus the euro has resulted in increased prices for finished goods and piecework performed in Europe. Recent elections in Italy and changed political climate have resulted in increases in wages paid to employees, increasing prices for Italian goods.*
- *Amalgamated Federated acquired Bergman-Goodall luxury department store during the year, continuing a general industry trend toward consolidation.*
- *Unusually long and harsh monsoon season in Southeast Asia severely disrupted shipping to and from Asian suppliers.*

Nature of the Client

In obtaining our understanding of the client and other internal factors, we considered the following matters:

- Business operations
- Investments
- Financing
- Financial reporting

Understanding Obtained in Prior Engagements

The company has been in business for over 50 years and has been a client of our Firm for 10 years. It was founded by Joseph Young (who died 5 years ago) and is now owned and managed by his children, Josh and Jane, who each own 30 percent of the company. Mr. Young's widow owns 20 percent and is not active in the business. Trusts for various grandchildren own the remaining 20 percent.

The company's main wholesale customers for the J Young Couture line are: Newman-MacLachlin, and Bernard's (a wholly owned subsidiary of Amalgamated Department Stores). The main wholesale customer for JY Sport is Amalgamated Department Stores, which includes Ford & Mailer, Mandelbaum's, Grosvernor's, and Daniel Fleisher's.

All the company's products are manufactured by independently owned, foreign manufacturers under long-term contracts. The company has two basic approaches to production:

- *Purchase finished goods. Young Fashions buys finished products from the supplier, who is responsible for the purchasing and carrying of raw materials, in addition to the manufacture of the product.*

- *Cut, make, and trim. Young Fashions buys raw materials and piece goods and then moves these to finished product assemblers who send the product to Young's warehouse or directly to the customer. The ending inventory is expected to be about 40 percent purchased finished goods, 40 percent finished goods under the cut, make, and trim program, 10 percent raw materials, and 10 percent work in progress at the assemblers.*

The company has two warehouses, one in San Diego and another in Philadelphia. As a way to prevent costly "stock outs," the company maintains a high level of "basic" products, such as shirts and blouses. Customers can order these products at any time, and they will be shipped within five business days.

The company does not undertake any research and development in the traditional sense of the term. However, they actively search for new fabrics for their designs.

The company owns its own headquarters. It finances its inventory and other operations primarily through cash and a revolving line of credit, secured by receivables and inventory.

Procedures Performed

We performed the following procedures to assess the continued relevance of the audit evidence obtained in previous engagements and to identify changes in the nature of the client:

- *Discussion with Jane Young Ching (8/15), Josh Young (8/15), Lori Feldman, Finance Manager (8/16), and Bob Maguire, Operations Manager (8/22)*

Changes to Our Understanding in the Current Period

As a result of performing the procedures indicated, we noted the following changes in the nature of the client that have occurred since the prior engagement and that may affect the current period audit:

- *As a result of its acquisition by Amalgamated Federated, Bergman-Goodall is now a major customer of Young Fashions. This company has a strong balance sheet but is known in the industry as being a tough negotiator on returns, disputes, and markdowns. We will address this issue in our tests of markdowns.*

- *In June, the company hired a full-time IT director, Robert Haner. (Previously, the function was performed by Lori Feldman, Finance Director, and one IT assistant. Most IT functions were outsourced.)*

- *Company is considering changing suppliers for some goods from Italian companies to those located in Romania or Poland.*

Objectives, Strategies, and Business Risks

In obtaining our understanding of the client's objectives, strategies, and related business risks, we considered the following matters:

- How the entity addresses industry, regulator, and other external factors that affect it

- Effects of implementing a strategy, including any effects that will lead to new accounting requirements

Understanding Obtained in Prior Engagements

The company's main objectives are [principle 6]

- *continued growth.*

- *repositioning of the brand as a value-priced luxury brand, competing against other luxury brands (for example, Giorgio Pirandello, Bosch, L'Estrada) on the basis of price. This positioning is different from its traditional position as a high quality, bridge-line brand competing against other bridge-line brands (Barry Ferris, Brutini, Amy Thomas).*

The main strategies for achieving these objectives include

- *expanding the line of women's and men's wear across the J Young Couture line, which generally has higher margins than the JY Sport line.*

- *expanding its retail outlet network.*

- *de-emphasizing sales to Amalgamated Federated to concentrate more on the luxury retailers (although still selling to Amalgamated Federated).*

- *maintaining a high quality IT system as a way to decrease the long lead time between the design of new garments and their sale. Decreased lead times allow the company to be more responsive to customers, reducing end-of-the-season markdowns and inventory carrying costs.*

The main business risks associated with the company's strategies include [principle 7]

- *there are fewer customers for the J Young Couture line than for the JY Sport line. Additionally, couture customers tend to be more loyal to their long-time brands, creating a barrier for expanding into this market.*

- *marketing costs for luxury brands are higher than the marketing for bridge-line brands. Additionally, competing successfully against other luxury brands will require significant image marketing.*

- *Amalgamated Federated is one of the company's main customers, and there is the risk that increased income from sales to luxury retailers will not offset any decrease in income from sales to Amalgamated Federated.*

- *constant upgrading of IT systems carries the risk that the new systems will not work as planned, will take longer than expected to implement, or will cost more than anticipated.*

Company Responses: The company has developed the following strategies and controls or dealing with these risks: [principles 4, 10]

- *Hired a new IT director to attempt to reduce the IT systems risks*
- *Changed the commission structure to offer higher commissions for sales of the Couture line*
- *Significantly increased the advertising budget and the co-CEOs review the results of advertising*
- *CEO meetings with key customers*

Procedures Performed

We performed the following procedures to assess the continued relevance of the audit evidence obtained in previous engagements and to identify changes in the client's objectives and strategies and related business risks:

- *Discussion with Jane Young Ching (8/15), Josh Young (8/15), Robert Haner, IT Director (8/24), and Bob Maguire, Operations Manager (8/22)*
- *Read letter from Josh and Jane dated 5/17/03 announcing launch of women's accessory line for spring/summer to its customers*
- *Read minutes of quarterly Board of Directors Meeting, 1/20, 7/18 and 9/05*

Changes to Our Understanding in the Current Period

As a result of performing the procedures indicated, we noted the following changes in the client's objectives and strategies and the related business risks that have occurred since the prior engagement and which may affect the current period audit [principle 9]:

- *Upgraded versions of order management application.*
- *Added a mid-range AS 400 computer to its configuration.*

- *Working to install a report-writing application that will provide management with more and better reports to help plan operations and manage the business.*

- *Expanded line of both men's and women's lines of J Young Couture. Launched a new line of women's accessories in Q4 (J Young Couture).*

- *Have not fully integrated new accessories line with the inventory management system, which has prevented management from monitoring inventory levels for accessories sold through wholesale customers. This condition creates a risk of material misstatement of the financial statements—see part III, risk #3, for additional comments and follow-up.*

- *Did not actively pursue repositioning of brand or de-emphasis of sales of JY Sport to Amalgamated Federated, due to higher labor and materials costs for Italian goods.*

Measurement and Review of Financial Performance

In obtaining our understanding how management measures and reviews the entity's financial performance, we considered the following matters:

- Key ratios and operating statistics
- Key performance indicators
- Employee performance measures and incentive compensation policies
- Trends
- Use of forecasts, budgets, and variance analysis
- Analyst reports and credit rating reports
- Competitor analysis
- Period-on-period financial performance (revenue growth, profitability, and leverage)

Understanding Obtained in Prior Engagements

Company management uses the following measures to monitor the company's financial performance:

- *Cash on hand, receivables, and payables. This gives management a quick assessment of liquidity.*

- *Total inventory balance. These balances will fluctuate depending on the season. Total receivables plus inventory compared with loan balance—these assets are pledged as collateral for loan. Loan agreement requires receivables and inventory to be at least twice the loan balance at end of each month.*

- *Budget to actual comparisons for sales and gross margins by product line and for the company as a whole, operating expenses, net income, cash on hand, receivables and payables.*

- *Sales, gross margins, inventory turnover, and receivables by product line. This is a primary measure of company performance. It is used to determine whether Company is meeting its financial goals. Markdowns and other credits are monitored by product line, since this is a risk area.*

- *Sales by product line by customer. Report provides information on sales channel inventory levels, which is necessary to estimate end-of-season markdowns.*
- *Net income. Also used as the internal primary measure of company performance.*

Note: Data in most reports is summarized at a highly aggregated level. See evaluation of entity-level controls (appendix K-2) for further consideration.

Procedures Performed

We performed the following procedures to assess the continued relevance of the audit evidence obtained in previous engagements and to identify changes in the way management measures and reviews the entity's financial performance:

- *Discussion with Jane Young Ching (8/15), Josh Young (8/15), Barry Gregg, Sales Manager (8/16), and Lori Feldman, Finance Director (8/16).*
- *Read minutes of quarterly Board of Directors meetings: 1/20, 5/05, 7/18 and 9/05.*

Read the following reports: Quarterly financial statements for quarters ended 6/30 and 9/30; quarterly budget to actual worksheets for 6/30 and 9/30; Sales Analysis Report 6/30 and 9/30.

- *E-mail thread from Barry Gregg, Sales Manager, to Bret Jensen, Salesman, and Lori Feldman, Finance Director; subject: "second quarter results." Thread was started 7/12 and asks for explanation of variances between budget and actual for sales to Newman-MacLachlin.*

Changes to Our Understanding in the Current Period

As a result of performing the procedures indicated, we noted the following changes in management's measurement and review of the company's financial performance that have occurred since the prior engagement and that may affect the current period audit:

- *Management is monitoring company-wide technology expenditures and marketing costs by product line*

Other reports that management will receive with new reporting application include

- *orders from customers, by customer and product line. This helps develop expectations of sales for the next month and also alerts management to possible stock outs.*
- *supplier reports. These reports show orders placed with suppliers, the status of shipments, the amounts paid and owed.*
- *sales, gross margins, and receivables by customer.*

Part II—Planning Analytical Procedures

Observations and Suggestions

The information you obtain by performing risk assessment procedures will help you perform more effective analytical procedures in planning the audit. This information about the client and its industry can help you form an expectation and then determine whether actual results are consistent with that expectation.

In this example, the auditor used the client's budget for 'X4 as a basis for the expectation, which was then compared to actual results. Significant differences between expected and actual amounts were discussed by management and will be tested during the audit. When analytical procedures are used as risk assessment procedures, these differences can help identify risks of material misstatement. They also may confirm or disconfirm information obtained through other procedures, such as inquiry.

For example, through inquiry and other procedures (as described in part I) the auditor learned that labor and materials costs for the J Young Couture line increased significantly during the year. The results of the analytical procedures confirmed this understanding. Had the analytical procedures indicated that labor and materials costs for J Young Couture were comparable to prior years, amounts, this difference between the expected trend and that reported by the client could indicate a risk of material misstatement.

Overall Company (*in thousands*)

	Budgeted	Year-End Reported Amounts	
	20X4	20X4	20X4
Wholesale sales, net	(basis of analytical expectation)	(estimated from 3rd quarter results)	Actual
J Young Couture	41,000	$35,063	27,597
JY Sport	68,000	70,126	70,965
Total wholesale sales	109,000	105,189	98,562
Retail sales, net	7,000	9,220	4,436
Total sales, net	116,000	114,409	102,998
Cost of goods sold			
J Young Couture	16,000	16,830	11,591
JY Sport	38,000	37,868	39,111

(continued)

	Budgeted	Year-End Reported Amounts	
	20X4	20X4	20X4
Wholesale sales, net	(basis of analytical expectation)	(estimated from 3rd quarter results)	Actual
Retail	3,000	4,942	2,301
Cost of goods sold	57,000	59,640	53,003
Gross profit	52,000	54,769	49,995
Marketing	12,000	10,414	8,025
General and administrative	26,000	30,989	28,460
Income from operations	14,000	13,366	13,510
Provision for income taxes	4,000	4,867	5,066
Net income	8,000	$ 8,499	8,444
Cash and cash equivalents	11,000	$ 15,538	13,008
Accounts receivable, net	34,000	35,988	32,902
Inventory	31,000	32,920	32,072
Other assets	9,000	9,757	9,354
Total assets	85,000	$ 94,203	87,336
Current liabilities	21,000	$ 24,930	22,886
Long-term liabilities	14,000	14,752	15,763
Total liabilities	35,000	39,682	38,649
Stockholder's equity	50,000	54,521	48,687
	85,000	$ 94,203	87,336

Inventory Levels by Product Line

Year		J Young Couture	JY Sport
X3	Year-end inventory balance	$ 12,688	$ 19,384
	Percentage of total inventory balance	40%	60%
	Inventory turnover	2.2	3.7
X4 (3rd Q estimate)	Year-end inventory balance	$ 20,752	$ 12,168
	Percentage of total inventory balance	63%	37%
	Inventory turnover	1.7	5.8
Budget X4 (basis for expectation)	Year-end inventory balance	13,000	18,000
	Percentage of total inventory balance	42%	58%
	Inventory turnover	3.2	3.8

Note: We based expectations primarily on the X4 budget. See XXX for an understanding of the budget process and our walkthroughs of that process.

Analysis

Overall Company

- *J Young Couture sales were budgeted for a significant increase over previous year. Actual sales were less than budgeted, though still 30 percent greater than the prior year. Because of significant changes in the cost of Italian labor and supplies, the division spent much of the year finding alternative, cheaper sources, which resulted in a lack of resources to pursue the repositioning of the brand. Because of this lack of marketing, JY Sport sales were flat. This change in product mix is consistent with the company's strategy of improving couture sales by expanding the line and introducing a new line of women's accessories products.*

- *Retail sales increased by approximately $5 million (100 percent). Approximately $3.5 million was due to women's accessory line. The company also increased its sales of J Young Couture due to expanded product line which accounted for the remaining difference.*

- *Margins on J Young Couture decreased from 58 percent in X3 to 52 percent in X4. Expected margins for X4 were expected to increase to 60 percent as a result of re-positioning the brand. This variance from expected results is attributable to higher labor costs in Italy, which is the source for nearly all of the J Young Couture products. During the audit, we will quantify the cost increase in Italy and determine whether it accounts for all the difference.*

- *Margins for JY Sport line remained relatively constant at approximately 55 percent, which is in line with expected margins and consistent with historical levels. JY Sport is manufactured in*

Southeast Asia using fabric from Hong Kong—not affected by Italian price increases.

- Increase in marketing costs due to launch of new accessory lines and expanded marketing efforts of J Young Couture.

- Increases in cash, receivables, and inventory commensurate with increase in sales. However, these amounts were not consistent with the budget. To be investigated—see XX.

Inventory

- Relative inventory levels of J Young Couture varied significantly from anticipated levels. Inventory turnover was significantly less than budget. These variances are due to

  — higher labor costs for Italian goods.

  — significant decrease in inventory levels for JY Sport items.

The effect will be further measured during the audit—See XX.

- For JY Sport, the company still has not been able to restore its inventory levels to normal levels after the disruption in the manufacture and shipping of goods from Southeast Asia (caused by unusually difficult monsoon season). This decrease in inventory levels has resulted in lower sales and a higher inventory turnover rate.

Subsequent to year-end this information will be updated for actual '03 amounts.

Part III—Summary of Identified Inherent Risks

Observations and Suggestions

- This section of the form summarizes the *inherent risks* identified in parts I and II. You should assess all identified *inherent risks* so you can develop an appropriate audit response.

- The *inherent risks* #1 and #3 in following table have been carried forward to appendix K-5, where they will be assessed with all other identified *risks of material misstatement* (which in this example, have been identified in appendixes K-2, K-3, and K-4). Because this example focuses only on sales transactions, risk #2 and the inventory part of risk #1 in following table have not been carried forward to appendix K-5. However, in practice, this risk would still need to be assessed in the same manner that all other identified *inherent risks* should be addressed.

| No. | Description of Risk | Overall Fin Stmt-Level Risk? | Relevant Assertion-Level Risks | | |
			Acct. Trans or Disclosure	Assertion(s)	Ref.
1	General downward pressure on prices and end-of-season markdowns may result in over- or under-reporting sales and receivables due to a poor estimate of markdowns owed to customers.	No	Revenue Receivables	Valuation	w/p XX-x
	Overvaluation of inventory.		Inventory Cost of Sales	Valuation	XX-x

(continued)

©2016, AICPA

| No. | Description of Risk | Overall Fin Stmt-Level Risk? | Relevant Assertion-Level Risks | | |
			Acct. Trans or Disclosure	Assertion(s)	Ref.
2	Reduced margins on J Young Couture line, combined with higher inventory balances and increase in competition for couture apparel, may result in over-valuing inventory.	No	Inventory and Cost of Sales	Valuation	w/p XX-x
3	Lack of integration of new accessories line with the inventory management system has resulted in a lack of information about inventory of accessories held by customers. Lack of information, together with lack of historical data about markdowns of this new product, may result in the inability to make a reliable estimate of markdowns for this line.	No	Revenue Receivables	Accuracy Valuation	w/p XX-x

Regarding controls: The previously mentioned risks are before considering controls. See referenced working papers where we consider controls in these areas and conclude on risk of material misstatement.

APPENDIX K-1-1

Young Fashions: Audit Strategy

Observations and Suggestions

As described in paragraph 3.02 of this guide, you should establish an overall audit strategy that includes

- determining the characteristics of the engagement that define its scope.
- understanding the reporting objectives of the engagement to plan the timing of the audit and the nature of the communications required.
- considering the important factors that determine the focus of the audit teams efforts.

As described in paragraph 3.141 of this guide, in addition to your preliminary overall audit strategy, you also should document significant revisions to that strategy to respond to changes in circumstances. This example documents such revisions.

In addition, you should determine materiality and performance materiality. Part II of this example documents this determination for Young Fashions.

All information that appears in this font style illustrates information completed by the auditor.

Instructions for Preparation

This form documents your audit strategy, including your determination of materiality and performance materiality.

Part I of this form should be used to document your audit strategy as well as any revisions to your preliminary audit strategy. Use part II of the form to document your determination of materiality and performance materiality.

Part I—Audit Strategy

Preliminary Audit Strategy—Prepared August 31, X4

Characteristics That Define Scope of Audit	
Basis of reporting	• Generally accepted accounting principles
Industry-specific reporting requirements	• None
Client locations	• Headquarters: Los Angeles • Warehouses: San Diego and Philadelphia
Timing of the Audit and Required Communications	
Reporting deadlines	• March 15, 20X5
Physical inventory observation	• December 31, 20X4
Confirmation of sales transactions	• December 31, 20X4
Risk assessment procedures	• Most risk assessment procedures will be performed at various dates in August and September and October and updated near year end.
Dates for expected communications with management and those charged with governance	• Communications of control deficiencies and misstatements will be made during the course of the audit, letter on controls targeted for May 15, 20X5.
Factors That Determine Audit Focus	
High risk audit areas	• Revenue and receivables, including markdowns and charge-backs • Inventory
Material locations and account balances[1]	• Inventory is kept at San Diego and Philadelphia warehouses, but all accounting is performed at headquarters in Los Angeles. • Material accounts include cash, receivables, inventory and debt.
Plans to test controls	• None because of weakness in IT access and security for most of X4.
Entity's use of IT and the need for an IT specialist as part of the engagement team	• IT is used to process orders, track inventory, and process financial reporting information. • For major customers, company's IT system integrates with customers IT system. • Use of IT specialist is warranted, since this is a complex IT environment.
Recent developments	• [See appendix K-1]

---

[1] This illustrative case study does not consider implications of AU-C section 600, *Special Considerations—Audits of Group Financial Statements (Including the Work of Component Auditors)* (AICPA, *Professional Standards*), related to group audit considerations.

Direction of Overall Inherent Risk

We believe the overall risk is overstatement of income. We based this on managements need to show growth (for example, growth in revenues) to the bankers, creditors, and customers and show profits to other owners. In addition, the bonus plan provides management with some incentives to overstate income. Accordingly, we will focus many of our tests on the risks of overstatement of income.

We did note deficiencies related to controls over spreadsheets. These deficiencies indicate misstatements are possible in either direction. Accordingly, we will test current spreadsheets for both overstatement and understatement of income. In addition, because this year was very profitable we will watch for understatement of income (the creation of excess reserves).

Subsequent Changes to Audit Strategy

Since the development of the initial overall audit strategy, the company made significant changes to its IT system, including hiring a new IT director, upgrading to a newer version of the order management system, and installation of more formal logical access controls and security. Because this is a sophisticated system, we will again include an IT specialist on the engagement team and, based on the findings of the specialist, reconsider the decision to rely on IT application controls for certain classes of transactions. In addition, we assessed there continued to be poor IT access and security controls for the first nine months of the year. Based on the advice of the IT specialist, we have assessed control risk for the first nine months of the year as high for all IT-related controls. We have changed our testing approach to extensively test transactions substantively. We already do most balance sheet testing at year end. See XXX. Note: The impact of the deficiency noted for the nine-month period may also preclude the determination of control risk for other (non-IT-related) controls as anything below high. However, for the purpose of this case study, that consideration has not been contemplated.

Part II—Determination of Materiality and Performance Materiality

---

Observations and Suggestions

As described in paragraph 3.06 of this guide, you should determine a materiality level for the financial statements as a whole to help you plan your audit. The determination of materiality is a matter of your informed professional judgment, which depends on a number of factors, including

- the nature of the client and circumstances, such as their financial position or results of operations.
- how the financial statement users use the company's financial statements. This consideration would include trends, such as profitability, key financial statement ratios, including working capital, and the potential impact on loan covenants.

After assessing the users and their likely perspective on what level of materiality might be influential to their use of the financial statements, one of the steps used to determine materiality is to apply a percentage to an appropriate benchmark, such as total revenues, net income, or net assets. In governmental entities, a measure such as expenditures may be more appropriate.

This example memorandum documents the auditor's thought process in determining the materiality for Young Fashions. In this example, the auditor has chosen to document materiality and performance materiality in a memorandum to the file.

Application of Percentage to a Benchmark

To help determine materiality for Young Fashions, we computed amounts using various benchmarks and estimates of company financial results.

Base	Estimated Amount	Illustrative Percentage	
Total revenues	$ 114,000,000	0.5%[1]	$ 570,000
Pretax income	$ 13,300,000	7%	$ 931,000
Net income	$ 8,500,000	5%	$ 425,000
Total assets	$ 94,000,000	0.5%	$ 470,000
Equity	$ 54,000,000	2%	$ 1,080,000

---

[1] For some entities, auditors may consider a range based on revenues (for example, 1/2% to 1%) or expenses (for example, 3% to 5%) if these measures are the "drivers" in the business and relevant to the financial statement users' interests. Some government audit engagements may follow more tailored guidance as to a target materiality base and percentage relevant to these engagements, such as basing the audit benchmark on expenditures.

Determination of Materiality and Performance Materiality

Observations and Suggestions

The determination of materiality is not simply a mathematical calculation or an averaging of several calculations. Rather, materiality is determined based on auditor judgment, which typically includes—but is not limited to—the consideration of calculations such as the previous one.

An important element of the determination is the consideration of the users of the client's financial statements and how they might use them and their expectations of materiality. The base used from which to assess materiality should align with the user's expectations and needs. In this section, the auditor describes the consideration of financial statement users and the overall thought process for determining materiality.

To illustrate the application of the guidance in the standards to this critical judgment, the documentation of the auditor thought process in this example may be more extensive and detailed than typical for such circumstances. A sentence or two identifying the users and the logic in selecting the relevant base and percentage or dollar amount may be appropriate.

In determining materiality for Young Fashions, we considered the intended users of the company's financial statements, which we believe are the following:

- *Lenders. The company has a revolving line of credit, secured by receivables and inventory. Restrictive covenants also must be met. See XX-x.*

- *Major customers. Most of the company's major customers annually review the company's financial statements and other business information before committing to significant purchases from a supplier such as Young Fashions.*

- *Major suppliers also assess the company's overall financial condition to determine whether the company is capable of fulfilling their purchase order commitments, which also is a function of cash flow, working capital, and profitability.*

- *Other owners. This group is focused on profitability.*

All of these main user groups use the company's financial statements primarily to assess cash flow and, to a lesser degree, profitability. We note that as a privately held company, the owners have wide discretion over the amount of cash to distribute to owners, primarily in the form of compensation. As a result, assets, equity, and expenses may not be reflective solely of business operations but may include factors such as the owners' desire to retain or distribute cash in or from the business.

Accordingly, we determined that total revenues were the most appropriate benchmark for determining materiality as they more effectively represented business cash flows. The 0.5 percent is based on our assessment of the financial statement users and our judgment about the magnitude of a misstatement that could influence their decision making process.

Given the previously mentioned considerations, we have determined materiality for the financial statements as a whole to be $500,000, which is based primarily on revenues ($114 million), but has been reduced slightly after considering *that users may also use net income as a secondary base for assessing company performance.*

We will consider the low past level of audit misstatements as well as the past practice of Young to adjust misstatements and Firm policy to use PPS-based sample sizes for substantive sampling.

Based on that determination of materiality for the financial statements as a whole, we determined performance materiality to be $350,000. The amount under which misstatements are considered trivial is $3,500 for this engagement.

We will ask management to adjust all factual (known) misstatements and investigate and consider the effects of all judgmental and projected misstatements. In addition, the bank is especially interested in receivables and inventory since these accounts are the basis for the restrictive covenants. Thus, we will exercise care in waiving any proposed adjustments to those accounts.

We will use tolerable misstatement in determining extent of testing using PPS samples, in identifying accounts that are less than significant, and in performing substantive analytical procedures.

See appendix K-5 for audit approach for revenue and receivables (after analyzing risk of material misstatement) and for overall issues of concern to the partner. See XX for audit approach for other cycles (not shown).

Appendix K-2

Young Fashions: Evaluation of Entity-Level Controls

This appendix is nonauthoritative and is included for informational purposes only.

Observations and Suggestions

You should document your understanding of the controls relevant to the audit, including the following:

- An evaluation of whether the design of the control, individually or in combination, is capable of effectively preventing or detecting and correcting material misstatements
- A determination of whether the control exists and the entity is using it

This appendix illustrates how you might achieve those two documentation objectives for entity-level controls, not including IT general controls, which are addressed in appendix K-3. Appendix K-4 provides an illustrative example of the documentation of your understanding of activity-level controls. Entity level controls are one of the "top down" elements that can make your assessment of risks and controls more effective and efficient.

Included in this example are all the financial statement controls that normally are relevant to the audit, as indicated in chapter 3, "Planning and Performing Risk Assessment Procedures."

In addition, you should document the risk assessment and other procedures you performed to gather information about internal control and the source of this information. Appendix K-2-1 provides illustrative documentation that satisfies these requirements.

All information that appears in this font style illustrates information completed by the auditor.

Instructions for Preparation

This form documents the understanding of entity-level controls, including

- an evaluation of whether the design of the control, individually or in combination, is capable of effectively preventing or detecting and correcting material misstatements.

- a conclusion of whether the control exists and the entity is using it.

This form also provides a cross-reference to a description of the information sources and procedures performed to gain the understanding of financial statement-level controls.

How to Complete Each Column

- *Control objectives.* These generic control objectives have been used in this illustrative case study as their use was common on many audit engagements. For each engagement, these control objectives might be reviewed and adjusted to make any necessary changes, based on your understanding of the entity and its environment. The principles of the COSO framework along with the associated points of focus and the entity's and auditor's identification of risks may serve a similar purpose to control objectives. For transactions, the assertions may also be a substitute going forward.

- *Risks of failure to achieve the objective.* For each control objective identified, you might then determine the risks the company faces to achieving the control objective based on the entity's objectives and an assessment of "what could go wrong" so as to not be able to achieve the objectives. Generic risks might then be reviewed and modified, if necessary, to reflect the unique circumstances of the client.

- *Indications that the control objective is not being met.* This column may be used to help you identify deficiencies in control design. Generic indicators might then be reviewed and modified, if necessary, to reflect the unique circumstances of the client.

- *Implemented control features.* This column may be used to describe your understanding of the control policies and procedures that the client has implemented to meet the control objective. These descriptions may be carried forward from prior audits once you have performed sufficient procedures to determine that the descriptions are still complete and relevant. New control policies and procedures may need to be added to the table.

- *Control design.* For each row (that is, control objective) you might then consider whether the identified control features could—if operating effectively throughout the audit period—provide reasonable assurance that the control objective will be achieved.

  Your conclusion about effectiveness may then be supported by your description of the control objective, the risk of achieving that objective, and the control features.

- *Reference to information sources.* This column may be used to cross-reference to the procedures you performed to gain an understanding of the design and implementation of controls, which are listed in "Audit Program: Understanding Financial Statement Level Controls."

Observations and Suggestions

The matrix layout of this example documentation is consistent with the framework in AU-C section 315, *Understanding the Entity and Its Environment and Assessing the Risks of Material Misstatement* (AICPA, *Professional Standards*).

- Reading left to right, an evaluation of control design begins with understanding the entity's broad and detailed objectives [principle 6]. In this example, these objectives are portrayed as being "prepopulated" in the form. That is, the auditor's audit methodology includes these example objectives for all audits. However, the auditor is reminded that these objectives are examples only, and they may often be tailored to meet the unique facts and circumstances of specific entities. In this example, the auditor of Young Fashions has modified several of these example objectives, for example in the section titled "Integrity and Ethical Values." In the absence of identified control objectives for some transaction based accounts, a practical approach might be to use the audit assertions, and identify how controls address these assertions. Assertions are generally broader than control objectives. Principles from the COSO framework are added to this example in brackets to the extent they may be consistent with the stated objectives herein.

- The second column of the matrix describes the risks to the entity if the objective is not met. This column will help the auditor design appropriate further audit procedures if he or she determines that certain objectives are not met. Again, the auditor's audit methodology includes examples, which the auditor may often modify as appropriate.

- The third column, "Indications That the Control Objective Is Not Being Met," is not required by any framework, but it has been added to this example because it may help the auditor identify deficiencies in control design. This optional column also includes examples, which the auditor may then modify as appropriate. It is derived from the risks column, and some auditors find it helpful to express the risks this way.

- In the fourth column, the auditor documents his or her understanding of the control features that have been implemented at the client to address the stated control objective.

- By comparing the control features to the objectives or principles, the auditor determines whether the design of control, either individually or in combination with other controls, is capable of effectively preventing or detecting and correcting material misstatements. In the fifth column of the matrix, the auditor documents the conclusion about control design.

In addition to the matters documented on this form, the auditor also should document the procedures performed to gather information about internal control and the source of that information. In this example, that documentation is provided in appendix K-2-1.

Part I—Understanding of Entity-Level Controls

Control Environment

The control environment reflects the overall attitude, awareness, and actions of management, those charged with governance, and others concerning the importance of control and its effect on establishing, enhancing, or mitigating the effectiveness of specific controls. The control environment includes such factors as

- integrity and ethical values. [principle 1]
- commitment to competence. [principle 4]
- those charged with governance. [principle 2 and principle 3]
- management's philosophy and operating style. [principle 1]
- organizational structure. [principle 3 and principle 5]
- assignment of authority and responsibility. [principle 3]
- human resource policies and practices. [principle 4]

Integrity and Ethical Values [principle 1]

Points to Consider:[1]

- "Tone at the Top"
- Standards of conduct
- Evaluates adherence to the standards of conduct
- Addresses deviations in a timely manner

---

[1] These points to consider are reflective of the points of focus included in the 2013 COSO framework for principle 1 and may be helpful for consideration regardless of the framework utilized by the entity.

Example Objectives, Risks, and Features:

Control Objectives	Risks of Failure to Achieve the Objective	Indications That the Control Objective Is Not Being Met[2]	Implemented Control Features	Control Design?	Ref.
Company establishes policies relating to acceptable business practices, the company's ethical values and employee integrity [principle 1]	• Employees enter into unauthorized company transactions that are not properly captured and recorded in the accounting system or disclosed in the financial statements. • Fraud. • Questionable accounting practices not reported to appropriate level of management for correction.	• Lack of time or interest in — initially stating company values. — regularly evaluating and revising values. • Failure to address all areas where policies on acceptable business practices should be established	• Management has established formal acceptable business practices for investments by key company personnel in vendors and suppliers. • Other policies are informal. • The company's focus is on operations and earnings growth, with an emphasis on bonus arrangements to increase sales and earnings. Management has not fully addressed how these incentives may motivate employees to improper behavior; however, ownership structure and monitoring mitigate against a significant risk.	Effective (in meeting control objective)	Inq – 1,2,3,10,4,5 Ins – 1
Effective communication of integrity and ethical values [principle 1]	• Employees enter into unauthorized company transactions that are not properly captured and recorded in the accounting system. • Fraud. • Questionable accounting practices are not reported to appropriate level of management for correction.	• There is lack of documentation of acceptable business practices and values. • Employees do not receive or read communication. • Communication is infrequent. • There is lack of training on ethics and acceptable business practices.	• There are few written policies regarding acceptable business practices. • Other policies are informal and discussed in employee orientation.	Deficiency noted—see part II CD-1	Inq – 1,2,3,10,4,5 1

(continued)

©2016, AICPA

Control Objectives	Risks of Failure to Achieve the Objective	Indications That the Control Objective Is Not Being Met[2]	Implemented Control Features	Control Design?	Ref.
Effective enforcement of stated policies relating to integrity and ethical values [principle 1 and principle 5]	• Fraud. • Questionable accounting practices are not reported to appropriate level of management for correction.	• Inappropriate conduct and violation of stated policies are not reported to management. • Management actions do not reinforce stated policies. • Management fails to act appropriately to known violations of company policy.	• No policies exist for anonymously reporting by employees of concerns regarding questionable accounting or auditing matters or business practices. However, top management has an "open door policy" and employees indicate that they would not hesitate to inform management of questionable behavior. • No real opportunity exists for management to demonstrate that they would take appropriate action, as there have been no reported violations. Employees interviewed believe that management would take appropriate action in the event of a violation of allegation of unacceptable behavior.	Effective	Inq – 5,6,7,8,9
Acceptable U.S. business practices are communicated and enforced with regard to overseas suppliers [principle 1]	• Illegal or unauthorized transactions entered into with overseas suppliers. • Increased risk of material misstatement due to fraud.	• Business practices that are common acceptable outside the United States (for example, labor relations, relationships with customs and other official) are not identified by the company. • Company policies are not communicated effectively to third-party suppliers. • Violations of stated policies are not reported.	• Management regularly reviews and revises policies relating to overseas suppliers. • Outside consultant periodically reviews and monitors business practices of major non-U.S. suppliers. • Annually, all suppliers are sent a letter stating company policies in key areas.	Effective	Inq – 2,7

[2] As noted, this column is optional and may be used if considered helpful.

Commitment to Competence [principle 4]

Points to Consider:[3]

- Establishes policies and practices regarding competence
- Evaluates competence and addresses deficiencies
- Attracts, develops and retains competent employees (and contract workers from outsourcing companies)
- Plans for succession

---

[3] These points to consider are reflective of the points of focus included in the COSO framework for principle 4 and may be helpful for consideration regardless of the framework utilized by the entity.

Example Control Objectives, Risks, and Features:

Control Objectives	Risks of Failure to Achieve the Objective	Indications That the Control Objective Is Not Being Met	Implemented Control Features	Control Design?	Ref.
Consideration of the competence levels for particular jobs and how those levels translate into requisite skills and knowledge [principle 4]	• Inaccuracies in the accounting records. • Failure to recognize unusual transactions, events, or circumstances that require special accounting consideration or disclosure. • Inability to prepare financial statements in accordance with generally accepted accounting principles.	• There is a failure to define and periodically review and update job requirements. • There is a failure to understand skills and knowledge necessary to perform jobs. • Personnel policies (for example, hiring, promotion, and compensation) give excessive consideration to factors other than performance.	In conjunction with human resource policies and practices, the company • defines tasks to be accomplished in a flexible manner to match its growth focus. • annually determines whether individuals possess the requisite knowledge and skills to perform their jobs adequately.	Effective	Inq – 2,5,6,9 Ins – 3

Note: Those charged with governance is discussed in a section to follow.

Management Philosophy and Operating Style[4]

Points to Consider:

- Dominance by one or a few individuals
- Management's attitude toward, and monitoring of, business risks
- Frequency of interaction between senior management and operating management
- Management's financial reporting philosophy
- Management's willingness to consult with its auditors on accounting issues and adjust the financial statements for factual, judgmental, or projected misstatements
- Management's responsiveness to prior recommendations
- Management priority given to internal control
- Control environment over accounting estimates

---

[4] May be classified as a principle 1 concept. This exact description is not a unique principle in the COSO framework.

Example Control Objectives, Risks, and Features:

Control Objectives	Risks of Failure to Achieve the Objective	Indications That the Control Objective Is Not Being Met	Implemented Control Features	Control Design?	Ref.
Management's philosophy and operating style are appropriate for the entity, including • direct senior management involvement in operations and financial reporting process. • close coordination of the three locations. • commitment to high quality financial reporting process and internal control.	• Business and financial reporting risks facing company are minimized or not recognized by management. • Management is not appropriately involved in the financial reporting process or in the design, implementation and monitoring of internal control. • Fraud.	• Management's philosophy and operating style are not appropriate considering factors such as the company's — size. — complexity of operations and financial reporting. — financing structure. — business risks. — financial reporting risks.	• Key management decisions are made by a few officers (see organizational structure). • Management is primarily concerned with the pressures associated with operations and earnings growth. • Management readily accepts proposed adjustments on clear-cut issues but is known to aggressively challenge proposed adjustments involving accounting estimates. • No formal controls over bonus arrangements (viewed as a key to increasing sales and earnings). • Management has made some changes to internal control based on auditor recommendations, but their priorities are in other areas.	Effective Effective Effective Deficiency noted—see part II CD-2 Generally-effective for major issues	Inq – 1,2,4,10 Ins – 7

©2016, AICPA

Organizational Structure [principle 3]

[Briefly describe the entity's organizational structure (with organizational chart attached if available).]

The company designs, manufactures, and distributes apparel along two distinct lines: J Young Couture and JY Sport. Company headquarters is in California with warehouse and distribution centers in New Jersey and California. All significant operating and financial decisions are centralized at company headquarters. A board of directors exercises oversight over a chief executive function that is split between Josh Young (responsible for design) and Jane Young Ching (responsible for operations). All significant decisions are made by the co-CEOs. Virtually all operating decisions relative to information technology have been delegated to the manager of IT.

The company does not own or operate any production facilities. All products are manufactured by independently owned manufacturers under long-term contracts. The company has two basic approaches to production:

- *Purchase finished goods. The company buys finished garments from the supplier, who is responsible for the purchasing and carrying of raw materials, in addition to the manufacture of the product.*

- *Cut, make, and trim. The company buys raw materials and piece goods and then moves these to finished product assemblers.*

All manufacturers are located outside of the United States: J Young Couture manufacturing is done primarily in Italy, while JY Sport is manufactured in Asia.

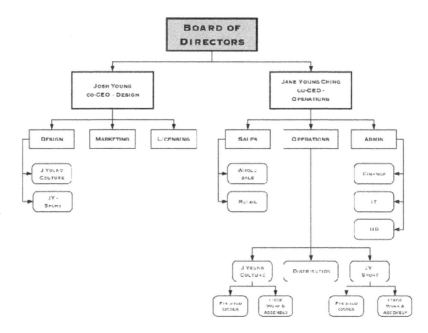

Points to Consider:[5]

- Considers all components (lines of business, administrative functions, locations and use of service organizations) of the entity
- Establishes reporting lines and flows of information
- Defines authorities and responsibilities and limits

---

[5] These points to consider are reflective of the points of focus included in the COSO framework for principle 3 and may be helpful for consideration regardless of the framework utilized by the entity. The points of focus included in the COSO framework for principle 5 may also be helpful for consideration here.

Example Control Objectives, Risks, and Features:

Control Objectives	Risks of Failure to Achieve the Objective	Indications That the Control Objective Is Not Being Met	Implemented Control Features	Control Design?	Ref.

Entity organizational structure enables its ability to achieve its financial reporting objectives. [principle 3]	• Company's financial reporting systems are not adequate to capture, record, and process properly all transactions, events, or circumstances that affect the financial statements or require disclosure.
	
	• Lack of resources may result in important control functions not being performed on a timely basis.
	
	• Information that affects financial reporting is not communicated between departments.
	
	• The internal audit function and others with responsibility for evaluating and maintaining internal control and the financial reporting process do not have adequate authority to perform their function.
		• Lack of clear lines of authority
		  Particularly between co-CEOs
		
		• Lack of communication and coordination between functions
		  Especially the design group, operations, and sales
		
		• Inadequate supervision
			See description of organization and organizational chart.	*Effective*	*Inq – 1,2,3,10,4*
					Ins – 8

Assignment of Authority and Responsibility [principle 3 and principle 5]

Points to Consider:[6]

- Considers all components (lines of business, administrative functions, locations and use of service organizations) of the entity
- Establishes reporting lines and flows of information
- Defines authorities and responsibilities and limits
- Enforces accountability
- Establishes and evaluates performance measures, incentives, and rewards
- Considers excessive pressures
- Evaluates performance and rewards or disciplines individuals

---

[6] These points to consider are reflective of the points of focus included in the COSO framework for principle 3 and principle 5 and may be helpful for consideration regardless of the framework utilized by the entity.

Example Control Objectives, Risks, and Features:

Control Objectives	Risks of Failure to Achieve the Objective	Indications That the Control Objective Is Not Being Met	Implemented Control Features	Effective Design?	Ref.
Responsibility and delegation of authority are consistent with the company's organizational structure. [principle 3]	• Failure to perform financial reporting or internal control procedures • Performance of key financial reporting or internal control duties by individuals who lack the necessary training or expertise	• Lack of clarity about responsibilities *Particularly for co-CEOs* • Delegation of responsibility without commensurate delegation of decision-making authority • Delegation of responsibility and authority without proper supervision and monitoring by management • Failure by top management to delegate jobs that require highly specialized skills	• Delegation of authority and responsibility is informal. • Key officers actively supervise business operations with the exception of IT. • Divisional management participates with key officers in making business decisions, but authority rests largely at the top.	Effective Deficiency noted—see part II CD-3	Inq – 1,2,3,4 Ins – 1
Adequate number of personnel to carry out responsibilities. [principle 3 and principle 4]	• Failure to perform financial reporting or internal control procedures • Performance of key financial reporting or internal control duties by individuals who lack the necessary training or expertise	• They are unable to hire and maintain sufficient personnel. • Pace of hiring does not keep pace with rate of growth of business.	• The company's growth periodically stretches — the accounting function. — IT function and systems. — operations.	Deficiency noted—see part II CD-4	Inq – 4,5,7,8,1

©2016, AICPA

Human Resource Policies and Practices [principle 4]

Points to Consider:[7]

- Establishing policies and practices regarding competence
- Evaluating competence and addresses deficiencies
- Attracting, developing and retaining competent employees (and contract workers from outsourcing companies)
- Planning for succession

---

[7] See footnote 3.

Example Control Objectives, Risks, and Features:

Control Objectives	Risks of Failure to Achieve the Objective	Indications That the Control Objective Is Not Being Met	Implemented Control Features	Control Design?	Ref.
Personnel policies, such as recruiting, orientation, training, evaluation, and compensation support the establishment and maintenance of an effective control environment. [principle 4]	• Individuals performing key financial reporting or control functions are not — qualified. — provided with the proper incentive to perform their assigned tasks. • Increased risk of error or fraud.	• Rapid turnover of key personnel. • Failure to integrate job requirements with personnel policies. • Lack of coordination between strategic business initiatives (for example, business expansion) and HR requirements.	• The CFO has been on the job only for 18 months. • HR manager is included in strategic planning discussions and is actively involved with senior management.	Effective	Inq – 9,1,2,45 Ins – 3

©2016, AICPA

Risk Assessment [principle 6 and principle 7]

Points to Consider:[8]

Specifies suitable objectives [principle 6]

- Reflects management's choices
- Considers tolerance for risk
- Includes operations and financial performance goals
- Forms a basis for committing of resources

Identifies and analyzes risk [principle 7]

- Include entity, subsidiary, division, operating unit, and functional levels
- Analyze internal and external factors
- Involve appropriate levels of management
- Estimate significance of risks identified
- Determine how to respond to risks

---

[8] These points to consider are reflective of the points of focus included in the COSO framework for principle 6 and principle 7 and may be helpful for consideration regardless of the framework utilized by the entity.

Example Control Objectives, Risks, and Features:

Control Objectives	Risks of Failure to Achieve the Objective	Indications that Control Objective is Not Being Met	Implemented Control Features	Control Design?	Ref.
Timely identification of risks relevant to the financial reporting process. [principle 7]	• Transactions, events, or circumstances that affect the financial statements or require disclosure are not captured, processed or recorded. • Financial reporting system is weak.	• Failure to identify changes in the entity or its environment that could create business or financial reporting risks. • Failure to determine how identified business risks affect the financial reporting process.	• Management has implemented a five-year strategic plan for the company that includes objectives and analyzes risk factors. • The strategic plan is developed on a top-down basis and reviewed by the board of directors. • The organizational structure allows for the timely communication and identification of both business and financial reporting risks.	Effective	Inq – 1,2,3,10,4 Ins – 9,8
Appropriate assessment of the significance and likelihood of financial reporting risks. [principle 7]	• Bias in making assumptions underlying accounting estimates, management's intent, and other subjective matters that affect the financial statements and disclosures.	• Lack of understanding of financial reporting matters. • Unchallenged assumptions or bias in the assessment of significance and likelihood of identified risks.	• CFO participates as a member of strategic planning committee. • Board of directors oversees the strategic planning process.	Effective	Inq – 1,2,3,10,4

Information and Communication [principle 13 and principle 14]

Points to Consider:[9]

Internal information [principle 14]

- Communicate internal control information
- Communicate with governance
- Provide separate communication lines
- Select relevant methods of communication

External information [principle 15]

- Communicate with external parties
- Enable inbound communications
- Communicate with governance
- Provide separate communication lines
- Select relevant methods of communication

---

[9] These points to consider are reflective of the points of focus from the COSO framework for principle 14 and principle 15 and may be helpful for consideration regardless of the framework utilized by the entity.

Example Control Objectives, Risks, and Features:

Control Objectives	Risks of Failure to Achieve the Objective	Indications That the Control Objective Is Not Being Met	Implemented Control Features	Control Design?	Ref.
Individuals involved in the financial reporting process receive the accurate, timely information that is necessary to perform their jobs. [principle 14 and principle 15]	• Inaccurate accounting records. • Failure to capture, record, and process all transactions and events that affect the financial statements or require disclosure. • Inconsistent application of manual control procedures. • Ineffective monitoring of financial results or internal control.	• Failure to identify information needed to perform financial reporting tasks. • IT systems cannot reliably deliver timely, accurate information in a usable format.	• There is only an informal understanding of the information needed to perform financial reporting functions. • Most of the purchased software is three to five years old and, based upon the company's rapid growth and diversification, is now somewhat limited in its ability to keep pace with functional business requirements. • Likewise, the hardware/technical environment is nearing its capacity.	Deficiency noted—see part II CD-5	Inq – 3,4,5,7

Monitoring

Points to Consider:[10]

Ongoing and/or separate evaluations [principle 16]

- Consider a mix of ongoing and separate evaluations
- Consider rate of change [see also principle 9]
- Establish baseline understanding
- Use knowledgeable personnel [see also principle 4]
- Evaluations integrate with business processes [see also principle 7]
- Adjust scope and frequency
- Objective evaluation

Taking corrective action [principle 17]

- Assess results
- Communicate deficiencies [see also principle 14, principle 3, and principle 5]
- Monitor corrective actions [see also principle 5]

---

[10] These points to consider are reflective of the points of focus from the COSO framework for principle 16 and principle 17 and may be helpful for consideration regardless of the framework utilized by the entity.

Example Control Objectives, Risks, and Features:

Control Objectives	Risks of Failure to Achieve the Objective	Indications That the Control Objective Is Not Being Met	Implemented Control Features	Control Design?	Ref.
The effectiveness of internal control is monitored regularly. [principle 16]	• Changes in the entity's business or its environment may create control deficiencies that are not addressed in a timely manner. • Deficiencies in internal control increase the opportunity for fraud and the resulting risk of material misstatement due to fraud.	• Lack of documentation of control procedure or performance of controls makes it difficult to monitor controls effectively. • There is a failure to identify changes in the business or its environment that should result in changes to internal control. • No individual or group at the entity has the responsibility to monitor control effectiveness. • The group or individual responsible for monitoring internal control does not have the expertise or authority necessary to effectively monitor controls and make necessary changes.	• Management and the board obtain evidence relating to how internal control is operating by performing the following review activities. — The board of directors compares performance with projected results on a quarterly basis. — Detailed budgets are set informally by key officers (rather than by more formal methods involving middle management). — Top management reviews actual results against budget monthly for each division. — Although variations from budgets are reviewed on a regular basis, management does not extensively document its follow-up activities. • Co-CEOs review annual financial statements.	Deficiency noted—see part II CD-6	Inq – 1,2,10 Ins – 4,10

Control Objectives	Risks of Failure to Achieve the Objective	Indications That the Control Objective Is Not Being Met	Implemented Control Features	Control Design?	Ref.
			• In addition, the bank loan officer meets regularly with Young Fashions' management to monitor the company's financial performance, which heightens management's consciousness about taking and monitoring business risks. The bank also monitors that the covenants are met based on the latest financial information. The bank has the right to test inventory and receivables and can (and has) confirmed transactions with customers.		
Results of monitoring process are used to initiate corrective action. [principle 17]	• Deficiencies in the design or application of internal control persist, increasing the risk of material misstatement. • Deficiencies in internal control provide an opportunity for fraud, increasing the risk of material misstatement due to fraud.	• Results of monitoring process are misinterpreted. • Group or person responsible for monitoring internal control do not suggest changes to internal control or suggest changes that cannot be implemented. • Management and those charged with governance fail to act timely on recommendations for improvements to internal control.	• Results of management's monitoring activities are reviewed primarily with an eye toward correcting misstatements in the accounting records, not toward identifying and correcting control deficiencies. • Our experience with the company indicates that management takes appropriate action when we identify and communicate to them internal control matters we note during our audits.	Deficiency noted—see part II CD-7	Inq – 1,2,10 Ins – 7

Antifraud Programs and Controls [principle 8]

Points to Consider:[11]

- Consider various types of fraud
- Assess incentives and pressures
- Assess opportunities
- Assess attitudes and rationalizations

---

[11] These points to consider are reflective of the points of focus from the COSO framework for principle 8 and may be helpful for consideration regardless of the framework utilized by the entity.

©2016, AICPA

Example Control Objectives, Risks, and Features:

Control Objectives	Risks of Failure to Achieve the Objective	Indications That the Control Objective Is Not Being Met	Implemented Control Features	Control Design?	Ref.
Mitigate the risk of fraud at the entity. [principle 8 and principle 10]	• Increased risk of fraud and therefore, the risk of material misstatement due to fraud.	• Inappropriate corporate culture and "tone at the top." • Lack of awareness or understanding of risks of fraud facing the entity. • Lack of a process for assessing fraud risks and responding appropriately to those risks. • Ineffective oversight of antifraud programs and controls.	• Management is highly sensitive to the risks of fraud at the entity and actively searches for ways to reduce the company's exposure to fraud. • Management has identified business processes most susceptible to fraud and has implemented appropriate controls. • IT manager has implemented various general and application controls to reduce error and fraud risk related to IT. • Also see comments relating to control environment.	Effective	Inq – 1,2,3,10,4 Ins – 6

                    ©2016, AICPA

Controls Over Nonroutine Transactions [principle 10 and principle 12]

Points to Consider:

- Identification of nonroutine transactions
- Identification of related-party transactions
- Proper accounting for such transactions
- Effective oversight of the accounting for the transactions

Example Control Objectives, Risks, and Features:

Control Objectives	Risks of Failure to Achieve the Objective	Indications That the Control Objective Is Not Being Met	Implemented Control Features	Control Design?	Ref.
Nonroutine transactions are accounted for properly and presented fairly in the financial statements. [principle 12]	• Nonroutine transactions and events are — not recognized in the financial statements. — recognized at improper amounts. — not disclosed appropriately.	• Failure to identify transactions that are considered "nonroutine" for auditing purposes. • Failure to consider proper accounting treatment for nonroutine transactions. • Bias or unsupported assumptions in the selection or application of the accounting policies for identified nonroutine transactions. • Ineffective oversight of the accounting for nonroutine transactions.	• The transactions for the company are relatively routine and recurring in nature. In the unusual event that a nonroutine transaction occurs (for example, business acquisition), the CFO will identify the transaction and research the proper accounting. • If necessary, the CFO will contact external CPA firm to confirm how to account for the transaction. • Nonroutine transactions are approved by the board, who reviews the accounting treatment.	Effective	Inq – 2,4,10

                                    ©2016, AICPA

Controls Over Estimates [principle 10 and principle 12]

Points to Consider:

- Identification by management of required accounting estimates
- Accumulation of relevant, reliable, and sufficient data upon which to base the estimate
- Review and approval of the estimate

Example Control Objectives, Risks, and Features:

Control Objectives	Risks of Failure to Achieve the Objective	Indications That the Control Objective Is Not Being Met	Implemented Control Features	Control Design?	Ref.
Estimates for all amounts that require estimation for their inclusion in the financial statements are reasonable and supportable. [principle 10 and principle 12]	• Accounting estimates or other subjective matters are not properly — recognized. — measured (for example, an asset valuation allowance, sales returns).	• There is failure to identify financial statement amounts or disclosures for which an accounting estimate is required. • There is failure to identify events or changes in circumstances that would require an accounting estimate where none was previously required (for example, asset impairment). • Data underlying the estimate does not support the estimate. • Assumptions underlying the estimate are inconsistent with other information. • Management has bias in the preparation of the estimate.	• Established processes and controls exist for the preparation and review (by the board) of routine estimates such as the allowance for doubtful accounts, inventory obsolescence, and sales returns. • CFO has technical accounting proficiency to properly consider and identify changes in circumstances or events that may trigger the need for an accounting estimate.	Effective	Inq – 2,4,5,10 Ins – 11 Obs – 1

Controls Over the Selection and Application of Accounting Policies [principles 6 and 10]

Although not directly linked to a principle in the COSO framework, deficiencies related to the selection and application of accounting policies may relate to the governance function (principle 2), management (principle 3), or to the improper specification of objectives in the risk assessment component (principle 6). The design of controls [principle 10] over financial reporting depends on the appropriate selection of accounting principles. A specific deficiency may also impact more than one principle, so considering the integrated nature of the internal control framework, one deficiency could have multiple impacts on the effectiveness of controls.

Points to Consider:

- Board oversight of the initial selection of and subsequent changes to significant accounting policies or their application
- Appropriate selection and application of accounting policies in controversial or emerging areas for which there is a lack of authoritative accounting guidance or consensus

Example Control Objectives, Risks, and Features:

Control Objectives	Risks of Failure to Achieve the Objective	Indications That the Control Objective Is Not Being Met	Implemented Control Features	Control Design?	Ref.
The selection and application of accounting policies result in financial statements that are fairly presented in all material respects.	• Financial statements do not represent the economic conditions or events that they purport to represent.	• There is failure to communicate to the board the initial selection and application or subsequent change to significant accounting policies. • Oversight of the board of directors is ineffective. • There is failure to identify controversial or emerging accounting areas. • Management has bias in the selection or application of accounting policies.	• The company has very few instances to select or change its accounting policies. • In the event that such an occasion were to arise, the CFO would most likely identify the matter and consider the possible accounting options. • The board of directors most likely would review the matter with the external CPAs and ask for their suggestions on the matter.	Effective	Inq – 6 Ins – 4,10

Oversight of the Financial Reporting Process by Those Charged With Governance [principle 2 (and also principle 3)]

Points to Consider:[12]

The Board: [principle 2]

- Establishes oversight responsibilities
- Applies relevant expertise
- Operates independent from management
- Provides oversight for the system of internal control

Structure, Authority, and Responsibility: [principle 3]

- Considers all components (lines of business, administrative functions, locations and use of service organizations) of the entity
- Establishes reporting lines and flows of information
- Defines authorities and responsibilities and limits

---

[12] These points to consider are reflective of the points of focus included in the COSO framework for principle 2 and principle 3 and may be helpful for consideration regardless of the framework utilized by the entity.

Example Control Objectives, Risks, and Features:

Control Objectives	Risks of Failure to Achieve the Objective	Indications That the Control Objective Is Not Being Met	Implemented Control Features	Control Design?	Ref.
Those charged with governance effectively participate in the financial reporting process. [principle 2]	• Increased risk of material misstatement for matters such as accounting estimates, or the accounting for significant unusual transactions. • Increased risk of material misstatement due to fraud, especially fraudulent financial reporting.	• Lack of an independent board. • Inability of the board to evaluate the actions of management. • Inability of the board to understand the client's business transactions or the financial reporting process. • Inability of the board to evaluate whether the financial statements are fairly presented.	• The board of directors consists of seven members: four officers of the company, a nonofficer shareholder, and two outside directors (a lawyer and a relative who is not a part of the immediate family or a member of management). • The board meets regularly and communicates regularly with the external auditors. • The company has not formed an audit committee.	Effective	Inq – 1,2, 10 Ins – 5,12

Financial Statement Preparation [principle 12]

The following describes the procedures the entity uses to prepare financial statements and related disclosures and how misstatements may occur.[13]

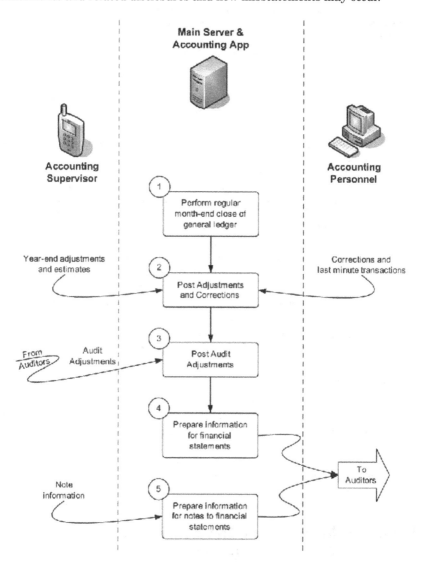

---

[13] The following dialogue illustrates a process description and not a controls description. Entities may maintain such documentation, and the auditor may reference that entity documentation but may focus in their documentation on the controls.

©2016, AICPA

Explanation

The attached chart separates the financial reporting process into three main information sources. The main server houses the accounting application. Routine, daily transactions are posted into this system. Additionally, the accounting supervisor and other accounting personnel will make post-closing adjustments to the accounting application.

1. *At year end, the company will perform its regular month-end close procedures.*

2. *Some adjustments and estimates are prepared only at year end, for example, the estimates of valuation allowances for inventory, receivables, and sales returns. The accounting supervisor prepares these estimates and posts them to the general ledger using a journal entry.*

    Additionally, a member of the accounting staff reviews significant accounts and performs reconciliations and as a result, may identify errors that need to be corrected. Also, operations personnel may have last-minute transactions (usually purchases and sales) that should be included in the year-end numbers, but occurred too late to be entered into the system through normal channels. The accounting clerk prepares journal entries to post these corrections and last minute transactions.

3. *Once the client agrees to post our proposed audit adjustments, the accounting supervisor posts them to the accounting system. We also will evaluate the auditor-identified adjustments as a potential control deficiency and evaluate the severity of any deficiency.*

4. *The resulting general ledger is then tied to the financial statements.*

5. *The accounting supervisor prepares information that should be disclosed in the financial statements. This information is reviewed by the CFO, who then works with the auditors to ensure that the draft disclosures are complete and understandable.*

How Misstatements May Occur

The most likely ways that misstatements may occur include the following:

*   *The last-minute transactions posted by the accounting personnel may not belong in the current accounting period.*

*   *Year-end estimates may be biased to achieve a desired result or may be based on unreliable information.*

*   *Spreadsheets used to prepare tables for the notes to the financial statements may not process the underlying data properly or they may use unadjusted or otherwise incorrect financial information.*

Part II—Evaluation of the Effectiveness of Design and Implementation of Entity-Level Controls [14]

Effectiveness of the design of implemented controls. Based on our understanding of the control policies and procedures that have been implemented, we have determined that these policies and procedures are capable of achieving the stated objectives, *except for the following matters, which we consider to be deficiencies in the design of controls:*

---

[14] The organization of documentation by entity and activity or assertion based controls is a user choice. Under the COSO frame-work, organization by principles and points of focus may achieve a similar objective.

Control Deficiency			Affects Risk of Misstatement?	Fin Stmt Risk?	Assertion-Level Risks		
Ref	No.	Description			Acct. Trans or Disclosure	Assertion(s)	Ref
CD-1	1	Few written policies regarding acceptable business practices. [principle 1]15	Yes	Yes— areas of risk include payables and inventory	N/A	N/A	N/A
CD-2	2	No formal controls over bonus arrangements, which are a fraud risk factor. [principle 8]	Yes	Yes	N/A	N/A	w/p XX-x
CD-3	3	Key officers do not actively participate in the supervision or monitoring of IT. Lack of active supervision is considered a fraud risk factor that could provide an opportunity for fraudulent financial reporting. [principle 2, principle 16]	Yes	Yes	N/A	N/A	w/p XX-x
CD-4	4	Company growth periodically stretches accounting, IT, and operational resources. [principle 4, principle 3]	Yes	Yes	N/A	N/A	w/p XX-x
CD-5	5	There is an informal understanding of all the information needed to perform financial reporting functions. Software is limited in its ability to keep pace with functional business requirements. [principle 14 and principle 15]	Yes	Yes	N/A	N/A	w/p XX-x
CD-6	6	Management's monitoring of internal control is only partially adequate, as it is based on a review of financial results and not on the design and operating effectiveness of internal control. [principle 2 and principle 16]	Yes	Yes	N/A	N/A	w/p XX-x
CD-7	7	Misstatements result in a correction of the accounting records but not always a consideration of underlying control deficiencies that caused the misstatement. [principle 17]	Yes	Yes	N/A	N/A	w/p XX-x

13 Note that to accurately assign a deficiency to a principle, the nature and cause of the deficiency may need to be considered. In addition, there remains some flexibility to assign deficiencies to different principles. A deficiency may relate to more than one principle and may need to be assigned to multiple principles when aggregating deficiencies. For example, a failure to properly apply a control over accounting for revenues under generally accepted accounting principles [principle 12] may be the result of poor training [principle 4] or errors in internal information [principle 14].

Response to Ineffective Design or Implementation

See W/P XX-x [appendix K-5], "Assessing Risks of Material Misstatement and Linkage to Further Audit Procedures," for documentation regarding the consideration of the risk of material misstatement at the financial statement level and the corresponding overall audit response.

All identified control deficiencies have been carried forward to the W/P XX-x [not included], "Summary of Control Deficiencies," for further evaluation of the severity of the noted deficiency, both individually and in the aggregate.

Observations and Suggestions

- This example takes a checklist and narrative approach to the documentation of financial statement level controls. That is, the auditor should describe the controls that have been implemented to meet the stated control objective. While a common procedure, the approach is not the most effective one for identifying control gaps. In many cases a better approach is to ensure controls are in place to address the risks flowing from the objectives. A missing control is a deficiency of some magnitude level.

- It is intended that a "blank" form would include standard control objectives or principles, and as appropriate, audit assertions. Individual engagement teams may tailor these objectives and associated risks for the specific facts and circumstances of the client.

   Note that under the integrity and ethical values element of the control environment, the auditor has added an additional control objective that is unique to the company (ethical business practices for non-U.S. suppliers). The default control objective related to management's philosophy and operating style also has been modified by the auditor to reflect specific circumstances of the company.

- Risks to achieving objectives might then be carefully reviewed to determine that they are at a level of detail and specific enough to address the particular circumstances at the entity. In several instances, the auditor has added language to the generic risks to address the unique characteristics of Young Fashions.

- On the initial audit, the audit team would describe the controls that were designed to achieve each control objective. Going forward, these control descriptions could be carried forward, assuming that the descriptions were still relevant.

   Each year, the auditor would perform risk assessment and other procedures to determine that the design of controls was still relevant and that the controls still were being used by the entity.

- In a checklist or form, the control objective usually is phrased as a question, for example, "How does the entity effectively communicate integrity and ethical values?" The auditor would then provide an answer, as appropriate. Evidence supporting that assessment would then be referenced or added to the documentation. Checklists comprising possible controls may not be effective. Checking a "yes or no" box to a specific control does not address how the control supports the objective or principle.

- Neither this form nor a checklist designed to achieve the same result, would—by itself—satisfy all the documentation points described in this guide. For example, in addition to the documentation on this form, you are required to document the sources of information used to gain an understanding of controls and the procedures you performed. For Young Fashions, those two items are documented in appendix K-2-1, "Procedures Performed to Evaluate Entity-Level Controls." The column on this form labeled "Ref. to Info. Source" provides the auditor with a chance to provide a direct link between the risk assessment procedures performed, the results of those procedures, and the auditor's conclusions.

  As another example, if the auditor was to write "yes" or "no" in answer to the question "Does the entity effectively communicate integrity and ethical values?" without providing a description of the information sources and procedures performed and evidence obtained to substantiate the "yes" or "no" answer, that documentation would be insufficient.

- The conclusion section of the form requires the auditor to summarize all identified *risks of material misstatement* and all control deficiencies. In our illustrative example, appendix K-5 illustrates how you might document your further consideration of *risks of material misstatement*.

  For guidance on evaluating control deficiencies, please refer to appendix G, "Assessing the Severity of Identified Deficiencies in Internal Control," which provides general guidance that is unrelated to this case study.

APPENDIX K-2-1

Young Fashions: Procedures Performed to Evaluate Entity-Level Controls

Observations and Suggestions

You should document the risk assessment procedures you performed to gather information about internal control and the source of that information. This audit program is an example of how you might satisfy those requirements. This program is not designed to document your understanding of internal control, only the procedures you performed to gain that understanding. See appendix K-2 for an example of the documentation of the auditor's understanding of internal control.

Some of the procedures performed to update the understanding of entity-level controls involve inquiries of company management. As a matter of audit efficiency, you may wish to make inquiries about the risks of fraud [as required by AU-C section 240, *Consideration of Fraud in a Financial Statement Audit* (AICPA, *Professional Standards*)] when making inquiries to gain an understanding of internal control.

This audit program illustrates example documentation for the procedures performed and information sources for *entity-level controls only*. Appendix K-4 provides an illustrative example of the documentation of the procedures and sources for assertion level controls.

This form includes a space to document the auditor who performed the work, the date, and the auditor who reviewed the work and the date of that review. Paragraph .09 of AU-C section 230, *Audit Documentation* (AICPA, *Professional Standards*), requires the documentation of this information.

All information that appears in this font style illustrates information completed by the auditor.

Instructions for Preparation

This audit program must be developed for each engagement to audit financial statements in accordance with generally accepted auditing standards. This program documents

- the sources of information from which the understanding of controls was obtained.
- the risk assessment procedures performed.

The audit program is divided into three sections, according to the nature of the risk assessment procedure performed. Separate audit programs exist for

- inquiries of management, appropriate individuals within the internal audit function (if such function exists), and others.
- observation.
- inspection of documentation.

How to Complete Each Column

- *No. / date.* The audit program steps may be numbered sequentially to facilitate the referencing between the procedures performed and the results of that procedure. For example, the first row of the inquiries program could be labeled "I-1," the next row "I-2," and so on.

  This column may also be used to indicate the date the procedure was performed.

- *Compl. by.* The auditor who completes the audit program step (for example, conducts the inquiry) may initial this column to indicate that he or she performed the procedure.

- *[Name, Title], [Process Observed / Procedure Performed].* Provide a brief description of the procedure performed to gather information about internal control. Note that

  — documentation of inquiries may include the name and job designation of the person interviewed.

  — documentation of an observation procedure would identify the process or subject matter being observed, and the relevant individuals and what they were responsible for.

- *Subject matter discussed.* Use these columns to indicate all of the financial statement level controls that your procedure pertains to. Financial statement level controls that are presumed to be relevant on every audit are as follows:

  a. *Control environment.* The attitudes, awareness, and actions of those charged with governance concerning the entity's internal control and its importance in achieving reliable financial reporting.

  b. *Risk assessment.* How management considers risks relevant to financial reporting objectives and decides about actions to address those risks.

  c. *Monitoring.* The major types of activities that the entity uses to monitor internal control over financial reporting, including the sources of the information related to those activities, and how those activities are used to initiate corrective actions to its controls.

  d. *Other financial statement level controls,* which include

    - controls over nonrouting transactions and estimates, to the extent that the existence of these items creates significant risks of material misstatement.

    - processes related to the selection and application of accounting policies, as described in AU-C section 260, *The Auditor's Communication With Those Charged With Governance* (AICPA, *Professional Standards*).

    - the responsibilities of those charged with governance.

Observations and Suggestions

- Paragraph .A14 of AU section 230 states that audit documentation of procedures performed should include the identifying characteristics of the specific items tested. In providing examples of "identifying characteristics," the standard notes

  > For a procedure requiring inquiries of specific entity personnel, the documentation may record the inquiries made, the dates of the inquiries, and the names and job designations of the entity personnel. For an observation procedure, the documentation may record the process or matter being observed, the relevant individuals, their respective responsibilities, and where and when the observation was carried out.

  > The first few columns of these audit programs allow for the documentation of these matters.

- All of the items except one that are listed under "Subject Matter Discussed" may be relevant for every audit. That is, with one exception, the auditor should obtain an understanding of the design and implementation of the financial statement controls listed here. The only exception is the oversight of those charged with governance. As described more completely in paragraph 4.39 of this guide, the auditor "should consider" certain matters related to the oversight of those charged with governance, which is considered to be an element of the control environment [for example, principle 2].

- Reviewers of the completed work programs would consider whether

  — the audit program includes inquiries and other procedures performed by the engagement partner or manager that provide information about internal control design or implementation.

  — sufficient procedures have been performed for all financial statement level controls.

  — an appropriate mix of risk assessment procedures have been performed for each financial statement level control (that is, procedures other than a single, uncorroborated inquiry have been performed).

  — all items required to be documented by AU-C section 230 have been documented.

Inquiries of Management, Appropriate Individuals within the Internal Audit Function (if such Function Exists), and Others

(See w/p xxx for details of questions and responses [not included in this illustration]).

No.	Date	Compl. by	Name, Title	Subject Matter Discussed			
				Control Environment	Risk Assessment	Monitoring	Other
1	10/03	mpr	Josh Young, co-CEO / Design	X	X	X	Antifraud Oversight
2	10/03	mpr	Jane Young Ching, co-CEO / Operations	X	X	X	Antifraud Oversight Nonroutine Trans Estimates Acctg. Pol
3	10/03	mpr	Robert Haner, IT Director	X	X	X	Antifraud Oversight
4	10/03	mpr	Lori Feldman, Finance Manager	X		X	Comm. Nonroutine Estimates Acctg. Pol. Journal entry process and controls
5	10/03	mpr	Jenny Hershberger, Accounting Clerk	X		X	Comm. Journal entry process
6	10/03	mpr	Bret Jensen, Salesman	X			
7	10/03	mpr	Bob Maguire, Operations Manager	X			
8	10/03	mpr	Harrison Hargrove, Distribution Director	X		X	Comm.
9	10/03	mpr	Patrick Anderson, HR Director	X			Antifraud
10	10/03	mpr	Sherman Howard, Board Member	X	X	X	Antifraud Oversight Nonroutine Trans Estimates Acctg. Pol
11	10/03	mpr	Carter Lillian, Chief Internal Audit Executive	X	X	X	Antifraud Oversight

©2016, AICPA

Observation

No.	Date	Compl. by	Process Observed/Procedure Performed	Subject Matter Discussed			
				Control Environment	Risk Assessment	Monitoring	Other
1	10/03	mpr	Perform planning analytical procedures (see w/p xxx)	X			
2	10/03	mpr	Observe implementation of suggestions from prior year's management letter (see w/p xxx)			X	

©2016, AICPA

Inspection of Documentation

No.	Date	Compl. by	Process Observed/ Procedure Performed	Control Environment	Risk Assessment	Monitoring	Other	Reference to Results
				Subject Matter Discussed				
1	10/03	mpr	Read Memo dated 2/13/X0 "Investments in Vendors and Suppliers" describing company policy re: investments by key company personnel in vendors and suppliers	X				CE-1
2	10/03	mpr	Reviewed memos dated 3/15/X4 and 10/20/X4 "Young Fashions Business Practices" which described acceptable business practices for non-U.S. suppliers	X			Info and Communications	CE-3,6
3	10/03	mpr	Reviewed Young Fashions Employee Handbook as of 8/X4 (most recent version)	X			Info and Communications	CE-3,6
4	10/03	mpr	Read company organization chart dated 7/X4 (most current)	X				CE-5
5	10/03	mpr	Read minutes of board meetings and agendas. For quarterly meetings held in X4, dated 1/20, 5/05, 7/18 and 9/05	X	X	X	Oversight	K-1,2 RA-1,2 O-1 CE-4
6	10/03	mpr	Read summary of significant accounting policies from 12/31/X4 financial statements				Acctg. Pol	SAAP-1

No.	Date	Compl. by	Process Observed/ Procedure Performed	Control Environment	Risk Assessment	Monitoring	Other	Reference to Results
					Subject Matter Discussed			
7	10/03	mpr	Reviewed summary of audit differences and their disposition, as documented in prior year's working papers. Noted that all proposed adjustments were made.				Oversight	O-1
8	10/03	mpr	Reviewed communications among design, operations, and sales groups related to planning and coordination efforts. E-mail thread dated 1/16/03 subject: Summer season projections E-mail thread dated 3/4/03; subject: re-stock tencel shorts and trousers E-mail thread dated 4/16/03; subject: boardshorts in short supply E-mail thread dated 6/20/03; fall/winter projections and standing orders E-mail thread dated 7/15/03 summer markdown plans	X			Info and Communication	O-1
9	10/03	mpr	Read five-year strategic plan dated September 02		X			O-1
10	10/03	mpr	Reviewed all four quarterly budgets for 03 and management's comparison to actual results			X	Info and Communication Oversight	O-1
11	10/03	mpr	Reviewed worksheets and other documents supporting accounting estimates. See further discussion on working papers X-X, X-X and X-X [not included in this case study]				Estimates	O-1
12	10/03	mpr	Read board of directors' charter dated 8/15/01 and included in Personnel Handbook	X			Oversight	O-1

Appendix K-3

Young Fashions: Understanding of Internal Control—IT General Controls

This appendix is nonauthoritative and is included for informational purposes only.

Observations and Suggestions

IT general controls [principle 11] typically are a significant component of entity-level controls that should be evaluated by the auditor. The information gathered in this example generally follows the guidance presented in this guide pertaining to the control objectives, risks, and control policies and procedures related to IT general controls.

The engagement team is assumed to have sufficient knowledge of many of the IT matters to gather some of the information included in this example, and to identify risks. The engagement team may nevertheless ask an IT specialist to assess certain risks and develop an appropriate audit response.

For example, in this case study, the company lacked logical access controls during the year. In this case study, the primary engagement team was able to identify the condition and recognize that lack of logical access controls created a *risk of material misstatement* of the financial statements. However, the primary engagement team did not have sufficient expertise to assess the significance of the risk or to develop the tests necessary to determine whether the lack of control might indicate a material weakness and have led to misstatements.

Because of the lack of logical access controls and other matters, the engagement team included an IT specialist. See appendix K-5 for the documentation related to that decision. The documentation of the procedures performed, findings, and conclusions reached by the IT specialist is not included in this case study.

All control deficiencies identified in this working paper have been evaluated to determine whether they represent a *risk of material misstatement* of the financial statements. These risks have been carried forward to appendix K-5 for further assessment and linkage to the auditor's response.

All information that appears in this font style illustrates information completed by the auditor.

Practice Considerations for Auditors of Entities Using the COSO Framework

In the COSO framework, IT general controls are contained in a separate principle (principle 11) within the control activities component.

The points of focus associated with principle 11 include that the entity

- determines the dependency between use of technology in business processes and technology general controls (ITGC).

- establishes relevant technology infrastructure controls.
- establishes relevant security management process controls.
- establishes relevant technology acquisition, development and maintenance process controls.

Instructions for Preparation

This form documents the understanding of IT general controls, including

- a description of the sources of information and procedures performed to gather the understanding of IT general controls.
- an evaluation of whether the design of the control, individually or in combination, is capable of achieving the control objective.
- a conclusion of whether the control exists and the entity is using it.

This form is divided into three parts:

- *Part I*, "Description of Procedures Performed," which documents the sources of information and procedures performed to gain an understanding of IT general controls.
- *Part II*, "Understanding of IT General Controls," which documents the understanding of the design of IT general controls and whether the entity is using them.
- *Part III*, "Evaluation of the Design of Controls and Risk of Material Misstatement," which summarizes the conclusions related to IT general controls and determines the degree to which those deficiencies create a risk of material misstatement.

Part I—Description of Procedures Performed

Describe the procedures performed to understand the design of IT general controls and their implementation. For all inquiries, list the title of the person interviewed.

No.	Description of Procedure	Identifying Characteristics	Matters Discussed
1	Inquiry of Robert Haner, IT Director	Conducted by mpr on 8/24, 9/1, 9/2	All
2	Inquiry of Lori Feldman, Finance Director	Conducted by mpr on 8/16	A-1, A-2, A-3, B-1, C-1, C-4, C-5, C-6, C-7, D-1
3	Inquiry of Jane Young Ching, co-CEO	Conducted by ryb on 7/25	A-1, B-1, B-3, C-1, D-1
4	Inquiry of Josh Young, co-CEO	Conducted by ryb on 7/25	A-1, B-1, B-3, C-1, D-1
5	Inquiry of Jenny Hershberger, Accounting Clerk	Conducted by mpr on 8/22	A-4, C-2, C-4, C-5, C-6
6	Inquiry of Junior Tatupu, Warehouse Manager, San Diego	Conducted by bt on 10/30	A-4, C-2, C-4, C-5, C-6
7	Observation of: • Location of server and midrange computer • Demonstration of logical access control • Operation of order management, inventory management, supply chain management, and financial management applications	Conducted by mpr on 8/24. Demonstration of logical access controls performed by Robert Haner, IT director. Observation of applications performed by mpr on 8/24	D-1 C-6 C-6, C-4
8	Read IT budget for X4 and X5	Most current budget dated 9/1/X	B-1
9	Read documentation prepared by Robert Haner regarding installation of overall security framework.	Notes, diagrams, and memos to file prepared by Robert Haner to prepare for and implement the security framework. Materials were undated, but according to Mr. Haner, were prepared at various times from late August to mid-September X4	C-6
10	Read e-mail from Robert Haner to all employees and also to third parties with access to the company's system (for example, software vendors and consultants) describing the installation of new security framework.	Memo dated 9/23/X4	C-6

(continued)

No.	Description of Procedure	Identifying Characteristics	Matters Discussed
11	Obtained and reviewed a listing of applications currently used by the company. List includes application name, version, and vendor.	Listing prepared as of 9/30/X4. Compared current year listing to that prepared for prior year audit	C-3, C-4
12	Obtained and reviewed copy of current policies for network configuration.	Policies were obtained by mpr on 9/2/X4 using network operating system utility.	C-6
13	Reviewed vendor supplied documentation of IT applications.	Reviewed documentation of current versions in-use for network operating system, order management, purchasing, and inventory systems.	B-2
14	Read documentation prepared by Robert Haner regarding the investigation of possible corruption of data when order management system was upgraded to a newer version.	Notes, diagrams, and memos to file prepared by Robert Haner to investigate upgrade performed by vendors. Materials were dated at various dates during the month of September.	C-3

Note: This is not a complete list of all the procedures performed in the review of general controls.

Part II—Understanding of IT General Controls

Control Objective

Develop, communicate, and plan an overall IT strategy that enables the achievement of entity-wide controls.

No.	Question	Yes, No, N/A	Comments on Control Design and Implementation
A-1	Does management coordinate their overall business plans and strategies with their IT strategy?	Yes	*U.S. apparel companies are highly dependent on their IT systems to manage their supply chain, since all manufacturing is done by third-party suppliers all over the world. Large retailers also require suppliers' IT systems (that is, Young Fashions' systems) to integrate with their own. In order to stay competitive, Young Fashions must constantly consider how operational strategies and plans will affect IT.*
A-3	Does management actively identify, assess, and respond to IT-related risks?	Yes	*Prior to hiring new IT director, Lori Feldman, finance director, was in charge of IT. To the extent her schedule allowed, she was involved. Since the hiring of the IT director during X4, issues are identified and responded to more quickly.* *Typically, issues are identified by accounting or operations personnel or by customers or suppliers. These are then forwarded to IT director (previously finance director) for resolution.*
A-4	Does management appropriately consider user needs for the following? • Planning of IT systems • Implementation of IT systems • Maintenance of IT systems	 Yes Yes Yes	*User needs are not formally documented, but IT director works closely with users, especially in the maintenance phases, to make sure that the system is operating in a way that is as responsive as possible to user needs. Working paper xxx explains what he does and the results achieved.*

Control Objective

Provide resources and organizational infrastructure necessary to implement the IT strategy.

No.	Question	Yes, No, N/A	Comments on Control Design and Implementation
B-1	Does management budget for the continued funding of IT systems development?	Yes	*Because of the importance of IT to the company's operations, management allocates significant funds to maintaining IT. Historically, most of these amounts were paid to consultants and other third parties.*
B-2	Does a structured approach exist for the following? • Training on IT matters • Service of IT hardware • Documentation of IT systems	*No* *n/a* *No*	*User training is done on an as-needed basis—there is no structured approach. The hardware owned by the company does not require regular servicing. The only documentation that exists is whatever has been provided by the hardware or software vendor. No structured documentation exists of other IT systems matters.* *See working paper xxx for an assessment of this deficiency.*
B-3	Is the level of expertise of the personnel assigned to manage IT operations commensurate with the complexity and needs of the IT system?	Yes	*Prior to hiring a full-time IT director, the company relied on IT consultants and other third parties to help manage its IT systems, under the direction of Lori Feldman, finance director. Since August, the newly hired IT director has taken over management of the IT function, and his level of expertise seems appropriate.*

Control Objective

Identify, acquire, and integrate IT applications and solutions that are necessary for implementing the IT strategy.

No.	Question	Yes, No, N/A	Comments on Control Design and Implementation
C-1	Has the entity developed specific IT functional and operational requirements?	Yes	The company depends on its IT system to manage its supply chain and also to meet the requirements of its customers. Management understands these operational requirements and actively considers how IT systems allow the company to meet these objectives.
C-2	Does the entity have policies such as the following to ensure that appropriate hardware and software are acquired and implemented? • Entity-wide standardized hardware and software standards • Regular assessment of hardware and software performance	Yes Yes	Company maintains standard hardware and software configurations. Assessing the performance of hardware and software is done on an as-needed basis, when customers require additional functionality, or when operational personnel identify IT issues.
C-3	Does the entity have a formal migration, conversion, and acceptance plan for new systems, vendor-provided version upgrades, and systems modifications?	No	No formal plan exists; the company typically relies on the third-party software vendor to install version upgrades and new systems. During the current year, the company upgraded its order management system to a new version. This upgrade was performed by the vendor. The new IT director was hired several months after the upgrade was installed. Based on observations made by system users, the new IT director determined that data from the previous version may not have been transferred properly to the new version.

(continued)

No.	Question	Yes, No, N/A	Comments on Control Design and Implementation
			This issue was eventually resolved, and the IT director determined that the data in the system as of 9/18/X4 was correct. However, the system operated for approximately four weeks using data that may not have been accurate. **See comment part III, risk number 1, for further consideration of this matter.**
C-4	Does the entity take appropriate steps to ensure that applications that have been provided by different vendors are integrated appropriately?	*Yes*	*The company uses software applications from three different vendors. The company does not have a formal process for integrating software from different companies. However, the existing system has been in place for several years, and all issues relating to integration of different software vendors have been worked out.*
C-5	Do controls exist over the development, modification, and testing of spreadsheets?	*No*	*The accounting supervisor, and to a lesser degree others within the accounting department, prepare spreadsheets to process or prepare information for inclusion in the accounting records or the financial statements. No controls exist over these spreadsheets, except for the review of output for significant unusual results.* **See comment part III, risk number 21, for further consideration of this matter.**

No.	Question	Yes, No, N/A	Comments on Control Design and Implementation
C-6	Has the company implemented logical access controls to restrict access to the following, which are used in the financial reporting process? • Systems • Data • Programs • Spreadsheets	 *No* *No* *No* *No*	*In the past, there was no overall security framework in place at the company. All individuals are granted complete access to all data, systems, and applications. Software vendors and third-party consultants also were granted access in order to help the company maintain its system.* *The new IT director has implemented a security framework, which became operational in October X4. However, for most of the year, the company operated without adequate logical access controls.* **See comment part III, risk number 3, for further consideration of this matter.**
C-7	Do the entity's IT operating policies and procedures include the following? • Development and testing of a business continuity plan • Installation of suitable environmental and physical controls	 *No* *Yes, (only after 9/30)*	*The company regularly backs up its data, but they have never tested to determine that the data can be reinstalled in the event of a disaster.* *The company's main hardware is a server and beginning in September, a new mini-computer. Both machines are located in a locked room that seems to be physically suitable.* *Prior to the hiring of the new IT director, the server was located in the accounting department in an unsecure location.* **See comment part III, risks number 4 and 5, for further consideration of this matter.**

Control Objective

Monitor IT processes to ensure their continued effectiveness.

No.	Question	Yes, No, N/A	Comments on Control Design and Implementation
D-1	Has management defined performance measures that are monitored on a timely basis?	No	*Management has not defined IT performance measures. With Lori Feldman, finance director, no longer involved directly in IT operations, the IT function is not actively monitored by anyone outside of the IT function.* **See comment part III, risk number 6, for further consideration of this matter.**

Note: The example previously mentioned illustrates some, but not all, of the understanding related to IT general controls. Other documentation [*not illustrated*] may address areas such as access controls, Web controls, physical security controls, and program and system change controls.

Part III—Evaluation of the Design of Controls and Risk of Material Misstatement

Effectiveness of the design of implemented controls. Based on our understanding of the control policies and procedures that have been implemented, we have determined that these policies and procedures are capable of achieving the stated control objectives, *except for the following matters, which we consider to be deficiencies in the design of controls.*

Control Deficiency				Assertion-Level Risks			
Ref.	**No.**	**Description**	**Affects Risk of Misstatement?**	**Fin Stmt Risk?**	**Acct. Trans or Disclosure**	**Assertion(s)**	**Ref.**
C-3	1	*Lack of formal integration plan resulted in possible loss or corruption of data when the order management system was upgraded to a new version.*	Yes	No	*Revenues Receivables*	*Completeness Accuracy Occurrence*	*w/p XX-x*
C-5	2	*Lack of controls over the development and maintenance of spreadsheets.*[1]	Yes	Yes			*w/p XX-x*
C-6	3	*Deficiency of logical access controls over data and applications for the first nine months of the year.*	Yes	Yes			*w/p XX-x*
C-7	4	*Lack of testing of a business continuity plan.*	Yes	Yes			*w/p XX-x*
C-7	5	*Network server was located in an unsecure location for majority of the year.*	Yes	Yes			*w/p XX-x*
D-6	6	*Management generally does not closely monitor and supervise IT operations. [principle 16]*	Yes	Yes			*w/p XX-x*

[1] This might be reflected also in further audit procedures that test the data processed and output produced by the spreadsheets [also principle 12].

Response to Ineffective Design or Implementation

See W/P XX-x, [appendix K-5] "Assessing Risks of Material Misstatement and Linkage to Further Audit Procedures," for documentation regarding the consideration of the risk of material misstatement at the financial statement level and the corresponding overall audit response.

All control deficiencies have been carried forward to the W/P XX-x, [not included] "Summary of Control Deficiencies," for further evaluation of the severity of the noted deficiency, both individually and in the aggregate. Interactions with other components (or principles) are considered further there.

Appendix K-4

Young Fashions: Evaluation of Activity-Level Controls—Wholesale Sales

This appendix is nonauthoritative and is included for informational purposes only.

Observations and Suggestions

You should document your understanding of the controls relevant to the audit, including

- an evaluation of whether the design of the control, individually or in combination, is capable of effectively preventing or detecting and correcting material misstatements.
- a determination of whether the control exists and the entity is using it.
- the risk assessment and other procedures you performed to gather information about internal control and the source of this information. In this example, the auditor has performed a walkthrough of a portion of the sales cycle.

As described in paragraph 3.95 of this guide, you are not required to obtain an understanding of all the information processing and activity-level controls related to each class of transactions, account balances, and disclosures in the financial statements or to every relevant assertion. Rather, your understanding of activity-level controls should be focused on significant transactions and material accounts and disclosures, that is, where you consider that material misstatements are more likely to occur.

Additionally, auditor documentation of his or her understanding of entity controls may be less than the level of documentation maintained by the entity to document its processes, procedures, and controls. Auditor documentation only needs to be sufficiently robust to assess the effectiveness of the controls and to serve as a basis for determining that they are in operation and for measuring changes in those controls over time.

This form is designed to achieve the three documentation objectives for *activity-level controls only*. Appendixes K-2 and K-3 provide illustrative examples of the documentation of your understanding of entity-level controls, including IT general controls. Further, this example is limited to one significant transaction and the related account balance for wholesale sales transactions. Separate documentation would be required for other significant transactions and material accounts and disclosures related to this client.

Many transaction-based controls such as those described here are evaluated under the COSO framework as part of principle 12. The points of focus related to this principle are that the entity

- establishes policies and procedures to support deployment of management's directives
- establishes responsibility and accountability for executing policies and procedures

---

- performs activities in a timely manner
- takes corrective action
- uses competent personnel
- reassesses policies and procedures

In addition, principle 10 addresses the necessity for and design of controls that flow from the risks that were assessed.

Points of focus associated with principle 10 include

- integrates with risk assessment.
- considers entity-specific facts.
- determines relevant business processes.
- evaluates the mix of control activity types.
- considers the level the activities are applied.
- assesses the segregation of duties.

Thus, many of the transaction-based control assessments may involve two principles. As a result, it may be efficient to revise audit documentation accordingly.

The example form that follows is divided into three parts:

- Part I is a series of walkthroughs that the auditor performed to confirm internal control design for revenue transactions. This part is designed to gather information. As a matter of audit efficiency, you may wish to make inquiries about the risks of fraud [as required by AU-C section 240, *Consideration of Fraud in a Financial Statement Audit* (AICPA, *Professional Standards*)] when performing walkthroughs.
- Part II of the form is the auditor's analysis of the information gathered in part one. This analysis is necessary to compare identified controls to stated control objectives and determine whether the design of those controls is effective.
- Part III of the form is a summary of identified control deficiencies and risks of material misstatement. These deficiencies and risks will be carried forward to appendix K-5 for further assessment.

All information that appears in this font style illustrates information completed by the auditor.

Instructions for Preparation

This form documents the understanding of activity-level controls, including

- an evaluation of whether the design of the control, individually or in combination, is capable of effectively preventing or detecting and correcting material misstatements.
- a conclusion of whether the control exists and entity personnel are using it.
- the risk assessment and other procedures performed to gather information about internal control and the source of this information.

A separate form may be completed for each related group of significant transactions or material account or disclosure. For example, documentation about the purchasing cycle would include information about the accounts payable balance, and the preparation of this form would document your understanding of both the transaction and the account. A separate form would be prepared to document your understanding of, for example, revenue recognition.

Instructions for Completing the Form

Part I—Understanding of Information Processing and Control Design

Your documentation should include

- how significant transactions are initiated, authorized, recorded, processed, and reported and the related accounting records, supporting information, and specific accounts.

- the process of reconciling the detail to the general ledger for significant accounts.

- if information technology is used to process transactions, how the incorrect processing of transactions is resolved.

- if applicable, control activities relating to authorization, segregation of duties, safeguarding of assets, and asset accountability.

- specific controls designed to mitigate specific inherent risks or risks of fraud.

- relevant control activities, to the extent not already documented.

Revenue Recognition

If the class of transactions is related to revenue recognition, complete the checklist[1] for Understanding the Design of Revenue Recognition Processes and Controls.

Part II—Evaluation of Control Design

Complete the matrix, "Evaluation of Control Design"; document your evaluation; and describe the control deficiencies, if any, identified in your evaluation.

Part III—Summary of Control Deficiencies and Risks of Material Misstatement

Your evaluation of the design of activity-level controls may lead you to identify control deficiencies or risks of material misstatement. These deficiencies and misstatements, if any, may be summarized in this section so they may be cross-referenced to the working paper that describes your audit response.

---

[1] Note that the completion of any such checklist is not a requirement, but illustrates in this case study a practice of this auditor.

©2016, AICPA

Part I—Understanding of Information Processing and Control Design

The following pages in this section document our understanding of the processes[2] and controls for sales to wholesale customers for both J Couture and JY Sport. This documentation includes sales only, and does not consider the processes related to cash receipts, inventory relief, or credit adjustments, which are documented in working papers XX-X, XX-X, and XX-X respectively [not included].

The flowchart on the next two pages documents our overall understanding of the processes. **The numbered circles in the diagram are cross-references to the walkthrough worksheets.**

The walkthrough worksheets that follow describe our understanding of the processes and procedures that have been implemented. They also describe the walkthrough auditing procedures we performed.

---

[2] For purposes of the case study, additional process information is included that is not required by auditing standards. The auditor's responsibility is to document his or her understanding of the controls and not processes.

Overview of Wholesale Sales

(Numbered circles are cross-references to the walkthrough worksheets that follow.)

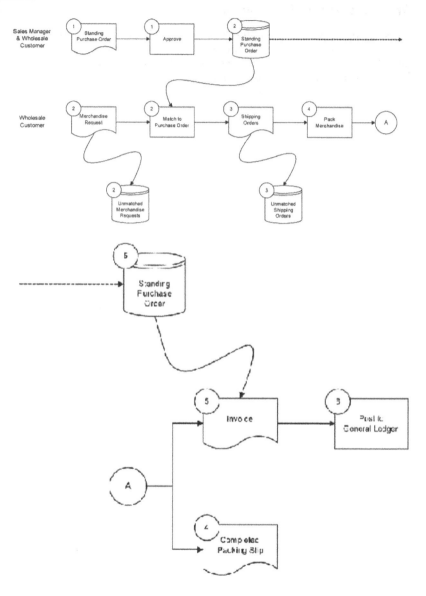

Understanding of Sales Transactions

Observations and Suggestions

As described in paragraph 4.09 of this guide, it important for you to obtain an understanding of matters relating to sales transactions that may affect your client's revenue recognition. This worksheet documents the auditor understanding and analysis of those matters.

Matters Potentially Affecting Revenue Recognition	Understanding	Comments
Products and services sold	Men's and women's apparel and furnishing. There are two separate lines: J Couture and JY Sport.	*See working paper XX-XX [appendix K-1] for additional comments relating to product lines.*
Customers	Large department stores and some specialty shops. J Couture sells primarily to high-end stores and specialty shops. JY Sport sells to other department stores. Most customers are strong financially, and bad debts have not been a problem. See markdown issue that follows.	*See working paper XX-XX [appendix K-1] for additional comments relating to customers.*
	The company also has a chain of retail stores that sell to the end consumer. These customers usually pay with bank cards and bad debts are rare.	*See XXX for procedures at the retail stores.*
Seasonal or cyclical variations in revenue	Significant sales (approximately 35% of total annual sales) are recognized during Q4 due to retailers stocking for holiday sales they expect to make during the month of December.	*There are two selling seasons, spring/summer (generally begins in February) and fall/winter (generally beginning in August). Except for Q4 (holiday sales) revenue generally is greatest in the month after season begins (as customers place their orders) and slowly decreases over the rest of the season.*

(continued)

Matters Potentially Affecting Revenue Recognition	Understanding	Comments
Marketing and sales policies	Marketing to retail stores is done through commissioned sales personnel, who meet regularly with customers. The company uses standard sales contracts, but pricing and other key terms are negotiated on a client-by-client basis.	See walkthrough worksheet #1 for additional comments on wholesale sales.
	To expand sales of J Couture line, the company has launched an image marketing campaign aimed at consumers who meet the targeted demographic for the product line.	See working paper XX-XX [appendix K-1] for additional comments relating to expansion of J Couture and related marketing.
Policies relating to pricing, sales returns, extension of credit, delivery and payment terms	Pricing and payment terms are negotiated on a customer-by-customer basis.	See working paper XX-XX [appendix K-1] for additional comments relating to pricing and sales concessions.
	The company compensates its customers for a portion of the price markdowns the department stores incur in order to move slow moving inventory.	
Assistance provided to distributors	See above for assistance provided to customers for slow moving inventory.	
Marketing and sales personnel involved with processes affecting revenue recognition, including order entry, extension of credit, and shipping	Order entry is done online by the customer.	See walkthrough worksheet #1.
	Operations CEO approves orders and extension of credit.	See walkthrough worksheet #1.

Matters Potentially Affecting Revenue Recognition	Understanding	Comments
	Shipping is performed by warehouse personnel, based on standard shipping terms.	*See walkthrough worksheet #4.*
Compensation arrangements that depend on the recording of revenues	*Sales personnel compensations are almost entirely a commission based on sales. Salespeople complain when they do not receive commissions for sales that should have been billed. Thus, completeness of sales/receivables is not a significant issue, but occurrence/existence might be.*	*See working paper XX-XX [appendix K-1] for additional comments relating to sales commissions.*
Accounting principles	*Revenue is recognized at shipment, which is when title to the goods passes.* *Revenue is recorded net of returns, discounts, end-of-season markdowns, and operational chargebacks.* *Estimates for end-of-season markdown allowances are based on historic trends, markdowns allowed after year end, correspondence with customers, seasonal results, an evaluation of market conditions, and retailer performance.* *Retailers sometimes overstate their markdowns to Young and then negotiate strongly.*	*This information is per the company's most recent financial statements and is consistent with industry practices.*

Young Fashions
Wholesale Sales
Walkthrough Worksheet #1

Prepared by: *BT*   Date Prepared: *8/15/X4*

The following documents the procedures performed, information gathered, and conclusions reached relating to walkthroughs of major transactions.

Planning

Person(s) we interviewed

> *Barry Gregg, Sales Manager*
> *Jane Young Ching, co-CEO*

Date of interview   *8/15/X4*

Accounts and assertions affected: Sales occurrence, accuracy; receivables existence, and valuation

Description of transaction discussed *Initiation of standing purchase orders*

Processing step(s) we discussed:

X Initiation of transaction

__ Transaction recording

__ Transaction processing steps

X Authorization of transaction

__ How the incorrect processing of transactions is resolved

__ Process for reconciling detail to the general ledger

Brief description of the company's prescribed processes and controls for the previously mentioned step(s)

Process	Control No.	Control Description	Relevant Accounts and Assertions
The Sales Manager (Gregg) is responsible for negotiating terms with wholesale customers and documenting these in the standing purchase order. The standing purchase order describes the quantities and terms of the items that may be ordered by the customer without further approval.	1-Con-a	The Operations CEO (Ching) reviews and approves the terms.	Sales Accuracy
	1-Con-b	The company uses standard purchase order contracts. Any changes to these standard contracts must be approved by in-house counsel in advance.	Sales Accuracy
The accounting department enters approved contracts into the system.	1-Con-c	Edit checks help prevent the input of incorrect information. See control 2-CD-3 (walkthrough worksheet #2) for additional controls that would identify and then correct errors in the standard purchase order file.	Accuracy

Identification and Resolution of Processing Errors

Describe how processing errors are identified and resolved.

Errors in the terms of the transaction (for example, credit limits or shipping terms) are identified by Operations CEO as part of her review. These errors are corrected before the standing purchase order is signed (1-Con-a). The IT system performs edit checks to ensure that information such as customer number, shipping address, and billing terms are correct or within an acceptable range. Any errors of this nature must be corrected before processing can continue.(1-Con-c)

Segregation of duties. Assess the adequacy of the segregation of duties for the prescribed processes and controls, as described. If segregation of duties is not adequate, describe compensating controls.

Control No.	Control Description	Assertions
1-Con-d	*Segregation is adequate. The sales manager initiates the transaction, which is then approved by operations CEO.*	All

Safeguarding of assets. Assess the adequacy of the safeguarding of the assets related to this transaction, if applicable. If safeguarding controls are not adequate, describe compensating controls.

Control No.	Control Description	Assertions
	Not applicable	

Asset accountability. Describe the process and related controls for establishing the accountability for the assets related to this transaction, if applicable. If these controls are not adequate, describe compensating controls.

Control No.	Control Description	Assertions
	Not applicable	

Procedures Performed and Results

We performed the following procedures, as indicated, to corroborate the responses to our inquiries.

Procedure		Audit Procedure Performed?		
Control No.	Description	Yes	No	Comments
Pro-a	Reviewed original documents	X		*We reviewed standing X4 purchase orders for Bernards, Mandelbaum's, Sonia's Boutique, and Mortons, for which the terms had been modified from the standard contract. For the Morton's X4 purchase order, we reviewed an e-mail message dated 11/21/X3 from in-house counsel to Barry Gregg, sales manager, approving the change.*
Pro-b	Made observations	X		*Gregg, sales manager demonstrated how purchase order information is entered into the system, and we observed the operation of the computer edit checks of purchase order input, including customer field, customer number, date, quantity, and price.*
Pro-c	Made inquiries of others	X		*On 8/18/X4 we spoke with James Gregory, in-house counsel, who confirmed that he reviews variations from standard contract terms. We also asked about the types of variations he has approved during the year and how these are communicated to accounting.*
				As a result of that inquiry, we identified several transactions for which the nonstandard rights of return may pose revenue recognition issues. See part III, "Summary of Identified Risks of Material Misstatement," for reference to audit response.
				On 8/24, we made inquiries of Robert Haner, IT Director, about the edit checks programmed into the IT system. We observed that he set the parameters for these checks using his systems administrator access privileges. We noted, however, that he or anyone else could change the terms using these privileges. Also, before 9/30 anyone could change the terms since logical access controls were ineffective.
Pro-d	Performed other procedures		X	

Observations and Suggestions

- There are several different ways to perform an effective walk-through. In this example, the auditor conducted inquiries and performed other procedures at each significant processing step, rather than tracing a single transaction through the system. When performing a walkthrough in this manner, you would take steps to ensure that the information controls are in place to ensure that the information that is transferred between processing steps remains complete and accurate.

- The auditor's procedures were not limited to inquiries of a single individual but include multiple procedures to determine that controls have been implemented.

- The auditor frequently expands inquiries to include questions about the types of errors typically encountered and other follow-up questions. In this walkthrough, these expanded inquiries resulted in the auditor identifying high risk transactions (sales involving nonstandard rights of return) for further audit consideration. In other walkthroughs the auditor might identify control deficiencies through these expanded questions. It helps to investigate not only what the client does to perform the control procedure, but also what they have found during the period as a result of performing the procedure.

- In walkthrough 6, the auditor may make inquiries about the reliability of the information used by management to monitor internal controls. Establishing the reliability of this information is important, as discussed in paragraph 2.104 of this guide.

Young Fashions
Wholesale Sales
Walkthrough Worksheet #2

Prepared by: *BT*   Date Prepared: *8/17/X4*

The following documents the procedures performed, information gathered, and conclusions reached relating to walkthroughs of major transactions.

Planning

Person(s) we interviewed

> *Barry Gregg, Sales Manager*
> *Jane Young Ching, co-CEO*
> *Robert Haner, IT Director*

Date of interview *8/15/X4*

Description of transaction discussed *Receipt of merchandise request from wholesale customer*

Processing step(s) we discussed:

X Initiation of transaction

X Transaction recording

__ Transaction processing steps

___ Authorization of transaction

X How the incorrect processing of transactions is resolved

___ Process for reconciling detail to the general ledger

Brief description of the company's prescribed processes and controls for the previously mentioned step(s)

Process	Control No.	Control Description	Relevant Assertions
When a wholesale customer wants to initiate a purchase, the customer sends an electronic merchandise request to the sales manager.	2-Con-a	The sales manager reviews the request for obvious errors or unusual terms. If nothing unusual is noted, the sales manager electronically approves the order and releases it for further processing, which includes the generation and sending of an order confirmation to the customer.	Accuracy
	2-Con-b	Unapproved merchandise requests remain in a suspense account until approval or rejection.	Accuracy
The terms of merchandise requests released for processing are automatically compared to the standing purchase orders.	2-Con-c	Errors in the terms of the transaction (for example, price) and transactions that exceed established limits are posted to the suspense account for unapproved orders.	Accuracy
	2-Con-d	The sales manager reviews the suspense account periodically and follows up on all unapproved merchandise requests.	Accuracy
	2-Con-e	Quarterly, co-CEO receives a report of all unapproved sales orders in suspense, and contacts sales manager to follow up on a timely basis.	Accuracy

Identification and Resolution of Processing Errors

Describe how processing errors are identified and resolved.

Identified by sales manager or IT system and placed into suspense account for follow up. See comments previously mentioned.

Segregation of duties. Assess the adequacy of the segregation of duties for the prescribed processes and controls, as described. If segregation of duties is not adequate, describe compensating controls.

Control No.	Control Description	Assertions
2-Con-f	*Segregation is adequate, as most controls are performed by IT system. CEO monitors manual follow up of suspense items that are cleared by sales manager.*	*All*

Safeguarding of assets. Assess the adequacy of the safeguarding of the assets related to this transaction, if applicable. If safeguarding controls are not adequate, describe compensating controls.

Control No.	Control Description	Assertions
	Not applicable	

Asset accountability. Describe the process and related controls for establishing the accountability for the assets related to this transaction, if applicable. If these controls are not adequate, describe compensating controls.

Control No.	Control Description	Assertions
	Not applicable	

Procedures Performed and Results

We performed the following procedures, as indicated, to corroborate the responses to our inquiries.

Procedure		Audit Procedure Performed?		Comments
Control No.	Description	Yes	No	Comments
Pro-a	Reviewed original documents		X	*This transaction is initiated electronically. No hard copy documents are available for review. Reviewed electronic files (see below).*
Pro-b	Made observations	X		*Sales Manager, Gregg, showed us electronic merchandise requests from Daniel Fleischers, Newman-MacLachlin, and Harold's Fine Furnishings that he received on 8/16/X3. He demonstrated how he reviewed these and then released them for further processing. He demonstrated that he could not make changes to the customer-initiated merchandise request.*
Pro-c	Made inquiries of others	X		*We discussed with the co-CEO her role in reviewing the suspense file.*
Pro-d	Performed other procedures	X		*We asked Gregg about the typical circumstances that would result in an order being placed in suspense. The most common reason is that the company has stocked out of the item requested and it is on back order. The other main reason is that the terms of the standing purchase order must be changed (for example, due to renegotiated terms). Only Ching (Operations CEO) can make changes to purchase orders in the standing purchasing file, and sometimes there is a delay of several days. If the customer places an order under the new, renegotiated terms, the system will post the order to the suspense account. We reviewed a printout of the suspense file on 8/31 and discussed it with Gregg. He showed us how the file was consistent with the previously mentioned explanations. We also reviewed a history of suspense items for the year and found no unusual items or exceptions.*

Young Fashions
Wholesale Sales
Walkthrough Worksheet #3

Prepared by: *mtn*   Date Prepared: *1/06/X5*

The following documents the procedures performed, information gathered, and conclusions reached relating to walkthroughs of major transactions.

Planning

Person(s) we interviewed

> *Harrison Hargrove, Distribution Director*
> *Junior Tatupu, Warehouse Manager, San Diego*
> *TJ Gordon, Warehouse Manager, Philadelphia*

Date of interview

> *8/23/X4(Hargrove)*
> *12/28/X4 (Tatupu and Gordon)*

Description of transaction discussed *Preparation of shipping orders*

Processing step(s) we discussed:

> __ Initiation of transaction
>
> __ Transaction recording
>
> **X** Transaction processing steps
>
> __ Authorization of transaction
>
> **X** How the incorrect processing of transactions is resolved
>
> __ Process for reconciling detail to the general ledger

Brief description of the company's prescribed processes and controls for the previously mentioned step(s)

Process	Control No.	Control Description	Relevant Assertions
Once the merchandise request is matched to a standing purchase order, the IT system generates a shipping order, which is sent electronically to the appropriate warehouse.	3-Con-a	Sequential shipping orders are assigned and subsequently accounted for. Also see working paper XX-XX for description of IT general and application controls related to the generation of shipping orders.	Completeness
After the warehouse receives the shipping order, they print a hard copy, and the goods are picked, counted, packed, and shipped.	3-Con-b	Unfulfilled shipping orders remain in a suspense account. Usually, these items relate to goods that the inventory system showed as being on-hand but were unable to be located. Once the right goods are received, the items are shipped. Periodically, the warehouse manager investigates and resolves items in suspense account.	Completeness
The system automatically logs the shipment and sends a shipping conformation to the customer.	3-Con-c	See working paper XX-xx for discussion of IT general controls related to the generation of the shipping log.	Occurrence Completeness

Identification and Resolution of Processing Errors

Describe how processing errors are identified and resolved.

Unprocessed items are posted to a suspense file and subsequently cleared.

Control No.	Control Description	Assertions
3-Con-d	Segregation is adequate. Warehouse personnel are included only in picking and packing items. IT system prepares shipping orders.	All

Safeguarding of assets. Assess the adequacy of the safeguarding of the assets related to this transaction, if applicable. If safeguarding controls are not adequate, describe compensating controls.

Control No.	Control Description	Assertions
	See working paper XX-X for description of safeguard controls over inventory. [not included]	

Asset accountability. Describe the process and related controls for establishing the accountability for the assets related to this transaction, if applicable. If these controls are not adequate, describe compensating controls.

Control No.	Control Description	Assertions
	Not applicable	

Procedures Performed and Results

We performed the following procedures, as indicated, to corroborate the responses to our inquiries.

All procedures were performed in conjunction with annual physical inventory count, which was performed on 12/31/X4 at both warehouses. Procedures described here were performed on 12/30, the day before warehouse activity ceased for the physical count.

Procedure		Audit Procedure Performed?		
Control No.	Description	Yes	No	Comments
Pro-a	Reviewed original documents	X		*Reviewed hard copies of shipping orders 15596–15604 printed by warehouse.*
Pro-b	Made observations	X		
Pro-c	Made inquiries of others	X		*On 12/30/X4, we made inquiries of Bret Jensen, sales person, and Barry Gregg, sales manager about problems reported by customers relating to delayed or incorrect shipments. They both indicated that these instances were rare and almost always related to items on back order (see walkthrough #2).*
Pro-d	Performed other procedures	X		*Warehouse managers (Tatupu and Gordon) displayed unmatched shipping orders in suspense accounts. These were for orders placed by Grosvenor's and Ford and Mialer. Tatupu and Gordon described the procedures they typically follow to investigate these items and ensure that orders are filled.*

©2016, AICPA

Summary of Identified Risks of Material Misstatement

As a result of the procedures performed as described in this worksheet, we identified the following *risks of material misstatement.*

Ref.	Description of Risk	Assertions	Response to Risk
	None		

Young Fashions
Wholesale Sales
Walkthrough Worksheet #4

Prepared by: *mtn*   Date Prepared: *1/06/X5*

The following documents the procedures performed, information gathered, and conclusions reached relating to walkthroughs of major transactions.

Planning

Person(s) we interviewed

> *Harrison Hargrove, Distribution Director*
> *Junior Tatupu, Warehouse Manager, San Diego*
> *TJ Gordon, Warehouse Manager, Philadelphia*

Date of interview

> *8/23/X4 (Hargrove)*
> *12/28/X4 (Tatupu and Gordon)*

Description of transaction discussed *Packing of merchandise and preparation of packing slip*

Processing step(s) we discussed:

__ Initiation of transaction

__ Transaction recording

X Transaction processing steps

__ Authorization of transaction

__ How the incorrect processing of transactions is resolved

__ Process for reconciling detail to the general ledger

Brief description of the company's prescribed processes and controls for the previously mentioned step(s)

Process	Control No.	Control Description	Relevant Assertions
Once the shipment is packed, warehouse personnel use the shipping orders to note any differences between what was ordered and what was actually shipped. The warehouse supervisor then enters actual shipping information (including any changes from original shipping orders) into the system.	4-Con-a	The warehouse supervisor reviews the shipping orders and makes inquiries about any shipments that were not able to be filled in their entirety.	Accuracy
The system automatically generates the packing slip included in the shipment to customers and dates the shipments. The system generates an e-mail message to the customer confirming the shipment.	4-Con-b	See working paper XX-XX for discussion of IT general and application controls related to shipping and order fulfillment.	Occurrence Accuracy

Identification and Resolution of Processing Errors

Describe how processing errors are identified and resolved.

_N/A_

Segregation of duties. Assess the adequacy of the segregation of duties for the prescribed processes and controls, as described. If segregation of duties is not adequate, describe compensating controls.

Control No.	Control Description	Assertions
4-Con-c	Segregation of duties may be circumvented at times. Warehouse supervisor has the responsibility for preparing packing slips, but per discussion with employees, sometimes the individual who packed the items will enter the information needed to prepare the packing.	Accuracy Occurrence

Safeguarding of assets. Assess the adequacy of the safeguarding of the assets related to this transaction, if applicable. If safeguarding controls are not adequate, describe compensating controls.

Control No.	Control Description	Assertions
	See working paper XX-X for description of safeguarding controls over inventory. [not included]	

Asset accountability. Describe the process and related controls for establishing the accountability for the assets related to this transaction, if applicable. If these controls are not adequate, describe compensating controls.

Control No.	Control Description	Assertions
	Not applicable	

Procedures Performed and Results

We performed the following procedures, as indicated, to corroborate the responses to our inquiries.

	Procedure	Audit Procedure Performed?		
Control No.	Description	Yes	No	Comments
Pro-a	Reviewed original documents	X		On 12/30/X4, we reviewed a marked-up sample of shipping orders used by warehouse personnel to prepare shipments. The shipping orders reviewed were numbers 15679, 15680, and 15682. Note: order 15681 was unfilled and we noted it in the suspense account.
Pro-b	Made observations	X		On 12/30/X4, prior to shutting down the warehouse for the physical count we observed warehouse personnel using shipping orders to prepare shipments. We noted that personnel compared items picked to those listed on the printed shipping orders.
Pro-c	Made inquiries of others	X		See walkthrough #3 for description of inquiries made of Jensen and Gregg.
Pro-d	Performed other procedures		X	

Young Fashions
Wholesale Sales
Walkthrough Step #5

Prepared by: *mtn*   Date Prepared: *1/06/X5*

The following documents the procedures performed, information gathered, and conclusions reached relating to walkthroughs of major transactions.

Planning

Person(s) we interviewed

> *Harrison Hargrove, Distribution Director*
> *Junior Tatupu, Warehouse Manager, San Diego*
> *TJ Gordon, Warehouse Manager, Philadelphia*

Date of interview

> *8/23/X4 (Hargrove)*
> *12/28/X4 (Tatupu and Gordon)*

Description of transaction discussed *Preparation of sales invoices to wholesale customers*

Processing step(s) we discussed:

__ Initiation of transaction

__ Transaction recording

X Transaction processing steps

__ Authorization of transaction

__ How the incorrect processing of transactions is resolved

__ Process for reconciling detail to the general ledger

Brief description of the company's prescribed processes and controls for the previously mentioned step(s)

Process	Control No.	Control Description	Relevant Assertions
All controls relating to the preparation of invoices are information technology controls. The computer multiples the quantities shipped per the packing slip by the prices to be charged per the standing purchase order. The system then generates an invoice that is sent to customers.		See working paper XX-XX for discussion of IT general controls related to billing.	Accuracy Occurrence Completeness
	5-Con-a	Errors in billing are reported by customers to and investigated by accounting department personnel.	Accuracy Occurrence Completeness
	5-Con-b	At the end of the season, customers submit billing corrections (chargebacks). Material items are reviewed and investigated by accounting personnel and sales rep.	Accuracy Occurrence Completeness
	5-Con-c	IT director also may identify billing errors related to incorrect pricing in standing purchase order file. All errors identified in this fashion are reported to accounting.	Accuracy Occurrence Completeness

Identification and Resolution of Processing Errors

Describe how processing errors are identified and resolved.

See table previously mentioned.

Segregation of duties. Assess the adequacy of the segregation of duties for the prescribed processes and controls, as described. If segregation of duties is not adequate, describe compensating controls.

Control No.	Control Description	Assertions
	Segregation is not adequate, as most controls are IT controls. The IT manager has complete control of the IT system. In addition, the access and security controls were inadequate for the first nine months of the year.	

Safeguarding of assets. Assess the adequacy of the safeguarding of the assets related to this transaction, if applicable. If safeguarding controls are not adequate, describe compensating controls.

Control No.	Control Description	Assertions
	Not applicable	

Asset accountability. Describe the process and related controls for establishing the accountability for the assets related to this transaction, if applicable. If these controls are not adequate, describe compensating controls.

Control No.	Control Description	Assertions
	Not applicable	

Procedures Performed and Results

We performed the following procedures, as indicated, to corroborate the responses to our inquiries.

Procedure		Audit Procedure Performed?		Comments
Control No.	Description	Yes	No	
Pro-a	Reviewed original documents	X		*Reviewed copies of August 15 invoices sent to: Bernard's Mandelbaum's, Harold's Fine Furnishings, and Sonia's and compared with shipping information and standard price.*
Pro-b	Made observations		X	
Pro-c	Made inquiries of others	X		*On 10/05/X4 we spoke to Jenny Hershberger, accounting clerk about billing errors reported by customers. These may either be pricing errors or merchandise not meeting the store's quality standards.*
				She stated that at the end of the season, customers prepared a "chargeback schedule" of billing errors and markdowns for which they were entitled to receive a credit. We reviewed chargeback schedules for Newman-Machlin and Grosvenor's relating to the spring/summer X4 season, which closed on 9/15/X4. These had been approved by Ching and were considered reasonable.
				We discussed with the sales manager and co-CEO their procedures for the review of chargebacks from major customers.
Pro-d	Performed other procedures	X		*See W/P XX-X [not included] for additional audit procedures performed relating to chargebacks and credits to customers.*

Young Fashions
Wholesale Sales
Walkthrough Worksheet #6

Prepared by: *BT*   Date Prepared: *8/17/X4*

The following documents the procedures performed, information gathered, and conclusions reached relating to walkthroughs of major transactions.

Planning

Person(s) we interviewed

> *Barry Gregg, Sales Manager*
> *Jane Young Ching, co-CEO*

Date of interview *8/15/X4*

Description of transaction discussed *Posting sales transactions to general ledger*

Processing step(s) we discussed:

__ Initiation of transaction

__ Transaction recording

X Transaction processing steps

__ Authorization of transaction

X How the incorrect processing of transactions is resolved

X Process for reconciling detail to the general ledger

Brief description of the company's prescribed processes and controls for the previously mentioned step(s)

Process	Control No.	Control Description	Relevant Assertions
Sales transactions are captured on a real-time basis and then transmitted to the financial reporting system for month-end processing.	6-Con-a	Accounting department reconciles accounts receivable detail to general ledger control totals.	Accuracy Occurrence Completeness
	6-Con-b	Each quarter, both the sales manager and the operations CEO receive a detailed sales package of numerous individual reports, including: sales by customer and comparison to budget (based on standing purchase orders), suspense account items, back orders, projected sales by customer for the next quarter. At the end of the season the package includes a summary of end-of-season markdowns and chargebacks. The sales manager and CEO review this package to identify anomalies that indicate possible errors or fraud. When chargebacks are entered into the system, sales commissions are adjusted to recover the commission on the sale, so sales personnel have an incentive to challenge incorrect chargebacks.	Accuracy Occurrence Completeness
	6-Con-c	Sales personnel receive monthly sales and commission reports, which they review primarily to identify missing sales, back orders, or other items for which they have not been credited.	Accuracy Occurrence Completeness

Identification and Resolution of Processing Errors

Describe how processing errors are identified and resolved.

N/A

Segregation of duties. Assess the adequacy of the segregation of duties for the prescribed processes and controls, as described. If segregation of duties is not adequate, describe compensating controls.

Control No.	Control Description	Assertions
	Segregation is adequate. Individuals responsible for performing the control activities are not responsible for initiating or recording the transactions.	

Safeguarding of assets. Assess the adequacy of the safeguarding of the assets related to this transaction, if applicable. If safeguarding controls are not adequate, describe compensating controls.

Control No.	Control Description	Assertions
	Not applicable	

Asset accountability. Describe the process and related controls for establishing the accountability for the assets related to this transaction, if applicable. If these controls are not adequate, describe compensating controls.

Control No.	Control Description	Assertions
	Not applicable	

Procedures Performed and Results

We performed the following procedures, as indicated, to corroborate the responses to our inquiries.

Procedure		Audit Procedure Performed?		
Control No.	Description	Yes	No	Comments
Pro-a	Reviewed original documents	X		Reviewed 2nd quarter sales packages sent to sales manager and operations CEO. Reviewed June X4 reconciliation of accounts receivable to general ledger. Reviewed July X4 sales and commission reports.
Pro-b	Made observations		X	

(continued)

	Procedure	Audit Procedure Performed?		
Control No.	Description	Yes	No	Comments
Pro-c	Made inquiries of others	X		*On 8/24/X4 we spoke with Robert Haner, IT Director, about the source of the information used to generate the sales packages and sales and commissions information. All information for these reports is generated from the wholesale order entry, except for* • *budgeted sales by customer, which is prepared on a spreadsheet by sales manager and input separately into the system, and* • *commission rates, which can vary by sales person, product line, and customer. These rates are maintained in a separate file, which is not documented in these working papers.*
Pro-d	Performed other procedures	X		*Reperformed June and December reconciliation of accounts receivable*

Revenue Recognition Controls Checklist

Indicate where your understanding of the following revenue recognition controls are documented.

	Reference
1. Controls over policies and procedures for:	
• Receiving and accepting orders	*Walkthrough 1*
• Extending credit	*Walkthrough 1*
• Shipping goods	*Walkthrough 4*
• Relieving inventory	*Inventory w/p [not included]*
• Billing and recording sales transactions	*Walkthrough 5*
• Receiving and recording sales returns	*Returns w/p [not included]*
• Authorizing and issuing credit memos (including markdowns)	*Returns w/p [not included]*

	Reference
2. Controls and procedures for determining the proper cutoff of sales at the end of the accounting period	*See additional comments below.*
3. The computer applications and key documents used during the processing of revenue transactions	*Walkthrough 1, 2, 3, 4*
4. The methods used by management to monitor its sales contracts, including	
• the company's policy about management or other personnel who are authorized to approve nonstandard contract clauses.	*Walkthrough 1*
• whether those personnel understand the accounting implications of changes to contractual clauses.	*See additional comments below.*
• whether the entity enforces its policies regarding negotiation and approval of sales contracts and investigates exceptions.	*Walkthrough 1*

Additional Comments

The company has not implemented preventive controls that function throughout the period. Rather, Young Fashions relies on controls in place during the physical inventory count to ensure proper cut-off at year-end. Thus, the company takes its physical at year end. Cut-off is not a major risk because of the point in the cycle in this seasonal business. The review and reconciliation procedures described in walkthrough 6 also would help to identify misstatements caused by improper cut-off.

Existing policies and procedures would be effective at detecting the accounting implications of some changes to contractual clauses such as changes to prices. However, other contractual changes, such as changes in shipping terms or rights of return, may not always be communicated from legal (who approves the change) to accounting. This condition is a control deficiency, which is included in working paper X-XX for evaluation and discussion of additional procedures. See working paper X-XX for additional procedures performed to address the risks of misstatement that may result from this control deficiency.

Part II—Evaluation of Control Design

Observations and Suggestions

The matrix layout of this example documentation is consistent with the documentation requirements described in the guide.

- Reading left to right, an evaluation of control design begins with understanding the entity's control objectives. In this example, these objectives are portrayed as being "prepopulated" in the form. That is, the auditor's methodology includes these example control objectives for all audits. However, the auditor is reminded that these control objectives are examples only, and they should be expanded and tailored to meet the unique facts and circumstances of specific entities. In this example, the auditor of Young Fashions has modified several of these example control objectives, for example in the section titled "integrity and ethical values."

- The second column of the matrix describes the risks to the entity if the control objective is not met. This column will help the auditor design appropriate further audit procedures if he or she determines that certain control objectives are not met. Again, the auditor's audit methodology illustrated here includes examples, which the auditor might modify as appropriate.

- You should document the procedures performed to gather information about internal control and the source of that information. Columns 3 and 4 of the matrix provide a cross-reference to that documentation, which was the documentation of the auditor's walkthrough of internal controls.

- In the fifth column, the auditor may document his or her understanding of the control features that have been implemented at the client to address the stated control objective.

- By comparing the control features to the control objectives, the auditor would then determine whether the design of control, either individually or in combination with other controls, is capable of effectively preventing or detecting and correcting material misstatements. In the sixth column of the matrix, the auditor can document the conclusion about control design.

Order Processing

Control Objective	Risk of Failing to Achieve Objective	Reference Walk-through	Reference Control Number	Control Activity	Effectiveness
Only process valid sales orders (existence)	Duplicate sales orders are processed.			Merchandise request is processed by IT system. Quarterly reviews by sales manager and operations CEO	With effective IT general controls the IT system will not process merchandise requests more than once. Effective in design and implementation. However, identified ITGC deficiencies will limit reliance on any automated aspect …
	Unauthorized sales are processed.	2 2	2-Con-e 2-Con-d 2-Con-d 2-Con-e	Merchandise request is submitted by customer, who must have a valid password to submit order. Merchandise requests are compared to standing purchase orders.	Effective in design and implementation. However, identified ITGC deficiencies will limit reliance on any automated aspect …
	Orders are accepted at unauthorized prices or terms unacceptable to management.	1 2	1-Con-a 1-Con-b 2-Con-d 2-Con-d 2-Con-e	Standing purchase orders approved by operations CEO. Standard purchase order contracts used. Merchandise request are compared to standing purchase orders.	Effective in design and implementation. However, identified ITGC deficiencies will limit reliance on any automated aspect … **[Note to the reader; this response is hereinafter noted as "Effective …"]**
	Large, unusual or related party orders are fulfilled.	2	2-Con-d 2-Con-d 2-Con-e	Merchandise request are compared to standing purchase orders. Processing cannot continue without valid purchase order.	Effective …

(continued)

Control Objective	Risk of Failing to Achieve Objective	Reference			Control Activity	Effectiveness
		Walk-through	Control Number			
	Unacceptable customers are added to the customer list.	1	1-Con-a		Operations CEO approves all standing purchase orders.	Effective ...
	Customer list is inaccurate or incomplete.	1 / 2 / 2	1-Con-c / 2-Con-b / 2-Con-d / 2-Con-e		IT input controls verify information on standing purchase orders. If a valid customer submitted a merchandise request for which there was no purchase order, (that is, incomplete standing purchase order file), the merchandise request would be posted to suspense account for further follow up. CEO and sales manager review suspense account items.	Effective ...
	Order processing procedures are implemented that circumvent existing internal control techniques.	2	2-Con-a		Merchandise requests can only be submitted electronically, greatly reducing the likelihood that other processing procedures could be implemented manually. (walkthrough 2)	Effective in design and implementation. However, identified ITGC deficiencies will limit reliance on any automated aspect.
	Transactions authorized by inappropriate personnel.	1	Con-a		Only CEO can approve purchase orders.	Effective ...

Control Objective	Risk of Failing to Achieve Objective	Reference		Control Activity	Effectiveness
		Walk-through	Control Number		
Process all valid sales orders (completeness)	Back orders are not fulfilled.	3 6	3-Con-b 6-Con-b	Backordered items are placed in a suspense file for review and follow up by sales manager. Operations CEO reviews backordered items quarterly.	Partially effective. There is no automated system for filling backorders, which are processed by sales manager or on an ad hoc basis. Risk is that sales manager could fail to process back orders in a timely manner. If this were to occur, the error would not affect the balance sheet or income statement (since no sale has occurred until the order is processed and shipped). However, at the end of the season backlog is reset to zero since the company will not manufacture out of season goods. The risks associated with this design deficiency are operational, not financial. See audit plan step xx-xx. ITGC deficiencies will limit reliance on any automated aspect …
	Orders are not recorded properly.	2	2-Con-a	Orders are recorded automatically upon submission of a merchandise request by the customer.	Only design and implementation considered as effective. ITGC deficiencies limit reliance.

(continued)

Control Objective	Risk of Failing to Achieve Objective	Reference			Control Activity	Effectiveness
		Walk-through	Control Number			
Distribution						
Ship the proper goods that were ordered and accurately record the shipment (accuracy)	Incorrect items are included or substituted in the order.	3	3-Con-b		Warehouse personnel use hardcopy of shipping order to pick and pack order.	Partially effective. Use of shipping orders helps ensure that correct items are included in shipment. However, this control does not address the inappropriate substitution of an order. The physical inventory count and review of credit activity in subsequent periods may catch some errors that could result from those errors that were more than inconsequential could go undetected. See part III for further consideration of this matter. ITGC deficiencies will limit reliance on any automated aspect …
Record sales in the proper period (cut-off)	Deliveries are recorded prematurely or in the incorrect period.	XX 6 6	XXX 6-Con-b 6-Con-a		The seasonal nature of the business makes this a low risk. Year-end physical inventory instructions also help provide proper cut-off. See inventory working papers. [not included] CEO, sales manager and salesperson review sales activity during period. (walkthrough 6) Accounts receivable trial balance is reconciled to general ledger account total. (walkthrough 6)	Controls are largely detective in nature, which reduces their effectiveness, but are adequate given the risk. See part III for further consideration of this matter. However, identified ITGC deficiencies will limit reliance on any automated aspect …

Control Objective	Risk of Failing to Achieve Objective	Reference		Control Activity	Effectiveness
		Walk-through	Control Number		
Input all shipments for further processing (accuracy, completeness)	Shipping orders are incomplete or missing.	3	3-Con-a	Shipping orders are numbered sequentially and accounted for. (walkthrough 3)	Effective …
		3	3-Con-b	Unfulfilled shipping orders are posted to a suspense account for further follow up by warehouse manager. (walkthrough 3)	
Properly post transactions to the accounting records (accuracy)	Human error in coding or entry.	6	6-Con-a	All postings are done automatically.	Effective, with the proper functioning of IT general controls. However, identified ITGC deficiencies will limit reliance on any automated aspect …
	Inappropriate access to delivery systems.	4	4-Con-c	Warehouse personnel may access delivery system due to lack of physical access.	See part III.
	Inadequate segregation of duties.	4	4-Con-c	Not adequate, as warehouse personnel can make changes to items shipped and then access the system.	This is considered a control deficiency. Further comments below. See part III for additional audit procedures performed to address the risk.

(continued)

Control Objective	Risk of Failing to Achieve Objective	Reference			Control Activity	Effectiveness
		Walk-through	Control Number			
Invoicing						
Sales are recorded in the appropriate period. (cut-off)	Revenue is recognized prematurely or inappropriately deferred until a later accounting period.	5	5-Con-a		Invoices are prepared automatically when goods are shipped.	Effective in design and implementation. However, identified ITGC deficiencies will limit reliance on any automated aspect.... However, see comments relating lack of communication between legal and accounting relating to changes in standard contract terms, which may affect timing of revenue recognition.
The price of goods and quantity shipped are invoiced accurately. (accuracy)	Formulae used for calculating invoice amounts and accounts receivables entries are inaccurate.	5	5-Con-a		IT application has been coded with the proper formulas.	Effectiveness depends on IT general controls. However, identified ITGC deficiencies will limit reliance on any automated aspect ...
	Selling price is inaccurate.	5	5-Con-a		Invoice is prepared from standing purchase orders.	Partially effective. Changes to standing purchase orders made from the time the client submits a merchandise request until the order is shipped may not be reflected in the invoice. See comments in returns and credits working papers XX-X. However, identified ITGC deficiencies will also limit reliance on any automated aspect ...
	Inaccurate price lists are used.	5	5-Con-a		Same as previously mentioned	

Control Objective	Risk of Failing to Achieve Objective	Reference		Control Activity	Effectiveness
		Walk-through	Control Number		
	Customer complaints regarding inaccurate bills are not investigated or monitored.	5	5-Con-a 5-Con-b	Customers report billing errors as part of end-of-season chargebacks.	Effective …
Generate a sales invoice for every shipment (completeness of sales)	Invoices are not sent out properly.	5	5-Con-a	Invoices are prepared and sent automatically. (walkthrough 5)	Effective …
Information Technology					
Generate a sales invoice for every shipment (completeness of sales)	Order data is not transferred completely from the order entry subsystem to the invoicing subsystem.	5	5-Con-a	Order entry and invoicing are integrated.	Effective …
Prepare invoice using authorized terms and prices (accuracy)	Data input into the invoicing system inaccurate compared to the order entry system.	1	1-Con-c	Order entry and invoicing are integrated. IT input edit checks verify key information.	Effective …
	Human error causes changes to standing data (master files) to be incompletely and inaccurately inputted.	1	1-Con-c	Order entry and invoicing are integrated. IT input edit checks verify key information.	Effective …

(continued)

Control Objective	Risk of Failing to Achieve Objective	Reference		Control Activity	Effectiveness
		Walk-through	Control Number		
	Periodic updates for batch processing are improperly executed.	N/A	N/A	Online – real-time order management system (maintained on server) and batch updates to financial management system (on AS400) are integrated.	n/a
	Inappropriate access to customer and price information and lack of segregation leads to inappropriate employee behavior.	N/A	N/A	See comments relating to access and security in IT general controls review.	Effective ...
	The process for approving changes standing customer information, account codes, and credit limits is insufficient.	1	1-Con-a	CEO is only person with access to standing purchase orders.	Effective ...
All changes to standing data are completely and accurately input. (security, access, accuracy)	The process for approving changes price lists approved is insufficient and leads to a price list that is not aligned with management's strategy or the entity's cost basis.	1	1-Con-a	CEO is only person with access to standing purchase orders. (walkthrough 1)	Effective ...

Part III—Summary of Control Deficiencies and Risk of Material Misstatement

Effectiveness of the design of implemented controls. Based on our understanding of the control policies and procedures that have been implemented, we have determined that these policies and procedures are capable of achieving the stated control objectives, *except for the following matters, which we consider to be deficiencies in the design of controls.*

	Control Deficiency				Assertion-Level Risks		
Ref.	No.	Description	Affects Risk of Misstatement?	Fin Stmt Risk?	Acct. Trans or Disclosure	Assertion(s)	Ref.
Walk-through #1 Pro-c	1	Communication of changes to standard contracts between legal and accounting is not reliable, which creates the risk that sales could be recorded at wrong amounts or in the incorrect period.	Yes	No	Revenue Receivables	Occurrence Existence/ Valuation	w/p XX-x
Walk-through #4 4-Con-c	2	Warehouse personnel have the ability to make shipments that vary from customer order and then access the system to record the changes.	Yes	No	Revenue Receivables Inventory	Occurrence Existence Accuracy	w/p XX-x
Walk-through #6 Pro-c	3	Use of spreadsheets to determine budgeted sales may contain inaccuracies that may reduce the effectiveness of management's monitoring.	Yes	Yes	N/A	N/A	N/A
Walk-through #6 Pro-c	4	Spreadsheets are used to calculate sales commissions. Because of general lack of controls over spreadsheets, the calculation of commissions may be incorrect.	Yes	No	Compensation	Accuracy	w/p XX-x

Response to Ineffective Design or Implementation

See W/P XX-x, [Appendix K-5] "Assessing Risks of Material Misstatement and Linkage to Further Audit Procedures," for documentation regarding the consideration of the risk of material misstatement at the financial statement level and the corresponding overall audit response.

All control deficiencies have been carried forward to the W/P XX-x, [not included] "Summary of Control Deficiencies," for further evaluation of the severity of the noted deficiency, both individually and in the aggregate.

Observations and Suggestions

- This evaluation matrix supports the auditor's evaluation about the effectiveness of the design of the controls over this transaction. The matrix starts with financial statement assertions and describes the risks of "what could go wrong" relating to those assertions. The controls that were identified in part I of the form are then described and the auditor makes an assessment of the design of the controls.

  Absent this exercise of evaluating controls on a risk-by-risk basis for each assertion, it would be difficult to support a conclusion about the design of the controls.

- Overall, the system seems to be designed effectively for the last three months, but not for the prior nine months (due to weaknesses in security and access controls). Note that many of the controls are IT controls. Many of these are preventive in nature, which tend to be more effective than detective controls. Additionally, the significant use of IT controls helps to establish adequate segregation of duties.

- Ultimately, the effectiveness of IT application controls depends on the effectiveness of related IT general controls. Thus, if the auditor were to design further audit procedures for these transactions based on reliance on controls, those IT general controls also would need to be tested.

- In this example, the auditor considered relying to some degree on the client's controls.

  - Unfortunately controls were not effective for the first nine months of the year, so for this period, assurance will be drawn from substantive audit procedures.

  - However, a significant amount of work already has been performed to evaluate the effective design of the controls in the latter part of the year, and the incremental costs of testing operating effectiveness may not be that great. Most of the controls are IT controls, the application of which can be tested only once, provided that IT general controls operated effectively during the period. You may determine it not to be efficient to test controls and rely thereon for only three months of the year.

©2016, AICPA

— The benefits of relying on controls in future periods could be significant. The auditor may be able to design more effective analytical procedures for revenue. With knowledge of and reliance on the system, the auditor could use computer assisted auditing techniques (CAATs) data extraction and other CAATs to perform many substantive procedures. Sample sizes, for example relating to revenues or accounts receivable confirmation or inventory test items, also could be reduced.

Appendix K-5

Young Fashions: Assessing Risks of Material Misstatement and Linkage to Further Audit Procedures

This appendix is nonauthoritative and is included for informational purposes only.

Observations and Suggestions

While performing risk assessment and other procedures, you may identify *risks of material misstatement*. You should then assess these risks at both the financial statement and the relevant assertion level. As stated in paragraph 5.68 of this guide, you should document these assessments of risk. This appendix illustrates one example of how you might prepare that documentation.

Appendixes K-1, K-2, K-3, and K-4 provide example documentation of the risk assessment procedures performed to gain an understanding of the client and its environment, including internal control. In these examples, the auditor identified conditions that indicate a *risk of material misstatement*, which were summarized in the last part of each appendix. Those conditions have been carried forward to this appendix so they can be assessed.

Carrying forward identified risks to a central worksheet such as the one included in this example will help the auditor assimilate risks that have been identified in different areas. For example, the auditor of Young Fashions observed that senior management does not actively supervise and monitor the IT department. On its own, that condition may be considered an isolated condition that would warrant only a narrow response. However, when aggregated with other, related conditions, the auditor may determine that a more robust response was necessary.

This example also includes references to risks of material misstatement due to fraud, which the auditor may identify as part of performing risk assessment and other procedures.

Once the *risks of material misstatement* are assessed, you should design an appropriate audit response. Your response to financial statement level risks will be different from your response to relevant assertion level risks. This appendix provides a summary of the auditor's response and then a cross reference to the working paper or audit program step where the auditor performed and documented the procedures that have been summarized in this appendix.

Determining whether a risk is a "*significant risk*" that requires special audit consideration is an important part of the auditors risk assessment process, and this appendix illustrates how you might document your determination of whether a risk is "significant."

Paragraphs 5.36–.37 of this guide provide guidance on determining significant risks at the financial statement and relevant assertion levels.

The *primary objective of this example* is to illustrate the documentation of the linkage between assessed risk and the design of further audit procedures. In

©2016, AICPA

reviewing this example, consider the summary of the audit approach and how the described approach is responsive to the assessed risk.

All information that appears in this font style illustrates information completed by the auditor.

Instructions for Preparation

This form documents your assessment of the *risks of material misstatement* that you have identified through the performance of risk assessment and other audit procedures. Your assessment should be performed at both the financial statement level and at the relevant assertion level for significant transactions and material accounts or disclosures.

This form also documents your determination of whether an identified risk constitutes a *significant risk* that requires further audit consideration.

You may then summarize your planned audit response to each identified risk. It is common for a single planned response to address more than one risk. The purpose of providing a summary of the planned audit responses is to establish a clearly defined link between the assessed risk of material misstatement and the auditors response. Audit working papers can be linked electronically or through cross references (with an explanation of the purpose and meaning of the linkage for clarity).

The summarized planned response could then be cross-referenced to the working paper or audit program steps where you provide more detailed documentation of the procedures performed, the results of those procedures, and your conclusion.

Financial Statement Level Risks

Observations and Suggestions

This section of the appendix summarizes the financial statement level *risks of material misstatement* identified as a result of performing risk assessment and other procedures. To the extent possible, financial statement level risks should be related to what can go wrong at the relevant assertion level. The risks summarized here are those that could not be related to a specific assertion or small group of assertions. These types of financial statement level risks require overall audit responses which, for this example, have been summarized in the table presented.

It is common for a single audit response to address several risks of material misstatement. For example, the auditor of Young Fashions has grouped all risks related to IT general controls, because they all are addressed by the work performed by the IT specialist.

The final column of the table, "Ref.," should be a reference to the working papers that describe in more detail the auditors overall response. These working papers have not been included in this example.

All information that appears in this font style illustrates information completed by the auditor.

(continued)

Ref. W/P	Ref. Risk No.	Description of the Condition	Risk Caused by the Condition	Significant Risk?	Summary of Response	Ref.
X-2 X-3	3 6	Key officers do not actively participate in the supervision or monitoring of IT. Lack of active supervision is considered a fraud risk factor that could provide an opportunity for fraudulent financial reporting. [principle 16]	IT system may not provide the data needed by users to perform accounting or internal control functions. [principle 13 and principle 14]	No	Our engagement team includes an IT specialist whose responsibilities include • gathering additional information related to these matters. • identifying and assessing risks of material misstatement. • identifying and assessing the severity of IT control deficiencies. • advising the team on developing an appropriate audit response to the assessed risks, including the design of further audit procedures. Based on our assessment, we will not be able to rely this year on IT general controls for the first nine months of the year; however, there do not appear to be any misstatements or failures of application controls as a result of these deficiencies.	w/p XX-x
X-2	4	Company growth periodically stretches accounting, IT and operational resources [principle 3 and principle 4]	Financial and nonfinancial information may not be processed accurately or in a timely fashion.	No		
X-3	6	Lack of controls over the development of spreadsheets used to process financial information. [principle 12]	Spreadsheets currently in use may process information inaccurately. New spreadsheets may be developed and used in other areas, creating the risk of error in those information streams.	No		
X-3	7	Deficiency of logical access controls over data and applications during first nine months of the year. [principle 11]	Financial data may have been changed inappropriately.	No		
X-3	8	Network server was located in an unsecure location during most of the year. [principle 11]	Financial data or logical access controls may have been compromised.	No		

Ref.					Ref.
W/P	Risk No.	Description of the Condition	Risk Caused by the Condition	Significant Risk?	Summary of Response
X-2	2	No formal controls over bonus arrangements, which is a fraud risk factor. The CEOs decide on the bonus amounts and distributions without formal policies. [principle 8]	Bonus arrangements may create an incentive/motivation for fraud by employees affected by the bonus arrangements	No	During the audit team brainstorming session, we emphasized the need to maintain professional skepticism when gathering information and evaluating audit evidence, particularly with regard to the reliance on information provided by the clients system that may be used to perform analytical procedures, especially during the period that IT general controls were not effective. More experienced audit team members performed key walkthroughs and made inquiries relating to fraud.	w/p XX-x
X-2	5	Informal understanding of all the information needed to perform financial reporting functions. Software is limited in its ability to keep pace with functional business requirements. [principle 13 and principle 14]	Company may not capture all information needed to prepare financial statements.	No		
X-2	6	Managements monitoring of internal control is only partially adequate, as it is based on a review of financial results and not on the design and operating effectiveness of internal control [principle 16]	Deficiencies in the design of internal control may not be identified or remediated on a timely basis, creating an opportunity for fraud if the deficiency is severe.	No		
X-2	7	Misstatements result in a correction of the accounting records but not always a consideration of underlying control deficiencies that caused the misstatement [principle 5 and principle 17]				

Relevant Assertion Level Risks

Observations and Suggestions

This section of the appendix summarizes the relevant assertion level risks that were identified as a result of performing risk assessment and other procedures. These risks have been carried forward from appendixes K-1, K-2, K-3, and K-4.

This case study focuses only on revenue, and so this worksheet includes only the risks that relate to revenue. In practice, the table presented would include *risks of material misstatement* that were identified for other significant transactions and material accounts and disclosures.

Each transaction, account or disclosure area is divided into two sections:

- *Overall risks.* There are nonspecific risks related to each assertion for the main transactions related to the account. For this example, the major transactions for revenue are gross sales and end-of-season markdowns and chargebacks.

- *Specifically identified risks.* These are the specific risks of material misstatement identified as a result of performing the risk assessment procedures.

In this example, the auditor has assessed the individual components of the *risk of material misstatement*, inherent risk, and control risk as well as a combined risk of material misstatement.

In the following example, other documentation provides support for the "high, moderate, or low" assessments. Such assessments without support would be inadequate for directing the nature, timing, and extent of other audit procedures.

The final column of the table, "Ref.," should be a reference to the working papers that describe in more detail the auditors overall response. These working papers have not been included in this example.

At the assertion level, the auditor should determine whether any of the risks of material misstatement are considered *significant risks*.

All information that appears in this font style illustrates information completed by the auditor.

| Ref. | | | | | Assessed Risk of Material Misstatement (see XXX explaining the basis for these determinations) | | | | Ref. |
W/P	Item No.	Description of Risk	Significant Risk?	Relevant Assertion(s)	Inherent	Control	Combined Risk of Material Misstatement	Summary of Audit Approach	Audit Program Step
Revenue									
Overall Risks									
		Gross receivables and gross sales	No	Existence / Occurrence	Moderate	High	Moderate	• Confirm receivables by PPS sample at 12/31. Ask about any disputes over invoices and compare to internal files to confirm accuracy of company records provided. — Perform limited sales cut-off tests — Be alert to sales existence issues related to sales from 1st 9 months re confirmations or allowances or write-off procedures.	
				Completeness	Moderate	High	Moderate		
				Accuracy	Moderate	High	Moderate		
				Cut-off	Low	High	Low		
		End-of-season markdowns and charge-backs	See below	Existence	Low[1]	High	Moderate	• Use computer assisted audit techniques (CAATs) data extraction to perform detailed substantive analytical procedures • Analysis of customer inventory levels • Analysis of historical end-of-season markdowns and chargebacks by product line and customer. • Confirmation with significant customers	
				Completeness	Low	High	Moderate		
				Accuracy	Moderate	High	Moderate		
				Cut-off	Low	High	Low[2]		

[1] Although inherent risk may be low, consideration may also be given to the likelihood and magnitude of misstatement when reaching an assessment of RMM. RMM is a judgment based on the facts and circumstances.

[2] The low exposure at year end due to closing the business around year end for an extended holiday was considered in reaching this conclusion and was documented. See Brainstorming Session documentation.

Ref.		Description of Risk	Significant Risk?	Relevant Assertion(s)	Assessed Risk of Material Misstatement (see XXX explaining the basis for these determinations)			Summary of Audit Approach	Ref.
W/P	Item No.				Inherent	Control	Combined Risk of Material Misstatement		Audit Program Step
Specifically Identified Risks									
X-1	1	**Inherent Risk Considerations** General downward pressure on prices and end-of season markdowns may result in over- or under-reporting sales and receivables due to a poor estimate of markdowns owed to customers. Markdowns are a significant estimate, which provides an opportunity for fraudulent financial reporting.	Yes	Accuracy Valuation	High	High	High	The customers inventory levels at the end of the season are a significant factor underlying estimated markdowns. Lack of availability of this information for new accessories line will make it difficult to make the estimate. Our audit approach is based on evaluating the reasonableness of the information used by management to make its estimate of markdowns on accessories. Audit procedures include obtaining confirmation of inventory levels from major customers, performing analytical procedures by customer and product, an analysis of post balance sheet sales of accessories by major customers, comparison of goods shipped to goods ordered and inquiries of sales reps for significant customers. As a significant risk, detailed substantive procedures will provide most of the audit evidence.	xx-x

(continued)

Ref.		Description of Risk	Significant Risk?	Relevant Assertion(s)	Assessed Risk of Material Misstatement (see XXX explaining the basis for these determinations)				Summary of Audit Approach	Ref.
					Inherent	Control	Combined Risk of Material Misstatement			Audit Program Step
WIP	Item No.									
X-1	3	**Control Risk Considerations** *Lack of integration of new accessories line with inventory management system has resulted in a lack of information about inventory of accessories held by customers. Lack of information, together with lack of historical data about markdowns of this new product may result in the inability to make a reliable estimate of markdowns for this line. [principle 11 and principle 12]*	Yes	Accuracy Valuation	High	High	High			

					Assessed Risk of Material Misstatement (see XXX explaining the basis for these determinations)				
Ref.									Ref.
WIP	Item No.	Description of Risk	Significant Risk?	Relevant Assertion(s)	Inherent	Control	Combined Risk of Material Misstatement	Summary of Audit Approach	Audit Program Step
XX		**Inherent Risk Considerations** The company processes a significant volume of sales orders. These transactions are processed electronically, and the proper functioning of the IT system is critical if orders (and ultimately revenue) are to be properly reported. Additionally, there is a presumption in the auditing literature that improper revenue recognition is a potential fraud risk.	No[3]	Accuracy Completeness Cut-off	High	High	High	Our engagement team includes an IT specialist whose responsibilities include • identifying and assessing risks of material misstatement. • identifying and assessing control deficiencies. • advising the team on developing an appropriate audit response to the assessed risks, including the design of further audit procedures, including — develop data extraction application to compare purchase order file pre-implementation to post-implementation file. — examine procedures followed by the company in implementing new system.	

(continued)

[3] The auditor considered and documented elsewhere that there was no specific revenue fraud risk identified for this engagement.

©2016, AICPA

| Ref. | | | | | Assessed Risk of Material Misstatement (see XXX explaining the basis for these determinations) | | | | Ref. |
WIP	Item No.	Description of Risk	Significant Risk?	Relevant Assertion(s)	Inherent	Control	Combined Risk of Material Misstatement	Summary of Audit Approach	Audit Program Step
X-3		**Control Risk Considerations** *During the year, the company installed a new version of its order management system. During upgrade, there was a potential loss or corruption of data that was transferred from old version to new.* [principle 11]	*No*	*Accuracy*	*High*	*High*	*High*		

©2016, AICPA

Ref.		Description of Risk	Significant Risk?	Relevant Assertion(s)	Assessed Risk of Material Misstatement (see XXX explaining the basis for these determinations)			Summary of Audit Approach	Ref. Audit Program Step
WIP	Item No.				Inherent	Control	Combined Risk of Material Misstatement		
XX		*Inherent Risk Considerations* Purchase orders define the terms of sales transactions, which affect revenue recognition.	No	Occurrence	Moderate	High	Moderate	• Read purchase orders for major customers to identify terms that may raise revenue recognition issues. • Confirm significant terms of purchase orders with customers. (Including a review of confirmation addressee to determine that customer individual should be knowledgeable of significant contract terms). • Inquiries of in-house legal counsel, sales reps for significant customers, and accounting	
X-4	1	*Control Risk Considerations* Communication of changes to standard purchase orders between legal and accounting is not reliable, which creates the risk that sales could be recorded at wrong amounts or in the incorrect period. [principle 14]	No	Occurrence					

(continued)

Ref. W/P	Item No.	Description of Risk	Significant Risk?	Relevant Assertion(s)	Assessed Risk of Material Misstatement (see XXX explaining the basis for these determinations)			Summary of Audit Approach	Ref. Audit Program Step
					Inherent	Control	Combined Risk of Material Misstatement		
		Inherent Risk Considerations The company processes a significant number of inventory transactions, and inventory balances are material. The companys inventory is vulnerable to theft.	No	Accuracy	Moderate	High	Moderate	• Physical inventory count will identify differences between inventory records and inventory on hand. • Identify communications from customers indicating inaccurate shipment. Procedures include, inquiries of sales reps, confirmation with customers, review and analysis of end-of-season chargebacks.	
X-4	2	**Control Risk Considerations** Warehouse personnel have the ability to make shipments that vary from customer order and then access the system to record the changes [principle 12]	No	Occurrence Accuracy					

Brainstorming for Fraud and Error Risk

After obtaining the understanding, the partner and engagement team (list attendees and date) brainstormed the risks of error and fraud. Here are the items discussed and the resolution:

Risk	*Discussion*	*Resolution*	*WP Reference/ Plan step*
Management override of controls, especially by IT director or Co-CEOs	*The CO-CEOs and IT director could override controls, mostly to show better financial statements;* *IT director could steal assets and manipulate the records, but he has no access to cash receipts (lock box) or inventory; he can't manipulate checks, since he does not sign checks*	*Exercise skepticism in dealing with Co CEOs (senior or manager to participate in all meetings with Co-CEOs); plan extensive tests of journal entries and estimates.* *Misappropriation of assets not a significant risk.* *No direct evidence of manipulation and cross-monitoring by executives mitigates this risk somewhat.*	*XX*
Bonus system	*Could cause employees to overstate income*	*Review of Bonus Program and annual decision process. Extensive tests of related journal entries and estimates.* *Include analytic procedures and comparisons within and between periods.* *Extensive inventory tests to ensure proper income basis for bonuses.*	*XX*
Lack of IT logical and physical security controls for the first 9 months of the year in a heavily computer-dependent environment	*Anyone could have changed data or formulas, either to misrepresent the financial statements or to cover a misappropriation of assets.*	*CAATs to detect unusual transactions and select sample of other transactions.* *Extensive tests of revenue and expense transactions.* *Be alert in tests to issues relating to automated controls in first nine months and any impact on application controls from the security and access deficiency.*	*XX*

(continued)

Risk	Discussion	Resolution	WP Reference/Plan step
Business risks for the client	Clients new strategies are risky, providing incentive for misstated financial statements; this is countered somewhat by strong balance sheet and earnings	Extensive analytic procedures. Plan review of strategies and financial statements by apparel industry expert.	XX
Estimate for markdowns	Misstatements could be either error or fraud; good controls over routine markdown estimate; problem with accessories	See separate discussion of approach to markdowns.	XX
Inventory in overseas locations and in-transit items	Inventory could be stolen by employees, vendors, manufacturers or others; however, Co-CEOs monitor shrinkage. Ending inventory will be fairly stated if counted, priced and extended correctly as of reporting date. Items could be included on inventory of 2 locations; however, check for transfer shipping near 12/31.	Our correspondent will observe and test inventory at major overseas locations; we will observe the U.S. locations and monitor closely any transfers or goods in transit at inventory date.	XX
Inventory pricing, given changing markets	Misstatements could be either error or fraud; good controls over costing; poor controls over lower of cost or market	Will ask management to correlate items that department stores have difficulty selling with inventory valuation; then will test using CAATs; will extensively test lower of cost or market.	XX
Spreadsheets	Lack controls primarily an error risk rather than a fraud risk	Use IT specialist to extensively test all spreadsheets; test formulas. Recommend a formal process to protect spreadsheets from accidental or deliberate unauthorized changes.	XX

Risk	Discussion	Resolution	WP Reference/ Plan step
Sales and shipping cutoff at year-end	Low risk because few shipments near 12/31 (seasonal business, and company closes for holidays)	Limited procedures needed.	XX
Collect ability of receivables (bad debts)	Low risk because customers strong financially or preapproved credit cards used.	Be alert for changes in risk. Inquire / observe re any new policies or programs of granting credit or accepting new customers with lower credit quality.	XX
Sales occurrence	Low risk in last three months since good controls; see above for IT weaknesses.	Be alert in confirmations and allowances or write-offs to any issues relating to first nine months.	XX

This is a section of the documentation and does not include all items discussed.

Appendix K-6

Young Fashions: Evaluation of Uncorrected Misstatements and Assessment of Control Deficiencies

This appendix is nonauthoritative and is included for informational purposes only.

Observations and Suggestions

Performing substantive procedures may result in your identification of misstatements. These misstatements, except those that are trivial, must be communicated to management. The auditor should request management to correct factual misstatements and to examine further the matters relating to the judgmental and projected misstatements and correct any misstatements identified as a result of that evaluation. The auditor needs to communicate uncorrected misstatements to those charged with governance; these misstatements also are included in the representation letter.

You then must consider the effect of the remaining uncorrected misstatements, both individually and in the aggregate, to determine whether the financial statements are presented fairly in all material respects and whether you have sufficient evidence to support the opinion. Your evaluation of uncorrected misstatements also should include the effect on the current period's financial statements of prior period's uncorrected misstatements.

Misstatements often indicate the existence of a control failure. However, the severity of the deficiency is not limited to the amount of the misstatement, but rather also involves consideration of what "could" result from the control deficiency. AU-C section 265, *Communicating Internal Control Related Matters Identified in an Audit* (AICPA, *Professional Standards*), guides the auditor in assessing deficiency severity and in communicating with management and governance.

Resolution of Matters Identified in This Case Study

In this case study, the auditor identified several risks of material misstatement. Appendixes K-1, K-2, K-3, and K-4 document the auditor's identification of these risks. Appendix K-5 illustrates how the auditor assessed these risks and developed an audit response that was directly related to this assessment. Included in appendix K-5 was a summary of the auditor's planned substantive procedures.

The documentation of those tests and their results are not included in this case study. However, as a result of those tests, the auditor identified several misstatements, which were addressed as follows:

- *Errors in Sales Commission Expense and Accrual at Year End.* Sales commissions are calculated by an accounting clerk using a spreadsheet, outside of the formal accounting system. Because of the lack of controls over spreadsheet development and use, the auditor identified this condition as a *risk of material misstatement.* (See appendix K-4, part III, risk number 4.)

The auditor's substantive procedures identified a miscalculation of sales commissions expense of $84,800. Client management chose not to adjust the amount of commissions because the commission information already had been released to sales personnel. The miscalculation of the sales commissions is not a financial statement misstatement because management has approved a new commission amount independent of the calculation. However, this is a control deficiency of some level of severity.

The auditor also was concerned about whether similar misstatements were made during the year and whether the misstatement was indicative of fraud. He asked his IT specialist to use audit software to check all rates and computations for the year. No additional misstatements were found. Based on discussions with the co-CEOs and these procedures, the auditor concluded this was not indicative of fraud.

- *Accounts payable.* In testing payables the auditor identified errors in the accounts payable to a new supplier based in Spain. (As indicated, in appendix K-1, due to rising costs in Italy, the company sought new suppliers for the J Young Couture line.) Spanish suppliers are paid in euros rather than U.S. dollars, which is the currency for other suppliers. An error in the conversion from U.S. dollars to euros resulted in an over-statement of inventory purchases and cost of sales of $185,000 and an over-statement of accounts payable for the same amount. There were no other transactions with this supplier and all other suppliers are paid in dollars.

- *Markdowns and chargebacks.* The auditor identified significant risks relating to the estimate of end-of-season markdowns and chargebacks. (See appendix K-5.) In general, these risks related to (*a*) a lack of information about inventory levels of certain products held by customers at the end of the season, and (*b*) possible loss or corruption of pricing data when the company upgraded its order management application to a new version.

  Having identified these risks, the auditor asked management to obtain the information necessary to make a reliable estimate of end-of-season markdowns and chargebacks. Client management contacted its ten largest customers, who comprise approximately 80 percent of total nonretail revenue for the year. Management then revised its estimate and corrected their financial statements based on this more reliable information.

  However, management did not obtain information or make any adjustments to its original estimate for its smaller customers. Based on an analysis of the revised information obtained from larger customers, sales volume to the smaller customers, and other factors, the auditor estimated that the company had underestimated its end-of-season markdowns and chargebacks for these customers. It is recognized that smaller customers have different bargaining power than the larger customers and therefore will likely have a lower markdown percentage. The estimated understatement was $245,000. The failure of the company to develop a functional control resulting in the misstatement may constitute a control deficiency of some magnitude.

- *Inventory pricing.* As a result of addressing the assessed inherent and control risks related to inventory pricing, the auditor selected a sample of inventory items and performed tests of details to determine that the pricing was accurate.

  As a result to these tests, the auditor identified several pricing errors. The auditor requested that the client investigate whether there were similar errors in the rest of the population. The client checked a few large items and found no misstatements. The client corrected the financial statements for the (factual) known errors, but not for the amount the auditor projected from the sample. The amount of this projection was $135,000. The projected amount was reduced by the amount of the factual error corrected by the client on the summary of errors prepared by the auditor. The control deficiency leading to the misstatement was evaluated as to its potential severity.

Prior period misstatements—in the prior year, all misstatements had been adjusted and none remained on the balance sheet.

This appendix documents how the auditor summarized uncorrected misstatements to determine whether the financial statements were free of material misstatement.

All information that appears in this font style illustrates information completed by the auditor.

Instructions for Preparation

This form documents the accumulation of factual, judgmental, and projected uncorrected misstatements to determine whether they are material to the financial statements.

When evaluating these misstatements you should consider (individually and in the aggregate)

- both the quantitative (size) and qualitative (nature) aspects of the misstatements.
- the effect of the misstatements to both the financial statements as a whole and to relevant classes of transactions, account balances, and disclosures.
- the particular circumstances related to the occurrence of the misstatements.

Evaluating Uncorrected Misstatements Individually

When evaluating an individual misstatement, you should evaluate

- its size and nature.
- its effect in relation to the relevant individual classes of transactions, account balances, or disclosures.
- whether, in considering the effect of the individual misstatement on the financial statements as a whole, it is appropriate to offset misstatements, such as when amounts are disclosed together in the financial statements.

Evaluating Uncorrected Misstatements in the Aggregate

Uncorrected misstatements should be aggregated in a way that enables you to consider whether they materially misstate the financial statements as a whole. This aggregation allows you to compare the misstatements to both the financial statements and to individual amounts, subtotals, or totals.

Summary of Uncorrected Misstatements

Observations and Suggestions

This table summarizes all the uncorrected misstatements in the form of a proposed journal entry that describes the nature of the misstatement and the entry that would be necessary to record the item. By itself, this summary is not adequate because it does not allow for the comparison of aggregated misstatements to both the financial statements and to individual amounts, subtotals, or totals. See paragraph 7.31 of this guide for additional guidance.

Uncorrected Misstatement		Balance Sheet		Income Statement	
Number	Description	Dr	Cr	Dr	Cr
1	Accounts payable	$ 185,000			
	Cost of sales				$ 185,000
	To correct amount payable to supplier paid in euros				
2	Sales (net)			$ 245,000	
	Allowances for Markdowns in Receivables		$ 245,000		
	To adjust estimate of end-of-season markdowns and chargebacks based on more reliable information				
3	Cost of Sales			$ 135,000[1]	
	Inventory		$ 135,000		
	To correct inventory balances based on an extrapolation of misstatement of pricing of individual inventory items				

[1] After correction of the factual misstatements by the client, this projected amount was reduced by the amount of the correction.

©2016, AICPA

Evaluation of Uncorrected Misstatements

Observations and Suggestions

This table aggregates the uncorrected misstatements in a way that allows them to be compared to individual amounts, subtotals, or totals in the financial statements.

This example does not include the consideration of the effect of prior year's uncorrected misstatements, as none remained. Please refer to appendix F, "Consideration of Prior Year Uncorrected Misstatements," of this guide for guidance on this matter.

Although a simpler presentation of this assessment might be supported by the facts in this specific case study, the illustrated format may be helpful in illustrating the concepts noted in AU-C section 450, *Evaluation of Misstatements Identified During the Audit* (AICPA, *Professional Standards*).

Engagements where materiality is based on specific user needs (for example, free cash flow in a family business that defines distributions based on this term) may add additional criteria to assess misstatements in those circumstances.

Misstatement		Assets		Liabilities		Income Statement			
Number	Type *	Current	Noncurrent	Current	Noncurrent	Revenue	Cost of Sales	S, G & A	Income
1	Factual	$ (245,000)		185,000			(185,000)		$ (185,000)
2	Judgmental					$ 245,000			$ 245,000
3	Projected	$ (135,000)					$ 135,000		$ 135,000
Total uncorrected		$ (380,000)		$ 185,000		$ 245,000	$ (50,000)		$ 195,000
Tax effect at 40%				78,000					$ (78,000)
After tax effect		$ (380,000)		$ 263,000		$ 245,000	(50,000)		$ 117,000
Effect of prior year's uncorrected misstatements								0	0
		$ (380,000)		$ 263,000		$ 245,000	$ (50,000)		$ 117,000
Totals per Financial Statements		$ 84,000,000	$ 10,000,000	$ 25,000,000	$ 15,000,000	$ 114,000,000	$ 60,000,000	$ 41,000,000	$ 8,500,000
Percent of uncorrected to financial statements		0.4%		1.1%		0.2%	0.1%	0.3%	1.3%

* [You are not required to describe the type of misstatement. However, doing so may assist you with your discussions with management and those charged with governance.]

Discussion with management and those charged with governance:

We discussed each of the misstatements with management and recommended correcting the financial statements for the first misstatement and performing a detailed review for the other two misstatements. Management was very willing to make the first proposed adjustment, because that would increase income and because it would correct the payable amount to the amount subsequently paid. We were concerned that if the first adjustment was made, that would still leave total potential misstatement of $380,000. We considered the work performed in the relevant accounts and overall on the audit and the conclusions we reached, and concluded that $380,000 was too close to materiality of $500,000 for us to be satisfied that there was a low risk of material misstatement. In addition, we considered that the loan covenants involved inventory and receivables and the bank would be concerned if these accounts were possibly overstated. Accordingly, we expressed these concerns to the Co-CEOs and key Board members (those charged with governance) and indicated that management should to do a proper investigation in both areas or we might have to increase the scope of procedures in order to provide a clean opinion. The client did that investigation and based on their procedures adjusted markdowns by $250,000 and ending inventory by $120,000.

We reviewed the client's work and concluded the work provided evidence that there was no longer any misstatement (see working paper xx for that review). Because the client's calculations indicated amounts close to the judgmental misstatement, we concluded the analysis was consistent with the result of our procedures, but that the client procedure was more precise than our estimate.

Conclusion

Based on a revised remaining uncorrected likely misstatement of $135,000, we conclude that sufficient work had been done so it is unlikely that the financial statements would contain additional misstatements over $500,000. Therefore, we conclude that we have sufficient evidence that the financial statements are not materially misstated.

Partial Analysis of Internal Control Deficiencies:

Deficiency	Reference	Classification	Reasoning	Communicated to Management and Those Charged With Governance
Key officers did not actively participate in the supervision or monitoring of IT. IT director has unlimited access to IT system without any direct supervision. [principle 8]	XX	Significant Deficiency	Limited compensating controls (see details in xx). More than a remote chance of material misstatement, especially since we found misstatements in audit. Limited oversight implemented in X3.	XX
Lack of controls over the development of spreadsheets used to process financial information. [principle 12]	XX	Material weakness	The employees and management generally assume the spreadsheets are correct. More than a remote chance of material misstatement, especially since we found misstatements in audit.	XX
Reliance on informal rather than formal integrity and ethical values policies. [principle 1]	XX	Deficiency	Management sets tone by their own good conduct; not an unusual risk for this size business. Employees feel the ethical values exist and are communicated and supported.	XXX Management only
There is only an informal understanding of the information needed to perform [x,y,z] financial reporting functions. [principle 13]	XX	Deficiency	Eventually the reporting gets done and checked (a compensating control); at that point, there are few misstatements; thus, we have had negligible proposed adjustments as a result of this lack of formality.	XXX Management only

(continued)

©2016, AICPA

Deficiency	Reference	Classification	Reasoning	Communicated to Management and Those Charged With Governance
User training is done on an as needed (ad hoc) basis—there is not a structured program. The only documentation that exists is whatever has been provided by the hardware or software vendor. No structured documentation exists of other IT systems matters. [principle 4 and principle 12]	XX	Deficiency	This has not been a major issue in the past and the documentation by the vendor is significant.	XXX Management only
Segregation of duties at the warehouse may be circumvented at times. Warehouse supervisor has the responsibility for preparing packing slips, but per discussion with employees, sometimes the individual who packed the items will enter the information needed to prepare the packing. [principle 12]	XX	Deficiency	Infrequent issue that may be unavoidable due to size. Management adequately oversees occasions where this happens due to illness or vacation to mitigate the exposure. In other cases the supervisor follows up and checks that the packer information was correct.	
Deficiency of logical access controls over data and applications during first nine months of the year. [principle 11]	XX	Significant Deficiency for first nine months; not a weakness thereafter	Limited analytical data monitoring (that is, compensating controls) in first nine months (see analysis in xx); More than a remote chance of material misstatement in that period. However, the monitoring of sales, payroll, and expenses by management mitigate the risk that material misstatement would be undetected at year end.	Communicated in X3 and again in X4. Noted that we believed the issue had been resolved in X4. See XX.

Deficiency	Reference	Classification	Reasoning	Communicated to Management and Those Charged With Governance
No formal procedures for bonus arrangements (who gets bonus and how much are decided by co-CEOs, without a formal process). [principle 10]	XX	Deficiency	Co-CEOs know who deserves a bonus and how to calculate this; not a major issue for this size company. Recommend documentation of process and monitoring.	XXX Management Only
Management's monitoring of internal control is only partially adequate, as it is based principally on a review of financial results and does not address all the issues related to the design and operating effectiveness of internal control. [principle 16] Misstatements detected internally result in a correction of the accounting records but not always a consideration of underlying control deficiencies that caused the misstatement. [principle 17]	XX	Significant Deficiency	Management is not focused on some of deficiencies noted previously; environment possible for misstatements to occur, but this is not the reason for the misstatement. Management has expanded its monitoring in X3 in response to X2 suggestions.	XX

Note: Issues of monetary misstatements identified by the auditor also indicate control deficiencies of some magnitude that need to be assessed as to their severity by the auditor.

Appendix L

The Effect of Group Audits on Planning and Determining Materiality

This appendix is nonauthoritative and is included for informational purposes only.

This appendix is intended to help auditors identify some of the key provisions related to planning and the determination of materiality under AU-C section 600, *Special Considerations—Audits of Group Financial Statements (Including the Work of Component Auditors)* (AICPA, *Professional Standards*), which supersedes Statement on Auditing Standards No. 1 AU section 543, *Part of Audit Performed by Other Independent Auditors* (AICPA, *Professional Standards*); and paragraphs .12–.13 of AU section 508, *Reports on Audited Financial Statements* (AICPA, *Professional Standards*). AU-C section 600 was effective for audits of group financial statements for periods ending on or after December 15, 2012.

Suggestions and Comments

When the AU-C section 600 applies to an engagement, it can have a profound effect on the planning and performance of an engagement. Auditors have noted difficulty identifying when the standard applies and how best to demonstrate compliance when it does. AU-C section 600 is broader in scope than the predecessor standard it subsumes, and the AICPA has posted numerous Technical Questions and Answers (Q&As) on the subject. AU-C section 600 may require audit firms auditing group financial statements of entities having two or more offices involved in the audit of group financial statements to consider a number of factors in the group audit that may not have previously been considered. An important criteria in determining whether the standard applies is whether components can be identified and not who performs the audit work. See the selected Q&As at the end if this appendix.

Auditors are urged to read the standard in its entirety as well as the AICPA Risk Alert *Understanding the Responsibilities of Auditors for Audits of Group Financial Statements—2013* that included a number of Q&As.

A best practice that has developed for some firms is to identify and develop a subject matter expert or two to help identify which firm engagements are subject to the standard, as they can include governments, non-profits and commercial entities even though these engagements may not involve other auditors.

AU-C section 600 introduces a number of new terms, concepts, and requirements related to group audits that will significantly affect current practice. Group financial statements include the financial information of more than one component. Paragraphs .11–.12 of AU-C section 600 define the following terms for purposes of generally accepted auditing standards:

> **component.** An entity or business activity for which group or component management prepares financial information that is

required by the applicable financial reporting framework to be included in the group financial statements.[1]

component auditor. An auditor who performs work on the financial information of a component that will be used as audit evidence for the group audit. A component auditor may be part of the group engagement partner's firm, a network firm of the group engagement partner's firm, or another firm.

component management. Management responsible for preparing the financial information of a component.

component materiality. The materiality for a component determined by the group engagement team for the purposes of the group audit.

group. All the components whose financial information is included in the group financial statements. A group always has more than one component.

group audit. The audit of group financial statements.

group audit opinion. The audit opinion on the group financial statements.

group engagement partner. The partner or other person in the firm who is responsible for the group audit engagement and its performance and for the auditor's report on the group financial statements that is issued on behalf of the firm. When joint auditors conduct the group audit, the joint engagement partners and their engagement teams collectively constitute the group engagement partner and the group engagement team. AU-C section 600 does not, however, deal with the relationship between joint auditors or the work that one joint auditor performs in relation to the work of the other joint auditor. (*Group engagement partner* and *firm* refer to their governmental equivalents when relevant).

group engagement team. Partners, including the group engagement partner, and staff who establish the overall group audit strategy, communicate with component auditors, perform work on the consolidation process, and evaluate the conclusions drawn from the audit evidence as the basis for forming an opinion on the group financial statements.

group financial statements. Financial statements that include the financial information of more than one component. The term *group financial statements* also refers to combined financial statements aggregating the financial information prepared by components that are under common control.

group management. Management responsible for the preparation and fair presentation of the group financial statements.

group-wide controls. Controls designed, implemented, and maintained by group management over group financial reporting.

---

[1] A component may include, but is not limited to, subsidiaries, geographical locations, divisions, investments, products or services, functions, processes, or component units of state or local governments. Equity method investments are also components that are scoped into the standard. However, other investments using fair value measurements are generally not considered components.

significant component. A component identified by the group engagement team (i) that is of individual financial significance to the group or (ii) that, due to its specific nature or circumstances, is likely to include significant risks of material misstatement of the group financial statements.

AU-C section 600 identifies a group engagement team's responsibilities in all audits of group financial statements as well as identifying performance requirements relating to risk assessment and materiality determinations for the group audit. This appendix will focus on some important performance requirements.

Group Auditor Responsibilities

An audit of group financial statements involves establishing an overall group audit strategy and group audit plan (including identifying the components and the extent to which the group engagement team will use the work of component auditors). The decision whether the auditor's report on the group financial statements will make reference to the audit of a component auditor should be made by the group engagement partner. When the auditor of the group financial statements assumes responsibility for the work of a component auditor, no reference is made to the component auditor in the auditor's report on the group financial statements. Alternatively, when the auditor of group financial statements does not assume responsibility for the work of a component auditor, the auditor will make reference to the audit of the component auditor in the auditor's report on the group financial statements.

Whether reference is made to the component auditor does not change the objective of the auditor to "obtain sufficient appropriate audit evidence regarding the financial information of the components and the consolidation process to express an opinion about whether the group financial statements are prepared, in all material respects, in accordance with the applicable financial reporting framework" (paragraph .10 of AU-C section 600).

Requirements of the Standard

The requirements of AU-C section 600 are enumerated in the following major section major headings:

- Responsibility
- Acceptance and Continuance
- Overall Audit Strategy and Audit Plan
- Understanding the Group, Its Components, and Their Environments
- Understanding a Component Auditor
- Determining Whether to Make Reference to a Component Auditor in the Auditor's Report on the Group Financial Statements
- Materiality
- Responding to Assessed Risks
- The Consolidation Process
- Subsequent Events
- Communicating with a Component Auditor
- Evaluating the Sufficiency and Appropriateness of Audit Evidence Obtained

- Communication With Group Management and Those Charged With Governance of the Group
- Documentation
- Additional Requirements Applicable When Assuming Responsibility for the Work of a Component Auditor

Planning Requirements

Paragraphs .18–.21 of AU-C section 600 require the group engagement team to

- establish an overall group audit strategy and to develop a group audit plan, which should be reviewed and approved by the group engagement partner;
- enhance its understanding of the group, its components, and their environments (including group-wide controls) obtained during the acceptance and continuance stage; and
- obtain an understanding of the consolidation process, including the instructions issued by group management to components.

Materiality

An important requirement when the standard applies is the allocation of audit effort amongst the components of the group. This is addressed through the identification of component materiality and component performance materiality. As stated in paragraph .31 of AU-C section 600:

The group engagement team should determine the following:

a. Materiality, including performance materiality, for the group financial statements as a whole when establishing the overall group audit strategy

b. Whether, in the specific circumstances of the group, particular classes of transactions, account balances, or disclosures in the group financial statements exist for which misstatements of lesser amounts than materiality for the group financial statements as a whole could reasonably be expected to influence the economic decisions of users taken on the basis of the group financial statements. In such circumstances, the group engagement team should determine materiality to be applied to those particular classes of transactions, account balances, or disclosures.

c. Component materiality for those components on which the group engagement team will perform, or request a component auditor to perform, an audit or review. Component materiality should be determined taking into account all components, regardless of whether reference is made in the auditor's report on the group financial statements to the audit of a component auditor. To reduce the risk that the aggregate of uncorrected and undetected misstatements in the group financial statements exceeds the materiality for the group financial statements as a whole, component materiality should be lower than the materiality for the group financial statements as a whole, and component performance materiality should be lower than performance materiality for the group financial statements as a whole.

d. The threshold above which misstatements cannot be regarded as clearly trivial to the group financial statements.

Additional requirements apply when the auditor of the group financial statements is assuming responsibility for the work of a component auditor.

Suggestions and Comments

The determination and documentation of the materiality (M) and performance materiality (PM) create complexities, as judgment is involved in setting these parameters.

The key relationships that are noted to be adhered to are:

- Group PM < Group M
- Component M < Group M
- Component PM < Component M
- Component PM < Group PM

These relationships are specified to control the risk that the aggregate of uncorrected and undetected misstatements from tests and procedures at the component levels will not exceed Group M.

The factors noted in appendix J, "Matters to Consider in Determining Performance Materiality," of this guide may be relevant in setting the relative relationship between these measures. These matters include, expected misstatement, resistance to adjustments, number of accounts where tests and estimation procedures are performed and number of locations or subsidiaries (for example, components). See table J-1, "Factors to Consider in Setting Performance Materiality."

When more of these factors are present, Group or Component performance materiality in many cases will be lower relative to group or component materiality. Other factors might also be considered when making this determination based on the facts and circumstances. The aforementioned risk alert on AU-C section 600 provides several examples of allocating group materiality to various components. The Audit Guide *Audit Sampling* notes in appendix E, "Multilocation Sampling Considerations" a model of risk and component planning for the number of locations to be selected and the depth of procedures to be applied that may be appropriate when all significant components cannot be practically audited or when significant components cannot be separately identified such as when auditing a chain of large stores.

Because of the combinatorial properties of separate tests and procedures performed at the component level, the aggregate (sum) component materiality for the various components may, and is likely to, exceed group materiality.

AU-C section 600 does not mention the concept of tolerable misstatement which is a concept applicable at the testing level within an account at the component level. Tolerable misstatement for tests and estimates at the component level may be set equal to or may be less than component performance materiality. When component performance materiality and tolerable misstatement are set the same at the component level, the performance

---

materiality may be set to a level such that when the various tests and estimations in the accounts are combined, the aggregate of uncorrected and possibly undetected misstatements will not exceed component materiality.

Selected Questions and Answers related to Common Issues

.09 Component Audit Performed by Other Engagement Teams of the Same Firm

Inquiry—Do the requirements of AU-C section 600 apply when a CPA firm uses auditors in different offices of the firm to perform various audit procedures related to the audit of a single entity's financial statements?

Reply—If the group engagement team identifies components in the financial statements of a single entity, it is a group audit, and AU-C section 600 applies. As defined in AU-C section 600, a *component auditor* may be part of the group engagement partner's firm, a network firm of the group engagement partner's firm, or another firm. (See paragraph .11 of AU-C section 600.)

[Issue Date: November 2012.]

.23 Use of Component Materiality When the Component Is Not Reported On Separately

Inquiry—Is it necessary to use a component materiality lower than group materiality when the component will not be reported on separately, and the audit of the entire group is being performed by the group engagement team as one audit?

Reply—If the component is a significant component on which the group engagement team will be performing audit procedures, the group engagement team is required to determine component materiality. (See paragraph .31 of AU-C section 600.) To reduce the risk that uncorrected and undetected misstatements in each component's financial statements, when aggregated, do not exceed the materiality for the group's financial statements as a whole, component materiality should be less than the materiality for the group financial statements as a whole. In circumstances when appropriate responses to assessed risks of material misstatement for some or all accounts or classes of transactions may be implemented at the group level, for example when accounts receivable for the parent and subsidiaries use the same system and the consolidated accounts receivable are audited as one aggregated amount, there is no risk of aggregation error and, therefore, no need to allocate materiality to components.

[Issue Date: November 2012; Revised, February 2013.]

.24 Applicability of AU-C Section 600 When Only One Engagement Team Is Involved

Inquiry—Company X consolidates the operations of Entity A. The same group engagement team that audits Company X also audits Entity A. Because only one engagement team is involved, does AU-C section 600 apply? If so, what does AU-C section 600 require that is not already covered by other auditing standards?

Reply—AU-C section 600 applies to all audits of *group financial statements*, which are financial statements that contain more than one component. In the circumstances when the same engagement team audits all components of the group, the considerations addressed in AU-C section 600 that relate to component auditors are not relevant. However, considerations addressed in AU-C section 600, such as understanding the components; identifying components that are significant due to individual financial significance and the significant risk of material misstatement; determining component materiality; understanding the consolidation process; and addressing the risks, including aggregation risk, of material misstatement in the group financial statements; are relevant in all group audits.

[Issue Date: February 2013.]

Decision-Making Flowchart

AU-C section 600 establishes specific requirements related to components that the group engagement team identifies as significant and those that are not significant. The following flowchart, found in paragraph .A79 of AU-C section 600, depicts how the significance of the component affects the group engagement team's determination of the type of work to be performed on the financial information of the component.

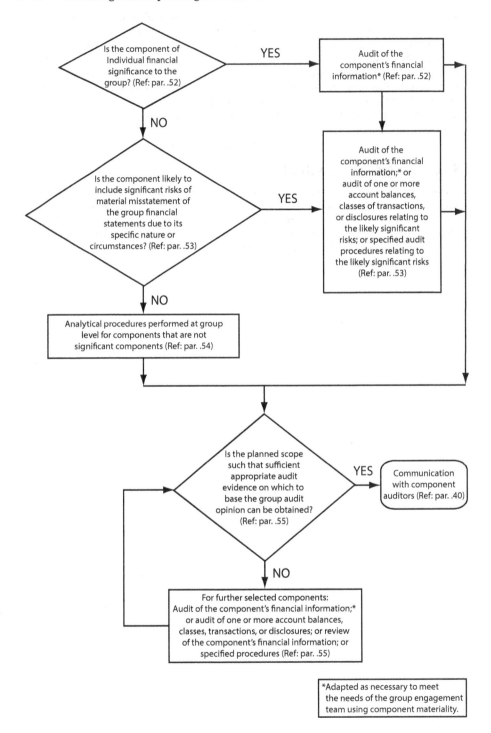

Appendix M

Overview of Statements on Quality Control Standards

This appendix is nonauthoritative and is included for informational purposes only.

This appendix is a partial reproduction of chapter 1 of the AICPA practice aid *Establishing and Maintaining a System of Quality Control for a CPA Firm's Accounting and Auditing Practice*, available at www.aicpa.org/interestareas/frc/pages/enhancingauditqualitypracticeaid.aspx.

This appendix highlights certain aspects of the quality control standards issued by the AICPA. If appropriate, readers should also refer to the quality control standards issued by the PCAOB, available at www.pcaobus.org/Standards/QC/Pages/default.aspx.

1.01 The objectives of a system of quality control are to provide a CPA firm with reasonable assurance[1] that the firm and its personnel comply with professional standards and applicable regulatory and legal requirements, and that the firm or engagement partners issue reports that are appropriate in the circumstances. QC section 10, *A Firm's System of Quality Control* (AICPA, *Professional Standards*), addresses a CPA firm's responsibilities for its system of quality control for its accounting and auditing practice. That section is to be read in conjunction with the AICPA Code of Professional Conduct and other relevant ethical requirements.

1.02 A system of quality control consists of policies designed to achieve the objectives of the system and the procedures necessary to implement and monitor compliance with those policies. The nature, extent, and formality of a firm's quality control policies and procedures will depend on various factors such as the firm's size; the number and operating characteristics of its offices; the degree of authority allowed to, and the knowledge and experience possessed by, firm personnel; and the nature and complexity of the firm's practice.

Communication of Quality Control Policies and Procedures

1.03 The firm should communicate its quality control policies and procedures to its personnel. Most firms will find it appropriate to communicate their policies and procedures in writing and distribute them, or make them available electronically, to all professional personnel. Effective communication includes the following:

- A description of quality control policies and procedures and the objectives they are designed to achieve

---

[1] The term *reasonable assurance*, which is defined as a high, but not absolute, level of assurance, is used because absolute assurance cannot be attained. Paragraph .53 of QC section 10, *A Firm's System of Quality Control* (AICPA, *Professional Standards*), states, "Any system of quality control has inherent limitations that can reduce its effectiveness."

©2016, AICPA

- The message that each individual has a personal responsibility for quality

- A requirement for each individual to be familiar with and to comply with these policies and procedures

Effective communication also includes procedures for personnel to communicate their views or concerns on quality control matters to the firm's management.

Elements of a System of Quality Control

1.04 A firm must establish and maintain a system of quality control. The firm's system of quality control should include policies and procedures that address each of the following elements of quality control identified in paragraph .17 of QC section 10:

- Leadership responsibilities for quality within the firm (the "tone at the top")

- Relevant ethical requirements

- Acceptance and continuance of client relationships and specific engagements

- Human resources

- Engagement performance

- Monitoring

1.05 The elements of quality control are interrelated. For example, a firm continually assesses client relationships to comply with relevant ethical requirements, including independence, integrity, and objectivity, and policies and procedures related to the acceptance and continuance of client relationships and specific engagements. Similarly, the human resources element of quality control encompasses criteria related to professional development, hiring, advancement, and assignment of firm personnel to engagements, all of which affect policies and procedures related to engagement performance. In addition, policies and procedures related to the monitoring element of quality control enable a firm to evaluate whether its policies and procedures for each of the other five elements of quality control are suitably designed and effectively applied.

1.06 Policies and procedures established by the firm related to each element are designed to achieve reasonable assurance with respect to the purpose of that element. Deficiencies in policies and procedures for an element may result in not achieving reasonable assurance with respect to the purpose of that element; however, the system of quality control, as a whole, may still be effective in providing the firm with reasonable assurance that the firm and its personnel comply with professional standards and applicable regulatory and legal requirements and that the firm or engagement partners issue reports that are appropriate in the circumstances.

1.07 If a firm merges, acquires, sells, or otherwise changes a portion of its practice, the surviving firm evaluates and, as necessary, revises, implements, and maintains firm-wide quality control policies and procedures that are appropriate for the changed circumstances.

Leadership Responsibilities for Quality Within the Firm (the "Tone at the Top")

1.08 The purpose of the leadership responsibilities element of a system of quality control is to promote an internal culture based on the recognition that quality is essential in performing engagements. The firm should establish and maintain the following policies and procedures to achieve this purpose:

- Require the firm's leadership (managing partner, board of managing partners, CEO, or equivalent) to assume ultimate responsibility for the firm's system of quality control.

- Provide the firm with reasonable assurance that personnel assigned operational responsibility for the firm's quality control system have sufficient and appropriate experience and ability to identify and understand quality control issues and develop appropriate policies and procedures, as well as the necessary authority to implement those policies and procedures.

1.09 Establishing and maintaining the following policies and procedures assists firms in recognizing that the firm's business strategy is subject to the overarching requirement for the firm to achieve the objectives of the system of quality control in all the engagements that the firm performs:

- Assign management responsibilities so that commercial considerations do not override the quality of the work performed.

- Design policies and procedures addressing performance evaluation, compensation, and advancement (including incentive systems) with regard to personnel to demonstrate the firm's overarching commitment to the objectives of the system of quality control.

- Devote sufficient and appropriate resources for the development, communication, and support of its quality control policies and procedures.

Relevant Ethical Requirements

1.10 The purpose of the relevant ethical requirements element of a system of quality control is to provide the firm with reasonable assurance that the firm and its personnel comply with relevant ethical requirements when discharging professional responsibilities. Relevant ethical requirements include independence, integrity, and objectivity. Establishing and maintaining policies such as the following assist the firm in obtaining this assurance:

- Require that personnel adhere to relevant ethical requirements such as those in regulations, interpretations, and rules of the AICPA, state CPA societies, state boards of accountancy, state statutes, the U.S. Government Accountability Office, and any other applicable regulators.

- Establish procedures to communicate independence requirements to firm personnel and, where applicable, others subject to them.

- Establish procedures to identify and evaluate possible threats to independence and objectivity, including the familiarity threat that may be created by using the same senior personnel on an audit or attest engagement over a long period of time, and to take appropriate action to eliminate those threats or reduce them to an acceptable level by applying safeguards.

- Require that the firm withdraw from the engagement if effective safeguards to reduce threats to independence to an acceptable level cannot be applied.

- Require written confirmation, at least annually, of compliance with the firm's policies and procedures on independence from all firm personnel required to be independent by relevant requirements.

- Establish procedures for confirming the independence of another firm or firm personnel in associated member firms who perform part of the engagement. This would apply to national firm personnel, foreign firm personnel, and foreign-associated firms.[2]

- Require the rotation of personnel for audit or attest engagements where regulatory or other authorities require such rotation after a specified period.

Acceptance and Continuance of Client Relationships and Specific Engagements

1.11 The purpose of the quality control element that addresses acceptance and continuance of client relationships and specific engagements is to establish criteria for deciding whether to accept or continue a client relationship and whether to perform a specific engagement for a client. A firm's client acceptance and continuance policies represent a key element in mitigating litigation and business risk. Accordingly, it is important that a firm be aware that the integrity and reputation of a client's management could reflect the reliability of the client's accounting records and financial representations and, therefore, affect the firm's reputation or involvement in litigation. A firm's policies and procedures related to the acceptance and continuance of client relationships and specific engagements should provide the firm with reasonable assurance that it will undertake or continue relationships and engagements only where it

- is competent to perform the engagement and has the capabilities, including the time and resources, to do so;

- can comply with legal and relevant ethical requirements;

- has considered the client's integrity and does not have information that would lead it to conclude that the client lacks integrity; and

- has reached an understanding with the client regarding the services to be performed.

1.12 This assurance should be obtained before accepting an engagement with a new client, when deciding whether to continue an existing engagement, and when considering acceptance of a new engagement with an existing client.

---

[2] A *foreign-associated firm* is a firm domiciled outside of the United States and its territories that is a member of, correspondent with, or similarly associated with an international firm or international association of firms.

Establishing and maintaining policies such as the following assist the firm in obtaining this assurance:

- Evaluate factors that have a bearing on management's integrity and consider the risk associated with providing professional services in particular circumstances.[3]

- Evaluate whether the engagement can be completed with professional competence; undertake only those engagements for which the firm has the capabilities, resources, and professional competence to complete; and evaluate, at the end of specific periods or upon occurrence of certain events, whether the relationship should be continued.

- Obtain an understanding, preferably in writing, with the client regarding the services to be performed.

- Establish procedures on continuing an engagement and the client relationship, including procedures for dealing with information that would have caused the firm to decline an engagement if the information had been available earlier.

- Require documentation of how issues relating to acceptance or continuance of client relationships and specific engagements were resolved.

Human Resources

1.13 The purpose of the human resources element of a system of quality control is to provide the firm with reasonable assurance that it has sufficient personnel with the capabilities, competence, and commitment to ethical principles necessary (a) to perform its engagements in accordance with professional standards and regulatory and legal requirements, and (b) to enable the firm to issue reports that are appropriate in the circumstances. Establishing and maintaining policies such as the following assist the firm in obtaining this assurance:

- Recruit and hire personnel of integrity who possess the characteristics that enable them to perform competently.

- Determine capabilities and competencies required for an engagement, especially for the engagement partner, based on the characteristics of the particular client, industry, and kind of service being performed. Specific competencies necessary for an engagement partner are discussed in paragraph .A27 of QC section 10.

- Determine the capabilities and competencies possessed by personnel.

- Assign the responsibility for each engagement to an engagement partner.

---

[3] Such considerations would include the risk of providing professional services to significant clients or to other clients for which the practitioner's objectivity or the appearance of independence may be impaired. In broad terms, the significance of a client to a member or a firm refers to relationships that could diminish a practitioner's objectivity and independence in performing attest services. Examples of factors to consider in determining the significance of a client to an engagement partner, office, or practice unit include (a) the amount of time the partner, office, or practice unit devotes to the engagement, (b) the effect on the partner's stature within the firm as a result of his or her service to the client, (c) the manner in which the partner, office, or practice unit is compensated, or (d) the effect that losing the client would have on the partner, office, or practice unit.

- Assign personnel based on the knowledge, skills, and abilities required in the circumstances and the nature and extent of supervision needed.

- Have personnel participate in general and industry-specific continuing professional education and professional development activities that enable them to accomplish assigned responsibilities and satisfy applicable continuing professional education requirements of the AICPA, state boards of accountancy, and other regulators.

- Select for advancement only those individuals who have the qualifications necessary to fulfill the responsibilities they will be called on to assume.

Engagement Performance

1.14 The purpose of the engagement performance element of quality control is to provide the firm with reasonable assurance (*a*) that engagements are consistently performed in accordance with applicable professional standards and regulatory and legal requirements, and (*b*) that the firm or the engagement partner issues reports that are appropriate in the circumstances. Policies and procedures for engagement performance should address all phases of the design and execution of the engagement, including engagement performance, supervision responsibilities, and review responsibilities. Policies and procedures also should require that consultation takes place when appropriate. In addition, a policy should establish criteria against which all engagements are to be evaluated to determine whether an engagement quality control review should be performed.

1.15 Establishing and maintaining policies such as the following assist the firm in obtaining the assurance required relating to the engagement performance element of quality control:

- Plan all engagements to meet professional, regulatory, and the firm's requirements.

- Perform work and issue reports and other communications that meet professional, regulatory, and the firm's requirements.

- Require that work performed by other team members be reviewed by qualified engagement team members, which may include the engagement partner, on a timely basis.

- Require the engagement team to complete the assembly of final engagement files on a timely basis.

- Establish procedures to maintain the confidentiality, safe custody, integrity, accessibility, and retrievability of engagement documentation.

- Require the retention of engagement documentation for a period of time sufficient to meet the needs of the firm, professional standards, laws, and regulations.

- Require that

  — consultation take place when appropriate (for example, when dealing with complex, unusual, unfamiliar, difficult, or contentious issues);

- — sufficient and appropriate resources be available to enable appropriate consultation to take place;
- — all the relevant facts known to the engagement team be provided to those consulted;
- — the nature, scope, and conclusions of such consultations be documented; and
- — the conclusions resulting from such consultations be implemented.

- Require that

  - — differences of opinion be dealt with and resolved;
  - — conclusions reached are documented and implemented; and
  - — the report not be released until the matter is resolved.

- Require that

  - — all engagements be evaluated against the criteria for determining whether an engagement quality control review should be performed;
  - — an engagement quality control review be performed for all engagements that meet the criteria; and
  - — the review be completed before the report is released.

- Establish procedures addressing the nature, timing, extent, and documentation of the engagement quality control review.
- Establish criteria for the eligibility of engagement quality control reviewers.

Monitoring

1.16 The purpose of the monitoring element of a system of quality control is to provide the firm and its engagement partners with reasonable assurance that the policies and procedures related to the system of quality control are relevant, adequate, operating effectively, and complied with in practice. Monitoring involves an ongoing consideration and evaluation of the appropriateness of the design, the effectiveness of the operation of a firm's quality control system, and a firm's compliance with its quality control policies and procedures. The purpose of monitoring compliance with quality control policies and procedures is to provide an evaluation of the following:

- Adherence to professional standards and regulatory and legal requirements
- Whether the quality control system has been appropriately designed and effectively implemented
- Whether the firm's quality control policies and procedures have been operating effectively so that reports issued by the firm are appropriate in the circumstances

1.17 Establishing and maintaining policies such as the following assist the firm in obtaining the assurance required relating to the monitoring element of quality control:

- Assign responsibility for the monitoring process to a partner or partners or other persons with sufficient and appropriate experience and authority in the firm to assume that responsibility.

- Assign performance of the monitoring process to competent individuals.

- Require the performance of monitoring procedures that are sufficiently comprehensive to enable the firm to assess compliance with all applicable professional standards and the firm's quality control policies and procedures. Monitoring procedures consist of the following:

  — Review of selected administrative and personnel records pertaining to the quality control elements.

  — Review of engagement documentation, reports, and clients' financial statements.

  — Summarization of the findings from the monitoring procedures, at least annually, and consideration of the systemic causes of findings that indicate that improvements are needed.

  — Determination of any corrective actions to be taken or improvements to be made with respect to the specific engagements reviewed or the firm's quality control policies and procedures.

  — Communication of the identified findings to appropriate firm management personnel.

  — Consideration of findings by appropriate firm management personnel who should also determine that any actions necessary, including necessary modifications to the quality control system, are taken on a timely basis.

  — Assessment of

    - the appropriateness of the firm's guidance materials and any practice aids;

    - new developments in professional standards and regulatory and legal requirements and how they are reflected in the firm's policies and procedures where appropriate;

    - compliance with policies and procedures on independence;

    - the effectiveness of continuing professional development, including training;

    - decisions related to acceptance and continuance of client relationships and specific engagements; and

    - firm personnel's understanding of the firm's quality control policies and procedures and implementation thereof.

- Communicate at least annually, to relevant engagement partners and other appropriate personnel, deficiencies noted as a result of the monitoring process and recommendations for appropriate remedial action.

- Communicate the results of the monitoring of its quality control system process to relevant firm personnel at least annually.
- Establish procedures designed to provide the firm with reasonable assurance that it deals appropriately with the following:
    - Complaints and allegations that the work performed by the firm fails to comply with professional standards and regulatory and legal requirements.
    - Allegations of noncompliance with the firm's system of quality control.
    - Deficiencies in the design or operation of the firm's quality control policies and procedures, or noncompliance with the firm's system of quality control by an individual or individuals, as identified during the investigations into complaints and allegations.

    This includes establishing clearly defined channels for firm personnel to raise any concerns in a manner that enables them to come forward without fear of reprisal and documenting complaints and allegations and the responses to them.

- Require appropriate documentation to provide evidence of the operation of each element of its system of quality control. The form and content of documentation evidencing the operation of each of the elements of the system of quality control is a matter of judgment and depends on a number of factors, including the following, for example:
    - The size of the firm and the number of offices.
    - The nature and complexity of the firm's practice and organization.

- Require retention of documentation providing evidence of the operation of the system of quality control for a period of time sufficient to permit those performing monitoring procedures and peer review to evaluate the firm's compliance with its system of quality control, or for a longer period if required by law or regulation.

1.18 Some of the monitoring procedures discussed in the previous list may be accomplished through the performance of the following:

- Engagement quality control review
- Review of engagement documentation, reports, and clients' financial statements for selected engagements after the report release date
- Inspection[4] procedures

---

[4] *Inspection* is a retrospective evaluation of the adequacy of the firm's quality control policies and procedures, its personnel's understanding of those policies and procedures, and the extent of the firm's compliance with them. Although monitoring procedures are meant to be ongoing, they may include inspection procedures performed at a fixed point in time. Monitoring is a broad concept; inspection is one specific type of monitoring procedure.

Documentation of Quality Control Policies and Procedures

1.19 The firm should document each element of its system of quality control. The extent of the documentation will depend on the size, structure, and nature of the firm's practice. Documentation may be as simple as a checklist of the firm's policies and procedures or as extensive as practice manuals.

Applying the Quality Control Standards to Four Hypothetical Firms

1.20 Subsequent chapters in this practice aid present four different hypothetical firms and the quality control policies and procedures each firm implements to address each of the quality control elements. Following is a description of those firms and their characteristics:

- Multioffice CPA Firm has 10 offices in 3 states and is centrally managed. It has approximately 15 partners and 100 professionals. Its accounting and auditing practice has a concentration of financial institution clients for which it performs audit and attest services. Multioffice CPA Firm has no issuer clients. (Chapter 2, "System of Quality Control for a CPA Firm's Accounting and Auditing Practice—Firm With Multiple Offices")

- Singleoffice CPA Firm has 1 office, 3 partners, and 10 professionals. Its accounting and auditing practice has a concentration of employee benefit plan audits. Singleoffice CPA Firm has no issuer clients. (Chapter 3, "System of Quality Control for a CPA Firm's Accounting and Auditing Practice—Firm With a Single Office")

- Sole Practitioner, CPA, is a sole owner who has no professional staff and occasionally hires per diem professionals. Her accounting practice consists only of engagements subject to Statements on Standards for Accounting and Review Services. (Chapter 4, "System of Quality Control for a CPA Firm's Accounting and Auditing Practice—Sole Practitioner") (Note: Sole practitioners who perform audit and attest engagements should refer to chapter 3)

- Closely Aligned CPA Firm and Non-CPA-Owned Entity are organized in an *alternative practice structure*, which is a nontraditional structure in the practice of public accounting consisting of an attest and a nonattest portion of the practice. The attest portion is conducted through a firm, Closely Aligned CPA Firm, owned and controlled by CPAs. The nonattest portion is conducted through a separate entity, Non-CPA-owned Entity, owned and controlled by individuals who are not CPAs. (Chapter 5, "System of Quality Control for an Alternative Practice Structure")

1.21 The policies and procedures described in each chapter are those that a firm of a similar size and type may consider establishing and maintaining. The policies and procedures used by an actual firm need not necessarily include nor be limited to all those used by the illustrative firms.

Appendix N

Schedule of Changes Made to the Text From the Previous Edition

This appendix is nonauthoritative and is included for informational purposes only.

As of October 1, 2016

This schedule of changes identifies areas in the text and footnotes of this guide that have been changed from the previous edition. Entries in the following table reflect current numbering, lettering (including that in appendix names), and character designations that resulted from the renumbering or reordering that occurred in the updating of this guide.

Reference	*Change*
General	Editorial changes, including rephrasing, may have been made in this guide to improve readability where necessary.
Preface	Updated.
Practice considerations in chapter 1	Added footnote and revised for the passage of time and to improve readability.
Paragraph 1.38	Revised to reflect the issuance of Statement on Auditing Standards (SAS) No. 130, *An Audit of Internal Control Over Financial Reporting That Is Integrated With an Audit of Financial Statements* (AICPA, *Professional Standards*, AU-C sec. 940).
Former practice considerations in chapter 2	Deleted to improve readability.
Paragraph 2.86	Revised to add reference to the "Report to the Nations on Occupational Fraud and Abuse" issued in 2016.
Paragraphs 2.87–.88	Revised to reflect the issuance of SAS No. 130.
Paragraph 2.111	Illustration 2-3 removed for passage of time.
Practice considerations in chapter 3	Revised to improve readability.

(continued)

©2016, AICPA

Reference	Change
Paragraphs 3.02 and 3.87	Revised to add reference to appendix L, "The Effect of Group Audits on Planning and Determining Materiality."
Paragraph 3.102	Revised to add reference to Audit Risk Alert *Revenue Recognition: Accounting and Auditing Considerations.*
Former practice considerations in chapter 4	Deleted to improve readability.
Paragraphs 4.20 and 4.50	Added footnote to reflect the issuance of AU-C section 9570, *The Auditor's Consideration of an Entity's Ability to Continue as a Going Concern: Auditing Interpretations of Section 570* (AICPA, *Professional Standards,* AU-C sec. 9570 par. .01–.10).
Former practice considerations in chapter 5	Deleted to improve readability.
Paragraph 5.09	Revised for the Committee of Sponsoring Organizations of the Treadway Commission framework considerations.
Former practice considerations in chapter 6	Deleted to improve readability.
Paragraph 6.89	Footnote added to improve readability.
Paragraph 7.44	Revised for the passage of time.
Paragraphs 7.47–.48, 7.50–.51, and 7.56	Revised to reflect the issuance of SAS No. 130.
Appendix C	Revised for passage of time.
Appendix J	Revised to add reference to appendix L.
Appendix L	Added to consider the effect of group audits on planning and determining materiality.
Appendix M	Added for quality control.
Index of Pronouncements and Other Technical Guidance	Updated.
Subject Index	Updated.

Index of Pronouncements and Other Technical Guidance

A

Title	Paragraphs
AU-C Section	
200, *Overall Objectives of the Independent Auditor and the Conduct of an Audit in Accordance With Generally Accepted Auditing Standards*	1.24, 2.02–.04, 2.10, 2.14–.15, 2.22, 5.07
230, *Audit Documentation*	1.06, 1.39–.40, 2.96, 5.17, 5.37, 5.70
240, *Consideration of Fraud in a Financial Statement Audit*	1.10, 1.15, 1.23, 2.81–.86, 2.92, 3.25, 3.34, 3.36, 3.88, 3.95, 3.100, 3.102, 3.121, 4.24, 4.65, 4.67, 5.20, 5.31, 6.89, 6.96, 6.117, 7.22
265, *Communicating Internal Control Related Matters Identified in an Audit*	1.01, 1.37–.38, 2.44, 2.87–.88, 2.111, 3.94, 4.38, 5.25, 6.21, 6.84, 7.44, 7.46–.47, 7.48, 7.52, 7.55–.56, 7.59, 7.61, 7.63–.65, 7.68–.69
300, *Planning an Audit*	1.01, 3.02–.05, 3.73, 3.143
315, *Understanding the Entity and Its Environment and Assessing the Risks of Material Misstatement*	1.06, 1.08–.09, 1.11–.12, 1.16–.19, 1.22, 1.26–.27, 1.30–.32, 2.06–.08, 2.15, 2.35, 2.39, 2.43, 2.46, 3.17, 3.21–.22, 3.26–.27, 3.32, 3.35–.37, 3.44, 3.48, 3.82–.83, 3.87–.89, 3.93, 3.95, 3.97–.99, 3.101, 3.103–.105, 3.112–.113, 3.131, 3.143, 3.146, 4.04, 4.06–.08, 4.15–.17, 4.19–.21, 4.23–.26, 4.33, 4.39, 4.44–.49, 4.52, 4.54, 4.56, 4.59–.60, 4.63, 4.69, 4.73–.74, 4.77, 4.84, 5.01, 5.03, 5.05, 5.07–.08, 5.11, 5.30, 5.31, 5.70, 6.111
320, *Materiality in Planning and Performing and Audit*	2.19–.20, 2.23, 3.06, 3.08–.09, 3.13, 3.87, 3.143, 7.05–.06, 7.38

Title	Paragraphs
330, *Performing Audit Procedures in Response to Assessed Risks and Evaluating the Audit Evidence Obtained*	1.31, 1.35, 2.17, 2.37, 2.100, 3.104, 5.04, 5.15, 5.30, 5.37, 5.40–.41, 5.53, 5.60, 5.70, 6.03–.05, 6.11, 6.25, 6.45–.46, 6.50–.51, 6.54–.55, 6.57, 6.59, 6.62, 6.78–.79, 6.83, 6.88–.90, 6.92, 6.108, 6.110, 6.114, 6.118, 7.03, 7.42–.43
402, *Audit Considerations Relating to an Entity Using a Service Organizations*	3.33, 3.79–.81, 3.84, 3.128, 6.06, 6.71
450, *Evaluation of Misstatements Identified During the Audit*	7.04, 7.09–.10, 7.23, 7.25, 7.27, 7.30–.32, 7.34, 7.38–.39, 7.41, 7.70
500, *Audit Evidence*	1.02, 1.06, 1.14, 2.93–.95, 2.99, 3.115, 5.45–.46, 5.54
505, *External Confirmations*	Table 5-3 at 5.42
520, *Analytical Procedures*	3.26, 4.25, 5.67, 6.88, 6.100, 7.12–.14
530, *Audit Sampling*	2.26–.27, 6.37, 6.39, 6.42–.43, 6.63, 6.113, 7.16
540, *Auditing Accounting Estimates, Including Fair Value Accounting Estimates and Related Disclosures*	3.33, 4.66, 6.97, 7.17, 7.20–.21
580, *Written Representations*	2.106, 5.48
600, *Special Considerations—Audits of Group Financial Statements*	2.27, 3.87
610, *The Auditors Consideration of the Internal Audit Function in an Audit of Financial Statements*	4.60
620, *Using the Work of an Auditor's Specialist*	3.33, 3.85
700, *Forming and Opinion and Reporting on Financial Statements*	7.40
AU Section 315, *Communication Between Predecessor and Successor Auditors*	1.01
Audit and Accounting Guide	
Audit Sampling	1.25, 2.18, 2.26, 5.59, 5.69, 6.15, 6.31, 6.35, 6.63, 6.74, 6.77, 6.86, 6.113, 7.16, 7.52
Auditing Revenue in Certain Industries	3.102, 4.10

Title	Paragraphs
Audit Risk Alert	
Revenue Recognition: Accounting and Auditing Considerations—2016/17	3.102
Understanding the Responsibilities of Auditors for Audits of Group Financial Statements	3.87

C

Title	Paragraphs
Code of Professional Conduct, ET section 1.295, "Nonattest Services"	2.115
COSO	
Internal Control—Integrated Framework	Appendix C
Internal Control—Integrated Framework Illustrative Tools for Assessing Effectiveness of a System of Internal Control	1.01
Internal Control—Integrated Framework Internal Control Over External Financial Reporting: A Compendium of Approaches and Examples	1.01

F

Title	Paragraphs
FASB ASC 606, *Revenue with Contracts from Customers*	3.102
FASB ASU No. 2014-09, *Revenue from Contracts with Customers (Topic 606): Summary and Amendments That Create Revenue from Contracts with Customers (Topic 606) and Other Assets and Deferred Costs—Contracts with Customers (Subtopic 340-40)*	2.08

P

Title	Paragraphs
Practice Aid *Fraud Detection in a GAAS Audit* (Revised Edition)	3.34

S

Title	Paragraphs
SAS	
No. 99, *Consideration of Fraud in a Financial Statement Audit*	2.86
No. 130, *An Examination of an Entity's Internal Control Over Financial Reporting That Is Integrated With an Audit of Its Financial Statements*	7.44

Subject Index

A

ACCESS CONTROLS, INFORMATION TECHNOLOGY (IT) 3.60–.62

ACCOUNTING ESTIMATES
· Assertion-level risks 5.37
· Audit findings 7.17–.19
· Controls related to non-routine transactions 4.66
· Further audit procedure design .....5.32–.34, ... 5.37
· Risk assessment process 2.92

ACCOUNTING POLICIES, SELECTION AND APPLICATION
· GAAP consistency 4.08, 4.69
· Internal controls over .... 3.94, 4.68–.70, ... Table 4-6 at 4.70
· Material misstatement due to fraud risk 4.67
· Understanding of 4.08, 4.13

ACCOUNTING RECORDS, TESTS OF 2.98

ACTIVITY-LEVEL CONTROLS
· Control activities 4.77–.80
· Deficiencies 4.81, 4.83
· Defined 1.06
· Design and implementation evaluation 4.73–.80
· Entity-level controls, distinguishing from 2.49–.53
· Information systems 3.96–.100, 4.73–.76
· Relevant activities 4.77
· Significant activity-level risk 3.103

ANALYTICAL PROCEDURES. see also substantive procedures .... 3.26–.28, ... 3.117, 5.42, Table 5-3 at 5.42

ANTIFRAUD PROGRAMS AND CONTROLS
· Communication with those charged with governance 2.86
· Elements .... 4.62, Table 4-5 at 4.62
· Evaluation 3.91–.92, 3.100
· Guidance .... Appendix D

APPLICATION CONTROLS, INFORMATION TECHNOLOGY (IT) ....3.58–.59, ... 3.67–.69, 3.101, 6.24–.26, ... Table 3-7 at 3.59

APPLICATION SUITE, DEFINED 2.71

ASSERTION-LEVEL RISKS
· Assessment of 2.07–.18, 5.21–.37
· Defined 1.06
· Detection risk 2.15–.16
· Financial statement-level 5.18–.20
· Further audit procedures 2.15
· Of material misstatement ....1.06, 1.11, ... 1.27, 2.07–.18, 2.34, 5.04, 5.59
· Significant risks 5.37

ASSERTIONS. see also financial statement assertions 1.06, 2.28

AUDIT DOCUMENTATION
· Audit planning 1.06, 3.143
· Audit strategy 3.143
· Case study .... Appendix K
· Further audit procedure design 5.70
· Further audit procedure performance ...6.118
· Importance of 1.06
· Internal control 3.40–.45, 4.36–.48
· Management's documentation of internal control 3.40–.43, 3.115
· Materiality level 3.143
· Misstatements 7.70
· Observation and inspection of documents 3.29–.30, 3.118–.120
· Performing tests of controls 6.73
· Risk assessment procedures 3.143
· Risk assessment process 1.39–.41
· Tests of controls 6.20–.21
· Understanding the entity and its environment, including internal control 4.84

AUDIT EVIDENCE. see also substantive procedures; tests of controls
· Appropriateness .... 2.101–.107, ... Table 2-7 at 2.104
· Audit risk (AR) model ....1.25, ... Illustration 1-1 at 1.01
· Characteristics, and risks of material misstatement 3.106
· Continuous reevaluation 3.142
· Defined 2.93
· Documentation 6.118
· Examples of information .....Table 2-6 at 2.98
· Further audit procedures. see entries beginning with further audit procedures
· Generally 2.93–.97
· Indirect information 3.43
· Nature of 2.93–.98
· From prior audits .... 1.17, 3.130–.133, ... 6.54–.58, 6.111
· Relevance 2.102
· Reliability .....2.103–.104, Table 2-7 at 2.104
· Substantive procedures. see substantive procedures
· Sufficiency of ...2.99–.100, 2.107, 7.42–.43, ... Table 7-2 at 7.43
· Summary 7.71–.78
· Tests of controls. see tests of controls

AUDIT FINDINGS 7.01–.41
· Accounting estimates 7.17–.19
· Financial statements as whole 7.38–.41
· Generally 1.06, 7.01
· Materiality, and evaluation of 2.21
· Misstatements in financial statements 7.02–.26

                                 ©2016, AICPA